Climbing in the Adirondacks

Adirondack
ADK
Mountain Club

Climbing in the Adirondacks

A Guide to Rock and Ice Routes
in the Adirondack Park

DON MELLOR

The Adirondack Mountain Club, Inc.

Lake George, New York

Published by the Adirondack Mountain Club,
814 Goggins Road, Lake George, NY 12845-4117
Visit our Web site at **www.adk.org**

First edition, 1983
Second edition, 1989
  Reprinted with Addendum, 1994
Third edition, 1995
  Reprinted, 1997, 2001

Book design: Christopher Kuntze
Photographs by the author unless noted otherwise.

Library of Congress Cataloging-in-Publication Data

Mellor, Don.
   Climbing in the Adirondacks : a guide to rock and ice routes in
the Adirondack Park / by Don Mellor. — 3rd ed.
      p.   cm.
   Includes bibliographical references and index.
   ISBN 0-935272-79-8
   1. Rock climbing—New York (State)—Adirondack Mountains—
Guidebooks. 2. Snow and ice climbing—New York (State)—Adirondack
Mountains—Guidebooks. 3. Adirondack Mountains (N.Y.)—Guidebooks.
I. Title.
GV199.42.N652A3454 1995
796.5'223'097475—dc20   95-10922
                                                               CIP

PRINTED IN THE UNITED STATES OF AMERICA
10 9 8 7 6 5 4   04 05 06 07 08 09

Contents

Cliff-Route Photoguides

USEFUL REFERENCE POINTS

1 AZURE MT.
2 WHITEFACE REGION
3 CASCADE LAKES REGION
4 HURRICANE CRAG
5 POKE-O-MOONSHINE
6 WALLFACE
7 AVALANCHE PASS
  (High Peaks area)
8 KEENE VALLEY
  & CHAPEL POND
  REGION

Adirondack Park Boundary

Santa Clara — 458 — 30 — 3 — Keeseville — 9N — 5 — 22

Paul Smiths — Wilmington — 56 — 2 — 73 — Keene — Elizabethtown

Saranac Lake — 86 — Lake Placid — 3 — Keene Valley — 4 — Westport

30 — Tupper Lake — 6 — 7 — 18 — 8

3 — Tahawus — 87 — Exit 30

30 — Newcomb — North Hudson — 22

Long Lake — 28N — 9 — Ticonderoga

Blue Mt. Lake — 10 — 11 — 12

28 — Indian Lake — 28 — 9 — 8

Old Forge — 13 — 9N

30 — North Creek

15 — 14

Speculator — 8 — Warrensburg

16 — Wells — Lake George

8 — 10

17 — 30 — Northville

Adirondack Park Boundary

9 MOXHAM DOME
10 PHARAOH MT.
11 BARTON HIGH CLIFF
12 ROGERS ROCK
13 LONG POND CLIFF

14 HUCKLEBERRY & CRANE MTS.
15 SHANTY CLIFF
16 ECHO CLIFF
17 GOOD LUCK CLIFF
18 GOTHICS MT.

ACKNOWLEDGMENTS

In a work such as this, the author is in many cases merely a compiler and editor of information. This guidebook reflects the travels, notes, and insights of people too numerous and too valuable to acknowledge properly.

Obviously, the guide is merely another step in building upon the work of Trudy Healy, and later, Tom Rosecrans. Trudy's were the first climbing guidebooks, setting a tone to which I hope I've adhered. Tom's 1975 guidebook expanded the scope of the guide and served as the platform for the first edition of *Climbing in the Adirondacks* in 1983. If some of these descriptions sound like theirs, it's only because their work was so good and their influence so strong.

Two notebooks got my process started: Dave Cilley's at EMS and Dave Hough's, documenting the explosion of routes at Poke-O-Moonshine. Chuck Turner, Jim Cunningham, and Alan Jolley were also instrumental in the formation of the 1983 edition.

Interviews proved invaluable and inspirational: Ben Poisson, Harry Eldridge, Jim Goodwin, Landon Rockwell, and John Case in particular were generous with their time and memories. Correspondence from Julien Dery, Pierre Gagnon, Andrew Embick, Yvon Chouinard, Hans Kraus, and Peter Metcalf helped to round out much of the picture.

And the list goes on: the tireless exploration and generous accounting of routes by people like Jon Bassett, Bill Widrig, Tom DuBois, Neal Knitel, and Dave Furman made much of this possible. For some of the newly discovered areas, I took the work of Jim Vermeulen and Dick Tucker almost verbatim, and credit for the research and writing belongs to them.

And finally, such a work as this could not even be attempted without the support of such friends as Patrick Purcell, Jeff Edwards, Patrick Munn, Bill Dodd, Ann Eastman, Geoff Smith, Dave Hough, Todd Eastman, Mark Meschinelli, Ed Palen, Dominic Eisinger, and Tad Welch. To these and many others who wrote and thus helped shape this project, thank you.

Wallface, the state's largest cliff, typifies the wilderness climbing experience.

PREFACE

What is climbing in the Adirondacks? It's getting away. It's figuring things out for yourself. It's a steep hike through the woods to the base of a cliff. The path along the base isn't really a path; someone's thrashed through there before, so a slight corridor separates the rock from the thick trees. You're not sure that you've found the base of the route. There are no wads of tape or cigarette butts to show the way. The climb takes you most of the day, and for a time you're a little lost, checking around that corner over there to see if there's a better way, digging out a clever nut placement from the dirt, sure that no one has ever protected this move before. You look out from the next stance over a luxuriant forest, and if you've chosen well, it is the sound of a river below, not that of a stream of cars that makes it hard to hear your partner. The last half pitch to the top has you fighting through tight spruce and balsam, and the black flies once kept at bay by the winds on the face drill at your ears and wade in the sweat of your brow.

What is climbing in the Adirondacks? It is not getting advice from a flock of chalkbags below. There are few colorful sling salads sprouting from fixed anchors. Those who have gone before you have tried their best to hide their passage, not advertise it. This is an untamed place, even in many ways an inconvenient place. Trails are generally unmarked, and many of the routes see so little traffic that the cracks might be choked with dirt and the grade given by the first ascent team way off the mark. Sure, you'll see a host of well-traveled roadside crags as you drive through the better-known areas like Chapel Pond Pass. But you might instead find yourself tempted to choose a place like Wallface, or Gothics, or some of the remote wilderness crags of the southern reaches of the park. There you'll rediscover the essence of a sport that has come so far in so very few years, but one which, thankfully, still retains the allure that has drawn people to the mountains from the beginnings of time.

You probably drove a long way to get here. It would have been easier to stop at the cliffs nearer to home. You would have seen all the familiar faces and cruised the routes you know so well. But you chose to drive the extra miles, to get away from the home crags, to be somewhere different. The Adirondacks. Maybe the best way to experience the place is to let it be, visiting and exploring, but leaving those elements you are escaping far behind as you do.

The Trap Dike on Mount Colden

INTRODUCTION

This is a guidebook to technical rock and ice climbing in the Adirondack Park of upstate New York. It also serves as a historical documentation of reported climbs. Thus, no description is necessarily a recommendation. Instead, the book is intended only to accompany you as you make your own decisions. The guide makes no claim to teach climbing or to instruct people in technique, safety, or equipment use. Nor does it serve as a dictionary to climbers' jargon. The language used in the guide is from the standard (though rapidly changing) American lexicon of climbing. There are several professional guide services in the region and instructional texts that cover these areas.

The idea for a guidebook to Adirondack rock climbs came from none other than Fritz Wiessner himself. In the fall of 1964, when John and Elizabeth Brett of the Alpine Club of Canada introduced Wiessner to Trudy Healy, advisor to the Penn State Outing Club, Wiessner mentioned his fear that the classic routes would be forgotten if no one took on the task of reporting. Trudy Healy accepted the challenge, and throughout the next year, notes were compiled, cliffs explored, routes re-climbed, and her "little blue guide" began to take shape.

Her original guidebook, *Climber's Guide to the Adirondacks,* was published by the Adirondack Mountain Club in 1967 and contained about 65 routes. One more edition followed before Healy moved west. Tom Rosecrans picked up the project, and in 1976 published *Adirondack Rock and Ice Climbs,* expanding considerably on Healy's work and reflecting the steady growth of the sport in the Adirondacks. With much the same spontaneity of Healy's initial involvement, Tom suggested that I take over the project, and in 1983 the first edition of *Climbing in the Adirondacks* appeared, to be followed by a short supplement in 1986 and a second edition in 1989. This third edition is merely another step in a never-ending process and a reflection of the sport more than thirty years after Wiessner first saw the need to record climbing routes.

This guidebook covers rock and ice climbs on state land. Although much of the climbing will continue to take place on private land, it isn't the right or place of a guidebook to invite others publicly to do so.

Added to the traditional, detailed descriptions of rock and ice climbs are two sections that cover remote cliffs and low-angled slides. The remote climbs in the High Peaks section includes only vague descriptions. Visitors can experience for themselves the joys and frustrations of searching things out. The section entitled Slide Climbs is included to bridge the gap between the hiking and climbing. It is also a response to the modern tendency to validate only technical difficulty. The wilds of the Adirondacks offer a whole lot more than just roadside crag climbs.

The Adirondack experience continues to be a unique one, and it grows increasingly so as the sport explodes around the country. Climbers visiting the region are refreshed to find a traditional approach to the sport: climbers here still enjoy adventure, solitude, and wilderness, and their methods reflect these values. With each passing year it becomes clearer and clearer that we need such sanctuaries. As crowded and increasingly sculpted crags become the norm, we must work all the harder to resist becoming the same. They have their place, but they need not be the blueprint for all climbing. Those of us who treasure the Adirondack experience climb with a respect for the land and its lore, and a restraint born of the hope that thirty years from now, when another writer describes climbing in the Adirondacks, the place will continue to stand refreshingly apart from the frenzy.

THE EVOLUTION OF AN IDEA

In 1985 we celebrated the 100th anniversary of the Forest Preserve. This legislation of 1885 and the constitutional amendment ten years later declaring that the lands of the preserve "be forever kept as wild forest lands" were the formal beginnings of what would become the largest park in the lower 48 states, a 6,000,000-acre tract of public and private land covering an area greater than Vermont. The predominant motivation of the legislation was the preservation of the watershed, which was under siege by indiscriminate logging. Today the Adirondack Park is prized more for its recreational potential than for the economic value of its natural resources, but regardless of the values behind the enactment of that 1895 amendment, we are the beneficiaries of one of the largest wild places in the United States.

Along with the privilege of enjoying the lands within the Park comes an enormous responsibility, both to the people of the state who made the sacrifice 100 years ago, and to the lands themselves. With our decision to use this resource must come a pledge to protect it. Every move we make here has an impact, and the preservation of the wilderness for the next 100 years and beyond will depend on the integrity of our own wilderness ethic. We must remember always that we chose to visit this place because of its special character; it would be a gross betrayal of all we claim to stand for if our visit jeopardized that very essence that brought us here in the first place.

Those of us who think of the Adirondacks in terms of the recreation it provides and the beauty that we find here are surprised to find out that neither was a primary reason for the creation of the Park. Many of the earliest explorers agreed with the Mohawk description of the land as "Couxsachrage," or "dismal wilderness." In fact, one of the most remote of the High Peaks today bears the name Couchsachraga. Others saw the region solely as a vast, untapped wealth of resources and envisioned a future of prosperity as settlers dug precious minerals, cleared land for farming, and cut the trees that would build a fast-growing America.

The view that wilderness had a value of its own came in slowly and unsteadily. Early visitors who would later be associated with the evolution of Adirondack wilderness thinking, such as geologist Ebenezer Emmons, surveyor and scientist Verplank Colvin, and even transcendentalist philosopher Ralph Waldo Emerson, all seasoned their awe of the region with an equal awe of the marching and progressive destiny of industrial America. Such ambivalence found these explorers in the still-prevalent philosophical bind which suggested that though the wilderness was awesome and even sublime, it would only become complete when humans added their own special touch and took fullest advantage of the land.

These various views were significant in the cultural development of the Park, but bore little weight in terms of the political debates that were to ensue. Only when the reckless overuse of the area threatened the wallets of the people of the state did the movement to preserve become viable. This occurred when clear-cutting of the forests began to alter the watershed that was the lifeblood of agricultural New York State. The Adirondack forests had acted like a huge sponge, retaining water during periods of heavy rain and rationing it out steadily during dry periods. When the land was left bare and erosion stripped the soils, farmers began to find their way of life threatened by alternating floods and drought. It was then, in the second half of the nineteenth century, that the idea began to take hold that New York's economic future depended on the retention of that vast regulating agent, the wild upstate forests.

In the latter part of the 1880s, visitors to the region began to think of it as both a healthful retreat and a place where sportsmen could pursue such noble and manly activities as hunting and fishing. Both of these new-found interests were probably a reaction to the urbanization that was upsetting the rural lifestyle on which the country had been built. The Adirondacks gave the stressed-out businessman a chance to relax and escape, just as it provided the new city-slicker the opportunity to prove that he still had those rugged essentials that had no outlet of expression in New York or Philadelphia. (Few stopped to reflect on the contradiction of hiring guides to do the real dirty work for them.) Additionally, tubercular patients, following the lead of Dr. Edward Livingston Trudeau, found in the Adirondacks the clear, dry air whose healing properties offered hope to suffering consumptives.

In the years that followed, the area became increasingly known for hunting and fishing, and these alone were enough to draw ever-increasing numbers from downstate. But in 1932, a new image was added to the region when the Winter Olympics came to Lake Placid. The sports world saw the mountains of upstate New York as a place for fun and competition. The existing camps and old inns proved insufficient for crowds of urban visitors, and hotels sprouted. Increasingly, the image of the Adirondacks became one of playground rather than retreat.

Preservation of wilderness remains a strong and growing cause, and this was no more evident than during the 1985 celebration of the first 100 years of the Forest Preserve. It gave us pause to reflect on the rapidity of change and the special heritage we have been given. It was a time to look back on the short-term sacrifices made in order to preserve a timeless resource. And it made us look ahead and plan for the new threats that would face the region in the 1980s and beyond.

The most publicized of these threats has been acid precipitation. As high-sulfur, coal-burning power plants and industries pour wastes into the upper winds over the industrial Midwest, the acidity of airborne water vapor rises to dangerous levels. The first topographical obstacle to these winds as they travel from west to east is the massif of the Adirondack Mountains. The air rises, cools, condenses, and falls as rain or snow with an acidity rivaling that of household vinegar.

This aerial bombardment would be harmful to any region, but it is especially so here in upstate New York. Acid precipitation can be partially leached or neutralized as it passes through the normally thick glacial soils that are characteristic of the Northeast. But in a mountain region such as the

Adirondacks, the soil cover may be as thin as a few inches, thus these areas are the most susceptible to acid pollution. Nor do we have the limestone buffers that are typical of many other areas and which would neutralize some of the acid. As a result of these factors, the areas in the western part of the region (those that get the first good dose of poison) and the uplands of the High Peaks, where the drenching is most continuous and the soils are thinnest, are showing the most severe effects of acid rain. A study concluded in 1988, for example, showed that 25 percent of the lakes in the Park were incapable of supporting fish life.

Another looming threat concerns development of the land for vacation homes and tourist recreation. Lawmakers downstate seem perfectly happy to preserve a wilderness area in someone else's backyard, but many Adirondackers are finding this stifling to the economic well-being of the region. Some of the poorest people in the state live in counties within the Park. How dare you, they ask, keep us from making a living just so you can keep your vacation lands? It is a question with no simple answer. Are we robbing local residents of their freedom when we legislate severe development restrictions, or are we actually preserving the freedom of all people to enjoy their world in as natural a state as possible? The answer, one hopes, may be one that works for both groups. Recent economic studies indicate that strict laws actually may have enhanced prosperity in restricted areas. This certainly has been the case in tourist towns such as Lake Placid.

Several citizens' groups have joined the effort to educate the public and protect the lands of the Adirondacks. Principle among them is the Adirondack Mountain Club (ADK), which since 1922 has worked hard for a more secure Forest Preserve as well as a Preserve that is better understood, experienced, and enjoyed in ways consistent with its wilderness character. ADK's conservation and lobbying efforts and its comprehensive outdoor education, trails, and publications programs stand out as fine examples of one organization's commitment to help ensure that present and future generations will experience the wilderness and magic of the Forest Preserve.

In recent years a bumper sticker expressed the views of some other local residents. It read, "I Loved New York—before the APA". The APA, or Adirondack Park Agency, was established as a regulatory agent to protect the wilderness and decide upon development issues. As such they are seen as both savior and tyrant. Yet without such an enforcement agency, we would quickly see development sprawl over the landscape as a one-way street that would preclude future debate on the value of a wilderness aesthetic.

The philosophy of the Adirondack Park Agency specifically, and of lovers of the wild in general, has been dedicated to responsible stewardship of the resource. It is inevitable that we are going to use the Adirondack region in some way; this seems beyond debate. But questions persist about how we are going to define this use. As we are working on this question, we should step back and look both at the increasing rapidity of change and growth and at other areas, the White Mountains of New Hampshire, for example, to see how growth is treating them. I suspect that when all of the pieces of the philosophical puzzle are put together, most of us will see that we have in our hands something unique, something to be treasured, and something worth sacrificing for.

Here this guidebook runs a risk: It will no doubt bring more people to the cliffs of the region, and their impact will be felt both in the diminution of solitude and the tracks they leave on the landscape. But I have greater confidence that the guide can bring together those who share the wilderness ethic, renewing their commitment and enlivening their active protection of this sanctuary. One theme, therefore, is the real heart of this book, and that theme is wilderness, something to be valued more deeply than any of the games we play during our visits to the wild places.

WILDERNESS ETHICS

One of the foundations of a park is that things are left in as natural a state as possible. As such, the mere cleaning of a route or the addition of fixed protection alters this natural state. Obviously, however, many routes, especially in the North Country, require cleaning, and many of our best routes are feasible only because they have protection bolts. Climbers everywhere operate somewhere within a spectrum between the absolutely unaltered route and the totally manufactured one, but in a designated wilderness area such as a park, it's best to be gentle.

In the 1980s American climbing, for the first time in recent memory, fell behind the pace of other areas of the world in terms of sheer technical difficulty. In response, many climbers advocated that we change our technique in order to keep up. In many American rock-climbing centers, the change was quick. Climbers rose to the challenge, duplicating Europeans' style in order to match their achievements. Crags like Smith Rock quickly replaced Yosemite Valley as the stage of America's hardest and most highly acclaimed routes. Other areas soon joined the movement.

PHOTO BY PAM GARRETT

Slide Rules, *on Big Slide Mountain, is one of the best climbs in the High Peaks.*

21

While the rules of the game are becoming standardized in most climbing centers, however, a few hold on to some regional traditions. It is interesting to consider how these traditions are often born of philosophies in the nature of the land and the values of the people using it. The Europeans, for example, favor numerous, rappel-placed bolts and frankly can't see what all the fuss is about. They are at home in an environment that is tamed and altered. Their cultural roots are deep indeed, and their forebears have been wresting a living for centuries from a dwindling area. The look of a European village speaks of their capacity to use every inch of space: the streets are tight, the homes stacked close, and gardens fill any gaps between buildings and hillside. European mountain regions follow suit. Summits are often adorned with crosses and cliffsides painted with route names and arrows to point the way. In fact, the term "red-point" refers to a German practice of filling in a painted circle of red at the base of the route to indicate that it has been led free.

At the other end of the spectrum are some of the wilderness areas of the United States, where visitors value preservation and tread gently upon the land. They know that essential to their trek or climb is that they are immersing themselves in a wild place. For climbers, part of this tradition has been the effort to follow natural lines of weakness, to rely on boldness and natural protection whenever reasonable, and to hide their passage by using rock-colored chalk, earth-tone bolt hangers, and rappel slings of dull brown or green. While it may be awesome to stand below a 5.14 and gaze at a line of bolts arching out on the most intimidating rock, it is also quite an experience to be high on a wilderness crag, looking out on a scene shaped by nature's hand and unaltered by human visitors.

Evidently, the area itself plays a key role in determining the ethic. If we were to come upon a manipulated landscape, a quarry for example, we would think little of altering it further. Additionally, if we found our climbing area small and shrinking, we might try to force artificial lines up the narrow, blank passages between other routes. We would feel little choice. But the settlers of America found themselves with options the Europeans did not have. We explored much of the land only recently, and we have the choice to leave some of it as it is. We also have the luxury of wide expanses of unclimbed rock, much of it cracked and offering natural climbing lines, and this gives the ambitious among us the opportunity to work a little closer with the landscape as we design an ascent. It takes an honest look at the climbing world around us to better understand our own. Within this context, the practice of bolting and trailwork here can continue to reflect our own special environmental and cultural heritage.

Although bolts are the lightning rods of ethical controversy, they are in fact only an emblem of the debate. Other problems, such as noise, litter, trail abuse, and graffiti, all threaten to creep into our climbing areas if we aren't vigilant. We can do our part by keeping to designated trails when the groundcover is fragile (as at the Beer Walls) and by cleaning up even the tiniest bits of tape or chalk wrappers at the base of the routes. Imagine the lasting impression you leave on the newcomer when you pick up the trash left by tourists near the parking area before you drive away. The behavior of the veteran climbers fast becomes the model for the novices.

In the last edition of this guidebook, I advocated a policy of limiting bolting by placing them on lead only. Surely this line is an arbitrary one, and just as surely, it isn't the full solution. Nor have I or anyone else been appointed official guardian. But somewhere must be a set of universally accepted values. Otherwise, even when we all agree that preservation is a good thing, climbers will operate according to their own definition. Some might think that a classic route needs better belay. Others might feel that a tree should be cut so that the rappel rope won't tangle. Another might find it easier to clip a bolt next to a crack on a hard route than to struggle with the clean gear. And so on. None of these climbers consider themselves blighters. Yet the net result is a transformation we may ultimately regret. With no intention of punning, I note that it is a slippery slope indeed. When bolts are added to old routes or placed next to cracks (as they have been), how long will it be before *Pete's Farewell* or *Gamesmanship* or even the *Empress* are safely bolted clip-ups?

No one wants a climbing world of hardened rules. But the need remains for a common understanding that every alteration adds to the one before and makes easier the next. And when climbers who are just learning the sport watch our actions, they not only imitate, but take them a step farther down the slope. Today, at least in the Adirondacks, it is agreed that it's wrong to bolt without a careful plan and without exhausting clean options, to add bolts to pre-established routes or in places where clean protection would suffice, to chip or to glue, or to cut prominent trees. The custom here continues to be a traditional "ground-up" style, and almost every route described in this guidebook was climbed accordingly. There are very few rappel-bolted routes. Even Purcell's modern-looking routes on the King

Wall and the impressive 5.12s of Martin Berzins and Patrick Munn at Poke-O-Moonshine were protected on the lead.

Each season it becomes ever more clear that we are at a crossroads. Today, we've only felt hints of the controversy, the resentment, the meanness, that would make some of us want to quit the sport. We have believed, perhaps naively, that the Blue Line marked a sanctuary, a place that need not necessarily keep up with the rest of the world. And we are slowly coming to know that in falling behind, we might actually be forging ahead. Looking back in a decade or so, we might well be proud of our priorities, our restraint, our decision to make the sacrifices ourselves rather than passing the burden on to our landscape.

A HISTORY OF CLIMBING
IN THE ADIRONDACKS

How does one decide just where to begin a history of climbing in the Adirondacks? The technical climbers of today, too often attribute the birth of rock climbing to the first man with rope and piton, the climber who did it our way. By this myopic definition, technical climbing in the Adirondacks began in 1916. If, however, we expand our vision and loosen our grip on the sport, we have to admit two things: first, that exploration of the peaks began with the tread of the first human foot, and second, that there is no hard line that separates technical climbing from hiking and scrambling on the trails and slides. The Adirondack story, thus, has no real beginning and no finite parameters. It is simply a story about the joy of mountaineering.

Historians frequently describe the course of human events in terms of the deeds of great men. They disregard social evolution and write that progress grew by the actions and decisions of its leaders. (Thus, Washington is credited with fathering our country and Ford with leading us to the assembly line.) Certainly, they were the catalysts, innovators fortunate enough to live in pivotal periods in history and strong enough to make their influence felt around the world. But history would have marched on without them; though their contributions were major, they were but representatives of the millions who were the true forces in the push that created today.

And so it is with our climbing history. One can vividly imagine the Adirondack climbing scene as having been a baton in a relay race, passed from Case to Goodwin, from Turner to Smith. Even this attempt to acknowledge the nameless as well as the famed follows too closely the great-man

The cliffs around Chapel Pond are among the most popular and varied.

method of analysis. Climbing here surged and ebbed over the years, and the periods of activity are best remembered when they are given names and labels. So as we follow the growth of the game we love from its quiet beginnings to its technological future, and as we define this growth as the Turner period or the Healy years, it will serve us well to remember that these were not the only innovators and that the successes of one cannot be measured against the successes of another. Truly, each climber, as he or she reaches ever higher, stands on the shoulders of those who have gone before.

Mount Colden, the Park's eleventh highest peak, might well be the best place to jump into the story. In July of 1850, Robert Clarke and Alexander Ralph, both employees at the MacIntyre Iron Works at Tahawas, climbed the deep slit known as the *Trap Dike* to the slides above and on to the summit. Today this ranks as perhaps the best scramble in the Adirondacks, taking a direct line from the precipitous Avalanche Pass to the mountain's summit and all of it on rock. Some modern parties carry a rope to belay the waterfall section, and the grade is hard third class or easy fourth. Clarke and Ralph weren't climbers by our definition; they knew nothing of rope work or belaying, but they were mountaineers in the truest sense.

Clarke and Ralph probably climbed the *Trap Dike* only to get to the top of Mount Colden. It was simply the most accessible route. It wasn't long, however, before climbers began to seek out harder routes and turn their attention to the climb rather than the summit. Perhaps we take this shift for granted, but we still share this philosophy as we shun holds to our left and right in the desire to squeeze harder routes between the logical lines of weakness.

One of the first to break away from the ranks of summit climbers was Newell Martin. A Yale graduate of 1875, Martin brought the "art of steeple climbing" from New Haven to the Adirondacks. It is difficult to discern from the existing records just what he climbed in his years upstate, but stories abound of his solo adventures on the slabs of Sawteeth and Gothics and the esteem that these exploits earned him from the ladies of Yale's house party weekends at the Upper Ausable Lake. It's comforting to know that some of these essentials haven't changed in the last hundred years.

The first Adirondack climber to use belaying techniques was probably John Case. A former president of the American Alpine Club, Case was a well-traveled climber who brought alpine climbing skills from Europe to New York. One of his partners in the Alps was Everest pioneer, George Finch. It was Case who bridged the gap between the *Trap Dike*–type exploration and modern rock climbing. Yet he never used protection, claiming that "it spoiled the rhythm of the climb," and he was proud to say that he never pounded a piton. Other climbers of his day were using pitons to protect climbs of higher standards, but Case adhered admirably to the law that "the leader must never fall." He believed that one must find his climbing capacity and stay within it. This shouldn't imply that Case was a timid or conservative climber. To the contrary, modern climbers should try the overlap near the top of Case's 1933 Wallface route and imagine what that 600 feet of exposure would feel like without protection. Later climbers called the route 5.0, but 5.3 might better rank that particular move. This route became a ritual for Case, who climbed it solo for many years.

Case's first climbs were on Indian Head and in Chapel Pond Pass around 1916. Shortly before this, he made a Christmastime ski descent of Whiteface Mountain, certainly one of the earliest of the millions to follow. John Case's best contribution to Adirondack climbing might well have been the knowledge and enthusiasm he shared with others. His early partners included Louis Thorne, Betty Woolsey, and Bob Notman, for whom *Bob's Knob* was named. None of his followers, however, contributed so much and for so long as Jim Goodwin. Like the others, Jim Goodwin was a complete mountaineer, combining skiing, bushwhacking, rock climbing, and ice climbing. As early as 1932, Goodwin and Notman made an attempt on Roaring Brook Falls, and in December of 1935, Goodwin climbed the *Trap Dike* using a long axe and ten-point crampons. In 1936, fresh from a season in the Canadian Rockies, Jim Goodwin and Bob Notman made the first ice ascent of *Chapel Pond Slab*.

As a rock climber, Jim Goodwin explored most of the major cliffs, slabs, and slides in the High Peaks. Included in his ascents were several early attempts on Wallface with John Case. They had picked out the depression and upper chimneys to what is now the *Wiessner Route* and climbed most of the height of the face. Wallface, known still for its route-finding complexities, thwarted the two climbers, but it wasn't long afterward that Case, along with his son and Betty Woolsey, traversed right from the depression and found the zigzagging but natural line of the *Case Route*. (Case maintained that the line is so easy that "someone must have found it" before his 1933 ascent.)

Another noteworthy ascent of Goodwin's was his climb of the high and slabby face of Porter Mountain with Edward Stanley in 1938. Goodwin would later call this a "darn-fool route" because they used no protection and doubtful belays. He remembers with regret nearing the top of the lichen-covered rock as the drizzle began and knowing that a slip would rip Stanley from his grassy stance. It is typical of Goodwin's humble approach to regret such a situation rather than brag about it later. How many of us share this philosophy? We have come to believe that there is something noble in risking our well-being, and Goodwin sees this as a perversion of our goals. In his many years as teacher to the growing numbers of climbers, his main emphasis was always fun and safety. It is also interesting to note that some 40 years later, the second recorded route on Porter was done by Jim's son Tony. Jim remembers watching Tony and Todd Eastman high on the face with a more than a little father's anxiety.

Adirondack climbing got a major boost when Bob Notman persuaded German expatriate Fritz Wiessner to visit the Adirondacks. Fritz was one of the world's leading climbers at the time, and he brought not only European but Himalayan experience with him. Climbers in his homeland near Dresden were climbing near the 5.10 level at the time, and only recently has the world acknowledged this. With Notman, Goodwin, and M. Beckett Howorth, Wiessner scoured the Adirondacks, adding routes to Indian Head, Wallface, Hurricane Crag, Chapel Pond, Rooster Comb, Noonmark, Mount Jo, and Mount Colden. Fritz Wiessner will always be remembered for his generous contributions to the Adirondack Mountain Club's annual rock climbing school. But perhaps more significantly, he gave Adirondack climbing an element of legitimacy: here was a world-famous climber who, though skeptical at first, saw potential here for excellent climbing, and it is this realization that is at the heart of first ascents today.

Under Jim Goodwin's direction, ADK's climbing school taught the essentials of safe and ecological climbing at Mount Jo in the mid-sixties. Here personalities, skills, and route information coalesced, and a surge of route exploration followed. Trudy Healy, with the support of Wiessner and Goodwin, planned the first official guidebook, and as advisor to the Penn State Outing Club, inspired several of her climbers to come to the Adirondacks to teach at the ADK school and help her research routes. There had been some notes around, but most of the information had to be discovered anew. Al Breisch and Craig Patterson took on the challenge and with Healy climbed much old and new terrain. With the publication of Trudy Healy's *A Climber's Guide to the Adirondacks* in 1967, Adirondack climbing had, in Jim Goodwin's words, "come of age."

One of the most active local climbers in the 1950s was Dave Bernays of

Saranac Lake. Dave learned to climb at Camp Treetops in Lake Placid and showed an energy not soon matched. As fifteen-year-olds, he and Harry Eldridge attempted Wallface with little gear and only a vague description of the route. They didn't finish, but Dave's interest had been piqued and he brought this to most of the other faces in both winter and summer. The Penn State crew, while researching for the 1967 guide, found pitons in the most unlikely places and usually assumed that Dave Bernays had been there first.

At Poke-O-Moonshine, the late fifties and early sixties were the years of the Canadians. A small group of experienced climbers from Quebec brought skills and boldness not yet seen in the Adirondacks. The leader during this period was John Turner. No climber since has so dominated the scene. Turner came from England in the fifties and established a new level of climbing in the Adirondacks and New Hampshire. On Cathedral Ledge in New Hampshire, he created *Recompense* and *Repentance,* routes that would remain the hardest north of the Gunks for many years. *Repentance* was especially severe: It is an overhanging off-width chimney that borders on 5.10. Modern climbers find the route intimidating, even though the crux can be protected by oversized cams and a fixed bong piton. Turner did it with his typical rack of a half-dozen carabiners and a few small pitons. Turner's partners would later say that he had a better eye for routes than anyone else, that he climbed slowly and surely and "never made a mess of a move." Routes like *Bloody Mary* and *The Cooler* stand today as testament to this drive and skill.

The Canadian group was a diverse collection of varied origins: they were of Irish, Scottish, English, French Canadian, and English Canadian backgrounds. The regular visitors to Poke-O-Moonshine included Claude LaVallee, Ben Poisson, Brian Rothery, Dick Strachan, Hugh Tanton, and Dick Wilmott. Like climbers everywhere today, they would finish their climbing days lounging across the road from the cliff (there was a small bar which, sadly, is missing today), drinking beer, gazing upward, and describing in myriad accents and great animation where the next route would go.

One can get a better idea of the accomplishments of an era when one examines the equipment used by the climbers. The Canadians were fortunate to have Bernard Foucard as a local importer of French alpine gear. He supplied them with carabiners and pitons, mostly thin blades and angle ring pitons. No pins were as large as modern chocks or Friends, and as Ben Poisson would later relate, "when the crack was wider than an inch, they just climbed without protection." This knowledge would certainly change our view of "routine" climbs like *Gamesmanship,* a 145-foot handcrack. The ropes were made locally in Montreal and were much like today's ⁷⁄₁₆" Goldline, but were white, supple, and of course, quite untested. On their feet these climbers wore mainly mountain boots, stiff-soled with rubber cleats, though in later years many switched to the more flexible klettershue: It was John Turner who brought back from Europe the first pair of PA's to the region.

The 1960s and early seventies brought more skilled and traveled climbers from the Gunks and elsewhere to the Adirondacks. The highlights of these visits were *Gourmet* on Wallface by Ants Leements, Jeff Wood, and Dave Isles; the direct off-width finish to *Bloody Mary* at Poke-O by Jim McCarthy (a variation still timidly avoided by most); the aid eliminations of *Body Snatcher* by John Stannard and *Psychosis* by McCarthy and Richard Goldstone; and the addition of *Cirrhosis* by Gunks guidebook author Dick Williams and Dave Loeks, all also at Poke-O.

During this period, the Adirondacks played host to a pivotal introduction of newer ice tools and technique. In 1969, Yvon Chouinard, with Jim McCarthy, introduced what would become the standard approach to ice-climbing to a group of climbers assembled at Chapel Pond. Chouinard brought out his radically short (though still long by our standards) axe and its partner handtool, both with drooped pick and sharp teeth. Thus armed, he and McCarthy front-pointed up the slab route without once resorting to step-cutting. Later that weekend, they also climbed what would become known as *Chouinard's Gully*. It was a revolutionary moment in American ice-climbing, one that would be followed the next year by a stepless ascent of New Hampshire's *Pinnacle Gully,* and one by which the climbing world would be forever changed. Within a few short years, "piolet traction" became the norm. The "big slab" at Chapel Pond would be considered forever a beginner's route, and the towering drips, flows, and waterfalls, like Poke-O's *Positive Thinking* and New Hampshire's *Black Dike*, unthinkable just a few years before, would become the climbs of a new standard.

Back on rock in the mid-seventies, the team of Al Long and Al Rubin added many fine routes to the area, most notably at Moss Cliff, where their routes rank as some of the finest in the East. Concurrently, locals and part-time locals Grant Calder, John Wald, Todd Eastman, and Dave Cilley were adding a host of good climbs of their own on Pitchoff Chimney Cliff and the Spider's Web. The step-brother team of Calder and Wald are best remembered for their spirit of commitment and adventure: the blind traverse on the then lichen-covered wall of *The El*, the overhanging stacked block line of *Keye,* and the unprotected slab climbing of *Rugosity* are good examples of their "go for it" attitude.

In 1976 Tom Rosecrans published *Adirondack Rock and Ice Climbs.* Perhaps the best result of his good detective work was the inclusion of Rogers Rock, a steep, clean slab that rises for over 500 feet out of the deep, blue waters of Lake George. *Little Finger,* the prize discovery of Jim Kolocotronis and Bob Perlee, is one of the best climbs of the area: It is a fingercrack that runs uninterrupted up the huge slab for over four pitches. Rosecrans added many routes of his own here to make this cliff a mandatory stop for visitors in their travels north.

Some of the finest climbers in the East and even in the country tried out the climbing upstate in the late seventies. Henry Barber made a few trips to Lake Placid to visit his close friend Dave Cilley, then manager of Lake Placid's Eastern Mountain Sports. Together they tore into the *Spider's Web,* where Barber found crack after crack slicing the slightly overhanging rock and brought free climbing here near the level of New Hampshire's. John Bouchard and John Bragg climbed the iced-up *Positive Thinking,* the Adirondacks' first NEI 5 ice route in 1975, and Jim Dunn joined the Poke-O crew to add top-quality routes such as *Summer Solstice* and *Firing Line.* On Pitchoff, Rick Fleming eliminated the aid from *Roaches on the Wall* on one of his brief visits from the Granite State.

Though occasional downstaters climbed at Poke-O-Moonshine, the mid-seventies explosion here was the work of a small, isolated group from nearby Plattsburgh. They called Poke-O their own and scoured it for new routes with a possessive passion, sure that if the word got out, the cliff would swarm with climbers and the road below would resemble the hairpin turn at the Gunks on a Sunday in July. Well, the word slowly spread, and the inevitable didn't happen, but as a result of their work, most of the routes on the cliff bear the names of Geoff Smith, Gary Allan, Drew Allan, Pat Munn, Dave Hough, and Mark Meschinelli.

The group, the Ski-to-Die Club, found their greatest thrills not on rock, but on three-pin ski descents of the High Peaks. In the tradition of Case's Whiteface ski, they made such notable runs as the north and south slides of Colden, the Marcy slide into Panther Gorge, the slides on Dix, Algonquin, Macomb, and a list of other exhilarating if not reckless downhills.

Their leader and mentor for both skiing and climbing was Geoff Smith.

As Hough would later say, "Geoff had insight." It was Smith who, like Turner twenty years before, could see the line and envision the route. Many of his best routes were actually creations: he'd often rappel, inspect, trundle, and clean before he climbed. Gary Allan was another leader of the group. He climbed with power and confidence and put up the hardest leads of the era at Poke-O, most significantly the first pitch of *Southern Hospitality* and the fingercrack of *Knights in Armor.* Pat Munn, Dave Hough, and Mark Meschinelli also added many fine routes of their own. But it was Smith who played the latter-day Turner, an example for a band of climbers and a symbol of the time.

Climbing in the Adirondacks was published in 1983, and it spurred the exploration for new routes once again, this time with a concentration in the Keene Valley and Lake Placid regions. Two climbers played key roles in this next surge of new routes: Jim Cunningham and Chuck Turner. Cunningham ran a guide service in Keene Valley, and his home there became a locus of operations for climbers in the area. With partners including Dave Flinn, Bob Hay, Rich Leswing, and Pete Benson, Cunningham discovered some excellent routes both on the already established Hurricane Crag and the newly discovered Beer Walls. Turner, joined by several partners including Bill Simes, added routes at the Washbowl and the Spider's Web. While no relation to John Turner, Chuck brought a similar energy to those who climbed with him.

On ice, it was the Alan Jolley show for a few years. He would find ice in the most unlikely places and climb most of it solo. Significant among these ropeless climbs were the first ascent of *Whip It Good* and the first pitch of *Positive Thinking.* Alan moved west shortly thereafter to take over the EMS climbing school in Boulder.

Continuing to explore for ice have been two other notables: Tad Welch and Tom Yandon. Over the last ten years, the best ice routes have been Tom Yandon's. There aren't too many other grandfathers who continue to climb at such a torrid pace. And Tom's achievements aren't limited to the Adirondacks: he regularly takes his leather boots and his homemade tools on the road for internationally acclaimed routes such as *Le Pomme d'Or,* and *Polar Circus.* Locally, with partners including his son Edmund, Dennis Luther, and Joe and Dave Szot, he continues to be the Adirondack ice climber, perhaps the only local climber who looks at summer as the "off-season." Tad's approach has obviously been influenced by his trips to Scotland. He seems happiest when his crampons are scratching bare rock and his tools are solidly planted into frozen turf. When following some of his descriptions, you would be well advised to bring along a file and some imagination.

Tad's exploits may be indicative of yet another revolution in ice climbing. With the most obvious routes already bagged, climbers are stretching the limits between what constitutes an ice climb and what is simply cold rock. In 1994, Jeff Lowe made his first trip to the region and, both literally and figuratively, "put on a clinic." Driving through the passes with veteran local climbers and looking up at the glazed rock, he'd ask, "Has that one been done? What's the name of that route? And what about that other one next to it?" while his hosts would look confusedly at each other and wonder if he could be serious. Obviously, and as in every other surge seen by the sport of climbing, it isn't tools and it isn't skill that leads us out beyond the limits of the day. It's vision, and Lowe's recent visits have widened some eyes.

No rock climber has covered as much new terrain over the past few seasons as Patrick Purcell. When Patrick was seventeen and just learning to climb, he took a 60-foot, protection-ripping groundfall at the Gunks, almost losing his foot. In fact, when he arrived at Vassar Hospital in nearby Poughkeepsie, there wasn't much holding it onto his leg, and doctors requested permission to remove it. But Patrick refused to give it up and after a dogged rehabilitation, he climbed again and was soon on his way to becoming a driving force behind many of our hardest climbs.

Climbing with various partners, most notably Jeff Edwards, Patrick's impact on the region continues right to the present, with him almost single-handedly developing the awesome King Wall. Many climbers had peeked around the corner at this giant and imposing wall, but few had ever contemplated the possibility of any free climbs here. No doubt the future will have the King Wall as one of the centerpieces of Adirondack, and even Eastern, climbing.

Another climber with a growing reputation for good routes is Tim Beaman. For many years, Adirondackers heard bits and pieces about this guy from Vermont who "really knows how to climb." All through the eighties Tim and his wife, Sylvia Lazarnick, were making trips across the lake to find some of the best climbs here, both on private and public lands. Frequently teaming up with Bill Dodd and Herb George, Beaman continues to build upon a legacy of good, hard crack routes. In fact, locals are coming to know that when they are on a Beaman route, they can expect stiff, strenuous crack climbing where perseverance is often the difference between success and failure.

One of the most exciting developments of the past few seasons has been the exploration of the southern Adirondacks. Here, climbers are finding cliff after cliff with enormous climbing potential. No longer does the climber from Syracuse or Albany feel confined to the High Peaks region to find good climbing. It is becoming increasingly clear that fine but virtually undeveloped cliffs lie deep in the woods in the "low peaks" section of the park. These aren't roadside crags like Pitchoff or Poke-O-Moonshine. Instead, climbers here are doing some hiking, and as they do, they are finding a climbing world free from both crowds and certainty. Jim Vermeulen, Tad Welch, Bill Widrig, and Dick Tucker have been the main forces in this recent push to discover. Together and with various partners, they have been instrumental in checking old maps, poring through hiking guides, and striking out on their rare days off in the quest to find new rock. Their efforts have paid off. The climbing map of the park is changing by the year; no longer is the greater Keene Valley region the only place people mention when they talk of Adirondack climbing.

At the same time climbers were exploring moderate routes on remote southern crags, other visitors were employing a more modern approach to climbing, and nowhere was this more evident than at Poke-O-Moonshine. It is here that the first purely bolt-protected face climbs emerged. Montreal's Julien Dery, along with partners including Pierre Gagnon and Gelu Ionescu, was drawn to the square-cut holds that pepper the blank sections of Poke-O, and his routes gained instant notice and acclaim. *Verdon* and *Maestro* were two of the first and best routes of this genre. Shortly thereafter, Dave Lanman put up two vicious test pieces, *The Howling* and *Salad Days*, the latter being upstate's first 5.13.

Interestingly, while these modern routes were going in, a British visitor reminded us that the 5.12 realm wasn't limited to bolted face routes. Martin Berzins, during his annual visits to the Adirondacks, has dazzled local climbers by picking out natural lines that had been right in front of everybody's noses but that looked just too improbable even to try. The Waterfall Face at Poke-O perhaps best demonstrates the tenacity of Berzins: Those three 5.12s in a row on a very sustained 140-foot wall will remind climbers for years to come that natural lines requiring nothing but traditional protection are still out there to be plucked by anyone who can muster the strength, the skill, and the vision.

Currently, the craft at its best is being demonstrated by Patrick Munn at Poke-O-Moonshine. *Calvary Hill, Messiah,* and *The Gathering* are the finest long-route achievements yet accomplished here. Pushed by Gary Allan's annual visits from the West, and joining forces most often with Dominic Eisinger, Patrick Munn has been setting a standard against which climbers will long be measured.

It was just over thirty years ago that Fritz Wiessner first proposed a climbing guidebook for the Adirondacks. The changes in the sport that followed might tempt one to believe that the march of climbing history is inevitable and linear. But upon closer scrutiny, we see that many things endure. Friendships are still forged on opposite ends of a rope. Climbers still feel a sense of belonging, of community, of shared values and experiences that sets them apart from the rest. They still cherish uncertainty as the spice that makes the game so special. And they still tread the landscape together, in awe both of its majesty and the scope of their responsibility for it.

SAFETY

Climbers have always treasured their independence, and in most places the sport, thankfully, remains relatively free of rules and regulations. We need no permits, nor must we demonstrate or standardize our procedures for any authority before we are allowed on the cliffs. Instead, we hold tight to the freedom that we might be on our own and make our own decisions.

We all, however, must heed at least one law, the law of gravity. Despite our temptation to defy it, gravity is constant, ready to pull us from a slippery stance the moment we let down our guard, tugging relentlessly at every loose rock poised above. Every so often, the law of gravity is harshly enforced. The falling leader crashes onto a ledge, the dislodged boulder accelerates toward a belayer tied snugly to an anchor with no place to run or hide. The freedom seems frivolous.

Please be aware that the degree to which we safeguard ourselves against the consequences of one law will probably determine the degree to which legal authorities will feel compelled to protect us with another. More plainly, if we climb responsibly and safely, we will probably remain free from interference. Safe climbing is an attitude, one that manifests itself in practices such as:

- wearing a helmet
- learning first aid and carrying a first-aid kit
- testing for loose holds .
- backing up all anchors
- presuming that the protection will pull out rather than admiring how solid it looks
- communicating clearly with your partners
- belaying out of the line of rockfall
- guarding ropes and slings against sharp edges
- practicing and using perfect belay technique 100% of the time
- knowing how to lock off a belay device and escape a belay with a prusik
- using a belay or a friction knot to back up every rappel
- retreating from a route when it just doesn't feel right

If, however, despite all safeguards, you are involved in or witness an accident, you must know how to respond. First, assess the situation to the best of your ability. Then, call for help. All search and rescue is under the authority of the Department of Environmental Conservation forest rangers.

Forest Rangers   897-1300

On weekends or after 4 pm, call:
Emergency Dispatch   891-0235

The third place to call would be the New York State Police (518-897-2000) in Ray Brook. They will use whatever means needed to contact persons able to help.

In remote sections of the park, state police or local rescue squads should be instructed to contact DEC forest rangers. The 911 system is not in place in all areas and may confuse or delay operations. If you do report an accident, have the following information in hand:

- Location (don't expect authorities to know cliff names not on the map)
- Time of accident
- Nature of accident (fall, rockfall, lightning, etc.)
- Age and sex of victim

- Apparent injuries:
    Level of consciousness of victim
    Bleeding
    Possible fracture, head or spinal injury
- Terrain:
    Will a technical, roped evacuation requiring trained personnel
    be required, or will a strong group of litter carriers suffice?
- Number of experienced climbers available to assist

GETTING ALONG WITH FALCONS
AND OTHER ADIRONDACK LOCALS

Years ago, the Adirondack cliffs were home to one of the most impressive predators in the wild, the peregrine falcon. In the last decade, a reintroduction project that began in the Shawangunks and moved north has culminated in the successful restoration of breeding pairs of falcons at over a dozen sites in the Park. Climbers have not only benefited from the thrill of being close to these majestic raptors, but they have also played an important role in bringing them back. Many local climbers regularly report to the experts at the Department of Environmental Conservation on the status of nests, assist them in bird banding, and advise them on the easiest and safest access to the nesting sites. Climbers have also shown deep respect for the temporary closures, understanding that while they may have limited access to a particular cliff for a short time, the benefits of successful nesting far outweigh any minor inconvenience.

Peregrine falcons ferociously guard their nests, and will strike climbers without hesitation or warning. As a volunteer and I were peering over the edge of a cliff during one authorized inspection, a female falcon screamed in, seemingly out of nowhere, and raked my partner across the face, leaving a line of blood trickling into her eyes from across her eyebrows. Such behavior is a necessary part of the survival of the species. Successful nesting requires that the eggs remain protected and warm during incubation and that the fledglings stay safely on the ledge until they are ready to fly. Any disturbance can be a disaster during this precarious time.

Recent nesting sites have included the Washbowl area (both upper and lower cliffs), Moss Cliff, Poke-O-Moonshine, Wallface, and a few privately owned and unpublished cliffs. The closures are posted on signs along the base of the cliffs or at cliff trailheads, with additional information available from the DEC office (518-897-1300). The typical nesting period runs from mid-April to mid-August, though the times vary according to each nesting pair. The officials in charge of the project, obviously grateful for the cooperation they've received from climbers, have been very accommodating, closing only the minimum amount of rock and opening the cliffs as early as possible once the birds have fledged and are no longer in danger from any disturbance. Remember that the state has authority to close huge areas of rock in order to protect the birds, and it is only because of our good behavior that they make access as liberal as they do. Keep it up.

ADIRONDACK WEATHER

The only predictable characteristic about Adirondack weather is its unpredictability. The temperature and precipitation chart should help in planning a trip to the area, but weather often interferes with the most carefully laid plans. It is also worth noting that the clouds seem to hang in over the mountains for a day or two after the national weather maps indicate a clear Northeast.

Typically, the rock-climbing season begins in late April or early May. The low cliffs and those without perpetual drainage from above begin to dry, and there is a brief grace period before the black flies move in and lay claim to the region. These "locals" seem to hatch to the clanging of hardware, and in late May and early June a variation of the beekeeper's outfit will retard insanity. The best attire for this season consists of a white turtleneck, white pants tucked into the socks, and a headnet stuffed in a pocket to ensure attentive belays. (Bugs seem to like dark colors best, with blue being a clear favorite. Perhaps it's some genetic predisposition. Maybe it's a fashion statement.)

Unlike most climbing areas in the United States, the Adirondacks seldom get too hot to climb, but in mid-summer one should certainly carry water on longer routes. The rock season draws to a close after a most spectacular autumn. This brief period is a favorite time for climbers. Cool weather, dry hands, and an explosion of color make these days in September and early October some of the year's best.

The first flurries fall in late October, and by mid-November, ice climbers, at great peril to both themselves and their tools, try to push in a season that more realistically gets under way in December. By mid-March, the

Monthly Average Temperatures, Snowfall and Precipitation

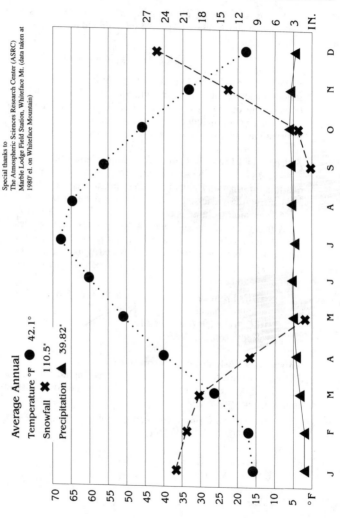

Average Annual

Temperature °F ● 42.1°

Snowfall ✖ 110.5"

Precipitation ▲ 39.82"

Special thanks to
The Atmospheric Sciences Research Center (ASRC)
Marble Lodge Field Station, Whiteface Mt. (data taken at
1980' el. on Whiteface Mountain)

ice begins to decay. Ice climbing in April is rare, but puffs of chalk begin rising again above sunny crags like Pitchoff and the Spider's Web.

WHAT IF IT RAINS?

If the weather conspires to ruin your trip, or if your tender fingertips refuse to touch another labradorite crystal, you needn't turn solely to the refuge of your tent or one of the local bars. There are countless other ways to enjoy the region. Included here are some that not only are entertaining or informative, but also should help you get a better feel for the Adirondacks.

Adirondack Mountain Club Information Centers

If you are headed to the Adirondacks from the south or east, ADK's Headquarters Information Center (HQIC) is an excellent stop for backcountry and general Adirondack information (May–Columbus Day, Mon.–Sat., 8:30–5:00; Tues. after Columbus Day–May, Mon.–Fri., 8:30–4:30).

Within the High Peaks region, ADK operates the High Peaks Information Center (HPIC) on its Heart Lake property. In addition to providing information, both centers host lectures and workshops, and offer educational displays, publications, souvenir merchandise, some outdoor equipment, and trail snacks.

> HQIC: From I-87 ("the Northway"), take Exit 21. Take 9N south approximately 0.2 mi. 518-668-4447
> HPIC: Take the Adirondak Loj Rd. 7 mi. south from Route 73 just south of Lake Placid.

Adirondack Park Visitor Interpretive Centers

These two educational and interpretive centers include hiking trails, nature exhibits, slide/lecture presentations, and numerous other displays on the Adirondacks.

> Paul Smiths Visitors Interpretive Center
> Route 30, Paul Smiths, NY
> and
> Newcomb Visitors Interpretive Center
> Route 28N, Newcomb, NY

The Adirondack Museum

This is a museum of Adirondack history that includes paintings and exhibits on mining, logging, and the exploration and settling of the region. It provides an excellent look at human interaction with the wilderness. Nearby is the Adirondack Lakes Center for the Arts offering films, concerts, workshops, and demonstrations in music, crafts, and other regional arts.

Routes 28N and 30, Blue Mountain Lake, NY 12812
518-352-7311

The Lake Placid Center for the Arts

Here one can find gallery displays, concerts, drama, and dance companies. It is located on Saranac Avenue in Lake Placid. 518-523-2512.

The Olympic Region

Lake Placid is filled with Olympic memories. The sites of the 1932 and 1980 winter events are open to the public. The ski-jumps (with an elevator trip to the top if you aren't afraid of heights), the bobsled and luge tracks, and the arena are some of the highlights. For information, call the Olympic Regional Development Authority at 518-523-1655.

Adirondack Flying Service

These scenic flights are the best way to get a quick overview of the lay of the land or the specifics of a remote High Peaks face. Within a few minutes of taking off from Lake Placid Airport, you'll be staring at the awesome Wallface or skimming the slides of Gothics. Tell the pilot what rock you want to check out, and bring a camera. The standard tour is about twenty minutes and costs $20 per person. 518-523-2473.

Keene Valley Library: The Alpine Collection

In the John Case Room of the library is a collection of mountaineering literature that will make any rainy day a short one. (Summer hours: Monday through Saturday 10–4, Tuesday and Thursday evenings 7–9. Regular hours: Tuesday and Thursday 9–12, 1–5, and 7–9 PM. Saturdays 9–12 and 1–4.)

Fort Ticonderoga

This is one of the region's most significant historical sites. It is here that key battles of the American Revolution were fought. Ticonderoga is close to the climbing areas of Pharaoh Mountain and Rogers Rock.

This short list was selected to provide an overview of what the region is all about. Days off the rock can also be spent fishing, golfing, hiking, sailing, eating, drinking, and napping . . . all of which are excellent in the Adirondacks.

USING THIS GUIDEBOOK

The climbs in this guide are grouped according to region. In order for most of this to make sense, you should have a good road map of the area as well as a trail map for some of the more remote climbs. Many of the verbal descriptions are supplemented with photos. I've done my best to make sure the descriptions are accurate, but there are certainly errors in this publication. Please note that many of the routes—many of the cliffs, for that matter—have had very little traffic. Some of the descriptions in the guide are the result of only one visit by one party. Always be ready to trust your own judgment over anything here in print.

The routes are evaluated by means of five classifications:

Grade (This tells how long a route should take.)
   I   A couple of hours
   II   Half a day
   III   Most of a day
   IV   A full day
   V   Usually includes a bivouac
   VI   A true big-wall climb of several days

Classification (This tells how hard or sustained the climbing moves are.)
   Class 1   Hiking.
                 Example: The trail to Mount Marcy

   Class 2   Rougher terrain.
                 Examples: The cable section on the Gothics trail or the slides on Whiteface.

   Class 3   Handholds necessary, increased exposure, dangerous falls possible.
                 Example: The *Eagle Slide* on Giant.

   Class 4   A rope is used to protect the hard sections, but the climbers generally move simultaneously.

*Wilderness crags like Good Luck Mountain in the
southern Adirondacks hold a wealth of new-route potential.*

Example: The waterfall section on the *Trap Dike* and most of the *Case Route* on Wallface.

Class 5 The climb is divided into "pitches" (sometimes referred to as p. 1, p. 2, etc.), and protection points are used between the leader and his stationary belayer. All progress is made physically; in other words, the gear is used only in the event of a fall. Class 5 climbs are further subdivided:

5.0–5.3 Easy
5.4–5.7 Moderate
5.8–5.10 Difficult
5.11–5.14 Extreme

(The open-ended system will grow to accommodate harder routes.)

We in the area have opted not to divide the classes further by adding the common a, b, c, d to the harder routes; this is because most of the severe climbs have had only one or two ascents and it would be very difficult to establish any consistency. When the routes seem especially easy or hard for a grade, a minus or a plus sign will be added.

Class 6 Artificial or aid climbing. The climber relies on equipment such as pitons or chocks to hold his weight. Class 6 climbs are subdivided as follows:

A0 (for a carabiner handhold or two) through A5 (where a fall of 150 feet could occur)

Further, though many routes have been upgraded in this edition, many visitors find Adirondack grades to be on the stiff side, especially when compared to gyms or the newer areas like Red Rocks or New River Gorge. You will find that areas that have been climbed since the early years—the Gunks, Seneca Rocks, the Adirondacks—adhere to an old-fashioned idea about the grading system.

Protection Rating

When possible, a protection rating is given. This presumes that the leader has a modern rack (Friends, RPs or other small wired nuts, Tri-Cams, TCUs and any of the other popular gadgets in common use at the time of this printing). It also presumes that the leader is skilled in seeing and utilizing the placement possibilities. Most leaders carry a nut tool for cleaning the cracks, especially where the tiny nuts are involved.

(E) The protection is excellent.

(S) The protection is satisfactory.

(D) The protection is poor or difficult to place.

(X) The pitch has virtually no protection and the climb is akin to a solo. Fall on one of these and it would be your last Adirondack "trip."

The protection rating takes into consideration the route's technical difficulty. If a route's 5.10 crux pitch has good protection but is followed by a 5.4 runout, the protection rating will still be (e), but the easier, unprotected section will be so noted in the description for that particular pitch.

Recommendation
A dagger (†) will be affixed to those routes that are especially recommended. Do not conclude, however, that the absence of a † means that the route isn't a good one. Experienced climbers make their own decisions rather than relying on the biases of a guidebook.

First Ascent Credits
Whenever possible, climbers are named as having completed the first ascent of a route. This probably matters more to those listed than to anyone else. But for those interested, the credits are abbreviated as follows:

FA	Means "first ascent by..."
FFA	Means "first free ascent by ..."
ACB	Means "as climbed by..." These climbers are the first reported on the route, and it is possible, but not certain, that they were actually first to climb it.

Obviously, these grades are subjective. Many routes have seen only one ascent. Thus, no consensus exists as to its quality or difficulty. There are few activities so esteemed by climbers as arguing over grades. Never will we all agree. So view these ratings as a rough guide, but be ready for anything. The grades are merely what some others have thought about the route, but as always, the decision and responsibility is yours alone.

The extraordinary King Wall with Patrick Purcell on Kingdom Come.

KEENE VALLEY

The greatest concentration of climbing in the Adirondacks lies around Chapel Pond. It and Poke-O-Moonshine make the most attractive destinations for visiting climbers. Included in this section are also some minor crags along Route 73 and I-87 to the south, but most of the rock described below lies on the numerous and often confusing cliffs, slabs, and outcrops scattered in every direction around the pond. The rock here is anorthosite, the rock type most characteristic of the Adirondack High Peaks. The older exposures are dark and rough, while more recently exposed faces, the Spider's Web for example, are smoother and closer to their original whitish color.

The small town of Keene Valley offers supplies, lodging, and a climbing shop, the Mountaineer (518-576-2281). The Noonmark Diner's breakfasts and homebaked goodies keep many a climbing team from making the promised early start. Camping is available in the boulders at the base of Chapel Pond Slab, at a dirt road that leaves Route 73 a few hundred feet north of Chapel Pond, or anywhere else that looks inviting. Park regulations allow camping anywhere on state land as long as you stay 150' from a road, a trail, or a water supply.

NORTHWAY EXPRESS WALL

This face lies on Forest Preserve land just off I-87 ("the Northway"), and it is visible to travelers heading north above milepost 92. The south-facing cliff is clearly visible from I-87. Approach from the interstate is easy, but parking is prohibited. Therefore, it is necessary to park at the nearest exit and walk the west side of the highway, keeping at least 30' from the road. Hike up to the first cliff band, an overhanging wall of about 70' with two lines on the right. The first is a 5.5 ramp, and the second a corner capped by an overhang that goes at about 5.6. The most obvious feature on the main cliff is a large, detached block that leads to a giant roof.

Great Spoof   I   5.9   175'   (E)

pitch 1 Climb the crack behind the right side of the block to the roof. Traverse right and up the corner to a belay. 5.7 80'

pitch 2 Follow the obvious corner/crack to the top.

FA Patrick and Mary Purcell 7/84

Screams of the Primitive   I   5.8+   175'   (E)

pitch 1 Climb the left side of the block, up the chimney to the roof. Continue through a small roof and right-diagonal crack to a stance. 85'

pitch 2 Climb out left to a small overhang (crux), and continue to the top.

FA Patrick Purcell and Andy Zimmerman 7/84

Strict Time   I   5.9   (D)

Near the left end of the cliff is a sheer wall with a finger crack that starts above a horizontal crack. This is *Greenhouse Effect*. The crux of these two routes is just getting off the ground.

pitch 1 Start 5' right of a beech tree; after the 5.9 start, move left 5' and climb face (5.8+).

FA Fred Abbuhl and Sue Dearstyne 4/28/90

Greenhouse Effect   I   5.9

pitch 1 Using the same start as for *Strict Time,* traverse the horizontal crack left and climb the perfect finger crack.

Variation Top rope left of beech tree start, diagonally to the finger crack. 5.11

FA Fred Abbuhl and Sue Dearstyne 4/28/90

Greenhouse Defect   I   5.11   (top-rope)

The face 20' left of the finger crack.

FA Fred Abbuhl and Doug Douglas 11/3/90

NORTH HUDSON DOME

A short distance past Exit 29 (between mileposts 96 and 97), the north-bound traveler sees this dark slabby face on the west side of I-87. It is illegal to park or even walk on the interstate, so one must park off the nearest exit (29), and walk north, staying at least 30' from the highway.

Burton Birch Route   II   5.7   400'   (s)

Near the center of the face (the clean, long central section) is a large oak, marked by an obvious "Y" about 8' up. To the right of the tree is a slab and left-facing corner.

pitch 1 Climb the slab for 40' to a dying oak and small grassy ledge. 5.4 90'

pitch 2 Climb out left to the left side of a small arch. Head back right and turn the arch on good holds. Belay at a unique, small crack in otherwise blank rock. 5.7 85'

pitch 3 Up steep moon rock to the top.

FA Patrick Purcell, Burton Ryan, and Birch 7/84

Easter's Force   II   5.7   300'   (e)

pitch 1 8' left of the oak mentioned above is a slab leading to an undercling flake. Climb the flake towards the left-facing corner and belay at flakes. 5.5 80'

pitch 2 Climb straight up to a crack/flake system beneath a steepening of the rock. 5.4 50'

pitch 3 Climb the flake and small crack right through the weakness in the steep section. Up the moon rock to a belay.

pitch 4 Scramble off left.

FA Patrick and Mary Purcell 4/85

ANOTHER ROADSIDE DETRACTION

This is a small but high-quality wall right on the west side of I-87, one mile south of Exit 30. It is only a short distance from the roadway, and upon closer inspection, it is much better than it seems from the car as one speeds by. A few good fingercrack and face climbs have been done in the 5.7–5.10 range. Approach by parking as for King Philips Spring off Exit 30 and walking parallel to the highway for one mile south to the wall. As with all climbs near I-87, stay at least 30' from the shoulder of the road.

KING PHILIPS SPRING

Just off Exit 30 of I-87 is King Philips Spring, source of springwater for locals and travelers and site of the Hotdog Man, considered by many to be haute cuisine in the world of roadside vendors. It is also the parking area for a popular series of cliffs. The climbing here is generally in the 5.4 range, and though the routes are easily top-roped, several lines offer enough protection for leading. The slabs lie at an angle of about 65 degrees and vary from about 30' to 100' in height. There are some drawbacks to this site: It is often crowded, the interstate is within sight and earshot, and the approach trail near the parking lot is littered with trash and toilet paper.

From the parking area, follow a dirt road back through the woods toward the interstate. The road becomes a trail, and though it diverges at one point, both paths emerge at the top of the cliffs.

Across the way and facing the main cliffs is another steep, clean slab. *Eighteen Wheeler* (5.9+ 90', FA Patrick and Mary Purcell 5/8/94) begins between two sets of birches, climbing up right using horizontal cracks and two bolts to a bolt belay. The second pitch climbs a bulge (bolt) to the top.

The Whitewater Walls

WHITEWATER WALLS

About halfway between Chapel Pond and Exit 30 are a small collection of slabs and faces above the Boquet River and easily seen from Route 73. There is parking (and swimming) at the bridge over the North Fork of the Boquet. From here it is necessary to cross the river and walk south along a high bank for about one-half mile. It is also easy to hop the guardrail right below the cliffs before crossing the river and heading up to the rock. The climbing here is similar to that at King Philips Spring, and it is easy to scope things out from the car. The routes are generally up unprotected faces and slabs ranging between 40' and 75' in height, and protection is generally poor. The climbs are usually top-roped.

SPANKY'S WALL

This minor south-facing 100' slab is easily visible to travelers approaching on Route 73 from the south, 1.5 miles south of Chapel Pond. It stands directly above a small pulloff on the east side of the road at a break in the guardrail. After a stream crossing, a short, steep hike takes one to the base of the cliff. The most notable feature here is an unclimbed line of roofs on the left side of the crag. The climbing done so far is all on less intimidating but higher rock to the right.

Kristin   I   5.4   90'   (E)

Near the left end of the slab, and right of the roof band, is a series of cracks and corners.

pitch 1 Follow the crack to a ledge. Step left and climb the corner and crack to the trees.

FA Ian Osteyee and Tom Skrill 10/85

Hangover Direct   I   5.4   80'   (s)

Following the large crack at the beginning of *Kristin*, veer off right over the face and up into a left-facing corner.

FA Ian Osteyee 1987

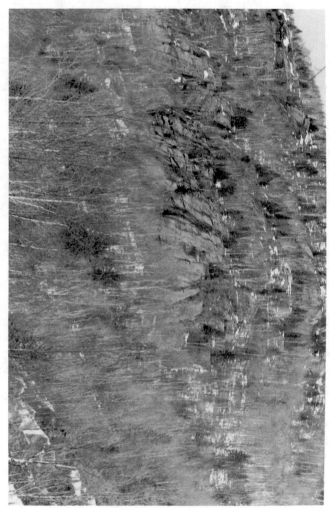

Spanky's Wall

Dancin' Buckwheat   I   5.9-   150'   (s)

Begin 25 yards right of the roof system at a yellow birch and a short, steep section.

pitch 1 Climb the short wall and gain the slab above. Belay at a tree ledge. 5.5 60'

pitch 2 Scramble right for about 30' to a right-facing corner/flake system. Undercling right to a break in the bulge.

FA Patrick Purcell and Matt McKenzie 8/83

Contos   I   5.3   80'   (E)

Begin about 30' from the right end of the wall.

pitch 1 Climb low-angled rock to a steeper wall and thin seam left of the more obvious crack.

FA Ian Osteyee and Dave Contini 3/86

Arrested Development   I   5.8   80'   (D)

Start 10' left of the toe of the buttress.

pitch 1 Boulder straight up to the right end of the ledge. Walk left, then climb the left side of the black streak for 15' to a foot traverse. Go left and slightly down on this for about 6', before making a delicate move to a hidden ledge. Obvious holds lead up and right.

Variation 5.9 The face right has good potential and has been top-roped.

FA Tad Welch and Jim Lawyer

BIKINI ATOLL

This is a very small outcropping of rock very close to the road on the east side of Route 73 one-quarter mile south of the Slab parking (the bridge).

Life's a Beach   I   5.9   60'   (s)

pitch 1 In the center of this rock, and visible from the road, is a thin crack.

FA Alan and Roger Jolley 8/83

JEWELS AND GEMS

This minor crag near Chapel Pond provides a few good climbs. Driving south from Chapel Pond, park at the beginning of the guardrail where the road bends to the left, 0.2 mi. south of the Chapel Pond Slab parking area (the bridge). Across the road to the east is a short, very steep slope hiding the cliff from view. The approach takes about a minute. The routes are described left to right, with the most obvious feature being the left-to-right diagonal *North Country Club Crack*.

Coal Miner I 5.9+ 65' (S)

Begin 25' left of NCCC, right of broken rock. Climb the steep buttress to a right-facing flake. Undercling right to a face-climbing finish.

FA Patrick Purcell 1985

Pearl Necklace I 5.8 65' (D)

pitch 1 From the left end of the low roof near the middle of the cliff, climb face holds to gain a shallow right-facing corner. The roof exit above and right is the crux.

FA Don Mellor, Alan Hobson, and Patrick Purcell 4/19/86

D1 I 5.11 65'

pitch 1 This is the vertical face left of *North Country Club Crack*.

FA Don Mellor and Patrick Purcell (top-rope 4/19/86

North Country Club Crack I 5.6 70 (E) †

pitch 1 Climb the obvious handcrack to its top, moving right around an unstable block to the top.

Variation The thin crack just right of the original route is 5.10

FA Patrick and Mary Purcell 5/8/85

Diamond and Coal I 5.6 70' (E) †

pitch 1 25' right of NCCC is an hourglass-shaped flake formation. Start on the right side of this and move around left at first opportunity. Climb an unlikely face to a layback finish at the top of *North Country Club Crack*.

Variation It is possible to handtraverse right from the top of these routes to gain the upper roof of the next climb. 5.8

FA Patrick Purcell and Bill Dodd 7/9/85

In the Rough   I   5.7+   70'   (s)

There are lots of options on this last route to the right.

pitch 1 Begin as for the previous route, on a ledge at the base of a right-facing corner, the right side of the hourglass. Up corner, out right at one point, and then through roof.

Variation **In the Buff** The shallow corner to the left, squeezed between the previous two routes, is 5.9.

KING WALL

Tucked around the corner from the Emperor Slab is one of the most impressive pieces of rock to be found in the Northeast. The King Wall resembles a giant drive-in movie screen, huge, slightly concave and seemingly unclimbable. Even now, most of the dozen or so routes that have challenged the overhanging main section of the wall end at rappel stations partway up. When routes finally work their way up the lower 200' and connect with the slabs above, the King Wall may well become the Adirondacks' chief hard-route attraction.

Park just past the crest of the hill south of the Slab parking. There is room for three cars at the north end of the wire guardrail. This is also the best parking for Jewels and Gems across the road. Walk left and uphill into the prominent streambed left of the Emperor Slab. About 15 minutes will bring one to the flat below the wall. The view of such an expansive piece of rock is worthwhile even for those not yet ready to take on this challenge.

The routes are described right to left from a dirty left-facing corner that affords a class 4 approach to the upper righthand section of the wall and from which some spectacular photographs can be taken. Most of the routes on the main face are predominantly bolt-protected, and as such, protection ratings aren't included.

Four Guns Blazing   I   5.11+   50'

The far right end of the cliff has a thin left-to-right diagonal seam, an old aid route with a fixed wire. Left of this is a good face route to an anchor point on the wall above.

FA Patrick Purcell and Chris Hyson 8/92

Kingdom Come   II   5.11+   165'   †

The most obvious face route on the right end of the cliff. Follow seven bolts through a slight left-facing corner to a belay at the long horizontal crack. The second pitch climbs a left-facing corner that arcs into a long roof above. The route has yet to be connected with *Clipping in Space* just above on the upper slab.

FA Patrick Purcell and Don Mellor 7/89 (p.1)
FA Patrick Purcell and Dominic Eisinger 8/92 (p.2)

Chronic Fixation   I   5.10   55'

Left of *Kingdom Come* is a large detached block/flake. Just left of this is a route with five bolts to a fixed anchor.

FA Patrick Purcell and Patrick Munn 9/92

Elusive Dream   II   5.10-   A2+   200'

300' left of the first face routes described is a right-facing corner that becomes a roof.

pitch 1 Up the corner crack to a belay at 60' 5.10-

pitch 2 Up to roof and artificial line of bolts and rivets to a fixed anchor.

pitch 3 Continue aid line to fixed belay and rappel.

FA Patrick Purcell 1979 and 1990

Another Whack and Dangle Job   I   5.8   A2

This is a prominent left-facing corner to a fixed anchor at its end.

FA Patrick Purcell 1985

Wall Ruler   II   5.10+   350'   †

This is the first and longest full-length route on the cliff. Begin from the right end of a large block/ledge.

pitch 1 A very committing 5.10 face leads to a ledge 20' up. Continue on a thin flake to a hanging belay below the large roofs. 5.10 70'

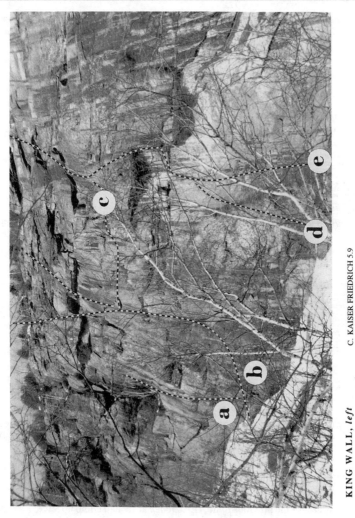

KING WALL, *left*

A. WORKING WIVES 5.11+

B. PRINCE 5.7

C. KAISER FRIEDRICH 5.9

D. MEDIEVAL TIMES 5.11

E. WALL RULER 5.10+

pitch 2 Face climb right (crux) into a huge left-facing corner and roof. Break out and up right with surprising ease, then left above to the spacious ledge and chain anchor.

pitch 3 and 4 A 165' rappel is possible from here. To continue upwards, join *Kaiser Friedrich.*

FA Patrick Purcell and Patrick Munn 1990

Medieval Times I 5.11 60'

From the left end of the large block/ledge, climb flakeholds on a black face. Traverse right to a fixed anchor.

FA Patrick Purcell and Chris Hyson 10/2/93

Kaiser Friedrich II 5.9 300' (s)

pitch 1 Same as for *Prince.* 5.7 80'

pitch 2 Out right from the block belay on a long traverse to the large fixed anchor ledge of *Wall Ruler.* 5.8 80'

pitch 3 Up an attractive series of right-facing corners.

pitch 4 The most direct line breaks straight up to a hard brown bulge right of dangerous-looking blocks 5.9 (bad protection). Alternatively, one could escape left on less attractive rock.

FA Don Mellor and Friedel Schunk 8/19/89

Prince II 5.7 300' (s) †

This is the easiest long route here. The first pitch is complex but climbable.

pitch 1 At the left end of the sheer section where the wall begins to look more featured (75' left of *Wall Ruler*). Start on a small ledge about 15' up. Climb out right, traversing easy ground to small roof. Turn this (5.7) and run it out to a belay. This is visible from below as a detached flake.

pitch 2 There are variations here: The fingercrack out left climbs past a tree to finish. 5.6. Alternatively, the face straight up is very committing (5.9) and leads to a handcrack roof.

FA Patrick Purcell, Mary Purcell, and Don Mellor 1989

Working Wives I 5.11+ 100' †

Start as for the previous route. Up to ledge at 15' and climb up left to a small

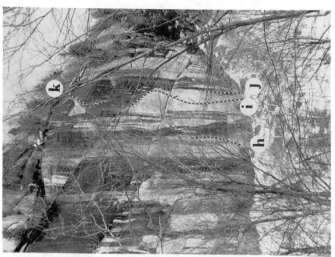

KING WALL, *right*

F. ANOTHER WHACK AND DANGLE JOB 5.8 A2

G. ELUSIVE DREAM 5.10- A2

H. CHRONIC FIXATION 5.10

I. KINGDOM COME 5.11+

J. FOUR GUNS BLAZING 5.11+

K. CLIPPING IN SPACE 5.12

arch. Follow bolts to an arete and a fixed anchor.

FA Patrick Purcell and Bob Martin

Pay the Troll's Bridge   I   5.10   50'   (E)

Walk uphill from the the previous route for about 100' to twin fingercracks. This route climbs the right-hand crack.

FA Tim Beaman, Sylvia Lazarnick, and Patrick Purcell 5/21/89

Trolls in Hiding   I   5.9   50'   (E)

The left-hand crack.

FA Tim Beaman and Sylvia Lazarnick 5/21/89

Amphibious Moat Monsters   I   5.8   150'   (S)

pitch 1 Start right of a wet diagonal 3" crack. Climb the pocketed face to the slab above. 40'

pitch 2 Continue easy slab to obvious prow. Belay (to eliminate rope drag) or turn prow on right and climb edge to the top. This attractive feature is invisible from below. 5.5

Variation From the upper slab, climb the wide corner crack to the top. 5.8

FA Patrick Purcell, Herb George and Herb George, Jr. 5/21/89

Sentry   I   5.10   90'   (E)

Start the 3" slanting crack. Traverse left to a face (bolts) to roof. Turn this on the left and on to the top.

FA Patrick Purcell and Patrick Munn 8/90

The following routes are on the left-most vertical section of rock before the cliff peters out into the hillside. The dihedral of Slave Labor *is a landmark here.*

Slave Labor   I   5.8   90'   (E)

This is the obvious right-facing corner. Approach the corner from the left.

FA Patrick Purcell and Jeff Edwards 5/22/89

Free the Slaves   I   5.12   (top-rope)

Not yet . . . but for now it's an excellent top-rope route on the arete of the previous route.

FA Patrick Purcell

Black Plague   I   5.4   80'   (E)

Climb the tiny right-facing flake/corner left of *Horses In Armor.*

Don Mellor, Jeff Edwards, and Patrick Purcell   5/2/89

Horses in Armor   I   5.7   90'   (s)

The unlikely face left of the corner is marked by right-facing flakes and hidden holds.

FA Patrick Purcell, Jeff Edwards, and Don Mellor   5/22/89

EMPEROR SLAB

This is the black slab that towers above Route 73 just south of Chapel Pond Slab. The rock appears wet and dirty, but it is actually quite clean; its blackened surface simply reflects the centuries of weathering since it was last scraped clean by glaciers some 9,000 years ago. This weathering has left a coarse surface that provides good, secure friction.

To date there are only a few established routes, and even with its proximity to the road, the slab sees almost no traffic. Nor are there any obvious lines of weakness; in many areas, the climber can simply wander at will. Protection is uniformly poor, but confidence in the adhesive properties of rubber on anorthosite can keep one from experiencing the consequences of a long run-out. The call for decision-making and the double-edged excitement of climbing far out from protection are what lure climbers out onto the blank stretches of the Emperor Slab. As with Chapel Pond Slab, there are no bolts, and most climbers would prefer this to remain so.

The slab can be approached either directly from the road or via the southern descent gully between the Emperor Slab and Chapel Pond Slab. This latter approach climbs the cleft between the two cliffs until it meets the cave. Here it is necessary to pass around to the north before cutting back left and straight out onto the upper two-thirds of the Emperor Slab. This bypasses the less attractive lower portion of the slab. Descend either

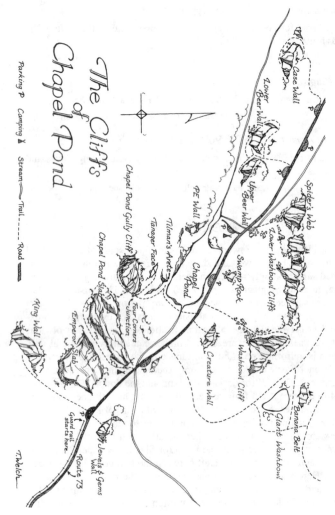

The Cliffs of Chapel Pond

Parking P   Camping ▲   Stream〰   Trail-----   Road▬▬

Case Wall
Lower Beer Wall
Upper Beer Wall
Spider's Web
Lower Washbowl Cliffs
PE Wall
Tilman's Arete
Tanger Face
Chapel Pond Gully Cliffs
Chapel Pond Slab
Chapel Pond
Swamp Rock
Washbowl Cliff
Four Corners Junction
Emperor Slab
King Wall
Creature Wall
Giant Washbowl
Banana Belt
Jewels & Gems Wall
Guard rail starts here.
Route 73

T. Welch

by rappel to this point or by walking back north into the standard southern descent from Chapel Pond Slab.

Listed below are the two earliest recorded routes. They will serve more as a general guide and a documentation of some of the history than as a suggestion of where one "should" go.

Fuhrer   II   5.6   400'   (D)

This route generally follows the left edge of the slab. Begin low on brush-covered rock.

pitch 1 Climb up and slightly left to a vegetated ledge. 130'

pitch 2 Continue up, zigzagging to contrive protection, to the second peninsula of trees.

pitch 3 Climb slightly mossy rock to the slanting overhang/corner. Follow this to its intersection with the prominent overhang that runs across the top of the slab.

pitch 4 Finish right on 5.6 friction, or escape left into the woods.

FA Tom Rosecrans and Joel Clugstone 9/4/75

Tone-Boneparte   II   5.7   400'   (D)

From the left end of the approach ledge (about one third of the way up), climb up and left. Climb past this to a belay at about 140'.

pitch 2 Another sustained rope-length brings one to another vegetation belay.

pitch 3 Continue to the prominent overlap at the top of the slab, and traverse right to a belay.

pitch 4 Continue right until a break through the overhang leads to the final slab.

FA Tony Goodwin and Tom Rosecrans 1974

CHAPEL POND SLAB

This long, clean slab is perhaps New York's most popular climb north of the Shawangunks. Not only does it provide clean friction at a relaxing angle, but its six or seven pitches of continuous climbing make it one of the longest ascents in the East. Here one can both learn the basics of the sport and at the same time make a real climb of it, an expedition with all the requisite exposure and decision-making required on the best of climbs.

CHAPEL POND SLAB

C. SOUTHERN DESCENT GULLY
D. EMPRESS 5.5
E. GREENSLEEVES 5.6
F. VICTORIA 5.6
G. THANKSGIVING 5.7
H. REGULAR ROUTE 5.5
I. BOB'S KNOB STANDARD 5.3

The Slab has the easiest approach in the region as well. Park just south of the pond next to the bridge at the height of the pass. A flat path leads to the rock about 200' from Route 73. Descent, however, isn't so simple and some of the down-climbing may require a rope.

1. The northern descent route heads right (north) towards the Gully Cliff and Chapel Pond. Skirt the top of the slabs and enter a tree-filled gully that brings one down to a forest (This is also reached near the top of *Bob's Knob Standard*). A well-worn path leads left with good views of the Gully Cliff. A short fixed rappel from a birch brings one down to the Gully trail, which leads eventually to the pond.

2. It is also possible to rappel *Bob's Knob Standard* (keep slings on birches to save trees) to the tree terrace and two more rappels below.

3. From the base of *Bob's Knob,* one can down-climb back (4th class) toward the center of the slab and dike start.

4. The southern descent gully sees much of the *Empress* traffic. It separates the Slab from the Emperor Slab to the south and provides a straightforward slither down the chute to a point about two thirds of the way down where it is interrupted by a 15' dropoff over a cave. Skirt this to the left (north) and re-enter the gully for its final 200'.

Perhaps the most intriguing element of climbing at Chapel Pond Slab is the long run-out on clean, open rock. Admittedly, the moves aren't really that hard. Instead, it is the whole picture of exposure and commitment that makes the climb so rewarding. Accordingly, the bolt-free tradition here is very strong. Not only have the standard routes been climbed countless times without resorting to the drill (in sneakers and hiking boots, not to mention the magic new rubber being introduced to the scene), but most obvious variations have seen ascents as well. Almost every one of the steep, smooth, and bulging sections between routes has been climbed in a style in keeping with this clean tradition. *Regular Route* has fair protection and would be a good introduction to the Slab before venturing out onto the more committing lines.

Empress   II   5.5   700'   (x)   †

This and *Regular Route* see most of the traffic. The route begins at a long left-facing corner, which is the main feature of the left side of the slab. The upper section is recognized by the offwidth chimney formed by an enormous flake high and left.

pitch 1 Climb the corner with good protection to its top and belay off right at a good crack. 5.3 145'

pitch 2 Though it is possible to continue in the right-facing corner system for two pitches of easier climbing to reach the "Hummock" belay of pitch 4, most parties choose to head diagonally right across a low-angled section to a belay at the base of the huge, arching left-facing corner.

pitch 3 Head across left on smooth rock, gaining a rolling ledge system comprised of three rock hummocks. These can be reached directly from atop the first pitch with a 165' rope.

pitch 4 A short pitch leads across to gain the highest of the ledges, directly under the wide crack high above.

pitch 5 This is an excellent friction/face pitch, but the best line offers no protection. A safer, though inferior, line heads off left a bit and finds protection in a hidden corner before getting back onto the blank slab. Belay at the birch ledge. 5.5 130'

pitch 6 Climb the off-sized crack on the buttress to its top; belay here or step out right onto a foothold and make a continuous, exposed run-out to a cramped belay. 5.5 150'

pitch 7 The going gets steadily easier toward the crest. (Resist the temptation to go for the top from the shelf belay atop the off-sized crack. It's about 190' with no anchor point.)

Variation 5.8 Climb the unprotected buttress right of the offwidth crack of pitch 6

Variation **Greensleeves** 5.6 300' (s) † From the birch belay of pitch 5, climb across right and gain a two-pitch right-facing corner.

FA Fritz Wiessner and George Austin
FA Alan Jolley 1982 (var. 1)
FA Alpine Club of Canada (var. 2)

Victoria II 5.6 700' (x)

This route is often wet and seldom climbed. In dry conditions, however, it is a recommended addition to the more familiar climbs. Begin at the hummock belay of the *Empress* pitch 4.

pitch 5 Climb the right side of the slab, belaying at a crack that splits a bulge at about 100'. 5.6

pitch 6 Continue up, stepping first right a bit, then back left to a belay below a large roof. 5.6 100' (A better option climbs across left to join *Greensleeves*.)

pitch 7 Turn the roof on the left and follow easier rock up the final right-facing corner.

FA Alpine Club of Canada

Thanksgiving   II   5.7   700'   (x)   †

This is the most sustained and committing of the routes here. Begin at the middle of the hummock ledge system of the *Empress* pitch 3.

pitch 4 Climb the ever-steepening left-facing groove above, emerging right onto coarse friction. Head up and right, belaying at rope's end (perhaps at wit's end as well) at the twin cracks of *Regular Route*. 5.7 150'

pitch 5 Climb the unlikely headwall slab on the left, tending left towards the huge overlap. A full rope is required to reach the belay. 5.7 165'

pitch 6 Instead of taking the easy line above, *Thanksgiving* opts to head across right to the base of *Bob's Knob*.

pitch 7 A short pitch climbs up and underclings out right under the roof. 5.7 40'

Variation **Pringles** 5.7 150' (x) It is possible to climb the downward sloping flaky holds between *Victoria* and *Thanksgiving*.

Variation **New Rubber** 5.7 150' (x) Instead of the groove of the opening pitch of *Thanksgiving*, this variation climbs out right and up on smooth rock with no protection to the twin crack belay.

FA Alpine Club of Canada

Regular Route   II   5.5   700'   (s)   †

The mundane title to this route belies its aesthetic nature. Rather than being regular, this route offers the most interesting and varied terrain of any on the Slab. And it has the best protection as well.

pitch 1 From the base of the major left-facing corner that begins *Empress*, rises a dike that leads up to a belay on low-angled rock. 5.0 150'

pitch 2 Climb up and slightly right to a ledge at the base of the huge right-facing, arching corner. 5.2 110'

Climbers high on Empress, with Greensleeves and Victoria to the right.

PHOTO BY MARK MESCHINELLI

pitch 3 Step out onto the face on the right and head for the low point in the wall above. Step through this dish and belay 30' higher at a fixed angle (1979). This can be backed up with camming devices. 5.3 130'

pitch 4 Head up and left to a left-facing corner. This leads to the twin crack belay at 145'. 5.4

pitch 5 Climb the right-hand crack (5.5) and head to the birch tree belay at the base of the *Bob's Knob* wall. The direct friction route is about 5.7; it's easier off in the bushes to the right.

pitch 6 Climb the black wall (5.5) for 20' to a huge terrace. (It is also possible to skip this by finishing off left on friction.)

pitch 7–8 Walk right around the corner and climb two class 4 pitches to the top.

Variation **Cave Finish** 5.6 120' (E) From the terrace, climb into the black cave and finish via a vertical jam-crack.

FA Ben Poisson 1960s (var.)

Bob's Knob Standard II 5.3 700' (s)

This is the original route here. It is now more frequently used for descent.

pitch 1–2 Same as for the *Regular.*

pitch 3 Same as for the *Regular* or to its right on easier rock.

pitch 4 Head up through the trees to the base of the large, overhanging wall of *Bob's Knob,* facing the road.

pitch 5 Hard moves lead up into the corner and moderate climbing brings one to a large tree-covered ledge.

pitch 6–7 Class 4 rock leads to the top.

Variations Routes on *Bob's Knob.* This is the huge, blocky buttress that dominates the upper right end of Chapel Pond Slab. It was named for Bob Notman, one of the first climbers of the region. In addition to those longer routes that climb *Bob's Knob,* there are several other short routes on its steep walls.

Dog's Breakfast I 5.11 A0 60' (E)

This impressive, curving, overhanging crack on *Bob's Knob* still hasn't gone free.

Hamburger Helper   I   5.8   70'   (D)

This is the open book between *Bob's Knob Standard* and *Dog's Breakfast.* Details and rating haven't been confirmed by a second ascent.

Eagle Crack   I   5.7   75'   (E)

On the vertical black wall just left of *Bob's Knob Standard* rises a crack. It is also possible to climb the face to its right with little protection. (5.6)

FA John Case and Bob Notman

FA Don Mellor and Bill Diemand 1981 (var. 1)

FA Rick Davis and Co. approx. 1980 (var. 2)

FA Helen Hibbert and Andy Helms approx. 1980 (var. 3)

CHAPEL POND GULLY CLIFF

To the right of the Chapel Pond Slab and just left of the south end of the pond is a dome-like buttress of nearly 500'. As seen from the road and from the Slab climbs, there are obvious sections of steep face-climbing up high, but the continuity is broken by tree-covered ledges. Nonetheless, it is a good climbing area, especially for those looking for long moderate-to-easy routes. In addition to the relaxed climbing on some of the older routes, there are a few test-pieces, *Tennessee Excursion* being perhaps the best.

The climbs are located on the northern descent gully from the Slab routes, and the approach is fairly easy. From the south end of the pond, cross the braided stream and hike up to the wall, passing the black and often wet 50' wall of the ice climb, *Crystal Ice Tower.* Off to the right is the obvious *Tilman's Arete,* the low-angled prow of white rock that rises from the pond. Turning left and uphill, follow a path past broken and dirty rock to the base of most of the routes.

For descent, one can hike a class 4 ramp back toward the gully and leading down just right of the *Tennessee Excursion* roof bands. A rope may be required for this short exposed section. Be prepared to rappel if this line is lost.

The first climbs described are short routes just above the south end of the pond.

CHAPEL POND GULLY CLIFF

A. OLD ROUTE 5.5

B. RIGHT-HAND ROUTE WITH FOR
ONCE A GREAT NOTION FINISH 5.6

C. SQUIRRELLESS JOURNEY 5.8

D. TOP OF TANAGER FACE

Shipton's Voyage   I   5.4   120'   (s)

At the southern end of the pond rise two parallel ridges of rock, separated by tree-filled gullies. This is the right-hand rib.

Tilman's Arete   I   5.7   150'   (D)   †

This is the more obvious left-hand rib that rises from the south end of the pond.

pitch 1 Climb the broad arete to a ledge belay. 5.3 75' (D)

pitch 2 Stay on the sharp edge, passing a quarter-inch bolt at the crux, and belaying on a small ledge with a cedar. 75' 5.7 (D) Rappel.

Variations The fingercrack on the wall left of the edge is 5.5. The main, dirty, right-facing corner is 5.4.

Ectoplasmic Remains   I   5.9   130'   (s)   P

Begin just left of the dirty corner mentioned above. Climb the face through an "apex" bulge and on to a bolt (five-sixteenths inch, 1988). Face climb past another bolt and slightly right to a yellow birch.

FA Patrick Purcell and Jeff Edwards 8/18/88

Thousand Faces of a Hundred People   II   5.7   275'   (s)

A wandering and obscure line that connects a few of the cliffs and slabs left of *Tilman's Arete*.

pitch 1 Start as for *Ectoplasmic Remains* and move left from the "apex" to a cedar and up arete to a grove of cedars above. 5.7 120'

pitch 2 Diagonal right to left across a second slab (5.5) to a lone birch on the third slab. 100'

pitch 3 Follow the arete to the top just below Chapel View Arete. 5.6 60'

Variation Top-rope the slab right of the lone birch mentioned above. 5.11+ 75'

FA Patrick Purcell, Mary Purcell, and Jay Holtz 8/11/88
FA Patrick Purcell and Jeff Edwards 8/18/88 (var.)

TANAGER FACE

The next routes are on a short, high-quality wall midway up the buttress and invisible from below. The Tanager Face is approached by a vague path that leads right from the gully at a four-corners cairn that also marks the entrance of the Slab descent route. Scramble up right across a slope to the base of the wall. The most obvious feature here is a left-facing corner with a tree. Left of this are four diagonal fingercracks.

Chapel View Arete   I   5.1   100'   (E)

About 100 yards right of Tanager Face (and just left of the mid-section of *Chouinard's Gully*) is a round buttress. Begin on the left side (or more steeply in front) and follow cracks and good holds to the top.

FA Don Mellor 8/88

Toodeloo   I   5.10+   50'   (D)

This is the right-most route on the Tanager. About 40' right of the obvious left-facing corner and at the top of the hill is a face climb. The first 15' is the crux and has no protection.

FA Bill Pierce 1988

Rough Cut   I   5.9   60'   (E)

Just right of the corner is a face climb past two bolts. Finish by heading left on a finger traverse to the top of the corner. This and its harder variation have since been altered by the removal and replacement of some of the bolts. Check first.

Variation A Touch Of Grey 5.11+   Climb straight up the grey face past bolts. Finish a few feet right of the next route.

FA Tad Welch and Jim Lawyer 10/24/87
FA Bill Pierce 1988 (var.)

Brightly Colored Males   I   5.6   50'   (E)

This is the obvious left-facing corner. It passes a cedar at mid-height.

Lifelong Affliction   I   5.8+   50'   (E)   †

This is the best-looking and most obvious of a superb series of finger-cracks. It is the right-hand crack of the group and the one just left of

75

Brightly Colored Males. From low on the corner, head left to a beautiful arching fingercrack.

FA Tad Welch and Jamie Savage 5/88

Tenacity I 5.10+ 50' (E)

This is the fingercrack left of *Lifelong Affliction.*

FA Bill Pierce and Don Mellor 8/88

Veracity I 5.9 50' (E) †

Another excellent finger exercise leads up the obvious finger crack to the left of Tenacity.

FA Bill Pierce 8/88

Golden Road I 5.10 50' (E)

This is the farthest crack to the left. Switch to the left crack at mid-height.

FA Bill Pierce 8/88

Vanishing Species I 5.9 50' (E)

Start at a ledge with a small birch on the left margin of the face. Up right on face holds, passing two fingercracks en route to the top.

FA Tad Welch and Bill Widrig 10/1/89

Silent Spring I 5.5 50' (S)

Follow flakes and cracks up the prominent outside edge of the left end of the face.

FA Tad Welch and Bill Widrig 9/18/89

High above Tanager Face, above tree-covered ledges, are a series of wide slabs.

Squirrelless Journey I 5.8 130' (D)

Purcell missed this one. About 100' above and slightly right of the top of Tanager Face is an excellent face route up a wide black slab to the top. Unfortunately, it's hard to get to.

pitch 1 Begin at a birch and climb unprotected face to steepening cracks and a ledge.

pitch 2 Up past a large corner to the top.

FA Don Mellor, Brad Hess, and Jason Piwko 5/8/92

The next routes begin in Chapel Pond Gully itself, the wide drainage right of Chapel Pond Slab.

Cheap Date I 5.4 150' (s)

This is the first climbable route one reaches on the approach up the gully. It is a distinct, small, right-leaning, stepped 20' corner. This and the next three climbs end at a huge ledge which is the start of some earlier climbs. This, the Base Ledge, is really a ramp that leads up from the gully and it provides easy descent, with a short rappel at the end.

pitch 1 Climb the right-facing corner to its top and step left onto the slab. Zigging and zagging a bit for protection, head up and slightly right to a belay at a birch in a wide crack. 100'

pitch 2 Scramble up to the large Base Ledge, from which easy descent can be down the ramp back into the gully. 50'

ACB Tad Welch and Ali Schultheis 6/11/87

Galapagos I 5.9 130' (E)

An evolutionary anomaly resulting from an isolation of the gene pool, this route was climbed without the usual inspection and cleaning. Just uphill from *Cheap Date* is a thin crack that angles slightly right on overhanging rock. Pull over onto the slab and follow any line to the Base Ledge.

FA Jeff Edwards and Don Mellor 5/14/88

Give It a Name, Man I 5.9 120' (E)

Just right of the overhang/bulge, about 40' left of *Cheap Date,* is another diagonal crack line. After the blank start, gain the crack, and exit any of three ways: the low traverse line to the right, another inobvious break right from the ramp about 15' higher, or the left-leaning ramp itself via a thin crack. Finish any of several slab lines to the Base Ledge.

FA Mark Meschinelli and Don Mellor 5/14/88

Duschara I 5.11 100' (E)

From under the left end of the bulge (20' left of the previous line), climb a short overhang and finish via the spectacular thin crack that angles off right on overhanging rock. An easy crack on the slab above brings one to the Base Ledge.

Variation It is possible to climb the line out left from the base of the overhanging crack. 5.11 (D)

FA Don Mellor 5/14/88

FA Chris Klein and Mark Abbott 8/18/88 (var.)

For Once a Great Notion II 5.6 400' (D)

This and its neighbors ascend the upper slabs seen from the road. This area offers so many variations that one can wander at will, seeking out hard, unprotected, clean face climbing, or opting more conservatively to zigzag from tree to tree. The route descriptions will be given as the first ascent party described them, but it is more likely that your own route-finding ability and ambition will determine the line of choice. It is worth noting that for any of the climbs that ascend the blank slabs on the upper part of the dome, #2–#3 Friends will vastly improve the protection in the prominent shallow horizontal cracks that distinguish the face.

pitch 1 Begin by climbing up broken and dirty rock above a birch clump about 30' right of *Right-Hand Route*. From the birch cluster traverse out right onto the face and over rotten rock to the trees.

pitch 2 Above and left is a large dead tree (or at least this was so in 1970). Climb the slab above and belay at a ledge with trees.

pitch 3 A long pitch of face climbing on large labradorite crystals leads to the top. This pitch can be split with another tree belay.

FA David Lovejoy and Dwight Bradley 1970

Note: The following three routes begin with good climbing, but degenerate into looser rock above. Be prepared to head off left for escape or move right to join the more exposed clean slabs described above.

Right-Hand Route I 5.4 250' (S)

Uphill from the Base Ledge ramp are three attractive corners. The most obvious is the large, overhanging, left-facing corner of the *Old Route*. Just right of this (and at a cluster of maples by a huge block against the wall) is a left-rising ramp/corner. This is the first pitch.

pitch 1 Climb the corner and step right over a small roof to a ramp. Belay at detached block (back it up!) above. 5.4 90'

pitch 2 There are three variations here: climb either the groove above the block, the parallel corner above the sorry-looking birch to the right, or better yet, traverse 40' right to a tree island.

pitch 3 Above the tree-sheltered belay ledge (option three above), climb excellent face past horizontal cracks to trees. 5.7 100'

pitch 4 Another long slab pitch finds its way to the top. Watch for loose rock.

FA Fred Gemmill (apparently via corners above block, late 1950s?)

Old Route *(originally Chapel Pond Gully route)*

I   5.5   250'   (s)

pitch 1 About 20' left of *Right-Hand Route* is a black slab between the large left-facing corner to the right and a broken crack line to the left. Run it out on good face holds, joining the corner and breaking out right at its top. Climb up and slightly right to a steep and loose groove, belaying at a ledge above. Use caution in this final, flaky section.

pitch 2 From this ledge, move left and take any of several steep corners to the top. It is also possible to effect a long horizontal traverse (5.5) to gain the tree island mentioned in the previous description.

FA Fritz Wiessner and Doug Kerr

Left-Hand Route   I   5.5   200'   (E)

Up and around the buttress to the left of the previous climbs (and quite near the stream below) is an attractive corner capped by a small, square block/roof about 40' up.

pitch 1 Climb the corner, passing the roof via a crack on the left wall. Belay just above the roof. 5.5 50'

pitch 2 Step right over the roof and climb a vertical jamcrack to a higher ledge. 5.4 50'

pitch 3 Continue in corners above or walk left off the cliff.

Left-Hand Direct   I   5.8   75'   (E)

Just before the wall turns left uphill in to final amphitheater is a left-facing corner capped by a block roof about 20' up. The route is partially hidden behind the trees.

pitch 1 Climb the corner past the roof, finishing in a short dihedral above.

Following the base of the climbs, it is now necessary to boulder-hop up the streambed for a few feet before entering the amphitheater of the overhangs. Climbs here will be described left to right, beginning with the most obvious feature in this section, the giant Tennessee Excursion *roof, the last and highest route in Chapel Pond Gully.*

Tennessee Excursion   I   5.11   50'   (E)   †

This amazing feature takes a climber 18' out horizontally in only 50' of elevation gain. The belayer almost has to turn around and look the other way in order to watch the final sequence.

pitch 1 Start at the left side of the amphitheater at the double-tiered roof-crack. Pass a chockstone in the lower roof before attacking the even bigger one above.

FA Patrick Purcell 7/30/87

Chattanooga Choo-Choo   I   5.11   55'   (E)

About 25' right of the previous route is another, harder roof system split by a crack.

pitch 1 Climb easier rock to the roof crack. Follow it past several hard moves, finishing on vertical rock.

FA Tim Beaman and Don Mellor 7/16/88

Pardon Me, Boy   I   5.10+   55'   (E)

The next crack is a fist-sized affair that ends with an overhanging squeeze.

FA Tim Beaman 6/88

Dodder   I   5.6   30'   (E)

At the right end of the ledge that leads out right above the amphitheater is a short vertical crack. This minor route is passed when descending the ramp from the summit.

FA Bill and Dianne Dodd 6/88

PHOTO BY MARK MESCHINELLI

The second on the rope emerging onto the ramp of Right-Hand Route.

Foot Patrol I 5.11 55'

On top of the amphitheater is a huge boulder with a fingercrack high up.

FA Patrick Purcell (top-rope) 7/29/87

P. E. WALL

Above the north (right) end of the pond is an outcrop with five distinct left-facing corners. Cross the outlet brook at the campsite and skirt the lake on an angler's path. The climbs are described right to left.

Synchronized Swimming I 5.7 120' (s)

pitch 1 At the right end of the cliff is a left-facing, blocky corner. Belay at the birch above. 5.5 70'

pitch 2 Climb crack above to the top. 5.7 50'

Variation From the birch, climb down left, turn corner onto the face and up left to a left-facing corner. After about 10', traverse right to handcrack. 5.5

FA Patrick and Mary Purcell 8/2/88
FA Patrick and Mary Purcell (var.)

Badminton 101 I 5.9 80' (E)

Start in the blocky corner, as for the previous route. The climb ascends the right-hand and lower-angled of two prominent offwidth corners visible from the pond parking lot.

pitch 1 A short traverse left leads to a tree-covered terrace.

pitch 2 Climb the obvious hand-/fingercrack (5.9) to the wide crack/corner.

FA Patrick and Mary Purcell 8/2/88

J.E. 26 I 5.8 100' (s)

This is the most prominent feature in this section of cliff: It is the left-facing offwidth chimney so visible from the beach.

pitch 1 Approach any of several ways to get to the birch at the base of the chimney.

pitch 2 A remarkable and unique pitch underclings left to a bolt (quarter inch, 1988) and up 15" crack past another bolt (five sixteenths). 5.8 70'

FA Patrick Purcell and Jeff Edwards 8/13/88

THE BEER WALLS

Since its discovery for climbing in 1982, this area has become one of the most popular upstate. It apparently has what climbers are looking for: short routes, moderate grades, easy access, and superb views of the High Peaks. Certainly there are other areas that provide better climbing, but this place fills the void that once existed between the low-angled slabs like Chapel Pond's and the higher, multipitch walls such as the Washbowl Cliff. The downside of this new-found popularity is that it will be crowded on weekends and holidays.

Climbers generally park at one of two areas: either on the east side of Route 73 at a large pull-off or on the west side of the road at a widened shoulder just north of the Spider's Web that provides room for about 10 cars. The trail leaves from between these two parking areas. Follow a well-worn path up the valley and right on an old logging road. The path splits at the crest of the hill and several minor trails shoot off in various directions. Generally, the left route leads to the Upper Beer Wall and the base of the Lower Wall. The right-hand path leads across the top of the Lower Wall. Most of the trails have been laid out sensibly so as to minimize trail erosion. Please do your part by keeping to these paths whenever possible.

OUTLET WALL

Separated from the main cliffs and with a separate approach, this cliff sees little traffic. The rock lies just above the popular camping spot across the road from the Spider's Web and at the outlet of Chapel Pond. Drive in to park, cross the small stream, and head uphill for a few minutes. The bolts described below have been removed.

Mother Nature I 5.11 50' (s)

pitch 1 In the middle of the wall is a route with two bolts (removed). Climb past the first to a left-facing flake, past the second bolt and up left.

FA Bill Pierce and Patrick Purcell 6/27/88

Silver Chicken   1   5.11   50'

pitch 1 Climb the crack left of the previous route through a bulge, passing one bolt (removed).

FA Bill Pierce 9/2/88

Pepe Le Pew   I   5.10   (top-rope)

The offwidth crack 12' left of *Silver Chicken*.

FA Christian Buckley 8/17/94

ENTRANCE WALL

This climb is found on the minor rock reached after the left-hand fork at the top of the pass a few minutes from the road.

Tie Me Up   I   5.8   30'   (E)

pitch 1 This is the first minor climb found as one reaches the crest of the hill, the steep handcrack behind the large birch.

FA Alan Jolley and Kathy Bright 8/83

UPPER BEER WALL

The label "Upper Beer Wall" refers to the steep rock left of the height-of-land and is reached by following the trail up to the crest of the hill and then down and left. The first climbs found are prominent short handcracks on a black wall.

Seven Ounces   I   5.7   40'   (E)   †

pitch 1 This route climbs the left-hand crack. The smooth lower crux grows increasingly polished as frustrated climbers burn rubber here.

FA Jim Cunningham and Pete Benson 6/2/82

Bouncer   I   5.10   40'   (D)

pitch 1 This is the intricate face between the two handcracks.

FA Bill Dodd (top-rope)
FA Ken Nichols and Chuck Boyd 10/9/84

PHOTO BY CHUCK TURNER

UPPER BEER WALL

A. ROARING TWENTIES 5.10
B. RADIOACTIVE 5.10
C. NEUTRON BREW 5.10
D. TEQUILA MOCKINGBIRD 5.10
E. THE STANDARD 5.10
F. PROHIBITION 5.11-
G. DARK HORSE AIL 5.11
H. FROSTED MUG 5.9 AND LABATT-AMI 5.7
I. BOILER MAKER 5.10
J. LAGER-RHYTHM 5.8

"3.2" I 5.4 40' (E) †

This is the right-hand obvious handcrack on this black wall. The strenuous crux is at the bottom.

FA Don Mellor 5/4/82

Red Hill Mining Town I 5.11 40'

This top-roped route climbs the face just right of "3.2," deliberately avoiding the crack.

FA Jim Belcer (top-rope) 1987

Guinness I 5.5 40' (s)

About 50' right of the previous climbs is a 4"–6" crack.

pitch 1 Climb the crack through a bulge.

FA Chuck Turner 10/82

The next climbs are located on the sheer wall to the right. The first few routes can be more easily reached by walking right from the top of the "3.2" and Seven Ounces *wall to the end of the tree-covered ledge to reach the shorter left end of the sheer wall.*

Spur of the Moment I 5.6 35' (D)

This is the first route on the terrace up and right of *3.2.*

pitch 1 Wander up the face at the left side of the clearing. Getting off the ground is the problem.

FA Steve Adler 1988

Day's End I 5.9 40' (D)

pitch 1 Just right of the previous route are a line of holds that lead to a roof. Break out of the roof via a left-to-right groove (or alternatively, up easier rock to the left).

FA Don Mellor 1988

Cover Charge I 5.11 60' (s) †

pitch 1 This is an excellent and sustained route that begins down and right at a fingercrack. The latter begins about 8' up between two trees. Stay in the right-diagonal fingercrack until it ends with a mantel at the top of the ramp. Climb left past a bolt and straight up to a crack finish.

History A route called *Pop Top* approached via the ramp high and left. FA Tom DuBois, 1988. The line as described above was first led by Patrick Purcell, 1988.

Center Stage 5.12 120'

An excellent route up steep rock right of the previous route. Climb a steep loose start to unrelenting climbing past thin cracks to a good rest ledge. A boulder problem begins the final wall. The climb had two bolts, but has since been led after their removal by practicing wire placements on rappel.

FA Patrick Purcell 1988

The next routes are located on the amazing and sheer 130' section of the Upper Beer Wall. The best part of the climbing here is above the roof barrier 30' up. The climbing on this unique expanse of rock is relentless, though seldom desperate. Holds are everywhere, but it may be tough to convince your weary fingers to stay on task. Caution is required in the looser roof section below. It's tough to figure these climbs out from the ground: the wall is a maze of cracks and holds. The descriptions that follow must be tempered with your own route-finding decisions.

Mouth That Roared I 5.10 120' (s)

The left end of the sheer wall is marked by black water streaks. Begin below this on a ledge with a twisted cedar.

pitch 1 Follow a short ramp out right to a ledge beneath the main overlap (5.10). Pull over the bulging overlap on sharp holds and follow a remarkable series of ledges and flakes to a right-facing corner. Finish via a right-diagonal flake/crack.

FA Ken Nichols and Bruce Jelen 9/9/88

Roaring Twenties I 5.10 140' (s)

At the left end of the biggest part of the wall are two parallel fingercracks about 5' apart and just left of a prominent cedar.

pitch 1 Take the left crack until it fades about 20' below the top. Traverse left 7' to a crack on the right edge of the black streaks.

FA Ken Nichols and Bruce Jelen 9/7/88

Radioactive   I   5.10   130'   (E)   †

pitch 1   This climb uses the right-hand of two fingercracks left of the cedar to meet the roof band and the excellent climbing above.

FA   Tim Beaman and Bill Dodd   1987

No Comments from the Peanut Gallery   I   5.10   130'   (E)

pitch 1   This route traverses left from *Neutron Brew* about 10' above the roof and heads for a "blocky pocket." The crack above leads to the top.

FA   David Smart and Dave Georger   9/2/85

Neutron Brew   I   5.10   130'   (E)

pitch 1   15' left of *The Standard,* climb the pointed block to an alcove with a small cedar about 25' up and left. Climb the roof directly above and follow a 1" –2" crack.

FA   Don Mellor and Bill Dodd   6/2/85

Tequila Mockingbird   I   5.10   130'   (E)   †

The most obvious and deep groove on the right end of the wall is *The Standard. Tequila Mockingbird* takes the crack about 7' to its left.

pitch 1   From the small cedar common to the previous routes, head out the roof on the right to gain the crack.

FA   Patrick Purcell, Don Mellor, and Bill Dodd   4/20/85

Standard   I   5.10   130'   (E)

This is the wide, dark crack near the right end of the wall.

pitch 1   Begin directly below at a handcrack, and follow a thin crack (5.10) to a stance below the roof. Turn the overhang and continue up the groove and the crack just to its left.

FA   Don Mellor   7/83

Prohibition   I   5.11-   130'   (S)

This route climbs between *The Standard* and *Dark Horse Ail.* Begin about 18' left of *Dark Horse Ail.*

pitch 1   Climb a crack and diagonal right to a narrow ledge, then back left to the main overhang. Above the lip, step right and follow a flaring crack to the rim.

FA Ken Nichols and Bruce Jelen 9/9/88

Dark Horse Ail   I   5.11   130'   (s)   †

This is the last crack on the right end of the sheer wall, about 6' left of the right end of the sheer wall.

pitch 1 Climb broken vertical rock under the Frosted Mug dihedral, following a crack through a roof to the top.

FA Steve Larson 8/83

Frosted Mug   I   5.9   130'   (s)   †

Few features anywhere beg so to be climbed. This is the striking inside corner on the arete just right of the sheer wall of the previous routes. Though the bottom section is obviously committing, there have been several dangerous, protection-ripping falls above. The climbing in this section demands enough control to stop and inspect the chocks rather than blindly stuffing things in as one laybacks past.

pitch 1 Begin uphill and right. Face-climb left with no protection out to the edge and onto the ledges above. 50' of pure dihedral leads to the top.

FA Chuck Turner and Bill Simes 5/1/82

Frosty Edge   I   5.10+   (top-rope)

The edge right of the dihedral.

Flying & Drinking and Drinking & Driving   I   5.10   100'   (D)

This route climbs the wall right of *Frosted Mug*.

pitch 1 Climb up and left to a thin crack just right of *Frosted Mug*. Continue up a narrow left-facing corner/flake, turn the roof right, and make a substantial run-out to the top.

FA Don Mellor 5/85

Labatt-Ami   I   5.7   120'   (E)   †

This route climbs the huge corner with the giant roof halfway up. Though the roof looks insurmountable, face holds lead around it on the left wall.

89

This was the first route climbed here. Turner and Simes returned the following day to climb *Frosted Mug*. Their fantasies on those hot spring days led to the first two route names and were the beginning of the race to name routes on the beer theme. The name "Beer Walls" gradually took over from what had been called Chapel Pond Canyon.

pitch 1 Climb loose rock in a corner to gain the large ledge. 5.6 50'

pitch 2 Climb the corner, under the roof and up to the top. These pitches can be combined.

Variation From the belay ledge, climb out left, angling on good holds towards the top of *Frosted Mug.* 5.7 (D)

FA Bill Simes and Chuck Turner 4/30/82

Boiler Maker I 5.10 80' (E)

From the large square ledge halfway up *Labatt-Ami,* is an overhanging crack that has seen chalk but no reported ascent. Right of this is an offsized chimney/jamcrack. This is the line.

pitch 1 Climb out right from the large cedar and climb the double-wide cracks to the top.

FA Tim Beaman and Sylvia Lazarnick approx. 1984

Lager-Rhythm I 5.8 150' (E)

This climb begins about 100' right of the previous route and follows a steep corner system facing right. The start is nondescript; one must scramble over loose rocks and trees to the first belay out of the firing line to the right. The climb is dangerous in its lower sections due to loose rock.

pitch 1 Climb into the corner and follow this to a roof; make a hard mantel here to a belay on the left. 5.8 75'

pitch 2 Step right over the void to the handcrack and weave a line up bulges and corners to the top. The first move is a riddle. 5.7 75'

FA Don Mellor and Alan Jolley 7/82

About 100 yards past the Upper Beer Wall toward Chapel Pond is a pair of smaller cliffs. The routes described are on the second of the two pieces of rock; the first cliff band is interrupted by a large roof above a ledge.

Pete's Wicked Flail   I   5.11   50'   (E)

The left-hand of two bolted routes passes through an A-shaped break in the roof. The bolts were placed earlier by another climber.

FA Frank Minunni 7/94

Tuesdays   I   5.11   60'   (S)

Follow the line of weakness on a rising traverse past four bolts to an anchor. The run-out to the anchor is on easier terrain.

FA Dave Furman 7/94

UPPER TIER

The routes in this and the next sections lie to the north (right on the approach trail) of the previous climbs. The path to this small cliff heads off right from the notch at the height-of-land.

Watch Crystal   I   5.11+   40'   (S)

pitch 1 Climb the blank face just right of the striking fingercrack of *Live Free or Die*.

FA Ken Nichols and Todd Eastman 10/10/84

Live Free or Die   I   5.9+   40'   (E)   †

pitch 1 A very popular climb, both as a sustained lead and as a top-rope. 10' of hard face leads to the classic finger crack.

FA Jim Cunningham and Rich Leswing 6/5/82

Jugs of Beer   I   5.3   40'   (E)

pitch 1 This route climbs an obvious blocky crack in the middle of the wall just left of the previous route.

FA Jim Cunningham and Pete Benson 6/27/82

Fast and Furious   I   5.8-   45'   (E)   †

pitch 1 Climb the right-slanting crack on the left end of the wall.

Variation Climb straight up right of the crack to meet the finish of this route. 5.11

FA Jim Cunningham and Pete Benson 6/27/82
FA Bill Pierce (top-rope) 1981 (var.)

Crazy Fingers   I   5.11   45'

pitch 1 Head straight up left of *Fast and Furious,* joining a crack to the top.

FA Bill Pierce 1988

LOWER BEER WALL

It is here that most of the climbing takes place. These climbs are found to the north of the Upper Beer Wall. Approach either by walking a good trail from just past the base of *"3.2"* and *Seven Ounces,* or by walking the crest of the walls above the Upper Tier. This path leads across the top of the climbs; it ultimately descends the north end of the crag past *Afternoon Delight.* The climbs are described right to left via the path from the Upper Beer Wall.

Barstool Direct   I   5.9   50'   (D)

Begin just around the corner of a small, broken buttress directly below the Upper Tier. This route climbs the right-facing corner/overhang at the top of this short wall.

pitch 1 Climb dangerous rock (crux) to the all-too-short good section above.

FA Dave Gillette and Chuck Turner 5/7/83

Moosehead   I   5.5   130'   (s)

This line stands alone on the expanse of rock between *Clutch and Cruise* and the Upper Tier. It passes much loose rock and several trees. Begin half-way between the right end of the cliff and the obvious, overhanging handcrack of *Clutch and Cruise.*

pitch 1 Climb the broken line to a belay at mid-height or continue in one long pitch.

FA Tom Rosecrans and Chris Knight 1983

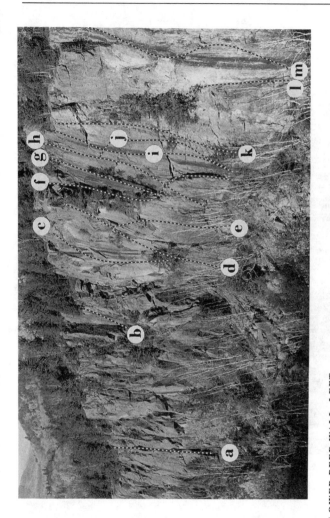

PHOTO BY CHUCK TURNER

LOWER BEER WALL, LEFT

A. ROLLING ROCK 5.9

B. SWORD 5.6 COORS CORNER 5.5
   WANDERING LUNATIC 5.10

C. DEATH TRAP 5.10

D. QUEST 5.8

E. TURBOCHARGE 5.10

F. DIAGONAL CHOCKSTONE
   CHIMNEY 5.4

G. PINE SHADOW 5.9+

H. PEGASUS 5.7+

I. BLACKSMITH 5.10

J. LICHENBRAU 5.7

K. PAT TRICKS 5.10

L. CLUTCH AND CRUISE 5.8

M. JOEY BAGGADONUTS 5.8+

93

LOWER BEER WALL, RIGHT

L. CLUTCH AND CRUISE 5.8

M. JOEY BAGGADONUTS 5.8+

N. MOOSEHEAD 5.5

O. UPPER TIER

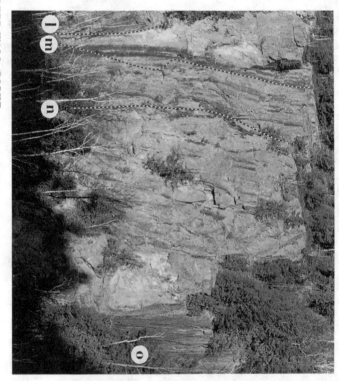

PHOTO BY CHUCK TURNER

Joey Baggadonuts   I   5.8+   150'   (D)   †

Locate the overhanging, bolted cave of *Clutch and Cruise*.

pitch 1 Start right of the cave at a short diagonal crack. Intricate climbing on fragile rock leads up right to a good ledge and a bolt under an overhang. Exit left on black rock and make a long easy run-out to the top.

FA Don Mellor, Patrick Purcell, and Bill Simes   8/9/89

Sumo Fly   I   5.9+   150'

Top-rope the black streak just right of *Clutch and Cruise*'s overhang. Start via the fragile flake.

FA Jim Cunningham and Todd Eastman   9/83

Clutch and Cruise   I   5.8   150'   (E)

The bottom of this route is what makes it unique and worthwhile; the rest is easier and less inspiring. Begin in an alcove with a handcrack leading out its right side.

pitch 1 Climb out the overhanging crack to the right-facing corner above. Follow this easily to a cedar belay.

pitch 2 The climb straight up over loose blocks above is very dangerous. Alternatively, drop down and right from the huge cedar belay and follow ledges up right to share the final black wall of *Joey Baggadonuts*. (5.4)

FA Rich Leswing and Jim Cunningham   6/2/82

Pats' Blue Ribbon   I   5.11+   60'   †

Start in the cave just left of the previous route. Climb out the roof past a series of bolts. Using the arete left is 11+; straight up the bolt line is 5.12.

FA Patrick Munn and Patrick Purcell   1993

Backs Against the Wall   I   5.5   150'   (E)

Begin this climb in the broken and irregular handcrack/chimney.

pitch 1 Follow the advice of the first ascent party and continue to a belay by the large tree.

pitch 2 The final pitch climbs over loose blocks and is very dangerous; opt instead for joining *Lichenbrau* (5.7), rappelling from huge cedar, or dropping down right from the cedar and climbing ledges up right to the black wall of *Joey Baggadonuts* (5.4).

FA Jim Cunningham and Peggy Collins 7/16/82

Pat Tricks I 5.10+ 150' (E) †

pitch 1 Start at a low bolt, climbing face just right of cedar bush belay of *Lichenbrau*. Climb directly to the top past two more bolts, keeping just left of the blocky chimney. Steep finish.

FA Patrick Munn and Patrick Purcell 1993

Lichenbrau I 5.7 175' (s) †

Just uphill from the previous routes is a short thin crack. Start just to the left.

pitch 1 Climb up past a tiny birch, then diagonally right up "Gunks" horizontals to a belay at or just right of cedar bush. 5.6 60'

pitch 2 Face-climb straight up, then head left across the face under a roof to the upper section of *Pegasus*. 5.7 90'

Variations **Lichenbrau Dark** 5.9 The fingercrack right off the ground makes a harder start.

FA Jim Cunningham, Rich Leswing, and Chuck Turner 8/82

Blacksmith 5.10 140' (E) †

pitch 1 This excellent pitch is one of the best in its class. Start as for *Lichenbrau* to the right of the right-facing gully flake. Up steep rock until level with the cedar bush. (Or use pitch 1 *Lichenbrau*). Up past two bolts and a pin. Straight through the roof is about 5.8, or harder yet, move right to bolt at biggest part of roof 5.10+.

FA Patrick Purcell and Bob Martin 1992
FA harder finish Mark Meschinelli

Pegasus I 5.7+ 140' (s) †

This is perhaps the best and most popular steep face pitch of its grade upstate. It is both thought-provoking and strenuous, and the protection is marginal. Back up the fixed pins (replaced in 1984) wherever possible.

pitch 1 Begin this climb at an off-sized fist crack that leads to the main belay. This ledge can also be reached by 4th-classing up the flake on the right. 5.7 40' *pitch 2* Climb out right, aiming to turn the roof at a right-facing corner. After this crux (pin), easier face-climbing leads to the rim. 5.7+ 100'

FA Rich Leswing, Jim Cunningham, and Peggy Collins 7/21/82

A-Frame

It is possible to top-rope the face just left of *Pegasus*, passing through the obvious A-shaped roof.

Pine Shadow   I   5.9+   140'   (D)   †

In 1985 we were reminded just how temporary things are. Before then, climbers belayed pitch 1 of *Pegasus,* etc., at a huge white pine that stood majestically out from the ledge, branches reaching as high as the cliff itself. If ever there was a solid belay anchor this was it; in fact, one had trouble just getting slings around its enormous trunk. *Pine Shadow* stands as a tribute and memorial to this fallen giant.

pitch 1 Begin between the obvious cracks of *Pegasus* and *Anteater.* Taking pains to avoid each crack, contrive a line up overhanging rock to the belay. 5.9 40'

pitch 2 Climb up and slightly left with no protection, turning the roof several feet left of *A-Frame*, and heading for a finish at a small right-facing corner.

FA Don Mellor and Chuck Turner 5/83
(with pitch 1 added later by Mellor, Ian Osteyee, and Patrick Purcell)

Anteater   I   5.8   140'   (E)

Begin at the broken handcrack just left of *Pegasus*.

pitch 1 Climb the crack through a low roof and belay at the Pine Tree Ledge, common with the previous climbs. 5.8 40'

pitch 2 Continue up the main dirty corner to the birch; head out right from here to a corner which leads to the top.

FA Jim Cunningham, Rich Leswing, and Hal Coghill 7/11/82

Diagonal Chockstone Chimney   I   5.4   150'   (E)

This climb was altered by the trundling of the loose boulder that formed the chockstone behind which one had to chimney. Without this deadly cork at the top of the climb, the route is neither a chimney, nor does it have a chockstone. (And it's not really diagonal either. Oh, well.)

pitch 1 Gain the Pine Tree Ledge by slithering up the right side of the large flake right of the previous starts. 5.0 40'

pitch 2 Cross the previous routes and continue up the corner. Watch for loose rock here.

FA Jim Cunningham and Rich Leswing 7/6/82

Mother Mantel   I   5.9   150'   (E)

pitch 2 From the belay ledge common to *Pegasus* and neighboring climbs, head left toward large cedar, then up arete with crack on the right to base of final short overhanging face. Thin crack and mantel to top.

FA Patrick Purcell 1990

Turbocharge   I   5.10   150'   (s)

Left of the *Pegasus* section and a few feet left of the *Anteater* crack is a thin crack that splits a roof about 8' up. This is the route's crux, though judgment and caution must be exercised on the obvious roof flake above.

pitch 1 Climb the finger crack through a frustrating crux. Follow a crack to the roof and turn it on the left. The huge flake that hangs under the roof *can* be avoided. The chalky handprints on it speak more of the recklessness of earlier climbers than of the security of the flake. Belay out left on small footholds.

pitch 2 Continue in the flaring corner above. 5.8

FA Chuck Turner, Alan Jolley, and Mark Meschinelli 8/82

Turbocharge Direct Finish   5.11

pitch 2 Instead of climbing the flaring final corner, break right through a hard roof and on to a crack in the outside of the buttress.

FA Patrick Munn

Quest   I   5.8   150'   (s)

This is the natural line that leads to the final pitch of *Turbocharge*.

pitch 1 Climb the steep blank face 5.7 with no protection to a cedar ledge. (Or the loose, blocky, right-facing corner to the right.)

pitch 2 Angle right past trees and some loose rock to join the upper *Turbocharge* corner.

FA Alan Jolley and Scott Provost 9/82

Death Trap   I   5.10   150'   (D)

High and left of *Turbocharge* is a right-facing flake system.

pitch 1 Same as for the previous route.

pitch 2 Follow a right-facing corner to a bolt (quarter inch,1986). Head right to a loose flake. Exit the flake right to the top.

FA Patrick Purcell and Andy Zimmerman 1986

Block Party   I   5.7   150'   (s)

About 100' left of *Pegasus* is a large, broken, dirty right-facing corner. This unappealing route begins to its left, crosses it, and finishes to its right.

pitch 1 Climb over blocks to a belay at a cedar stand.

pitch 2 Traverse right 25' to the main corner, cross out onto the face, and follow a thin crack to the top.

FA Alan Jolley and Scott Provost 9/82

Redrum   I   5.5   140'   (s)

Just left of the large *Block Party* broken corner is a smaller flake/corner that rises left.

pitch 1 Climb the flake and crack to a birch at its top.

pitch 2 Face-climb up and left to the first diagonal crack line that heads up right. Follow this past a bush to the outside edge and continue up a short corner.

FA Jim Cunningham and Rich Leswing 5/7/83

Wandering Lunatic   5.10   90'   (top-rope)

At the top of the cliff is a good vantage point from which to view *Sword;* the black face to the right is a good face climb.

FA Patrick Purcell and Bill Dodd (top-rope) 9/8/88

Coors Corner   I   5.5   120'   (E)

This and its neighbor, *Sword,* are virtually invisible from below. Their first pitches are so overgrown that they are easily missed.

pitch 1 About 50' left of *Block Party* is a line that leads up through the woods on 5.3 rock and belays below the obvious right-facing corner.

pitch 2 Climb the dirt-filled corner past a tree.

FA Jim Cunningham and Hank Andolsek 7/83

Sword I 5.6 120' (s) †

The upper pitch is outstanding and can be reached via rappel from above. It is easily seen from the trail across the crest of the wall.

pitch 1 Climb the forested first pitch of *Coors Corner*. (Or better yet, rappel from the top.)

pitch 2 Stem the bottom of *Coors Corner* and step left to the sword itself, a sharp edge of superb rock. There is one quarter-inch bolt on this pitch.

FA Jim Cunningham and Alan Jolley 5/7/83

Passion Corner I 5.10+ 40' (E)

Just left of the the previous routes and about 150' left of *Pegasus* are three open books. This route climbs the short, right-hand smooth corner. Begin at a birch clump below.

FA Patrick Purcell and Jeff Edwards 1987

Draught Dodger I 5.9 100' (E)

pitch 1 Climb the middle open corner, exiting out overhanging rock to the top.

FA Don Mellor and Alan Jolley 10/19/82

Octoberfest I 5.9 120' (E)

This is the left of the three open books.

pitch 1 Climb easy rock to a flake below the roof. Climb out right (crux) to a belay just above.

pitch 2 Step left to the ridge and follow it to the top.

FA Chuck Turner and Don Mellor 9/26/82

Rolling Rock   I   5.9   140'   (E)

Down and left of the three open books is obvious black dihedral partway up the face.

pitch 1 A tricky start leads into the corner. Hard moves up and out right lead to a large right-leaning flake. Pull over and on to the rim.

FA Don Mellor and Alan Jolley 10/19/82

On Tap: Special Brew   I   5.9   110'

Near the left end of the cliff is a shield-like wall split by the diagonal fingercrack, *Rockaholic*. Begin 10' to the right.

pitch 1 Climb up the weakness to a cedar. Move right onto a black streak to a roof and left-facing corner. Turn this on the right and face-climb to the top.

FA Jim Cunningham, Hank Andolsek, and Mark Eckroth 7/8/83

Equis   I   5.7   100'

This is the natural continuation of the *On Tap* start.

pitch 1 Climb up to the cedar and continue up the face and flake system to the finish.

FA Jim Cunningham and Rich Leswing 5/7/83

Rockaholic   I   5.8   80'   (E)   †

This is the enticing fingercrack rising right to left.

pitch 1 A hard move leads to the crack and the gateway flakes above.

FA Mark Meschinelli, Dave Hough, and Chuck Turner 5/6/83

Detoxification   I   5.8   80'   (D)

pitch 1 Just left of *Rockaholic* is a left-leaning shallow arch.

FA Tad Welch 10/19/86 (roped-solo)

Dos   I   5.7   200'   (s)

This is a rising girdle of the left end of the cliff.

pitch 1 Follow the diagonal line that begins 15' left of *Rockaholic*. Belay at the right-leaning flake of *Rolling Rock*.

pitch 2 Climb over the flake to the trees.

FA Jim Cunningham and Don Mellor 5/6/83

Delirium Tremens   5.10+   50'   (top-rope)

Right of the *Afternoon Delight* face is a buttress. Climb the right side.

FA Jeff Edwards 8/30/90

Duty Free   5.10   50'   (top-rope)

The blocky arete on the left side of the buttress.

FA Jeff Edwards 8/30/90

Afternoon Delight   I   5.5   60'   (s)   †

An excellent face climb up an unlikely wall.

pitch 1 Any number of variations climb this unlikely black face at the far left end of the Lower Beer Wall.

FA Mike Heintz and Ron Briggs 9/26/82

CWI   I   5.6   50'   (E)

This is the crack line that runs up the left end of the wall.

pitch 1 Climb from the tree up the steep handcrack through two bulges.

FA Jim Cunningham and Pete Benson 6/27/82

CASE WALL

About 15 minutes left (north) of the Lower Beer Wall is yet another section of rock. The name was suggested by Tad Welch to commemorate John Case and his many contributions to Adirondack climbing. The cliff can be approached any of three ways. It is possible to walk down past the Lower Beer Wall; it is also possible to park at the Ausable Club lot across from Roaring Brook Falls (though this approach trespasses for a few yards through Club property). Alternatively, one may head up through the woods from Route 73 at the large parking area (where the road begins its steep descent to Roaring Brook Falls) north of the normal Beer Walls parking area. A small cairn marks the beginning of this marked route.

The most obvious feature, and the one from which other routes can be found, is the huge right-facing chimney/corner near the right end of the disconnected cliffs. This is Gunpowder Corner.

Amateur's Edge   I   5.5   120'   (D)   †

pitch 1 This route ascends the broad arete right of GPC. Climb the wide crack to the large, stacked blocks (these aren't too stable; they detract some from the quality and safety of the climb). Join the crest of the ridge to the top.

Variation **Last Swim or Dive**   5.7   (D)   It is also possible to face-climb up and right from near the base of *GPC,* passing just left of the stacked blocks, and joining the edge above.

FA Tad Welch and Jamie Savage 5/88

FA Tad Welch and Ali Schultheis 7/88 (var.)

Gunpowder Corner   I   5.5   80'

This is the most prominent feature on the wall, the sandy, right-facing chimney. A bottom belayer would have been gunned down by falling rock on the first ascent.

pitch 1 Climb the chimney and corner, then out onto the face.

FA Tim Broader, Bob Hey, and George Carroll (top-rope) 6/85

Standing Room Only   I   5.7   140'   (S)   †

pitch 1 From the lower left side of *GPC,* climb dirty rock to bolt belay.

pitch 2 Step right to edge and up to the top. This is a worthwhile pitch that could also be reached from above via rappel.

Variation **Bone Games**   5.6   From the bolt belay, climb up the corner for a few feet, then step left. Up into the corner again and with easy face finish.

FA Bill Widrig, Steve Jervis, Ali Schultheis, Tad Welch, and Chuck Yax 9/23/88

FA Tad Welch and Ali Schultheis 10/29/89 (var.)

Walking left from Gunpowder Corner, *one passes several ravines that cut into the cliff band. The first, about 200' left of* GPC, *has a prominent, unclimbed overhanging wall. About 200' farther is another, less distinct ravine. It is here that the following routes are found.*

Mule Kick   I   5.10   75'

pitch 1 This is a top-roped climb right of the obvious *Lives of the Hunted*. Climb the face to the right and over looser rock to the top.

FA Tom DuBois 6/88

Lives of the Hunted   I   50'   5.8+   (E)

On the right wall of the ravine is an attractive crack with a long, thin flake pasted on its left side.

pitch 1 Begin at a large hemlock and climb the crack and flake to a surprise finish.

FA Tad Welch and Jamie Savage 5/88

Tita   I   5.8   40'   (E)

pitch 1 On the left side of the ravine, about 50' away from the other two climbs, is a large roof. Climb out left and steeply up the groove right of the roof, past a small cedar at 20', and up the fingercrack to the trees.

Variation **Tanks of Beer** 5.10   This is a top-roped variation that climbs the 6' roof left of the previous route on amazing buckets.

FA Don Mellor, Jeff Stewart, and Ben Wallace 8/23/88

FA Mellor and Stewart (var.)

NOONMARK

Climbing on Noonmark embodies all that is special to this area. Climbers here have more to do than just stare at the holds in front of them. Over their shoulder is a panorama that spreads from the slides on Dix to the backbone of the Great Range. Layer upon layer of uninterrupted mountain wilderness reaches back into the heart of the High Peaks. It is the place itself that makes the climbing so much better.

The area's earliest climbers recognized these qualities, and it was on Noonmark that some of the first climbs were done. The *Wiessner Route,* for example, stood for many years as one of the hardest cracks upstate. This classic climb on the typical, rough and weathered anorthosite of the higher mountains is just one of the many fine routes to be savored on this spectacular summit.

NOONMARK MOUNTAIN

A. CRACK CHIMNEY 5.3
B. KERR ROUTE 5.6
C. WIESSNER ROUTE 5.8
D. 5.9 VARIATION
E. CENTER CLIMB 5.7
F. 5.8 VARIATION
G. OLD ROUTE 5.4

Approach via the Stimson Trail from the Ausable Club Road across from Roaring Brook Falls off Route 73. The trail begins at the golf course. Please respect the parking restrictions on the private land of the Adirondack Mountain Reserve. A stiff uphill hike of 2 miles leads to the summit. Approach the climbs by scrambling down around to the right (facing outward). The climbs can be led or top-roped, but either way, one will have some trouble setting up anchors at the top. Large nuts are helpful; so is a long spare rope to anchor back from the crest. The routes are described left to right.

Crack Chimney I 5.3

pitch 1 This is the prominent vertical crack that begins about 60' from the left end of the cliff, just past the broken rock.

Kerr Route I 5.6

Begin just right of *Crack Chimney,* below finger of rock. Climb up a few feet, then traverse right to a crack that leads to the summit.

FA Douglas Kerr and Fritz Wiessner

Wiessner Route I 5.8 90' (E) †

This obvious handcrack/chimney, which runs the full length of the face, is Noonmark's most prominent route. Begin at an ancient lag bolt driven into the crack.

pitch 1 Sustained crack climbing leads to a lower-angled finish.

FA Fritz Wiessner and Garfield Jones

Center Climb I 5.7 90' (E)

Under the right end of a roof are twin fingercracks.

pitch 1 Climb the left-hand crack into a corner and ledge. Traverse left about 10' to a good handcrack (5.5). This pitch can be split.

Variation 5.9 It is possible to climb out the left side of the roof.

Variation 5.8 The right fingercrack provides a good alternative to this or the *Old Route.*

FA Fritz Wiessner

Old Route   I   5.4   90'   (E)

The right end of the cliff is more broken and lower-angled. The *Old Route* offers several variations up the left side of this section.

pitch 1 Take any of three starts just right of the twin fingercracks to gain the easy rock in the middle of the climb. The standard finish climbs the short chimney through the roof, or alternatively and harder, cracks to its left.

CREATURE WALL

This fine cliff sees little travel, despite its solid rock, easy access, and pro-liferation of moderate crack routes. It lies directly across Route 73 from the south end of Chapel Pond, and the exit cracks for several routes can be spied over the treetops from the road. The sheer, cracked wall stands about 90' high and rests at a comfortable angle of about 80 degrees. The prevalent theme here is the vertical handcrack, and most of the routes follow such obvious features.

A well-defined path leads to the wall, starting at the south end of Chapel Pond. Leave the road by climbing up over a bank and down into the woods. The most obvious features and those from which the routes will be described are the huge, orange, arched alcove of broken rock on the right side of the cliff and the half-dozen or so chest-freezer-sized blocks that lie at the cliff's base near the center of the wall. The routes are described right to left.

Cujo   I   5.8   90'   (E)

Begin on the left side of the arched alcove.

pitch 1 Climb broken rock up the left side of the alcove, breaking out left and following a crack to the top.

FA Dave Szot, Tom Rosecrans, and Dennis Luther 6/84

Pet Sematary   I   5.8   90'   (E)

Begin 25' left of the arched alcove at the right end of the large blocks.

pitch 1 From the right end of the blocks, head for a crack with a cedar high and just right of the more obvious finish crack of *Christine*. It is also possible to begin right of this, joining the main route or moving over to *Cujo* higher up.

FA Tom Rosecrans and Mike Hay 1/24/84

Christine   I   5.10   90'   (E)   †

This is a superior route that breaks a hard roof and finishes in the clean crack to its right. Begin left of the blocks at a triangle block or 20' farther left at another triangle block leading to a diagonal crack.

pitch 1 Either of the two starts takes one to twin cracks that angle across right to the base of the roof. Hand traverse the higher of these and climb the roof at a crack just left of some loose blocks. Belay off right at the finish crack.

pitch 2 This second pitch climbs the obvious crack right of the roof. 5.8

FA Dave Szot, Tom Rosecrans, and Dennis Luther 6/84
FFA Unknown

Gob Hoblin   I   5.7   90'   (E)

Begin as for *Christine.*

pitch 1 Climb up from either of the triangle blocks and finish the natural line left of the *Christine* roof.

ACB Tom Rosecrans 6/6/84

The Shining   I   5.9+   90'   (E)

pitch 1 Start at a crack and climb straight up past a bolt to *Gob Hoblin* tree; step right to a crack system to the top.

FA Ken Wright, Tom Rosecrans

Black Moriah   I   5.8-   90'   (S)

Begin at the left of the two triangle blocks.

pitch 1 Instead of arching with the obvious crack off right for *Christine,* continue in the vertical line, past a cedar, aiming for a huge cedar at the top of the crag.

FA Dave Szot and Dennis Luther 7/22/84

CREATURE WALL
Jump Bat Crack and Arachnid Traction take the parallel cracks on the left.
Christine finishes in the prominent crack in the center of the photo.

Diamondback   I   5.8-   90'   (s)

This is a vague line left of *Black Moriah*. Begin about 40' left of the chest-freezer blocks.

pitch 1 Follow a discontinuous vertical line to the top.

FA Dennis Luther, Dave Szot and Tom Rosecrans 7/29/84

Arachnophobic Reaction   I   5.10   90'   (E)

pitch 1 Climb the face and cracks between *Diamondback* and *Arachnid Traction* past two bolts.

FA Tom Rosecrans and Ken Wright

Arachnid Traction   I   5.8   80'   (E)   †

This is the most popular route on the cliff, finishing with the right of two classic diagonal handcracks.

pitch 1 This and the next route follow parallel lines. From the large birch at the base of the wall, climb up; then, switching cracks right, finish in the sustained handcrack that angles sharply left.

FA Tom Rosecrans, Dave Szot, and Dennis Luther 5/28/84

Jump Bat Crack   I   5.8   75'   (E)

pitch 1 Climb the line parallel to and left of *Arachnid Traction*, passing a good-sized tree low on the route. Finish in the sister crack to the previous route.

FA Tom Rosecrans and Chris Knight 6/2/84

Octo-Pussy   I   5.7   70'   (E)

This and the next route climb up to and through a horizontal alcove.

pitch 1 First locate the horizontal alcove/roof about 30' up. Take the right-hand of the parallel lines.

FA Tom Rosecrans and Mike Hay 6/22/84

Night Mare   I   5.7   70'   (E)

pitch 1 This is the parallel route, about 6' left of *Octo-Pussy*.

FA Tom Rosecrans and Mike Hay 6/26/84

Fire Starter I 5.5 60' (E)

The last lines on the left end of the cliff climb the black wall at thin cracks.

pitch 1 Traverse in from the left to two pitons (1984) and finish right of a large cedar. This climb is about 10' left of *Night Mare,* and near the descent path.

Variation ***Tarantula*** 5.9+ It is possible to face-climb directly to the pins at the junction of the thin cracks, finishing at the large cedar.

FA Tom Rosecrans and Dave Szot 6/22/84

FA Dennis Luther 7/84 (var.)

CLIMBS AROUND WASHBOWL POND

These undeveloped and nondescript crags lie scattered around the north-eastern shore of the Washbowl Pond. Neither the cliffs nor the pond is visible from the highway; both are reached via the Ridge Trail to Giant Mountain. The trail sign and hikers' register lie at the south end of Chapel Pond. The steep hike of just over a half mile is worthwhile in itself: it brings one to a dramatic overlook from which to view Chapel Pond and the various climbing spots along the southwest side of Route 73.

Once at the pond (0.7 mile from the road), many of the various crags described here are visible across the way, the most prominent being the Banana Belt, a prominent rounded spur of rock that extends toward the water and which has climbs on both of its sides. Find this in order to get a bearing. Above either side of the Banana Belt spur is a "gunsight" notch. The rock that makes up the right side of the right-hand notch is the *Asterisk,* and *Chameleon* is visible as the prominent vertical crack. High and to the left of the spur, in the left-hand notch, is The Nubble Cliff, with the top of *High Anxiety* only barely visible from the pond. Down and left of the Banana Belt buttress is the steep and unclimbed Future Cliff, offering perhaps the best potential for new hard routes. This 100' cliff faces the trail and is seen only by walking the path north past the pond.

ASTERISK

Approach as for the Banana Belt buttress, and walk around and up the right side until just below the upper gully (which ultimately leads to the Nubble

Trail). Head directly right over boulders for 150', passing under a prominent overhanging nose of rock. Fifty feet beyond is the obvious vertical crack route. With some imagination the crack configuration resembles an asterisk.

Chameleon 5.8 75' (E)

Climb the prominent crack.

FA Tom DuBois 10/9/93

BANANA BELT

This is the largest mass of rock above the pond, and it is reached easily by bushwhacking to its base. The routes are described left to right.

Chiquita I 5.9- 50' (S)

On the left (west) side of the buttress, locate a prominent orange right-facing corner. Climb the face 6' to the left of the corner using three bolts and small nut protection.

Jeff Edwards and Patrick Purcell 5/18/89

El Niño I 5.7 100' (E)

pitch 1 The prominent orange right-facing corner begins with difficulty and climbs past a crux corner/overhang about 50' up. Above, follow a narrow rising ledge to the right to a belay at a good crack.

pitch 2 Stay in the crack on the edge to the top. Thrash right through the trees to a rappel down the backside of the buttress.

FA Don Mellor and Chuck Bruha 4/11/95

The right (east) wall of the buttress is steep and impressive, sporting two excellent crack lines about 8' apart. Both have apparently been climbed. The next route begins uphill on the right side of a broken tree-filled line.

Banana Republic 5.9+ 60' (top-rope)

The arete and broken crack three-quarters up the slope on the east side of the spur.

FA Jeff Edwards 5/18/89

FUTURE WALL

There are other outcrops to the left of the Banana Belt and only partially visible from the pond. These hold a lot of potential for new routes for those willing to put in the time. Approach from the trail at the far north end of the pond and head easily through the woods to the rock. Beginning from the right end of the cliff, walk left under a steep cliff toward a nasty gully. (*Solitude* can be reached from here.) Here, the cliff line breaks left and the lower right end, just left of the gully, is a distinct black face. This is *Second Chance* 5.8- 45' (E). The route is a good one that begins at the right edge of the black face, angling up left to the roof, before finishing back up right. Above this is the Upper Tier, so named because it lies in a similar position with respect to the main wall as does the Upper Tier at the Beer Walls. *Solitude* 5.4 45' (E) climbs the prominent crack. Both routes by Tom DuBois 9/18/94.

NUBBLE CLIFF

This uppermost crag lies just below the tiny summit of the Nubble. Take the Giant Mountain trail past the right end of the pond, bearing left on the Nubble Trail (1.0 mi. from highway). The climbs lie directly below the first wide, open outlook. *High Anxiety* ends down right at a ledge about 50' below the outlook at a prominent pine. To reach the base, follow the trail into a sag, and head down a gully to the left (signs of a path here), swinging around left to the base of the rock.

High Anxiety   5.5   75'   (E)

This is the second and obviously cleaned corner. Up corner to steep, exposed arete on big holds. Recommended.

FA Tom DuBois 10/3/93

Steve's Flakes   5.7   50'

15' up previous route, move right onto large ledge and climb worrisome flakes just right of *High Anxiety's* arete.

FA Steve Adler 9/93

Howdy Hiker   5.8   60'   (s)

15' up *High Anxiety,* move right onto large mossy ledge. Walk right past the previous route to a second corner. The crux is short and not well protected.

FA Tom DuBois 9/93

WASHBOWL CLIFF

This imposing face is the largest vertical rock in the Chapel Pond Pass Region. It stands some 350' high and towers over Chapel Pond from its position high on the east side of the valley. It offers good climbing and a number of moderate routes. This, together with basically good rock, sound protection, and a sunny exposure, makes the crag a popular one. The cliff is popular with birds as well: in recent years both ravens and peregrine falcons have made their home in the central section of the rock. Just left of the exposed final lead of the *Overture* is an obvious nest marked by copious white stains under a roof. Originally a ravens' nest, this has more recently been the home of peregrines, who either politely asked the former occupants to leave, or simply ate their young, thus precluding competition from the next generation of ravens. In the nest is a rotting pair of men's underwear (Hanes size 34, tighty whiteys). One can only wonder what happened to the rest of this unfortunate free-soloist.

The cliff is reached by a 20-minute climb following a path that leaves Route 73 just south of the parking lot at the pond. A trail descends steeply from the guardrail, crosses a swampy section and a small stream, and follows a break in the cliff band to the talus beneath the wall. There are some cairns enroute, and newcomers should follow closely in order not to get cliffed by wandering too far left or right. Partway up the approach trail is a rock band with a prominent right-facing corner. (*Jack Straw* 5.6, Ben Kremers and Don Mellor). The path passes this to the right before emerging through a groove with huge cedars. Cairns continue to the cliff.

The cliff is vaguely diamond-shaped, and the key to route-finding is its toe, or very lowest, central point, where the trail emerges from the scree. The major right-facing corner of *Hesitation* is above this point. *Wiessner's* and other routes nearby are to the left. Another key is the huge Slanting Ledge that dominates the left section of the wall, about 150' up and not really visible from the base of the cliff: Locate this from the road before

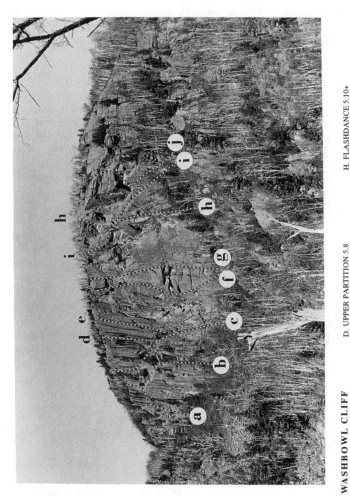

WASHBOWL CLIFF

A. BBC 5.6
B. MASTERCHARGE 5.11
C. WIESSNER ROUTE 5.5

D. UPPER PARTITION 5.8
E. TILL THE FAT LADY SINGS 5.11
F. WEEKEND WARRIOR 5.10
G. HESITATION 5.8

H. FLASHDANCE 5.10+
I. OVERTURE 5.9+
J. PRELUDE 5.8

embarking. Descent for all routes is best effected by walking around the crag on its north end. It is also possible to scramble and rappel down the south end of the cliff.

The climbs are described left to right.

BBC   II   5.6   200'   (D)

Once known as the RPI-OC Route (observing the long tradition of activity in the Adirondacks by students of the Rensselaer Polytechnic Institute), this full-length climb ascends the steep wall at the far left end of the cliff, joining the upper section of the Slanting Ledge for a belay.

pitch 1 Climb the blocky wall above and left of the huge low-angled slab at the cliff's base. Belay here or continue right across an exposed black wall and ledge system, belaying at a cedar. 5.5 (D)

pitch 2 Traverse a good ledge right, climbing, then descending to a belay at the Slanting Ledge. 5.2

pitch 3 Climb the steep, orange corner at the very left end of the Slanting Ledge 5.6. (or the crack to its left above the traverse of pitch 2?)

FA Richard Bailey, Dave Bernays, and Tris Coffin 7/30/50

Cul de Sac   I   5.7+   40'   (E)

Right of BBC is a handcrack in a left-facing corner. Not really a route, this climb is more a short exercise in pure jamming.

pitch 1 Climb the short but striking dihedral to a ledge. Once up, there is no place to go and no fixed anchor for descent. One must either rappel from a sling atop the corner, downclimb the corner, jump for the large tree, or scream for help.

Master Craft   I   5.10+   120'   (E)

This route climbs the farthest right side of the large wall above the slab.

pitch 1 Begin on a ledge with cedars and climb the arete past bolts to a large ledge belay of *Mastercharge*. 5.10 80'

pitch 2 Make difficult face move (bolt) to gain the fingercrack and the Slanting Ledge at the huge cedar. 5.10+ 40'

FA Patrick Purcell and Bob Martin 6/10/94

Mastercharge   I   5.11   150'   (E)   †

Two excellent pitches make this one of the best hard routes around. The wild finish provides a fitting climax. Begin under the orange/brown over-hanging wall that forms the left side of a corner below the right end of the Slanting Ledge. The first pitch follows a very obvious handcrack below this.

pitch 1   Climb up the corner and move left to the handcrack. Follow this (5.9) to a good ledge belay on the left at 90'.

pitch 2   Climb out right onto the brown wall. Face moves (5.10) right of the thin crack lead to the twin thin cracks (5.11) on the overhanging headwall.The climb finishes at the huge cedar on the Slanting Ledge.

FA David Lovejoy, Dwight Bradley, and Ray Crawford 8/70
FFA Don Mellor and Patrick Purcell 8/27/85

Butterflies are Free   I   5.9   150'   (s)   †

This route climbs the handcrack of *Mastercharge* and traverses right near its top, finishing up the steep, rust-colored corner (5.7). In this way, it is possible to take advantage of the classic handcrack without having to tackle the 5.11 twin-crack headwall.

FA Greg Newth and Wayne Palmer 8/27/75

I'm Committed   I   5.8+   150'   (s)

Or should be. This route begins as for the previous route and battles loose rock before finishing up and right on much better climbing. The ascent party described some loose sections; later in the summer, a climber pulled a sizable block—the crash echoed across the valley and the climber was for-tunate to survive the fall.

pitch 1   Begin as for *Mastercharge,* but head straight up instead of left. A crack leads to a tree, behind which is a good corner (right of *Butterflies*). Left hand slapping the edge and right fingers jamming the crack lead to the top.

FA Peter Ulrich and Mark Rechsteiner 5/22/94

Partition   II   5.8   250'   (s)   †

Above the middle of the Slanting Ledge is an enormous right-facing corner. This is the final pitch of this sustained Adirondack classic. The initial pitch, however, is loose and unappealing. An alternate start is recommended.

pitch 1 Begin between the *Mastercharge* wall and the *Wiessner Route*. A nondescript pitch wanders up corners, past some old pins, around an outside corner, and finally up a left-leaning ramp to the Slanting ledge. 5.7 140 (s)

pitch 2 No route-finding problems here: Stay in the huge right-facing corner. This is one of the best pitches of its grade in the region. The huge loose flake (it hung from the final offwidth slot) that terrorized leaders for 30 years was cut loose with a frighteningly gentle pry from a crowbar in 1993, making the climb safer, and apparently not much harder. Sustained 5.8

FA John Turner approx. 1960

The following routes leave from the Slanting Ledge and must be approached via one of the full-length routes from below.

Mann Act I 5.9 75' (s)

This is a unique single-pitch route that climbs the left end of the wall above the Slanting Ledge. Approach via any line to this point. Begin about 30' right of the final corners of *Wiessner*.

pitch 3 A downward handtraverse right across the wall gains the bottom of the right-facing flake/corner. Once in the upper corner, the going gets a bit less traumatic.

FA Don Mellor and Bill Simes 10/14/84

Feet of Fire I 5.11+ 90' (s) †

This and the next few routes climb the severe sheer wall right of the *Partition* corner, starting from the Slanting Ledge. Each is quite demanding, and each is highly recommended. Combine any with *Mastercharge* for a superior long, hard route.

pitch 3 Gain a low flake/ledge and make a hard traverse left to pick up the fingercrack, passing three pegs along the way. The vertical route stays about 15'–20' right of *Partition*.

FA Patrick Purcell and Don Mellor 7/27/90

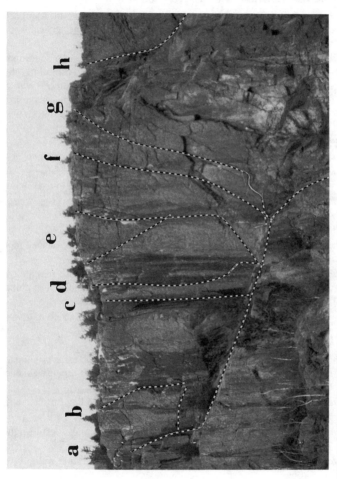

THE WASHBOWL CLIFF *(close-up of upper section)*

A. WIESSNER ROUTE 5.5

B. THE MANN ACT 5.9

C. PARTITION 5.8

D. FEET OF FIRE 5.11+

E. FLIGHT INTO EMERALD CITY 5.11

F. TILL THE FAT LADY SINGS 5.11

G. TOO WET TO PLOW 5.12

H. HESITATION 5.8

PHOTO BY MARK MESCHINELLI

Flight into Emerald City   I   5.11   90'   (D)

This route takes the prominent slanting crack on the upper wall. Approach via any of the longer routes and begin at the birch belay at the very right end of the Slanting Ledge.

pitch 3 Climb up onto a ledge to a bad bolt. Climb out right on questionable rock (short piton 1985) to gain the crack above. At the fork, the free ascent went left, while the aid ascent took the crack straight above.

FA Patrick Purcell, Mary Purcell, and Tom Skrill 9/83
FFA Harry Brielmann and Tony Trocchi 1985

Till the Fat Lady Sings   I   5.11   90'   (E)   †

Start on the right end of the Slanting Ledge at *Wiessner*'s birch belay.

pitch 3 Climb right-diagonal cracks out over the void to a large roof (bolt). Straight up on unrelenting but not severe climbing to the rim.

FA Don Mellor and Bill Dodd 7/11/90

Too Wet To Plow   I   5.12   90'   (s)

The previous route climbs the left of several "peaks" in an M-shaped roof band. This route takes the next one to the right.

pitch 3 Traverse straight right from the birch belay on loose rock past a bolt. Up increasingly difficult rock to the crux roof (bolt). The going stays hard until escape right is possible.

FA Don Mellor and Patrick Purcell 7/27/90

Whoops   I   5.8   350'   (s)

This route maintains a separate line a few feet left of the more prominent *Wiessner Route*. Begin at a right-facing corner under the extreme right end of the Slanting Ledge.

pitch 1 Climb the wall just left of the broken *Wiessner* line (or the crack above the tree to its left) to a belay ledge. 5.8 75'

pitch 2 Climb the shallow corners above the ledge, gaining a left-to-right diagonal handcrack that leads to the Slanting Ledge. 5.8 75'

pitch 3 Walk left the full length of the terrace to the final short wall.

pitch 4 Climb the steep thin crack just right of the orange open book of *BBC*. 5.8 35'

FA Joe Szot, Tom Rosecrans, and Rob Norris 9/79

Wiessner Route   II   5.5   350'   (s)   †

A highly recommended route that finds a relatively easy way up an impressive wall, this climb is one of the region's oldest. The crux is the block/overhang about 30' up. Begin in the large right-facing corner under the far right end of the Slanting Ledge.

pitch 1 Climb cracks to the square block/roof. Climb over its right side and belay above at a good, flat ledge. 5.5 75'

pitch 2 The second pitch climbs the depression to its end before escaping left (5.4) and belaying about 20' above at a birch on the Slanting Ledge. 75' It's possible to combine these pitches.

pitch 3 Walk uphill across the Slanting Ledge to the final short wall.

pitch 4 The original route climbs the right side of a huge block to a 5.5 finish. Other options include: (1) the left side of the block, (2) the 5.8 Whoops finish crack, (3) the excellent 5.6 orange corner of *BBC* (hidden out left on the edge), (4) the 5.6 arete that makes up the left edge of *BBC,* or (5) the hidden crack out to its left.

FA Fritz Wiessner, M. Becket Howorth, and Bob Notman 5/38

Third Time for Mrs. Robinson   I   5.10   180'   (s)

This is an unfinished route that leads toward the central buttress from the base of *Wiessner.* Unfortunately, the initially-appealing Nose Buttress of the central Washbowl Cliff is characterized by loose rock and disappointing climbing.

pitch 1 Begin right of *Wiessner* and climb a right-facing corner past a bolt to a belay at a small ledge and fixed anchor. 5.10

pitch 2 It is possible to make a rising traverse on dangerous rock right to the arete and a ledge below the *Hesitation* roof.

FA Michael Stone and Ian Wedmore 4/30/84
FFA Don Mellor and Patrick Purcell 8/27/85

Weekend Warrior   II   5.10   350'   (s)

This is another futile attempt at the Nose Buttress. *Weekend Warrior* stays a bit right of the prow and follows some good features to the top.

pitch 1 Follow a bolted face out left from the base of *Hesitation*. (This excellent pitch was led after the first ascent, which joined higher up. The pitch is fast becoming a route in itself. Rap anchor at top)

pitch 2 Move left to a corner and crack. The crux moves lead up and through the roof to a belay ledge under the roof.

pitch 3 Walk right to a boulder move, followed by easier climbing to a prominent right-facing corner. Belay at ledge above.

pitch 4 Climb out left and wander up toward the final corner with a cedar tree about 30' left of the final pitch of *Hesitation*.

FA Patrick Purcell (p.1)

FA Tim Beaman and Patrick Purcell 10/16/88

Hesitation   II   5.8   350'   (s)   †

This is an outstanding and consistently challenging line that bisects the cliff, taking the single crack line up from the toe of the wall to its very highest point, four pitches above. Both the leader and the second are exposed to long falls on the second pitch.

pitch 1 Begin in the major, clean right-facing corner above the approach trail. Follow the corner crack until it is possible to traverse right to a large sloping belay with old pins. The lower move out right, formerly one of the technical cruxes of the climb, disappeared when the key block fell. (Hundreds of people had laybacked strenuously on this block for years; when it was agreed that the block was probably unsafe and should go, Bill Dodd just grabbed it and threw it off. Don't get in this man's way.) 5.8 70'

pitch 2 This is another demanding pitch. Regain the corner and climb to the roof. Head right across the exposed wall to the roof's end, and watching rope drag, face-climb back left with no protection to a belay at the main crack about 20' above the roof. 5.7 75' The roof has been climbed directly on top-rope.

pitch 3 A less interesting pitch leads up broken rock to a belay beneath the final dihedral. 5.4 100'

pitch 4 The final steep corner leads to the rim. 5.6 75'

FA John Turner, Brian Rothery, and Irwin Hodgson 1958

Flashdance II 5.10+ 350' (s) †

Right of *Hesitation* is a major depression in the cliff. Though there are old pins up high, and though climbers have linked it with *Flashdance,* no other route history is known. *Flashdance* begins in a lesser corner to its right and heads for the huge red right-facing flake. The route is long and good, and is the first climb on the cliff to dry in early spring.

pitch 1 Boulder up to the corner and gain the right-facing corner. Follow this to a bolt belay atop a pedestal. 5.9 75'

pitch 2 Traverse right across the red wall, gaining another right-facing corner. A hard exit leads to a major ramp. 5.9+ 60'

pitch 3 Follow the ramp up left (just right of the ravens' nest) to a belay below the final crux pitch, the right-facing, double-capped roofs.

pitch 4 Climb into the hollow and turn both roofs on the right. 5.10+ Or join *Overture,* making for an easier finish.

History The route as described was climbed by Chuck Turner and Bill Simes in 1983. During the prior summer they had climbed the crux pitch (known originally as *Accord*) as a solution to the elusive direct finish to *Prelude.* The bolts at the first belay remain a mystery and seem to be 1960s vintage.

Overture II 5.9+ 350' (s) †

This is a superb route with a wild final pitch. It's possible to skip the lower crux by joining *Prelude* to its right at several points, making the route 5.8. Locate *Prelude,* the major left-facing corner that diagonals up and left at the right end of the cliff.

pitch 1 Climb the wall left of the dihedral, easy at first, then harder past two bolts (hidden from below). 5.9+ 150'

pitch 2 Wander up left on the ramps to their end below the double-decked, right-facing undercling pitch of *Flashdance.* 100'

pitch 3 Step down (right above the birds' nest) left and gain slab and arete out left to a bolt. Continue up ridge, then left around the edge to a corner and a bolt above. Dive left to the finish corner. This is Keene Valley's most exposed pitch. 5.8 100'

FA Patrick Purcell and Don Mellor 3/11/90 (p.1)

FA Don Mellor, Bill Dodd, and Jeff Edwards 7/10/90 (p.2 & 3)

Prelude   I   5.8   225'   (s)

At the right end of the cliff is an attractive left-facing dihedral below a large ceiling about 140' above. The name refers to the first pitch as a "prelude" to the more direct finish envisioned.

pitch 1 A frustrating move off the ground begins a good pitch to a belay below the roof. The move at the piton is hard.

pitch 2 Traverse right around the corner and across right to a belay.

pitch 3 The ramp and chimney lead to the top of the crag.

FA Grant Calder, John Wald, and Mike Levenson approx. 1975

Green Beer   I   5.8   90'   (s)

pitch 1 Climb the red wall right of *Prelude,* following flakes.

FA Mark and Terry Saulsgiver 3/85
FFA Joe Szot, Tom Rosecrans, and Mike Hay 1986

LOWER WASHBOWL CLIFFS

Far from being a developed climbing area, this broken band of cliffs is an explorer's delight. Stretching from the Spider's Web to the Washbowl Cliff, seven fairly distinct walls and buttresses loom above the road and long talus approach. There isn't much documentation of routes done in the past (though its climbing history dates at least as far back as John Case's explorations here, around 1916), but wherever climbers search for new lines, old, rusted pitons hint silently of earlier, forgotten passage.

The biggest problem of reporting in the past and perhaps a reason for the crags' nebulous history has been the difficulty of breaking the area down in one's mind, lending name and form to the walls: At first the cliffs seem a maze of towers and gullies that defy description. Just before the 1983 guidebook, some local climbers got together and gave each cliff a name. In this way, it would become easier to make some sense out of this rock pile. Even so, the place will probably continue to defy description, and climbers will have to approach these crags with the explorer's mind-set.

This east wall of Chapel Pond Pass consists of many separate pieces of rock. The first as seen when approaching from Keene Valley is the spectacular, crack-laced wall called the Spider's Web. This is described separately. The highest, largest, and last cliff in the rising series is the Washbowl Cliff.

LOWER WASHBOWL CLIFFS

A. LOST ARROW FACE (SHOWN: SERGEANT PEPPER, VIRGIN STURGEON, EXCALIBER)

B. THE TICKET

C. THE FAN

D. LONG BUTTRESS

E. CONCAVE WALL

F. EIGHTH WALL

Between these well-traveled walls stand several minor crags, the Lower Washbowl Cliffs. These are described left to right, or north to south.

The best place from which to view the cliffs and the most convenient starting point to approach the climbs is the mysteriously fenced-in parking lot just south of the Spider's Web. From this boulder-lined terrace, one's sense of depth and distance is lost as the eye is drawn up and over the enormous talus and on to the band of rock above from this most spectacular of viewpoints.

Unique about this broken wall of the valley is that it has ample drainage and strong afternoon sun. As a result, it has been climbed during every month of the year. Note the dates of some of the first ascents, and consider this as an option during those inevitable warm spells that conspire to ruin your well-laid plans for an ice-climbing trip to the North Country.

Note: The size of the talus slope bespeaks the instability of the cliffs here. All routes have at least some loose rock.

WHIP IT WALL

Between the Spider's Web and the Lost Arrow face is a short steep wall that is the site of the *Whip it Good* ice climb.

Whip It Bad I 5.10 75' (E)

The ice climb route. Up the right-facing corner, finishing out right in a tight handcrack.

Variation The vertical fingercrack just left of the handcrack finish is 5.9+.

FA Patrick Purcell and Bill Dodd 4/27/89

Whips and Chains I 5.10 40' (E)

Approach via the main corner; from on top of the block ledge, climb right-diagonal fingercrack.

FA Patrick Purcell and Dennis Luther 5/89

FALSE ARROW FACE

Down in the talus one spies a blocky spire thrusting a few feet above the trees. Most people mistake this for the Lost Arrow, which stands invisible from the road below the wall higher up. The False Arrow face is a minor formation that provides some fun climbing with a unique pinnacle summit. Descent is best made by down-climbing the 15' wall (5.1) back to the notch behind the rock.

Spire Route I 5.4 70' (E)

pitch 1 Begin below the highest point on the rock, at the left end of the wall. From a large cedar, climb the prominent crack line to the top. The classic belay here is the old loop around the summit itself.

Short Order I 5.5 40' (E)

pitch 1 This is the crack in the right-facing corner below and right of the summit. It does not climb the spire itself.

New Year's Day I 5.8 40' (E)

pitch 1 On the right wall of the crag, a few feet right of the previous route, is a thin crack line that angles left as it leads through a roof.

ACB Don Mellor, Mike Heintz, and Bill Dodd 12/31/84

LOST ARROW FACE

The first major cliff right of the Spider's Web is named for the spire that stands at its base. It stands about 100' up the slope from the False Arrow.

Chunga's Revenge I 5.6+ 150' (S)

Near the left end of the crag is a shallow left-facing corner right of a fresh orange rock scar. Two parties have experienced large rockfall on this section of the route, with one serious injury resulting.

pitch 1 Climb the crack for 40'; then move left across the scar to a belay at a large cedar ledge.

pitch 2 Climb straight over blocks to a ledge below an overhang. Climb through the hang at a crack and follow this to the top.

FA Tom Rosecrans and Rob Norris 8/9/74

Sergeant Pepper   I   5.8   150'   (E)

This is the prominent cleft capped by a roof. Begin as for *Chunga*'s.

pitch 1 Climb up to the cedar belay, passing through the loose section en route.

pitch 2 Follow the steep, left-facing corner above and out the roof to the right.

FA George Bennett and Rob Wood approx. 1968

Unnamed   I   5.11

The bolt-protected arete making up the right edge of *Sergeant Pepper* is reported to be a really good challenge.

Virgin Sturgeon   I   5.9   150'   (S)   †

This is a sustained route that attacks the highest portion of the cliff. Begin below a bolt 40' up.

pitch 1 Ascend the crack past the needless bolt (placed by another party around 1977) toward the larger crack above. An unrelenting finish in the right-facing corner system leads up and right.

FA Rob Wood and Dave Keefe 4/20/68

Excaliber   I   5.8   120'   (E)   †

This is an excellent route, combining a deceptively hard corner and an impeccable handcrack. Begin just right of center at an obvious 50' left-facing dihedral formed by a pillar.

pitch 1 Climb the ever-steepening corner to a pedestal belay. 5.8 50'

pitch 2 Follow the handcrack above past a pesky cedar. Exit right. 5.7 These pitches can be combined.

ACB Alan Jolley and Scott Provost 7/81

Cozy Corner   I   5.4   120'   (E)

This route climbs right of the *Excaliber* pedestal.

pitch 1 From the base of the obvious corner of the previous route, climb up and right via a tricky face move and small tree. It's not too hard, but it has puzzled many leaders. Continue up the corner and broken rock to the top (though it's possible to belay at any of several locations along the way).

ACB Tony Goodwin and Steve Healy 4/20/68

Hummingbird   I   5.7   150'   (s)

This route begins below and right, just left of the right end of the cliff, and 20' below the notch formed by the Lost Arrow. The first pitch can be by-passed from the left. There is much loose rock.

pitch 1 Climb the outside ridge past a large pine to a good belay at a cedar tree. 5.4 75'

pitch 2 Climb into the crack on the right, into a groove, and up to a point below the square-notched *Direct* variation. From here it is possible to exit either left to *Cozy Corner* or right over loose rock.

Variation **Hummingbird Direct** 5.9   A good finish alternative is to climb the roof slot above the first belay via the twin cracks.

FA P. Bennett, P. Baggely, and P. Ferguson 5/3/68
FA Bill Simes and Bob Bushart 1980 (var.)

Recital   I   5.8   60'   (E)

Behind the Lost Arrow is a thin fingercrack.

pitch 1 Climb the crack to its top and exit right.

ACB Don Mellor and Ian Osteyee 4/85

Rope Toss Wall   I   5.5   100'   (s)

Behind the *Lost Arrow* is a slab.

pitch 1 Climb the face directly or move right for protection; belay at a ledge level with the top of the Lost Arrow. 5.3 50'

pitch 2 Climb broken, orange rock to a loose finish. 5.5 50'

Sugar Plum Fairy   I   5.5   100'   (D)

Begin on the right side of the slab behind the Lost Arrow.

pitch 1 Climb the right side of the slab until it is possible to step out left onto the narrow spine of rock. Follow this unprotected arete to the top or until better judgement leads you right into the trees.

FA P. Baggely, P. Ferguson, and John Leggett 5/4/60

LOST ARROW †

This is the amazing rock that stands like a tractor trailer on end at the base of the right end of the wall. Its history speaks of the spirit of Dave Bernays and Stanley Smith. During their explorations of the valley walls in April 1950, they climbed several of "The Pinnacles of Chapel Pond" as reported in their article of that name in *Adirondac*, the magazine of the Adirondack Mountain Club. This rock was certainly the most alluring of the splinters that had peeled free from the walls. Yet there just didn't seem a way up. They solved the problem by anchoring Smith to a piton on the main wall behind; he threw a weighted rope over the spire to Bernays. They then hand-over-handed to the summit, dragging up rocks behind to serve as the mandatory summit cairn. These rocks still adorn the flat top of the spire. The descent is standard to those areas like the Needles of South Dakota: keep a rope secured below, toss the other end over the opposite side, and rappel. This keeps the top free of an artificial bolt anchor.

Southeast Face   5.8   (D)

pitch 1 Begin on the southeast face of the rock, or that which faces Chapel Pond. Face-climb past an old pin to a harder finish in a small groove/crack.

FA unknown

Southwest Face   5.9

Top-rope the side facing the road, past an old pin.

Irene   I 5.3 150' (S)

This and the next route climb the vague and broken wall above and right of the Lost Arrow Face. Begin 50' up and right of the Lost Arrow.

pitch 1 Climb up to a vegetated ledge; then climb the half-moon crack on the face to the right. Continue up left over loose, easy rock.

pitch 2 Continue up and left.

FA Mark and Terry Saulsgiver 6/2/84

B Gentle I 5.7 (s)

Begin directly above the Lost Arrow on the right face of an alcove (directly below a white patch).

pitch 1 Face-climb (5.7) to easier ground, then up and right to a cedar belay at 110'.

pitch 2 Diagonal up and right to gain the loose, blocky arete above an old cedar.

FA Mark and Terry Saulsgiver 6/84

THE TICKET

This is the next rock face to the right. It is the steep face split by several vertical crack lines and which stands directly above the fenced-in viewing area. The most visible crack line is *More Tea, Vicar?*

Sunday Funnies I 5.6 120' (s)

This route climbs the major V-groove left of the main face. Begin about 15' left of the buttress at a large birch.

pitch 1 Blocky rock leads to an awkward step around a flake/arete at 40'. Continue in the 4" crack to an alcove from which a spectacular escape left brings one to the top.

FA Don Mellor and Bill Dodd 12/30/84

Swept Away I 5.9 70 (E) †

This is the superb crack on the left wall of the main buttress. It is the hand/fingercrack behind a block/flake starting 12' up and just left of the outside edge of the cliff.

pitch 1 Climb out right from the base of the major corner (crux) to gain the crack. A rappel is possible from the top of the crack.

FA Don Mellor and Bill Dodd 12/30/84

Winter's Tale I 5.10 100' (E)

Near the left side of the crag is a crack that leads to an obviously difficult, overhanging, fist-sized finish.

pitch 1 Climb into the brief off-sized crack before attacking the overhanging fistcrack.

FA Don Mellor and Chuck Turner 12/27/82

More Tea, Vicar?   I   5.9   120'   (E)   †

This is the most prominent line on the cliff. Begin at the obvious 8" crack.

pitch 1 Climb the crack through the overhanging corner to a chimney finish. This can be broken into two leads.

FA Bob and Brenda O'Regan 5/6/68
FFA Chuck Turner and Mike Young 7/5/81

Chocolate City   I   5.7   100'   (E)

Right of the previous route, and the third of the prominent vertical crack lines that split the face.

pitch 1 Climb up and past a left-facing corner at mid-height.

FA Don Mellor and Paul Carlson 10/83

THE FAN

This cliff can be identified as the next major crag right of The Ticket, and by the right-slanting traverse cracks on the right side of the wall after which the wall is named. The route possibilities begin on a large tree-covered ledge that is approached by a loose, flaky wide crack on the right. This awful start is about 5.3. The best (or least ugly) line appears to be the vertical crack, the leftmost of the series. The cliff is about 150' high, including the lower section.

BALCONY CLIFF

To the right of the fan and left of the long, blocky ridge known as the Long Buttress is a wall split by vertical cracks that lead up from a large ledge, the balcony, about 40' up.

Wear Four   I   5.8   80'   (E)

This route climbs the most prominent crack just left of center.

pitch 1 Climb the left of two obvious blocky lines to the ledge. 5.6 40'

pitch 2 Continue up the most obvious crack, exiting left into a right-facing
corner to finish. 5.8 40'

FA Chuck Turner and Don Mellor 12/27/82

LONG BUTTRESS

Above and right of the boulder-lined viewing terrace is a long, blocky,
tree-covered ridge. It is the longest piece of rock on this side of the valley,
but it is too discontinuous to offer really good climbing potential. It was
here that the first successful peregrine falcon nest was established in 1984
with the birth and banding of three healthy chicks. They have since moved
uptown to the Washbowl Cliff. The first recorded human reconnaissance
was an ascent by Chuck Turner and Rich Leswing in 1981. Instead of a
route description, they simply reported that it wasn't worth the effort. The
two routes listed here certainly weren't the only ones attempted or finished.

Dodge and Dangle   II   5.8   240'

Halfway up the buttress on its left side is a deep diagonal gully. Below
this is an indistinct ramp. The final pitch is reported to be a payoff for the
inferior terrain below.

pitch 1 Climb the broken ramp into a corner. Continue up the wall to the
left to a large, tree-covered ledge. 130'

pitch 2 Traverse right 10' along the ledge and climb the tricky face to a
corner/ledge with a large tree. 50'

pitch 3 The obvious corner (5.8) leads to the top. 60'

FA Jim Vermeulen and Eric Dahn 8/83

Bad Advice   I   5.8   200'   (s)

"Look's easy, Chuck. I'm sure you won't need any big pieces of gear." On
the right side of the buttress, about halfway up, is an attractive fingercrack.

pitch 1 Climb the good crack to its top. Head left toward the ridge for a
belay.

pitch 2 Climb into the prominent corner capped by a roof with a hand-/

fistcrack. This final crux can be seen from the road at Chapel Pond.

FA Chuck Turner and Don Mellor 1982

CONCAVE WALL

Right of the Long Buttress is a large wall that rears upward and overhangs at the top. It is identified by the eye-catching, rust-colored right-facing dihedral, best viewed from Chapel Pond. This corner, *Cinnamon Girl,* is perhaps the most attractive feature on this end of the Lower Washbowl Cliffs.

Middle Earth   (easy)

Near the junction of the Concave Wall and the couloir to its left is a flake formation that forms a spelunker's chimney.

Tubular Bells   I   5.7   160'   (s)

To the right of *Middle Earth* and left of the steep gully that splits the face just left of *Cinnamon Girl* is a large slanting corner.

pitch 1 Climb the corner to just below the overhang. 5.7 70'

pitch 2 Break out left and belay. 40'

pitch 3 Follow the ramp up left to the top. The pitch is loose and may be avoided by rappelling.

FA Chuck Turner and Jim Cunningham 1981

Cinnamon Girl   II   5.8   A1   (E)

This route climbs the attractive orange corner. Begin about 40' to its right.

pitch 1 Climb the wall left of the gully/chimney to a bulge. Traverse left to a cedar belay.

pitch 2 A short pitch follows broken rock to a good ledge at the base of the rusty corner. 30'

pitch 3 This is the main feature of the route. The first ascent party climbed the corner mixed free and aid, traversing off left (and discovering *Tubular Bells*) at the top. Above, the wall hangs a bit.

FA to high point: Chuck Turner, Rich Leswing, and Jim Cunningham 1981

EIGHTH WALL

The last wall below the Washbowl Cliff contains some vertical cracks. It is convenient to approach as for the Washbowl Cliff and head down left to the base of the wall.

Land of the Lost   I   5.9+

pitch 1 Follow the vertical crack system roughly 10' left of *The Fang*.

pitch 2 Two parallel handcracks go at about the same grade.

FA Jon Barker, Chris and Ward Smith, and Jim Ainsworth 1989

The Fang   I   5.10   150'

pitch 1–3 Climb the striking vertical hand-/fingercrack near the center of the face with tree ledges offering good belays. The first pitch is identified by the large cedar at the top of the crack. This climb has been compared to routes at the Spider's Web.

FA Tim Beaman and Sylvia Lazarnick 8/14/83

SWAMP ROCK

Below the Long Buttress and the Concave Wall, in fact quite close to the road, is another partially hidden minor cliff. Approach this via an old tote road that heads off toward the talus from the north end of Chapel Pond. The rock stands at about the same height as Route 73.

Swamp Gas   I   5.8   75'   (E)

On the left side of the crag is a left-facing corner/crack.

FA Jeff Edwards and Patrick Purcell 6/25/86

Swamp Thang   I   5.11+

Start uphill and right, climbing up the center of the face past four bolts.

FA Dave Furman 8/15/94

Swamp Arete   I   5.7   60'

Climb the short overhanging handcrack on the right side of the rock to a ledge and outside edge above.

FA Jeff Edwards and Patrick Purcell 6/25/86

SPIDER'S WEB

For sheer sustained difficulty and purity of crack climbing, the Spider's Web has no peer in the region. Standing down at the lower left end of the Giant's Washbowl group, this slightly overhanging 150' wall seems to have been sliced clean from the mountainside by the Giant's saber itself. Its full-length crack lines are virtually uninterrupted by either ledges or rests, and it is this unrelenting verticality that is the essence of the challenge here. The difficulty of most of the climbs is a reflection more of the sum of the moves strung together than any particular boulder problem.

The cliff is best approached from the fenced-in parking area on the east side of Route 73 between Roaring Brook Falls and Chapel Pond. Parking next to the guardrail is common, but there is also room in the camping area across the road as well as at the pond itself. The approach down the bank and over the talus is straightforward. Descent is easiest to the north; the south end descent is steep and loose.

The climbs are described left to right.

Retrograde   I   5.11-   35'   (E)

pitch 1 This is the first thin crack problem on the very left end of the wall.

FA Bill Dodd 1988

Wrong Again, Chalkbreath   I   5.11-   35'   (E)

pitch 1 Climb the thin crack just left of *Bird's Nest*.

FA Tim Beaman and Herb George 1988

Bird's Nest   I   5.10   45'   (E)

pitch 1 Right of the two minor fingercracks is a longer, more prominent hand-/fingercrack.

FA Unknown

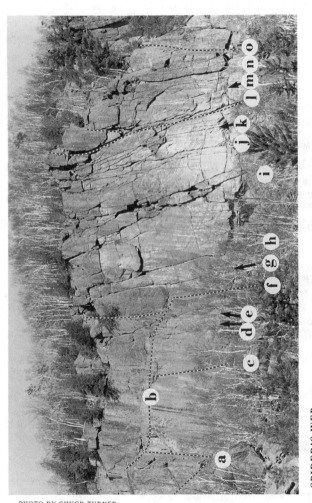

PHOTO BY CHUCK TURNER

SPIDER'S WEB

A. IT'S ONLY ENTERTAINMENT 5.11+,
   ESTHESIA 5.9+, SLIM PICKENS 5.9+

B. WALK-OFF LEDGE

C. TR 5.10-

D. ONLY THE GOOD DIE YOUNG 5.11

E. FEAR AND LOATHING IN KEENE
   VALLEY 5.11

F. MR. ROGERS' NEIGHBORHOOD 5.8

G. MONKEY SEE, MONKEY DO 5.11-

H. DROP, FLY, OR DIE 5.11

I. THE KEYE 5.8

J. ROMANO'S ROUTE 5.11

K. WHITE KNIGHT 5.11

L. ON THE LOOSE 5.9+

M. GRAND HYSTERIA 5.12

N. ETERNITY 5.10

O. YVONNE 5.9

Five Hundred Rednecks with Guns   I   5.11   50'   (top-rope)

pitch 1 Between the obvious handcracks of *Bird's Nest* and *Dacker Cracker* is a left-rising, tiny stepped staircase of holds. It begins at a mysterious low bolt.

FA Patrick Purcell 1986 (top-rope)

Dacker Cracker   I   5.10   50'   (E)   †

pitch 1 This is the most prominent vertical crack on the lefthand wall of the Web. Climb the crack past a wider section to a strenuous finish.

FA Don Mellor 5/82

Jelly Arms   I   5.11   55'   (s)   †

pitch 1 Right of *Dacker Cracker* is a thin crack that angles off right. Climb the increasingly difficult crack to a finish in a short chimney.

Variation **Hit by a Car** 5.11+   Instead of diagonalling right, head straight up.

FA Chuck Turner 10/82
FA Bill Dodd (top-rope) 1993 (var.)

Chicken Wire   I   5.11+   55'   (s)

pitch 1 Below the finish of *Jelly Arms* is another thin crack line. Difficult face moves from the ground lead to a tiny right-facing corner and an easier finish.

FA Don Mellor 6/85

Peace in Our Climbs   I   5.11+   60'   (E)   †

Start 15' right of the previous route.

pitch 1 Stick clip a bolt for hard face-climbing that leads to an incredible fingercrack.

FA Chris Gill 1991

It's Only Entertainment   I   5.11+   100'   (E)   †

This amazing route, one of the premiere single-pitch crack routes in the region, is increasingly becoming known for the whippers taken from the end of the handtraverse. The photogenic possibilities from the large boulder (use fast film) are exceeded only by the pure intensity of the climbing itself. It is the all-too-obvious left-slanting fingercrack that leads from the base of *Esthesia* and *Slim Pickins* and seems to end just short of the top. Chuck Turner aid-climbed the line and sky-hooked straight to the top in the early eighties, creating *Captain Hooks* A3. The free version hand-traverses left.

pitch 1 From the ledge at the base of the enormous right-facing corner of *Slim Pickins,* head out left on an unrelenting finger journey to the top of the crack. Hand-traverse left to share the finish with the previous route.

FA Tim Beaman and Bill Dodd 1988

Esthesia   I   5.9+   90'   (E)   †

This is another gem. Tucked into the arete formed by the huge inside corner that dominates the left end of the Web is yet another corner.

pitch 1 Climb the ever-widening finger-to-fist crack past two roofs to the top. The second roof is the crux: The parallel-sided crack here is about 4"–5" wide.

FA Grant Calder, John Wald, and Dave Cilley 7/28/76
FFA Todd Eastman and Dave Cilley 4/77

Jungle Fever   I   5.12-   85'   (E)

The wall and edge left of the *Slim Pickins* dihedral is sustained and excellent. Make sure bolts are in place before heading up.

FA Patrick Purcell and Jeff Edwards 1992

Slim Pickins   I   5.9+   90'   (E)   †

pitch 1 This climb follows the most obvious feature on the left end of the wall, the huge right-facing corner.

FA Henry Barber and Dave Cilley 4/77

Zabba   I   5.12+   80'

Right of *Slim Pickins* and just left of the cave start of *TR* is a thin crack with a bolt near its top. The former aid route has been top-roped free.

FA Bob Bushart and Bill Diemand 7/79
FFA (top-rope) Chris Gill 1991

TR I 5.10- 120' (E) †

About 60' right of the huge *Slim Pickins* corner is a crack system that rises from a small cave. (TR stands for Tom Rosecrans, initials scribbled onto the diagram in the new route book at EMS by Dave Cilley, who was keeping early track of the climbs.)

pitch 1 Exit the cave right and climb steep holds and cracks to a good ledge. 5.10-

pitch 2 Exit left or climb the short fist crack above.

FA Tom Rosecrans and Paul Laskey
FFA Steve Hendrick and Jay Philbrick 4/80

Pumpernickel I 5.11 80' (E)

This route climbs the cracks just right of *TR*. The lower section requires deliberate avoidance of the other route.

pitch 1 A series of hard moves just right of the cave leads up to a small stance. Twin fingercracks above make up the crux. The pitch ends on the main exit highway which walks (4th class) left off the wall.

FA Chuck Turner, Bill Simes, and Alan Jolley 7/82
FFA Patrick Purcell and Don Mellor 6/87

Only the Good Die Young I 5.11 80' (E)

This arm pumper begins just right of *TR*'s cave.

pitch 1 Climb out right on broken rock to the thin crack. The crux is just above, but hanging on to finish might prove to be the real problem. Exit left.

FA Chuck Turner, Alan Jolley, and Roger Jolley 1982
FFA Ken Nichols and Mike Heintz 9/84

Fear and Loathing in Keene Valley I 5.11 120' (E) †

Begin below the narrow right-facing corner of *Mr. Rogers' Neighborhood*.

pitch 1 From the sloping shelf at ground level, climb the unlikely wall to gain the obvious diagonal finger crack. Like so many of the routes here, success depends mainly on hang time.

pitch 2 Mantel to the next ledge and finish the short chimney.

FA Steve Hendrick and Jay Philbrick 5/80

PHOTO BY JEFF EDWARDS

Adam Clayman on Slim Pickins. Esthesia is the obvious crack to the left.

Mr. Rogers' Neighborhood   I   5.8   150'   (E)   †

This, the easiest route on the Spider's Web, climbs a prominent right-facing corner. The second pitch, added later, makes this a full-length route.

pitch 1 Step out from a large boulder onto the broken wall. Above the roof (5.8), step left and follow the corner (5.6) to a belay at the right end of the exit ledge.

pitch 2 Take the first crack left past a cedar stump at the top. 5.8

FA Don Mellor, Chuck Turner, and Rich Leswing 4/24/82

FA Mark and Terry Saulsgiver 1985 (p.2)

Monkey See, Monkey Do   II   5.11-   150'   (E)

Near the middle of the wall are two parallel, diagonal cracks.

pitch 1 Climb out of the recess on broken rock (as for *Mr. Rogers'*) to a ledge at 20'. Continue in the crack right of the right-facing corner. At the height of the exit ledge, traverse left to establish a belay. 5.9 80' The first ascent party climbed the route as one long pitch, but most subsequent teams have sought refuge off left.

pitch 2 Head back to the crack line, through a wide crux section, to a perfect handcrack finish.

FA Henry Barber and Todd Eastman 9/78

Drop, Fly, or Die   II   5.11-   150'   (E)   †

After a dramatic photo of Barber on the first ascent and a macabre route name, this climb soon became the most sought-after on the Spider's Web. It continues to be popular for its clean, sustained line, its good protection, and its place on the low end of the 5.11 grade.

pitch 1 From the hollow behind the large base rocks, climb up (5.10) from a spike of rock to a stance below the roof. Traverse left to join the crack, belaying at a semihanging stance at a six-inch ledge or at a fixed anchor below the roof.

pitch 2 Climb over a hard roof (5.10+) to a looser but easier finish. Though Barber originally climbed this route as a single pitch (asking Dave Cilley to tie on more rope after he had back-cleaned the protection from the traverse), most parties split the pitches.

Variation **Direct Start** 5.11   Join the main crack directly from the ground via a harder thin crack.

Variation **Captain Chips Traverse**   *pitch 2* 5.10 Climb out right under the roof at the upper belay and up the scary slot on the left or the broken line to the right.

FA Henry Barber 4/77

FA Don Mellor and Hans Johnstone 6/5/91 (var. 1)

FA Steve Hendrick and Jay Philbrick 5/80 (var. 2)

Lycanthropia I 5.12 165'

Another impossible route falls to the visiting Berzins. Impressive.

pitch 1 Start as for the previous route, but instead of moving left, climb straight up using either crack to a break. Step into *Drop, Fly, or Die,* up 6', the back right using fragile flake. Stay in crack to hanging belay at roof.

pitch 2 Head out right and climb the 5.9 slot over a scary block.

FA Todd Eastman and Chris Hyson 7/77

FFA Martin Berzins and Richard Felch 8/4/91

The Keye II 5.8 160' (E)

This was the first complete free route on the Spider's Web and it takes the most obvious line up the block-filled cracks in the center of the wall. The huge stacked blocks that make up the route seem insecure, and as such, it is up to each aspirant to judge whether he or she is willing to climb them.

pitch 1 Climb around a roof from the left or, more directly, start down below at an off-sized crack. Belay at 50'. 5.8

pitch 2 Continue on the left side of the stack to another sheltered belay. 5.8 50'

pitch 3 The exit from the alcove takes the left-hand crack and constitutes the route's technical crux.

Variation **Deviant Finish**   From the high cave belay, it is possible to hand-traverse right onto the face and up a good crack to the top. 5.10

FA Grant Calder and John Wald 7/76

FA Chris Lyons and Jerry Hoover 9/77 (direct start p.1)

FA Tim Beaman, Dill Dodd, and Herb George (var.)

Skeleton Key I 5.10+ 100' (E)

This link-up climbs the obvious crack just above and right of the off-sized fistcrack start of *The Keye* and heads out right to join *Romano*'s mid-section.

pitch 1 Climb *The Keye*'s direct start crack to a ledge on the right. Continue in a hand-/fingercrack until a traverse right is possible at a crack. Hard moves lead up to join *Romano's Route* just below the blocky mid-section belay.

FA Tim Beaman, Herb George, and Sylvia Lazarnick 1987

Romano's Route II 5.11 160' (E) †

This is perhaps the most obvious vertical hand-/fingercrack line on the white right-center section of the Spider's Web; it is also one of the best.

pitch 1 From a sloping ledge just left of the high block start to the right-hand routes, climb a thin hard fingercrack (5.11) to a ledge at about 40'. Belay here or continue in the handcrack, thin at first, to the belay on a blocky ledge off right.

pitch 2 There are several options above; several cracks, all loose, lead to the top. Most groups join *On the Loose*.

FA Rich Romano late 70s

White Knight I 5.11 90' (E) †

The purest fingercrack on the Web, this route climbs the vertical crack midway between *Romano's* and the obvious, blocky *On the Loose*. Begin atop the blocks under the right side of the wall. (The short, direct start crack was only later climbed at 5.12: *Ku Klux Ken,* Martin Berzins)

pitch 1 Climb out to the right at first (or use the direct start), then traverse back left to gain the bottom of the crack. Superior finger- and tight handcrack climbing leads to the roof under the blocky midsection belay. Exit up and left a bit to gain the ledge.

FA Bob Bushart and Bill Simes (as part of a hanging bivouac party) 1979
FFA Ken Nichols and Mike Heintz 9/19/84

On the Loose II 5.9+ 160' (E) †

This popular climb has some of the most secure jams on the cliff; it also follows the most overhanging section. As such, and like so many of the

routes here, the route's challenge is simply to hang on. The route is identified as the obvious crack system that dominates the right side of the wall,
about 30' from the end of the cliff.

pitch 1 From the boulder belay, climb up easily to a stance under the crack.
70' of strenuous but not severe climbing brings one to the sheltered belay
atop loose blocks.

pitch 2 The original and standard finish sneaks out left under the roof (5.9)
and follows a 4"–5" crack to a spectacular cave exit. Alternatively, it is
possible to exit right of the roof via handcracks above the slot (5.8).

FA Henry Barber and Dave Cilley 4/77

Grand Hysteria   I   5.12   150'

A steep crack between *Eternity* and *On the Loose.*

pitch 1 Climb the first 20' of *On the Loose,* then right 10' to a crack. Up
crack and seam to a good hold. Swing right into the crack, through overlap
and an easier finish.

FA Martin Berzins and Richard Felch 8/16/89

Eternity   I   5.10   110'   (E with wide crack protection)

On the very right edge of the main wall is an offwidth crack in a shallow
left-facing corner.

pitch 1 Below and right is a chimney/slot with a loose chockstone. Climb
this crack (*Yvonne* 5.6) to a large ledge. Belay here is possible. Duck
under the roof left and climb the unrelenting and little-traveled wide
crack to the top. To descend, wipe the blood from your elbows and
knees and scramble the loose gully around right.

FA Henry Barber and Dave Cilley 4/77

Yvonne   I   5.9   110'   (E)   †

This route lies in a prominent corner system right of the smooth main wall.
Though it lacks the exposure typical of the other routes here, each of its
three short pitches has a distinct character, and the route is, understandably,
quite popular.

pitch 1 Climb the wide crack past the loose chockstone to the ledge.
5.6 40'

pitch 2 The obvious bottomless handcrack in the corner ends at another good ledge. 5.8 35'

pitch 3 The finish moves in the corner above constitute the crux.

Variation 5.10 The short crack right of the regular start can link to the route above.

FA Rob Wood, Dave Thomas, and Bob Rice 4/68
FFA Grant Calder and Todd Eastman 6/76

The following routes are on a separate buttress of rock right of and behind the main cliff.

Stone Face   I   5.9+   100'   (E)

This is the right edge when viewed from Upper Washbowl area. Climb edge to the top.

FA Patrick Purcell 4/89

Running on Empty   I   5.7+   100'   (D)

Around to the right, not visible from the road, is a narrow face, just right of the previous route.

FA Patrick Purcell and Mary Purcell 4/89

ROARING BROOK FALLS

This is by no means a complete rock-climbing center, but it has at least one pitch of good slab climbing. Left of the falls itself is a white, smooth face of about 100' of 5.2, making a fine place to learn some of the basics on a top rope (there is no protection). Climbers have on numerous occasions completed the climb to the top of the falls (and more than one hiker has died here), but the rock above is broken and dirty. Parking for the trail to Roaring Brook Falls and on to Giant Mountain is at the base of the hill on the north end of the pass. The waterfall is seen easily from Route 73.

PEREGRINE PILLAR

Between the Hurricane Mountain hiking trail and Hurricane Crag on Route 9N is a well-hidden wealth of rock, so low and close to the road that it is easily overlooked when driving by. The dominant feature of these cliff bands is Peregrine Pillar, a pyramid-shaped cone standing at least 150' high. This is visible from the road if one stops and takes the time to look. Left of this are steep, red bands of hard-looking rock. The climbing described below is located on the Peregrine Pillar feature, so named for the nearby nest.

Park along the road near telephone pole # 121. About 10 minutes of hiking brings one to the base of the rock. Begin by locating the toe, or lowest point of the cliff, just left of the bottom of the main buttress.

Gale Force   I   5.9+   110'   (s)

50' left of the toe of the cliff is a disconnected fingercrack that diagonals right through a roof and left-facing corner, then straight up. Two trees, a cedar and a spruce, stand on a ledge about 15' up just right of the start. There is some loose rock, but otherwise, it's an excellent route.

FA Tom DuBois 9/1/91

Storm Warning   I   5.8+   150'   (E)

This direct climb follows a series of cracks up a prominent chimney system, past several large trees, to the top of the cliff. The route describes only one of several options for ascending this obvious line of weakness.

pitch 1 Start 20' left of the toe at a wet, broken, triangular alcove with a short, overhanging fingercrack out its top. Out alcove and left to vegetated stance. Climb ramp right and ledge left to belay tree. 50'

pitch 2 Back right onto the ledge and up short crack to easier rock. Rejoin the chimney, past some roofs to a cramped belay at a tree. 60'

pitch 3 Continue in chimney line past very loose block. (This block must go before the route can be recommended.) 40'

FA Tom DuBois and Steve Adler 8/18/90

A Felony in Georgia   I   5.8   (E)

Just right of the toe is an obvious, decomposing wide crack line that looks like the prominent route on the cliff. The route hasn't topped out, and some of the rock is loose.

pitch 1 Up offwidth to a ledge, then fingercrack to bad rock. Rap from tree on right or escape to Sea Gull Ledge.

FA Don Mellor and Patrick Purcell 4/2/86

For the following routes, use Sea Gull Ledge as a reference. This sloping, forested ledge is about halfway up on the right side of the pillar. DuBois and Adler found the remnants of a falcon snack here while helping with a peregrine research project, thus the name.

Sea Gull   I   5.2   50'   (E)

The broken gully leading to the lower corner of *Sea Gull* is mostly 4th class. Start 15' right of twin offwidths.

FA Tom DuBois, Steve Adler, Clint and Beth Telford

Ornithologists from Hell   I   5.8   150'   (E)

pitch 1 *Sea Gull* to ledge. 5.2 50'

pitch 2 At the back of Sea Gull Ledge is a major left-facing corner. Start here for the blocky crack, up through roofs and left to finish.

FA Tom DuBois, Steve Adler 7/28/90

Weird Science   I   5.7   150'   (E)

pitch 1 *Sea Gull* to ledge. 5.2 50'

pitch 2 Up to small tree, then into main corner. This pitch is a good one. Note falcon aerie 20' right toward the top of the pitch.

FA Tom DuBois, Steve Adler, Clint and Beth Telford 7/22/90

Deep Cleanser   I   5.5   40'   (E)

About 35' right up and around the broken right edge of the cliff is a series of cracks and blocks at a small maple.

FA Tom and Ellen DuBois

Talons of Power   I   5.11   120'   (S)

About 40' right of the previous route is an unmistakable line: A thin crack that diagonals slightly right. This is a prize and a test piece.

pitch 1 Climb the 40' fingercrack in black rock to the forested ledge on the left. 5.10

pitch 2 Follow the thin line up right on very steep rock, passing horizontal and vertical cracks.

FA Eric Wahl and Ann Eastman

Nameless Corner   I   5.6   60'   (s)

Up and right of the obvious crack of the previous route is this dirty corner. Up this and exit right to woods.

FA Tom DuBois and Steve Adler 8/90

Fledgling   I   5.7   35'   (E)

40' right of *Nameless Corner* is a rounded arete with a crack line on a distinct minor buttress. There are some loose blocks.

FA Tom DuBois 6/91

HURRICANE CRAG

On the north side of Route 9N between Keene and Elizabethtown is a high cliff known as Hurricane Crag (formerly Pitchoff 9N), which looks down over the road from its position on Spruce Hill. The climbing here is generally quite good; moderate routes abound and potential exists for more. Climbs on the central and right-hand portions of the crag pass through some loose, easy rock at the top, but this does little to detract from the overall quality of the experience. Once on top, climbers find an unusual bald summit with lone pines separated by smooth expanses of clean rock, more fitting the Sierras than the Adirondacks, usually topped by tight spruce and balsam.

Approach is fairly direct: Allow about 20 minutes through steep open woods from the road. There is a slight path that begins a bit east of the face (this may be marked), but if this path is lost, the approach is still fairly straightforward. Descent isn't so easy. The best descent is probably the rappel line marked in the photo. Be careful in the upper scramble down to the tree ledges.

The key to route-finding is the obvious right-facing dihedral that dominates the lower left end of the cliff. This is the start of *PSOC* and *Forever*

Wild. Quadrophenia climbs the two right-facing roofs in the high center of the face. Toward the right end of the cliff is a deep chimney; this is the *Old Route*. The routes are described left to right.

Handle with Care   II   5.8   250'

Begin left of the huge corner *(PSOC)* mentioned above.

pitch 1 Climb cracks and grooves on the outside of the buttress to its top.

pitch 2 From the left end of this ledge, climb up and right onto the face to a right-leading foot-traverse. Follow flakes up and head right to a steep crack. Climb the crack to a ledge leading left. Climb the face at a break in the wall, then step right to a flake belay ledge.

pitch 3 Easier ground leads to the summit.

FA Al Long and Al Rubin approx. 1975

Forever Wild   I   5.10   100'   (E)

pitch 1 On the left wall of the main corner is a prominent hand- and fingercrack. Scramble to its base and finish at the forested ledge.

FA Don Mellor, Mark Meschinelli, and Bill Simes 1987

PSOC   I   5.   250'   (E)

This begins at the base of the huge right-facing corner, climbing first to its right, before joining it and heading left over nondescript rock and ledges. The first pitch is worthwhile, and the entire route can be used as a rappel descent.

pitch 1 Climb the small left-facing corner on the face to the right, joining the upper section of the main corner to the large forest at its top. The pitch may be split. 5.7 120'

pitch 2–3 Head left and up over broken rock, ledges, and trees.

FA Craig Patterson and Fred Cady 1966

Quadrophenia   II   5.7   350'   (s)   †

This is an outstanding climb; it rivals the Washbowl's *Hesitation* as a long, varied, sustained, and direct route up the center of one of our larger cliffs. It calls for crack, roof, and face technique, as well as some good loose-rock

HURRICANE CRAG

A. HANDLE WITH CARE 5.8	C. QUADROPHENIA 5.7	E. LOOK, ROLL, AND FIRE 5.9+
B. PSOC 5.7	D. XENOLITH 5.8	F. OLD ROUTE 5.4

judgment for a brief moment at the top. Begin near the center of the cliff about 40' right of the prominent *PSOC* corner.

pitch 1 Climb a vertical crack past a small tree, to a left-leaning ramp, exiting right at its top to a large open ledge. 5.7 75'

pitch 2 Above the small tree is a flaring groove. Face-climb with little protection to a crack, and belay at a ledge below the first big roof. (Watch huge loose block just left of belay.) 5.7 75'

pitch 3 Turn both roofs to the right and up to a belay ledge.

pitch 4 Head up and slightly left to join the *Old Route,* or face-climb up and right to a 10' crack, followed by face-/slab climbing to the top. 140'

FA Jim Cunningham and Bob Hey 3/27/84

Xenolith II 5.8 350' (s) †

This route parallels the previous climb. Begin up and left of a huge double-trunked oak, 20' right of *Quadrophenia.*

pitch 1 Climb a crack line up a shallow corner and thin crack to a crux finish onto the huge open ledge. 5.8

pitch 2 From ledge (just right of fallen pine tree) climb a left-facing corner, joining *Old Route* for a few feet in a depression, then breaking left up thin crack in a V groove. Up to a headwall, traversing left 7' to the prominent groove past cedars to a belay. 5.7

pitch 3 Finish at will.

FA Don Mellor, John Connell, and Jeff Erenstone 1992 (p.1)
FA Ed Palen and Bob Martin 10/93 (p.2)

Look, Roll, and Fire II 5.9+ 350' (D)

This route follows the general line of *Quadrophenia,* starting to its right, sharing its middle, and crossing left to find a harder line through the roofs at the cliff's center.

pitch 1 Down and 30' right of *Quadrophenia* is a left-facing chimney (not to be confused with the large, straight-in chimney of the *Old Route*). Climb flakes just to its left, continuing on the right side of an arete, and emerging left (no protection) onto the large open ledge. 5.8 100'

pitch 2 Same as *pitch 2 Quadrophenia.* Instead of belaying under the first roof, traverse up and left to a rock pedestal. The traverse is loose and awful.

pitch 3 Step left into the cedar groove and up to overhang with three diverging cracks. Climb out the overhang via the right crack (though an easier exit appears possible right), and run it out over loose rock to the top. 5.9+ 150'

Variation **Tommy** 5.8   Instead of climbing the face/flakes of pitch 1, it is possible to use the chimney to join the arete/corner above.

FA Jim Cunningham and Ken Reville 4/3/84

FA Jim Cunningham and Dave Flinn 4/84 (var.)

Hooligans   I   5.8+   120'   (s)

pitch 1 Begin on the outside corner just left of the smooth, high-angled face at the toe of the buttress right of *Look, Roll, and Fire*. Up past hidden pin, then tricky moves to left margin of wall. Follow a slanting crack up left past a bulge to finish the last few feet of the previous route. 5.8+

pitch 2 From the big ledge, layback easy crack to a small cedar and the black face above via an incipient crack to the tree ledge. 5.8+

pitch 3 and 4 Numerous variations link on to the top.

FA Bill Widrig, Jim Lawyer, and Tad Welch 5/91

Afraid of the Dark   5.8   70'   (E)   †

First locate the awesome chimney of the *Old Route*. Take the handcrack a few feet left of the chimney until it is possible to face-climb right to the giant chockstone. Large holds and stemming on the chimney's edge lead to a spacious belay.

FA Tad Welch (roped solo) 5/23/91

Old Route   II   5.4   350'   (s)

This historic route climbs the amazing deep chimney, emerging out left over steep, loose rock at the top.

pitch 1 Around the corner from the central routes is the chimney. Follow this to its top. 110'

pitch 2 Head into the trees to a dihedral; climb loose rock to a ramp and finally back left to a belay.

pitch 3 A depression of easy rock leads diagonally left across the face to a finish at the highest point of the crag. There are a few piton relics and much loose rock en route.

Variation   II   5.8   300'

pitch 1 Climb the chimney.

pitch 2 Continue straight up to a ledge with a tree. 60'

pitch 3 Follow the steep, thin crack to a ledge. Stay in the line while the crack disappears for about 25'. Regain the crack and finish on slabs.

FA George Austin and Fritz Wiessner
FA Al Long and Al Rubin 6/4/75 (var.)

Schizophrenia   I   5.9   95'

pitch 1 Just right of the chimney of the *Old Route* is a large pile of blocks. Turn the overhang/flake above on the left to a steep corner. Face climb past the overhang at its top.

FA Jim Cunningham, Bob Hey, and Dave Flinn 3/28/84

Spring Equinox   I   5.8

Right of *Schizophrenia* is a steep wall with cracks with an overhang at its base.

pitch 1 Climb easy rock right of the overhangs to a ledge or approach via the corner/crack (5.8) to its right.

pitch 2 On the right edge of the steep wall is a steep crack/flake. Climb this to its top. Rappel or link up with the *Old Route*.

FA Jim Cunningham and Bill Dodd 3/24/84

New Route   I   5.5

pitch 1 At the far right end of the cliff is yet another wide chimney. Climb the arete down and left of this for 20'. Face-climb the black streak to a large ledge.

pitch 2 Finish with the slab above.

FA Jim Cunningham and Bob Hey 3/26/84

Contact Buzz   I   5.7 or 5.8

pitch 1 Between the chimney and the *New Route* is a steep, short, broken wall with a crack. Follow this to the ledge above. Rappel or finish as desired.

FA Ken Reville and George Carrol 3/28/84

TYPHOON WALL

Climbers often stumble upon two smaller crags in the woods on their way in. The first is a 40' dirty wall, about 150 yards from the road, with short cracks on the left. They were once cleaned and climbed. The second cliff is actually a destination in itself. It is called the Typhoon Wall, and is located about 100 yards down and left of the main face. The first routes described are here, beginning with three good crack routes at the right end.

Small Craft Advisory   I   5.8   40'   (E)

pitch 1 Approach this climb from a ledge about 20' up. Climb the short crack to the obvious open book. Watch loose rock at the top.

FA Jim Cunningham and Bill Dodd

Wimp Crack   I   5.11   40'   (E)

pitch 1 An excellent thin crack route that saves the best for last. Start on the ledge up and right; climb the vertical crack between the more prominent cracks on either side.

FA Don Mellor and Bill Dodd 8/12/88

Force Nine   I   5.9   50'   (E)

pitch 1 This is the obvious hand-/fingercrack, the left-hand of the three crack routes.

FA Jim Cunningham and Bill Dodd

Sports Psychology   I   5.8   60'   (E)

pitch 1 About 40' left of the cracks is a tall block. Climb its left side to a stance. The right-facing thin flake above leads to a tree.

FA Don Mellor, Bill Dodd, and Alan Hobson 1985

No Name   I   5.3   60'   (E)

About 100' around and left of the first climbs is a loose scree slope. At its top is a chimney formed by a block. The chimney has a fingercrack that provides good protection.

FA Patrick Purcell 5/1/88

Ward Cleaver   I   5.11+   60'

Left of the chimney is an incredible blade/arete of rock.

FA Patrick Purcell (top-rope) 5/1/88

Sweat Man   I   5.10+   60'   (E)

pitch 1 Around left of the blade is a handcrack on an overhanging, orange wall.

FA Patrick Purcell 5/15/88

CASCADE LAKES

With its proximity to Lake Placid and Keene Valley, this area sees a lot of climbers. The rock is good and varied, with the popular roadside Pitchoff Chimney Cliff and the scenic Barkeater Cliff being the most interesting of the lot. All tourist-town amenities are available in Lake Placid. Climb-ing gear can be found at Eastern Mountain Sports (518-523-2505) and High Peaks Cyclery (518-523-3764) in Lake Placid, and at the Mountaineer (518-576-2281) in Keene Valley.

BARK EATER CLIFFS

Legend has it that the Iroquois Indians referred to the Algonquins as "adirondacks" or "barkeaters" because they were forced to live off bark and buds to survive the harsh winters. The name was an insult to the allegedly inferior hunting abilities of the Algonquins, but Adirondack climbers will find the appellation quite fitting as they thrash their way around the base of some of the region's less-traveled cliffs. The legend may well be a simplistic or inaccurate account of the origin of the name Adirondack, but it holds on because it still colorfully depicts the wilds of the place. These cliffs, formerly called Pitchoff Northeast Cliffs, gradually took on the name Bark Eater Cliffs (after the Bark Eater Inn at the foot of the road) to avoid confusion with the Pitchoff Chimney Cliff on the other side of the mountain.

This is perhaps the quintessential Adirondack crag: From its heights on the northeast shoulder of Pitchoff Mountain, one looks out over a wilderness that embodies all that is special to the region. Below the vast trailless Sentinal Range is a broad hardwood valley interrupted only by a beaver pond. No hint of man's intrusion is visible.

For climbers, this place has been a real sleeper. Only recently have folks begun to realize the potential for one- and two-pitch routes offered by this crag. The rock is sound and relatively clean, the cracks are deep and varied, and the collection of giant boulders at the cliff's base tempts one not only to find routes on these rocks themselves, but to bring along a sleeping bag on the next trip to bivouac in any one of the countless boulder caves surrounding the cliff. But with all the good climbing to be found here, it is still probably the views and the serenity of the wilderness all around that make the place so special.

The approach takes about 20 minutes and begins off Route 73 just uphill from the town of Keene. Drive past the Bark Eater Inn and Cross-Country Ski Center to the end of Alstead Hill Road about 2.5 miles beyond. Park at Adirondack Rock and River Guide Service (lodging available). Hike the Jackrabbit Ski Trail for less than a mile to a cairn on the left, just past a wide wooden bridge. If you go too far, you'll find yourself at a beaver pond and the only good view of the rock. From the cairn, the path crosses the brook and heads uphill to the boulder field. There are several options for passage here; the most obvious brings one to the base of *Mr. Clean,* a striking handcrack in a right-facing corner. To the left is the Dog House.

The key to finding the climbs is the Dog House, the towering boulder that leans against the center of the cliff, forming a high-ceiling cave. The first routes are described right to left from this feature.

Canoes for Feet   I   5.9   50'   (top-rope)

This is the edge just left of the Dog House. A top rope is easily dropped from *Overdog*, pitch 1, atop the boulder.

FA Patrick Purcell and Mark Abbott 7/88

Pump it Up   I   5.8   90'   (E)

pitch 1 Climb the huge inside corner left of the Dog House.

FA Tad Welch 9/6/86

Lick it Up   I   5.10   50'   (E)

On the shorter wall 75' left of and facing the Dog House are attractive fingercracks.

pitch 1 Climb the right-hand thin crack to a crux exit.

FA Adam Clayman and Jeff Edwards 7/24/85

Wipe it Off   I   5.10+   60'   (D)

The wall just left of *Lick It Up* is a top-roped face climb, passing an unstable flake one-third of the way up.

FA Ken Nichols 1992

Finger it Out   I   5.10   60'   (E)   †

pitch 1 This is the obvious left-hand fingercrack. The start is the crux.

FA Chuck Turner and Bill Simes 5/82

Way Hairball   I   5.9   60'   (E)

pitch 1 From a chimney formed by a right-facing block/flake, climb out the offwidth to the right.

FA Tim Beaman, Herb George, and Sylvia Lazarnick early 80s

In the Chimney   I   5.5   60'   (E)

pitch 1 It's hard to get off the ground, but once in the chimney, interesting tunneling leads to daylight above.

Way in the Chimney   I   5.5   40'   (S)

pitch 1 Deep in the chimney is a shorter, purer chimney exercise that leads to nowhere. Once your eyes adjust to the darkness, you'll spy the single bolt anchor at the top.

FA Patrick Purcell 6/88

Joshua Climb   I   5.5   60'   (E)

pitch 1 This is the logical handcrack finish just left of the chimney. Approach via a short traverse.

FA Tad Welch and Mike Cross 9/6/86

Traverse City   I   5.11   60'   (S)

pitch 1 This starts with the same entry move into the chimney as for the previous climbs and traverses a horizontal fingercrack left across the wall.

pitch 2 From the ledge at the end of the traverse, climb face above. 5.7 30'

FA Patrick Purcell and Jeff Edwards 5/8/88

Wronged Again   I   5.9   50'   (S)

Down around left of the *Finger It Out* wall is a pair of cracks, the left of which has a jammed block.

pitch 1 Climb the right-facing flakes/crack on the right to slab (crux) and low-angled crack topout.

FA Patrick Purcell and Tom Dodd 5/88

Pronged Again   I   5.4   70'   (E)

This is the crack with the jammed block 5' off the ground.

FA Tom Dodd and Patrick Purcell 5/88

Friends in Business   I   5.8   50'   (E)

Left of these routes is a wall split by two cracks.

pitch 1 This is the left-hand crack. The frustrating start may become easier with more traffic.

FA Patrick Purcell and Ed Palen 5/88

The next climbs are described from the Dog House, left to right, on the larger right and central sections of the cliff.

Hair of the Dog   I   5.10   100'   (E)   †

Begin in the Dog House.

pitch 1 Climb the chimney (left of *Overdog*) to the chockstone. Then step onto main cliff (loose 5.6) to a ledge at equal level to top of Dog House (possible belay). Climb through roof at weakness (5.10), then up 20' crack to comfortable belay ledge under and left of larger roof. 90'

pitch 2 The big roof is climbed via a rightward undercling to a block and long reach over lip. 5.10 (This can be avoided by 5.6 climbing straight up.)

FA Ed Palen, Ann Palen, Patrick Purcell 1990

Beam Me to Leoni's   I   5.10   150'

This route takes the obvious cracks above the Dog House boulder.

pitch 1 Begin this route as for *Overdog*.

pitch 2 From the ledge on top of the Dog House, climb up the corner to the left and through the offwidth crack. Then walk right and climb the crack in the face to the top.

FA Greg Koop and Hugh Rose 1985

Overdog   I   5.9   150'   (s)   †

This unusual route climbs up behind the left side of the Dog House, crosses over it, and finishes out the square roof to the right.

pitch 1 Climb the triple cracks on the back wall and emerge back into the sunlight on top of the boulder. 5.5 60'

pitch 2 From the birch above, traverse out right and up past a bolt to a belay on the large, sloping shelf below the roof. 5.7 50'

pitch 3 The square roof above has two exits. The standard route begins in the left crack, and finishes roof via the right crack. 5.9 40'

Variation The left-hand roof exit is 5.10.

Variation ***Air Line*** 5.11 50' (s) From the right end of the large sloping belay ledge, climb an exposed wall via a thin seam.

FA Don Mellor, Chuck Turner, and Bill Simes 5/82

FA Don Mellor 7/10/88 (var. 1)

FA Don Mellor 7/10/88 (var. 2)

ASPCA I 5.7+ 100' (s) †

On the Dog House boulder itself is an amazing route.

pitch 1 From boulders at the right side of the cave, traverse left on "Gunks" holds to a roof. Turn this and belay at the lip. 5.7+ 40'

pitch 2 Climb the unprotected face to the top. 5.7 40'

FA Patrick Purcell, Tom Dodd, and Jeff Edwards 5/88

On the Leash I 5.7 35' (E)

pitch 1 Just right of the Dog House is a short, right-facing ramp/corner.

FA Patrick Purcell 5/88

Eat Yourself a Pie I 5.8+ 125' (E) †

This outstanding pitch climbs a narrow path up a prominent rib about 40' right of the Dog House.

pitch 1 Climb onto the arete from the right, sneaking right under the roof, and emerging onto the edge. Two bolts protect the upper section.

pitch 2 From the sloping belay, finish via *Overdog* or its variations.

FA Patrick Purcell and Tom Dodd 4/88

Big Bertha I 5.6 60' (E) †

pitch 1 Just left of the very obvious *Mr. Clean* corner is a left-facing crack and corner that leads to a fixed anchor.

Mr. Clean I 5.8 60' (E) †

About 50' right of the Dog House is a striking right-facing dihedral. A second pitch climbs the offwidth (5.9) above to a fixed tube chock, but most parties rappel from the top of the corner.

pitch 1 The 5.8 handcrack in the corner ends at a small tree and a bolt anchor.

FA Chuck Turner and Bill Simes 5/82 (p.1)

FA Patrick Purcell and Jeff Edwards 5/8/88 (p.2)

Radio-Flyer 5.11

Top rope the face just left of *Flexi-Flyer* via a short finger slot.

Flexi-Flyer I 5.9 70' (s)

pitch 1 About 15' right of *Mr.Clean* is a superb face climb. Start in a short, sharp-edged left-facing corner; head left to a pocket (bolt) and straight to the top. The direct start crack to the left is harder. Rappel.

FA Patrick Purcell and Bill Dodd 8/88

Mr. Dirty I 5.6 70' (x)

pitch 1 Begin 35' right of *Mr. Clean* and climb a face and thin crack to the two-bolt belay of *Flexi-Flyer*. The route closely parallels the huge offwidth to the right.

FA Bill Dodd and Patrick Purcell 8/88

Because Dogs Can I 5.8 45' (E)

pitch 1 50' right of the dirty, left-facing offwidth is a good fingercrack in a left-facing corner that ends at a fixed wired nut at the base of the overhanging headwall.

FA Patrick Purcell and Bill Dodd 8/88

A 2 Brute? A2

Above and left the previous route is an exposed and overhanging thin line with pitons to fixed belay.

FA Ed Palen

Doc Theo 5.11+

Just left of the upper aid section is a thin crack, invisible from below, that is reached via rappel.

FA Patrick Purcell

200' feet right of the Dog House is a huge broken gully with a "gunsight" spire.

What about Bob? I 5.11 130' (s) †

pitch 1 Start on the left side of the Gunsight Notch, climbing a series of cracks followed by a crux face with some bolts. Follow fingercrack to slab above.

FA Patrick Purcell and Bob Martin 10/26/93

Coy Dog I 5.9 90' (E)

This short but unrelenting crack can be seen only after walking left from the base of *Fun City.*

pitch 1 Traverse left into the crack/corner and follow the crack to the top. A belay midway will reduce rope drag.

FA Tim Beaman and Patrick Purcell 5/27/88

Fun City I 5.7 100' (E) †

About 100' right of "the gunsight" is a wall split by twin cracks in a slight depression.

pitch 1 Climb the crack in the right-facing corner.

Variation **Fun Country** 5.9+ (E) This climb takes the right-hand crack.

FA Rich Leswing and Pete Benson 5/82
FA Jeff Edwards and Adam Clayman 7/24/85 (var.)

Takes All Kinds I 5.10 80' (E)

This route has a little bit of everything. Begin at the left end of the prominent, low roof band.

pitch 1 Follow a fingercrack (crux), then left to corner and belay at base of the roof.

pitch 2 Traverse right 15' to a crack that leads to the summit slabs. 5.8

FA Tim Beaman and Patrick Purcell 5/27/88

The following routes are located on Celibacy Wall. (Edwards was awaiting his August marriage as any decent fellow should.) This lower-angled section is at the extreme right end of the cliff, past a long, low roof. Tunnel under a boulder and out into the open area below the climbs. From the top of these climbs, there is a good descent trail around to the southwest.

Skillyabuda   I   5.7   120   (D)

Left of *Yakapodu* is a bulging face. Up crux face, and right to vertical crack finish.

FA Jeff Edwards and Ryan Van Loon 7/26/90

Yakapodu   I   5.6+   90'   (E)   †

This is the obvious left-hand route.

pitch 1 Start at a crack in a slab, avoiding the bush-filled crack if possible. Continue in a right-facing corner and headwall above.

FA Adam Clayman, Jeff Edwards, and Todd McDougall 6/17/85

Barking up the Wrong Climb   I   5.8   90'   (D)

Between the two more obvious routes in the middle of the biggest part of the face is a popular top-rope problem.

pitch 1 Face-climb in from the right to a left-facing corner move (or roof to its right). Unprotected slab climbing leads to the easier headwall finish.

FA Don Mellor, Brian Ballantine, and Ed Ballantine 1993

Bachelors and Bowery Bums   I   5.7   90'   (S)

pitch 2 Begin 20' right of *Yakapodu* at a crack and tiny crescent flake. Wander to a large right-facing corner, eventually stepping left out onto the face. Finish in the crack above.

FA Jeff Edwards and Adam Clayman 7/24/85

Good Dough   I   5.5   80'   (E)

Up around the corner to the right is the last route on the face.

pitch 1 Start in a large right-facing corner at a tree. Climb a series of cracks to the top.

FA Jeff Edwards and Ryan Van Loon 7/26/90

PITCHOFF RIDGE TRAIL DOMES

This is certainly no area for the hard man or woman; instead it is a loosely connected collection of slabs on the northeast end of Pitchoff Mountain that might appeal to an explorer. Rising above the trailhead of the Pitchoff Ridge Trail are three vague domes of open rock, one on top of the other, the highest of which is the northeast end of the Ridge Trail. The rock can be seen from Route 73 south of Cascade Lakes.

Scope out the rock before heading up because there is really no way to see the rock once on the trail.

Dome One: Sunshine Slab   I   5.3   300'   (D)

This lowest outcrop can be seen on the flanks of Pitchoff as one drives south through Cascade Pass. It is a long, easy green slab with generally clean rock and no protection whatsoever.

FA Alan Hobson, Don Mellor, Rusty Geh and Kevin Kearns 5/7/84

Dome Two: N.O.C. Route   II   5.5   300'   (E)

From the top of Dome One, one spies the most obvious and attractive line here. The Northwood Outing Club route takes this prominent crack line for two pitches up the largest section of rock visible from the road.

pitch 1 Climb the obvious crack for 140' to a ledge. 5.5
pitch 2 The 3' crack above leads to a headwall and a slab finish. 5.5 140'

FA Don Mellor, Rusty Geh, Kevin Kearns, Sabine Weber,
Jim Williams, and Ian Osteyee 5/17/84

Dome Three

Although no roped routes have been recorded here yet, there is plenty of good bouldering on this final summit to the Ridge Trail.

OWLS HEAD

This little summit pokes its pointed head above the landscape about a mile below the Cascade Lakes on Route 73. Over the years it has become the most heavily used top-roping area upstate. And for good reason. Its cliff stands right on the summit itself, and the 30'–50' crack climbs are clean

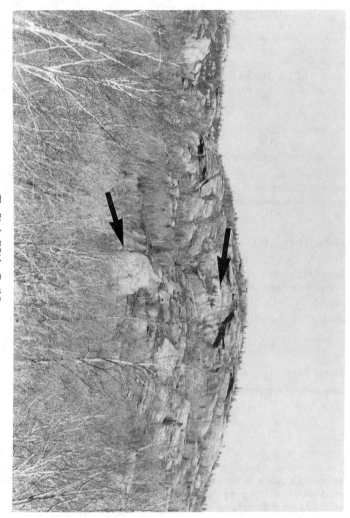

The Pitchoff Ridge Trail Domes

and moderate. It seems to be the perfect setting for instruction, and numerous church and school groups, as well as guide services, have made it their home away from home.

Given its popularity, climbers should be reminded of their responsibility to each other and the place itself. This responsibility can be practiced in many ways:

1. Limit the number of climbers in your group.
2. Avoid trampling the already receding summit vegetation by restricting traffic around anchor trees.
3. Clean up your route when it's not in use if there are others waiting to climb. Share the climbs.
4. Finally, if you plan to bring groups out for instruction regularly, why not consider another, more obscure cliff? Many guides have done this already, and though they can't find another Owls Head, they do find places they can almost call their own.

Owls Head is reached via a trail that leaves Route 73 at Owls Head Acres development. Most of the approach trail is a courtesy given by the private owners here. Please respect their wishes and park at the first lot right off Route 73. The uphill hike takes about 20 minutes.

PITCHOFF CHIMNEY CLIFF

This roadside crag, with its easy access from Route 73, its high visibility to travelers passing through the region, and its proliferation of moderate-to-difficult routes, has seen considerable and continual development. The multiple crack and face lines that stand out as lichen-free stripes on the rock give testament to the incredible potential such a small cliff can offer.

The cliff holds routes of all difficulties, and the climbs are generally well protected. The typical feature is the horizontal crack that closes at the lip and takes the kind of nut placement that puts even the most timid leader at ease. The rock, a syenite gneiss, has a character unlike that of any other in this guide, and once one becomes acquainted with the techniques required, each route seems a bit like the last, and each is typically Pitchoff.

The unique feature of the cliff is that it is really a slab of rock, some fifteen to 15'– 20' thick, that stands detached from the mountainside by a chimney. Frost action, the mechanism by which water, expanding as it freezes, slowly forces the cracks apart, will eventually push this wall into

169

the lake, but as it does, one hopes that some equally fine lines will be discovered underneath!

This chimney was the line of the cliff's first ascent and still offers fantastic opportunities to explore. The cave below, accessible by way of a tight squeeze at the back of the chimney (20' straight below the final belay of *Pete's Farewell*), extends for over 100', giving one of the only true spelunking adventures in the High Peaks region. Added to it all is a fine, easy slab below (5.1–5.4) that has evidently dropped from the cliff and now provides good top-roping potential for learning the sport.

Landmarks that will serve as guides to the starts of routes are the Great Chimney, which is best viewed from the south, and the waterfall at the extreme left end of the cliff. The best approach follows a trail from the southernmost of two parking areas on Lower Cascade Lake. Descend via a path around the north end or through the chimney with a short rappel at its base.

The routes are described left to right, beginning on the terrace just right of the waterfall and under the prominent roof high above.

Vermontville Redneck   I   5.10   (top-rope)

pitch 1 At the extreme left end of the terrace, behind some trees, is a cleaned, smooth wall.

FA Patrick Purcell 1986

Anniversary Waltz   I   5.10+   75'   (s)

At the left end of the terrace is a wet, mossy seep just left of the obvious fingercrack of *Rock and Roll Star.* Begin left of this at a vague, short, right-facing corner.

pitch 1 Climb the short corner to a horizontal crack and up to a bolt. Climb up and left to the right-facing flake finish.

FA Patrick Purcell and Steven Bailey 6/22/86

Uncontrollable Desires   I   5.8   100'   (s)

This route fittingly begins at the wet spot.

pitch 1 Climb up to a horizontal crack at 15' (angle piton, 1981). A run-out on steep holds leads up and right, keeping right of the dirty slot, to the triple-crack finish (5.7) common to the next few routes.

FA Bob Bushart and Bill Simes 5/81

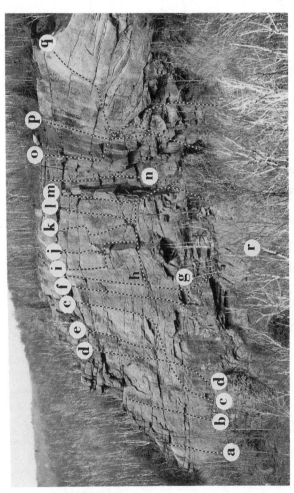

PHOTO BY MARK MESCHINELLI

PITCHOFF CHIMNEY CLIFF

A. ANNIVERSARY WALTZ 5.10+
B. ROACHES ON THE WALL 5.10
C. WALD CALDER 5.9
D. RUNNING OF THE BULLS 5.11
E. RAINY NIGHT ROAD TOADS 5.8

F. DYNAMO HUM 5.9
G. RUN HIGHER, JUMP FASTER 5.11
H. THE EL 5.8
I. PETE'S FAREWELL 5.7
J. P.F. FLYERS 5.10
K. HIDDEN CONSTELLATION 5.11+

L. STAR SAILOR 5.10+
M. THE DISPUTED 5.8
N. CRACK MECHANIC 5.11+
O. BRRRIGHT STAR 5.9+
P. SPACE RACE 5.11
Q. RUGOSITY 5.8
R. PRACTICE SLAB

Rock and Roll Star   I   5.10+   100'   (E)

pitch 1 The most obvious route on the left end of the cliff climbs the obvious, awkward fingercrack just right of the wet spot.

FA Eric Rhicard, Morris Hershoff, and John Deladucca 1977

Flying Squirrels   I   5.11   100'   (S)   †

Just right of the fingercrack of *Rock Star* is a face climb marked by a bolt about 10' up.

pitch 1 Start right of the bolt and follow a thin crack line to a bulge finish, about 6' right of *Rock Star.* Join the triple cracks on the final headwall.

FA Patrick Purcell and Jeff Edwards 6/7/86

Roaches on the Wall   I   5.10   100'   (E)   †

This is the most popular 5.10 on the cliff; it provides a safe and easy siege for those aspiring to the grade. Begin 30' right of the *Rock Star* fingercrack.

pitch 1 Begin at a low roof and traverse left to face moves past a bolt. The deceptively easy roof leads to the crux fingercrack.

Variation The direct start is 5.11.

FA Jerry Hoover and Bob Bushart 9/79
FFA Rick Fleming 5/80

Waiting for the Son   I   5.11   140'   (D)

Nicholas Edwards 7 lbs., 7 oz.

About 40' right of *Rock Star* is a low bolt. After a difficult face-climbing crux, move left to a roof just right of *Roaches.*

FA Jeff Edwards and Don Mellor 7/93

Roof   I   5.9   40'   (E)

pitch 1 This is a very obvious feature high above the previous routes. The fistcrack out the right side is slightly easier if one cheats a bit to the right.

Several of the following routes gain access to the central portion of the cliff by using the same start: The low alcove that is climbed via its left side out a roof about 8' off the ground. Too Early Spring *heads left and up, while most other routes traverse right to a ledge system. The start and the traverse are 5.8.*

Too Early Spring I 5.9+ 140' (s)

This route was discovered and top-roped in February, thus the name.

pitch 1 At the right end of the terrace is a small alcove. Climb the roof to a stance (5.8). An insecure traverse left leads to the thin crack that breaches the bulge (crux) above. Continue in small right-facing corners just right of the triple cracks to a belay under the huge roof.

pitch 2 Though it's practical to rappel, a dirty second pitch is possible: traverse right onto a hanging block and up crack above. 5.7

FA Don Mellor, Bob Bushart, and Bill Simes 5/81
FA Don Mellor and Mark Ippolito 7/83 (p.2)

Pine Cone Eaters I 5.10 100' (D)

This route continues up the initial crack of *Too Early Spring* and up flaky rock to the top. Not recommended.

FA Jeff Edwards and Adam Clayman 8/31/87

Too Burly Bulls I 5.9+ 140' (s)

Bushart and Simes, having come out of retirement to eke out another route in the vicinity of *Too Early Spring* and *Running of the Bulls,* found a really good climb and an apt route name.

pitch 1 Just right of *Too Early Spring* is a thin fracture. Climb this, past the large flake common to the other routes, and out a Gunks roof (5.8) to a good belay ledge.

pitch 2 The FA went straight up loose rock (5.10?). Subsequently, climbers have finished via the handcrack of *Easy Off* (5.5), or traversed farther right to finish with *Running of the Bulls* (5.8).

FA Bob Bushart and Bill Simes

Easy Off I 5.8 160' (s)

This and several of the following routes begin with the roof moves of *Too Early Spring* and diverge at various points along the rightward traverse line. This seldom-climbed route is 5.5 after the crux ground moves.

pitch 1 From the right end of the terrace, climb the roof (5.8) to a short traverse right and belay.

pitch 2 Head around up and left to meet a left-facing corner and handcrack.

FA Bob Bushart and Bill Simes 6/81

Running of the Bulls   I   5.11   140'   (s)   †

An excellent route that combines a strenuous and technical crux with a very exciting face pitch above.

pitch 1 Begin at the far right end of the terrace common to the previous routes. Follow two bolts and a pin (5.11) out right to a semihanging belay at a horizontal crack.

pitch 2 Face-climb straight above, heading left at the bulge, using a fragile flake. 5.9 Rappel from birch.

FA Patrick Purcell and Don Mellor 7/13/89

Rainy Night Road Toads   I   5.8   140'   (s)

The first pitch is common to other routes; the upper pitch is distinct.

pitch 1 Begin as for *Too Early Spring,* climbing out the alcove roof and traversing right about 35' to a semihanging belay from the horizontal crack. 5.8

pitch 2 Climb a thin, vertical wire crack. Face-climb to a bulging exit.

FA Don Mellor and Patrick Purcell 7/27/89

Drawing Mustaches on Dangerous Dogs   I   5.9   175'   (s)

It might just be safer to chase canines around with a marking pen than to take on this good route without being ready for some commitment. Though cleaned before the first ascent, the route has gotten quite dirty since.

pitch 1 Start as for *Too Early Spring;* traverse right (5.7) to a good belay ledge. 100'

pitch 2 Head back left a few feet and turn a roof at a right-facing corner. Continue up the crack line to two distinct finishes: hand-traverse left to a hard exit, or follow the cracks right and up for a slightly longer pitch.

FA Bill Dodd and Patrick Purcell 7/1/85

Wald/Calder Route   I   5.9   175'   (s)

This was the first route on this left central face.

pitch 1 Start as for *Too Early Spring* and follow a finger traverse right for 50' to a superb belay ledge/seat. 5.8 100'

pitch 2 Take the thin crack above to a flaring finger section and a loose flake move; finish with the hand-/fingercrack out the short overhanging headwall.

FA Grant Calder and John Wald 1976
FFA John Wald 6/79

Raging Raven   I   5.11   70'   (E)   †

Down and right of the Roaches Terrace, just about in the center of the cliff, is a line of bolts up a steep wall. It passes about 30' left of the ravens' nest ledge.

pitch 1 A hard start leads to long reaches on big holds and a fixed anchor.

FA Patrick Purcell 1993

Widow Maker   I   5.12   70'   (D)

In the lowest center of the cliff is a right-facing corner that leaves a dirt-covered ledge. Berzins described the rock as dubious and despicable, especially after having fallen from the roof to the ledge when gear pulled out of the corner. The original aid route left the belay and nailed right to what would become *Run Higher, Jump Faster.*

pitch 1 Up the corner and left out the roof on loose rock past tatty rurp slings. Up to a bad bolt belay next to the ravens' nest.

FA Alan Jolley and Bill Diemand 2/81
FFA Martin Berzins 1992

The next routes begin on the tree-covered ledge above the Practice Slab under the central section of the cliff. It is also common to approach most of these upper pitches via the Wald-Calder *start.*

Dynamo Hum   I   5.9   200'   (D)   †

At the left end of the tree-covered ledge above the Practice Slab is a right-facing, bottomless corner.

pitch 1 Up the corner (as for *Run Higher*) to a ledge under a roof. Traverse left across loose rock, around a corner and up to a two-bolt hanging belay. 5.9

pitch 2 Climb out right and up unprotected rock to a ledge (possible belay). The final pitch parallels *The El,* some 15' to its left. 5.9

FA Don Mellor, Jeff Edwards, Joe Quackenbush 7/92 (p.1)

FA Don Mellor and Bob Bushart 6/81 (p.2)

Run Higher, Jump Faster   I   5.11   100'   (s)   †

The 1950s commercial for P.F. Flyers sneakers promised that you'd be able to "run faster and jump higher." Early attempts on this route proved that EB's could offer the converse prospect. The main section of the route follows an earlier aid climb called *Widow Maker.*

pitch 1 From the left end of the large ledge above the Practice Slab, climb the right-facing corner to a ledge under a roof. Climb straight up past two bolts to the ledge belay common to other routes.

pitch 2 Finish as desired.

FA The route was first envisioned and bolted by Alan Jolley.

Chuck Turner was the first to succeed 8/82

P.F. Flyers' Flying Circus   I   5.7   A2   150'   (D)

After an artificial start, this route ascends the outside corner/arete left of *Pete's Farewell.*

pitch 1 From the tree-covered ledge above the Practice Slab, aid the left-hand thin crack to the face 20' above. Free climb the face up right of the large overhang before striking out left onto the edge.

pitch 2 Finish *P.F. Flyers,* etc.

fa Jim Cunningham and Mark Saulsgiver 5/84

(The aid start had been climbed earlier by Alan Jolley.)

Chuting Star   I   40'   A2

This is the right-hand thin crack under *Pete's* traverse. It is the parallel crack right of the previous route above the tree-covered ledge.

FA Mark Saulsgiver and Jim Cunningham

The Lonely   5.5   I   5.6   60'   (s)

This is a seldom-climbed start to routes at the right end of the cliff.

pitch 1 From the right end of the tree-covered ledge, climb up 8' (as for *Pete's* or the *Chimney*) and head out left past some loose rock to pick up a crack leading to the traverse line. It is the natural start to *Hidden Constellation*.

FA Bob Bushart and Bill Diemand 9/80

The El   I   5.8   175'   (E)   †

Perhaps *the Pitchoff* classic, *The El* combines two excellent but distinct pitches to create one of the best lines in the Adirondacks. Begin below the Great Chimney.

pitch 1 A short pitch is necessary here: climb up and out left to the ledge on the outside corner. 5.2 30'

pitch 2 Traverse left into the large right-facing corner *(Pete's Farewell)*. Continue left around the dihedral and out of sight (5.7). Stay in this line for about 40' more and move up 10' to a small stance.

pitch 2 The corner above combines good protection with several varied challenges. 5.8

Variations There are three separate pitches that link the traverse of *The El* to the final *Pete's Farewell* belay. They are especially useful for the *Run Higher* teams who desire a harder finish like *Eurotech* or *P.F. Flyers*.

> **Linkup** 5.8   Climb diagonally up from the belay of *The El* towards the handcrack of *Pete's*.
> **Beam Us Up, Scotty** 5.8   This is the left-facing flake mid-traverse.
> **Pointless And Hard** 5.9   There is a fingercrack left of the edge and right of the *Beam Us Up, Scotty* flake.

FA Grant Calder and John Wald 7/76

FA Steve Larson and Don Mellor '83 (var. 1)

FA Pete Benson, Rich Leswing, and Chuck Turner '81 (var. 2)

FA Purcell, Edwards, Mellor '87 (var. 3)

Death by Mini-Van   I   5.11   80'   (E)   †

Squeezed between two of the cliff's most popular routes is yet another superb pitch.

pitch 1 Run Higher, Jump Faster. 5.11

pitch 2 Climb out right from *The El* belay to a curving thin crack and excellent climbing. Resist the temptation to drift towards *The El* for the last move. 5.11

FA Dave Furman and Don Mellor 1994
(Eric Wahl and Ann Eastman did at least part of this prior to '94)

Pete's Farewell I 5.7 150' (E) †

This is a classic handcrack route, the most popular on the cliff. It is the easiest route on the main face, but the crux is no giveaway. Begin under the *Great Chimney*.

pitch 1 Leave the cool wafts of air dropping out of the chimney and climb 30' to the belay on the outside corner. 5.2

pitch 2 Traverse left into the corner (or slightly higher to avoid the hard part of the dihedral). Climb the crack past a birch to a good, exposed belay. Careful nutcraft in the horizontal crack can provide a secure back-up to the scrawny cedar 5.6 75'

pitch 3 Walk left across the narrow ledge to the diagonal handcrack finish. 5.7 50'

FA Pete Gibb and Dave Gilyeat (using a wooden wedge in the final crack) 8/24/68

Eurotech I 5.11+ 60' (s)

This elusive face climb begins at *Pete's* final belay.

pitch 1 Climb the face right of the *Pete's* handcrack past a bolt. Head straight up or (better) hand-traverse right to join *P.F. Flyers* crack.

FA Patrick Purcell and Jeff Edwards 1987

P.F. Flyers I 5.10 60' (E) †

Directly above the final *Pete's* belay is a smooth face with a bolt. The crux move on this popular finish is so puzzling that many grab the bolt and swear they've been sandbagged.

pitch 1 Climb past the bolt to a horizontal crack. Traverse left to an excellent fingercrack finish.

FA Don Mellor and Bob Bushart 6/81

Hidden Constellation   I   5.11+   100'   (E)   †

This outstanding and unlikely route climbs the thin seam just right of *Pete's Farewell*.

pitch 1 Begin the traverse (as for *Pete's*) and climb the shallow right-facing corner midway across. Follow this crack line, left at one point, to the seam about 15' right of *Pete's*. Climb up and hand-traverse right 10' to the last of several consecutive cruxes, the thin seam above.

> FA Don Mellor 5/17/85 (The upper half was originally climbed by traversing in from *Pete's* above the crux fracture.
> FA Don Mellor, Bill Dodd and Jim Cunningham)

Star Sailor   I   5.10+   70'   (E)

pitch 1 Begin the traverse as for *Pete's Farewell* and climb the beautiful and bulging fingercrack near the right side of the wall.

> FA Don Mellor 4/81

The Disputed   I   5.8   60'   (E)

pitch 1 Directly above the birch stump belay is a handcrack at the very right end of the cliff.

Great Chimney   I   5.4 to 5.6   100'   (S)

The first ascent at Pitchoff climbed this feature to its very top at chocked blocks. Most parties now use its lower half as access to (or descent from) the cave or upper routes.

Variations There are a few climbing routes on the walls inside the chimney. There's not much of a view, but the place provides a welcome air-conditioned environment on the hottest of days.

> FA Fritz Wiessner and Jim Goodwin 1949

Cave   3rd class   †

Though not an actual climbing route, this unusual trip is worth the effort. Approach can be made by hiking around the left end of the cliff to its top and across the exposed traverse to the blocks atop *Pete's Farewell*. From here there are several squeeze options that lead to the floor of the chimney 20' below. Alternatively, one can climb (5.4) into the gap via the *Great Chimney* route.

The cave itself begins at an unlikely hole at the very back end of the chimney. Squirm through and head inside for about 100' of amazing spelunking. There is rumored to be a linkup to the outside entrance of the *Great Chimney* route, though this is in no way a recommendation to get stuck en route.

Crack Mechanic   I   5.11+   100'   (E)

Strenuous and technical, this really good route climbs the wall just right of the *Great Chimney*. Begin at the base of the chimney.

pitch 1 Climb through the 5.10 crux of *Coffee Achievers* (bolt) and out left past a second bolt (quarter inch, 1987). The thin cracks lead to a belay on the left at the top of the *Great Chimney*.

pitch 2 A short 5.9 pitch follows a crack above.

FA Patrick Purcell 1986

Coffee Achievers   I   5.10   100'   (E)

This is a popular route that climbs the crack system in the back of the depression just right of the chimney.

pitch 1 From the base of the chimney, climb blocks through a fistcrack to a vague corner system. The moves past the bolt are the hardest, but there are some tests above as well.

FA Don Mellor and Mike Heintz 5/11/85

Wild Man From Borneo   I   5.10   100'   (s)

Arm-stretching jungle moves make this one unique.

pitch 1 Climb a low roof to gain the large, red, left-facing corner right of the *Great Chimney*. Above, make a long stab out right to a hold on the arete. This is followed by another reach right to gain the belay as for *Brrright Star*.

pitch 2 Climb the obvious crack line to the top. 5.6

FA Patrick Purcell 6/13/84

Upright and Locked   I   5.10+   100'   (s/D)

pitch 1 At the right edge of the large corner of *Wild Man* is a roof. Climb this (bolt) to a scary face move above. Join *Brrright Star*.

FA Patrick Purcell 1990

Brrright Star   I   5.9+   175'   (E)   †

An excellent and unusual route that tests both footwork and arm strength, this climb takes the left-rising traverse under the black, stepped roof system right of the chimney.

pitch 1 Climb a short, left-facing chimney (about 80' right of the *Great Chimney*) to a belay atop the huge block. 5.8 50'

pitch 2 A fingertip odyssey heads off left under the roof to a small stance at its end. 5.9+ 75'

pitch 3 An easier finish pitch (5.6) takes the obvious crack above.

FA Chuck Turner and Alan Jolley 11/14/82
FFA Chuck Turner and Alan Jolley 1983

Space Race   I   5.11   120'   (E)   †

Amazing. A puzzling crux down low is capped by one of the area's best roofs.

pitch 1 Climb the left-facing chimney formed by the giant block. Face-climb left across the wall to a hard series of moves (bolt). Belay here in slings, or make a long reach out to a jug (bolt) and over the roof to a sloping belay.

pitch 2 Moderate face-climbing (bolt) leads up the waterworn rock above. 5.8

FA ROOF Patrick Purcell and Dominic Eisinger 1990
FA Don Mellor, Bill Dodd, and Jeff Edwards 1991 (p.1)

Rugosity   I   5.8   120'   (S)

One of Pitchoff's original routes; the first pitch gets some traffic, but the green slab is rather dirty.

pitch 1 Climb the chimney facing the *Great Chimney* to the block belay. 5.8 40'

pitch 2 Step up and traverse right 20', then back up and left to a grassy ledge. Finish in the slight, right-angling depression.

FA Grant Calder and John Wald approx. 1976

Bogeyman   I   5.8   150'   (s)

An unusual route involving creative tunneling and really good face climbing.

pitch 1 Begin down around the corner from the Rugosity chimney. Climb nondescript, broken rock to enter the chimney above. Squirm left to a good belay at blocks.

pitch 2 Climb face above, heading left at the crux. Belay at horizontal crack or continue to the top. 5.8

FA Patrick Purcell

For those satisfied with horizontal mobility, there are two lines to consider. These are known as the Girdle Traverses.

Crosstown Traffic   II   5.9

From the top of *Disputed,* traverse left to the diving board flake near the top of *Pete's Farewell.* Continue under the roof of *The El* to a logical grassy exit. This was once cleaner.

FA Jim Cunningham, Bill Dodd, and Rich Leswing 5/25/84

Low Plains Drifter   II   5.9

Begin as for *Uncontrollable Desires.* Stay just under the *Roaches* roof and link the *Wald/Calder* traverse with pitch 1 of *The El* in reverse. Cross to *Rugosity* and finish *Bogeyman.*

ICE AGE WALL

This is a minor but amusing crag above the Upper Cascade Lake. Though it is very close to the road, it isn't visible from anywhere below. Along the Cascade Lakes are a series of gabions, large wire baskets filled with rock that serve as retaining walls. Along Upper Cascade Lake are three of these. Find the crag by scrambling steeply uphill for about a minute above the middle gabion (actually, just about the midpoint of the lake). The 40' wall lies just left of an ice climb known as *Indescretion.* There are three separate routes here (5.8–5.10). An excellent 5.10 bolted face route leads to a tree from which neighboring climbs can be top-roped.

FA Patrick Purcell and Jeff Edwards 4/30/91

CASCADE CLIFF

This is the huge wall that forms the southeast side of Cascade Pass above the mile-long Lower Cascade Lake. It has long attracted attention because of the easy access and spectacular views. Climbers, however, have been somewhat disappointed in their efforts here because loose rock and abundant vegetation spoil what would otherwise be a lovely area. Two routes seem popular and unique: *Lichen Delight* and *Overhanging Gutter.* Perhaps others will come into use with repeated use.

The cliff is located on Route 73 about 10 miles south of Lake Placid. The easy approach to the cliff is made by parking at the picnic area between Upper and Lower Cascade Lake and following a crude trail to the talus.

Route-finding at Cascade Cliff can be difficult; a few distinguishing features must first be recognized. The major feature of the left end is the large right-facing dihedral that dominates the section. This is the start of *Lichen Delight* and others in the area. The central region of the rock is fractured into several parallel, diagonal cracks that run up most of the face, forming such routes as *Malarkey Direct, Trundle Fodder,* and *Overhanging Gutter.* To the right is a large, crackless triangular slab of rock at the foot of the cliff; while some imagination is necessary here, this will be referred to as the "pyramid." Acquaint yourself with these formations before trying to decipher the following descriptions.

The routes are described right to left. The first three climbs are actually on Upper Lake Cliff, an outside corner of rock that stands above the lower end of Upper Cascade Lake, a few hundred yards right of the Main Wall. Approach via an angler's path along the upper lake until a steep uphill bushwhack leads to the rock.

My Favorite Martian   I   5.9   120'   (E)   †

On the outside of the obviously cleaned buttress is a long crack.

pitch 1 Climb through a low crux roof and up the excellent crack just right of the arete.

FA Patrick Purcell and Rich Leswing 5/12/88

Cosmic Thing   I   5.10   60'   (E)

Several feet right of *Mr. Spaceman* is a small roof close to the ground.

pitch 1 Climb the short fingercrack, then face climb up and right (crux) to the hidden inside corner. Up corner to the obvious mantel.

FA Tad Welch and John Thackray 6/10/90

Mr. Spaceman I 5.10- 50' (E)

On the left wall of the buttress/arete is a diagonal handcrack.

FA Dale Frisbey and Tom Coffin 3/79
FFA Don Mellor and Dale Frisbey 7/79

Dirty Diana I 5.3 50' (E)

Just to the right of Cascade Cliff is a low crag that faces the waterfall drainage. The crack through the roof is 5.3; shorter routes to the right are easier.

Beehive II 5.6 400' (S)

This route, the easiest on the cliff, follows a wandering line of corners and ramps. Begin a few feet right of the pyramid slab. Actually, the best starting point is on a tree-covered ledge about 40' up and directly right of the pyramid, under a large, dripping overhang about 100' above.

pitch 1 From the tree ledge, scramble across to the broken, tree-filled line that makes up the right edge of the pyramid. Belay in the trees above. 5.3 75'

pitch 2 Move left and follow a ramp up right to a belay above and left of the overhang. 5.4 75'

pitch 3 Climb left again a few feet and follow another ramp up twin cracks. Continue in this right-rising line to an overhang that can be climbed with the help of a dead tree to a belay in a small forest. 5.6 120'

pitch 4 Escape is easy to the right. The route, however, wanders up over walls and corners to the left, heading for a right-facing corner at the very highest point of the wall. 5.5 150'

History The line as described was climbed by the Penn State Outing Club in 1965. They found evidence of earlier passage on the lower section.

Overhanging Gutter II 5.7 300' (S)

The main feature of this climb is the overhanging, right-facing corner at the top of the central section of the cliff. The crux pitch climbs this crack. It's clean now, but one can only admire the tenacity of the first climbers who

CASCADE CLIFF

A. LICHEN DELIGHT 5.9

B. UNDERHANGING GARTER 5.6

C. MALARKY DIRECT 5.6

D. TRUNDLE FODDER 5.6

E. WHERE BEAGLES DARE 5.10+

F. OVERHANGING GUTTER 5.7

G. BEEHIVE 5.6

tackled this when it was choked with dirt. The lower pitches aren't great, but there are several ways to reach the climactic gutter pitch. *Trundle Gutter* seems the more direct linkup. It follows the first pitch of *Trundle Fodder*, moves left a bit joining the best pitch of *Underhanging Garter* (pitch 5), and eventually meets directly with the gutter pitch. Begin at the left side of the pyramid at the top of a wide, vegetated gully at a birch below a diagonal overhang.

pitch 1 Climb over this overhang/block and up over an open slab to a birch at the base of a sloping slab with a drop-off on the right.

pitch 2 Climb the slab and traverse right to its edge, climbing under an overhang and up to an exposed outside corner. Step around this and head for a belay bush at 110'.

pitch 3 Continue up toward the large slab below the final gutter corner, the obvious overhanging crack in the right-facing corner. The slab is best negotiated on its right side. Follow the crux crack to the top.

FA Craig Patterson, Dave Zimmerman, and Tony Goodwin 6/66

Where Beagles Dare II 5.10+ 300' (E)

Wander up to prominent alcove right of central *Underhanging Garter*, directly below the *Gutter* pitch.

pitch 2 Exit left side of alcove, then right across the face via a 5.8 finger crack. Belay at large ledge, same as for *Overhanging Gutter*.

pitch 3 From left end of ledge, face-climb left past bolts and up exposed face to top. 5.10+

FA Patrick Purcell and Joe Quackenbush 6/91

Trundle Fodder II 5.6 300' (S)

This climb begins in the prominent chimney left of the *Overhanging Gutter* route, actually almost directly below the final gutter pitch. As with all Cascade climbs, there is abundant loose rock: the climb is named for what almost happened to a canoe below.

pitch 1 Climb the chimney past a chockstone and continue up left to the base of a right-leaning corner. 110'

pitch 2 Climb out left around the corner to a thin, steep slab. Follow this and continue from its top to a slab with an old bolt on the left below a bulge. This old bolt, of unknown origin, reminds us that many of the routes described on this cliff are actually linkups of new and old terrain. Climb the bulge and belay in the corner of the large flake.

pitch 3 Traverse back to the original line, and chimney to the rim. Alternatively, from the belay at the large flake at the end of pitch 2, one may chimney to the top, following a dirty crack to the trees.

FA Tom Rosecrans and Ken Jackson approx. 1975

Malarkey Direct   II   5.6   300'   (s)

This climbs the second major crack right of the huge dihedral at the left side of the cliff.

pitch 1 Begin below the main right-facing dihedral. Climb broken rock to a sheltered belay below the corner.

pitch 2 Continue over easy and broken rock, tending right to a belay at the obvious birch.

pitch 3 A long pitch up a dirt-filled crack leads to the top.

FA Grant Calder and John Wald 8/14/75

Underhanging Garter   II   5.6   600'   (s)

This is a long and wandering line that starts at the lower left end of the cliff and finishes at the upper right. Begin at the base of the large right-facing corner.

pitch 1 Climb up the corner to a large, sloping platform. 50'

pitch 2 Traverse right 25', then upwards to a "sentry box" belay. 85'

pitch 3 Climb the corner and wander right along a mossy shelf. Continue on moss up to a birch. 80'

pitch 4 Traverse right to a diagonal chimney/crack. Climb this to a birch belay in a corner. 90'

pitch 5 Rappel off the birch to a stand below. One is now in the same crack line as the *Overhanging Gutter.* Continue up the crack, through a roof via a fistcrack, to the large sloping terrace below the gutter. 85'

pitch 6 Climb the slab to the steep wall and traverse right around a corner and up a slab above. Traverse right again and down to a stance. 135'

pitch 7 Climb the right side of the buttress, the slab above, and the corner above that. Cross another slab and stay right under short walls to a tree belay.

Calvin Schmid on the fine arete of Eat Yourself a Pie.

PHOTO BY JEFF EDWARDS

pitch 8 Climb the wall above, past a slab, and up the final corner. 40'

FA Tom Rosecrans and Ken Jackson 10/74

Kirby Corner   II   5.9   300'   (s)

This is the most obvious feature on the left end of the cliff that has, no doubt, lured many parties up only to thwart their efforts by blanking out just short of the rim. This route makes the best of what's offered by climbing the good section and fixing a rappel descent.

pitch 1 Climb broken rock as for the neighboring routes to establish a belay at the base of the corner. 5.3 150'.

pitch 2 Climb the crack in the corner, past the bulge at about 60', and traverse up and right on sloping shelves, then down right to a two-bolt belay.

FA Patrick Purcell and Rich Leswing 1988

Super Cell   5.11   (top-rope)

From the airy perch belay of *Lichen Delight* buttress, top rope the face below, about 15' right of the obvious *Atmospheric Pressure* crack.

FA Patrick Purcell 1992

Atmospheric Pressure   5.12   (top-rope)

This is the all-too-obvious crack on the overhanging right wall of the huge corner.

FA Patrick Purcell 1988

Lichen Delight   II   5.9   300'   (D)   †

This route climbs out a hand traverse partway up the huge right-facing corner.

pitch 1 Climb up to a stance below the corner. 5.3 150'

pitch 2 Continue up the corner until a spectacular traverse can be made to an exposed belay on the arete-like outside corner. 5.7

pitch 3 The original ascent dropped down and left below a tree, and continued leftward to a flake. From this point, Calder and Wald climbed the unprotected slab. An improved version heads straight up past a bolt.

FA Grant Calder and John Wald 8/28/76

FA Direct Finish Bob Bushart and Bill Simes approx. 1978

The Whiteface Region is dominated by the magnificent Moss Cliff.

WHITEFACE

The climbs here are located in Wilmington Notch, the narrow, glacially carved pass through which Route 86 connects Lake Placid and Whiteface Mountain. The towering cracks of Moss Cliff, the friendly slabs on Notch Mountain, the wild exploration at Olympic Acres—all bespeak the variety this region has to offer. Camping, motels, and supplies can be found in both Lake Placid and Wilmington, and there is a state campground right in the Notch itself near the entrance to the Whiteface Mountain Ski Center and across from Cloudspin Cliff.

NOTCH MOUNTAIN SLABS

Notch Mountain is the informal name given to the rocky buttress that makes up the southeast wall of Wilmington Notch. (It is most evident when approaching from Lake Placid.) It is a very scenic collection of slabs with 60'–100' routes of 5.2–5.6 range. The best climbing is confined to the small, south-facing slabs on the far right when viewed from the road. There are also a few routes on the summit crags above and to the left. Finally, the largest section of rock, that just across the road from the Moss Cliff parking lot, remains unclimbed.

The climbing here is scenic and unspoiled. Please do your best to keep it this way. Additionally, it is vital that the belay trees at the top of the cliff be preserved. Excessive walking near their roots, or unnecessary congregation of groups atop the climbs, could jeopardize this.

The best approach begins at the northern trail to Copperas Pond off Route 86 about 6 miles from Lake Placid. Follow the trail for about 10 minutes; then traverse left just below the height of land. No distinct path exists. When approached this way, the first climbs reached are on the distinct and attractive main slab. This is a pyramid-shaped 80' slab resting at about 60 degrees. Along its right edge is easy access to pine-tree anchors. Alternatively, it is possible to hike around right from the base of the main slab to gain the summit of Notch Mountain. (This easy bushwhack brings one to a spectacular overlook and provides access to the better part of *Fenris* and *Ormis*). The climbs are described right to left from this feature. There are numerous variations to the routes listed below.

Return Home I 5.2 60' (E)

pitch 1 Follow the curving, right-facing corner near the right edge of the slab. At its top, break diagonally left from a small spruce, following a crack just below the crest.

FA Tim Riley and Dick Tucker 11/25/77

Roast and Boast I 5.6 75' (S) †

pitch 1 Perhaps the best route here. Break through a low overlap in the center of the face and follow cracks to the lone pine above.

FA Bill Widrig and Tad Welch 8/28/85

And She Was   I   5.2   80'   (E)   †

This is an excellent beginner route.

pitch 1 Climb the diagonal footcrack to the detached block at the left edge of the face. Traverse right to the lone pine. Finish at will.

FA Tad Welch and Ali Schultheis

T.L.   I   5.5   80'   (s)

Just around the corner to the left of the main slab is another low-angled section.

pitch 1 Climb the clean slab, passing shallow diagonal cracks, and finishing in the main corner to the trees.

Variation A short second pitch is called ***After Golf***: From behind the large cedar, climb a short dirty slab to clean rock. Finish over obvious pointed rock.

FA Tad Welch and Bill Widrig 8/28/85
FA Dick Tucker and Tim Riley 5/25/87 (var.)

Men of Iron   I   5.4   80'   (s)

This route parallels *T.L.* to its left. Stay left near the black streak until a large crack is reached. Follow crack rightward and finish on steeper rock to a large cedar.

FA Dick Tucker and Tim Riley 4/12/87

Fat-Free Warrior   I   5.5   300'   (s)

This long route follows the very left edge of the middle slab, passing through a large tree-covered ledge en route.

pitch 1 Climb the left edge of the slab (as for *Men Of Iron*). Belay at pines. 50'

pitch 2 Stay on left edge of slab to a clump of cedars. 130'

pitch 3 Climb to a shallow V and large horizontal crack. Move left and on to the top.

FA Dick Tucker and Tim Riley 9/25/88

Daddy, Where Are You? I 5.4 300' (E)

This is a long route with some good climbing interspersed with trees and loose rock.

pitch 1 Begin at the lowest left edge of the third slab (the left-hand of three). Climb the shallow arch and up to a sloping belay ledge. 120'

pitch 2 Continue up right along the base of the wall to its end at a bush-filled corner. Climb a dirty chimney and slab, belaying in a small alcove with trees. 90'

pitch 3 Climb back wall of the alcove through trees to a wide slab. Turn the top bulge to the right.

FA Dick Tucker and Tim Riley 9/7/86

Fenris I 5.5 235' (S)

This route is best approached by scrambling directly uphill from the road; the traverse from the south-facing slabs is awful. The best part of the route—the last 60'—could be reached by rappel.

pitch 1 Thrash to the base of a large gully that dominates the right side of the face. An unappealing pitch generally up left of the gully brings one to a dirty tree-filled corner. 150'

pitch 2 Up the corner to open rock. Follow large crack and face to top.

FA Dick Tucker and Tim Riley 7/9/89

Ormis the Viking God I 5.4 60' (E)

This is a tight chimney formed by a detached flake. It is found near the summit, about 30' left of *Fenris*. Approach by rappel.

HIGH FALLS CRAG

This is the steep wall of the well-known ice climb, *Multiplication Gully*. It is distinguished by two appealing crack routes that run parallel up the center of the face. The cliff is located above a pull-off on the Ausable River between Moss Cliff at the height of the Notch and High Falls Gorge, the tourist attraction closer to Whiteface Mountain. From the angler's parking area, the impressive twin cracks can easily be seen on the wall on the southeast side of Route 86.

Route of Oppressive Power   II   5.10   300'   (s)   †

This striking crack begins with the obvious bottomless chimney; it is the left-hand crack. It is thought by some to be one of the best climbs in the Adirondacks.

pitch 1 Locate the bottomless slot about 70' up. Begin by thrashing past trees and nondescript rock to a belay at its base. 5.   50'

pitch 2 Climb a thin crack on the left wall of the depression (5.9) and run it out up the arete on the left to enter the chimney. The crack steadily narrows to a handcrack crux. Belay at an amazing balcony/seat out left. 5.10   75'

pitch 3 Stay in the crack to the forested ledge. 5.8   50'

pitch 4 Follow a ramp up left to a boulder problem (5.8) finish. Rappel with two ropes to avoid a nasty bushwhack.

FA Rich Romano late 70s

There Be Dragons   II   5.10+   300'   (E)

This is the right-hand crack.

pitch 1 Same as for *Oppressive Power.*

pitch 2 Bridge up the slot and climb the right-hand crack (tight hands) out the roof and up until it deteriorates. Traverse straight left to the balcony belay of the previous route. Rappel or continue to the top via *Oppressive Power.*

FA Don Mellor, Bill Dodd, and Patrick Purcel 6/85

High Falls   II   5.10-   350'   (s)

Right of the obvious twin cracks of the previous routes is a black and orange depression. Right of this is a high wall with an obvious crack above huge, impenetrable orange overhangs. The crack is reached via a pitch up the left wall of *Multiplication Gully,* the winter climb in the deep cleft on the right side of the wall.

pitch 1 Climb bushes up the gully to a ledge on the left with four large cedars. 4th class   50'

pitch 2 Just left of the cedars is an overhanging corner with a four-inch crack. Climb the corner and blocks to the face above. Continue on easy rock just right of the arete to a cedar tree belay stance. 5.6   50'

HIGH FALLS CRAG

A. ROUTE OF OPPRESSIVE POWER 5.10

B. HIGH FALLS 5.10-

pitch 3 Head out left over an open book and the void below to a huge flake under the roof. (This frightening monster can be seen from the road.) Tread gently left to a hanging belay at the base of the crack. Pitches 2 and 3 can be combined. 5.9 40'

pitch 4 The climactic crux pitch climbs the steep and airy fingercracks on the headwall visible from the road.

FA Jeff Edwards, Don Mellor, Patrick Purcell 9/88

CLOUDSPIN CLIFF

This is a minor crag above Route 86 a mile or so southwest of Whiteface Mountain Ski Center; it is obvious to drivers coming from Lake Placid as they take the sharp curve before the state campground. The rock stands about 100' high. In recent years some good routes have been discovered, and under the lichens, bushwhacking straight uphill. The going is easier in the woods just left of center. The uphill walk takes about 10 minutes.

The most obvious feature to use when searching out climbs is the high, right-to-left diagonal offwidth crack. (This route is called *1968 Offwidth Pants,* seen easily from the road.) To its left is a sheer face; to its right the rock is more broken and featured. Most climbs will be described relative to this crack.

Demolition   I   5.6   90'   (s)

pitch 1 Near the right end of the cliff is a large triangular roof. Begin under this and climb to a ledge below a crack/corner that leads to the top.

FA Jeff Edwards and Dan Stauft 5/4/87

Pink Lynch   I   5.7   100'   (s)

pitch 1 Near the right-center of the cliff, right of *Offwidth Pants,* is a slab/ramp. From its left side, climb up to a tree, then right a bit to an awkward overhang and corner above.

FA Don Mellor, Jamie Bellanca, and Tim Lynch 5/4/87

Trouser Gallery   I   5.12   140'   (E)

High in the center of the cliff, just right of *Offwidth Pants,* is a prow of rock, across which runs a diagonal fingercrack. Begin directly below *Offwidth Pants*.

pitch 1 Start as for the next two routes, pulling trees to gain a hidden corner behind a cedar. Belay up right on a block ledge. 5.7 70'

pitch 2 Instead of taking the obvious fingercrack, face-climb (5.10) just right of it, heading towards the diagonal offwidth (5.7 x). Hand-traverse strenuously right, then up and left to gain the crux fingercrack. Exit right.

FA Don Mellor 6/24/91

Frippery I 5.8 120' (E) †

The best moderate tour of the cliff.

pitch 1 Same as for *Trouser Gallery*. 5.7 70'

pitch 2 Climb the obvious fingercrack to a flake system at the bottom of the offwidth. Climb up right in a short corner and make an exposed hand traverse right to finish with *Trouser Gallery*. 5.8 70'

FA Don Mellor and Scott Peterson 4/16/92

1968 Offwidth Pants I 5.8 140' (D)

This most obvious feature on the cliff is awkward and hard to protect.

pitch 1 Same as for *Trouser Gallery*. 5.7 70'

pitch 2 At the top of the fingercrack, enter the chimney, emerging left at its top. 5.8 70'

FA Don Mellor, Jeff Edwards, and Brad Hess 5/91

Hop on Pop I 5.11 140' (E) †

This route climbs the face just left of the *Offwidth Pants* crack.

pitch 1 Approximately 40' left of the start of the previous routes is a rising right-to-left series of dirty ledges to a birch belay. 3rd class 40'

pitch 2 Climb a 10' red, right-facing corner just left of the prominent birch. Out roof to thin crack and belay ledge. 5.10 50' (Gear to 4'' for belay flake.)

pitch 3 Step right to sharp flake; from top of the flake climb a steepening grove to a bolt (crux) and a hand traverse left.

FA Don Mellor 5/6/92

Grand Ole Osprey   I   5.10   140'   (E)   †

An excellent two-pitch route.

pitch 1 Same as for *Hop on Pop.* 5.10

pitch 2 From top of the belay flake, step up to a bolt and follow a wandering line past two more bolts to the top. 5.10

Destined for Obscurity   I   5.10   80'   (S)

pitch 1 Near the left-center of the cliff (and right of a striking short arete) is a full-length chimney. Start left of this at a handcrack to cedar belay. 5.7 30'

pitch 2 Move left and head (no protection) to a fingercrack. The final moves are the hardest.

FA Jeff Edwards with Chris Lees 5/14/87

SUNRISE MOUNTAIN SLAB

Approaching Whiteface from Lake Placid on Route 86, about a mile before reaching Moss Cliff and the Notch, one sees a dome-like slab, divided by a water-groove, high on the left. This is a seldom-visited rock that offers good, clean friction and face climbing. Wade the river and climb a very steep, wooded slope to its base. There is no trail.

Half-Baked Flake   I   5.6 (?)   200'   (D)

This route is reported to climb the left side of the slab via a loose flake.

FA Jerry Hoover and Dan Gugliantta 1977

Helms-Jolley   I   5.6   200'   (D)

Right of the water-groove is a long friction face with a surprisingly steep headwall above. Begin at the slab's lowest point.

pitch 1 Climb past a bolt (quarter-inch, 1982) to a belay at the base of the headwall. 5.6 120'

pitch 2 Step left and climb an amazing, pocketed wall with no protection. Exit right. 5.4

Variation **Best of Friends** 5.6   From the right end of the slab, climb past a bolt (quarter-inch, 1984), converging with the previous route at the headwall belay.

FA Andy Helms and Alan Jolley 1982
FA Alan Jolley and Kathy Bright 1984 (var.)

MOSS CLIFF

Nowhere is a cliff name so misleading. The appellation probably resulted from a faulty reading of the USGS topographic map, which gave the name "Moss Cliff" to one of the open slabs closer to Lake Placid. The cliff that climbers now refer to is the clean, unbroken sweep of rock that soars above the Ausable River at the height of Wilmington Notch on Sunrise Mountain adjacent to Whiteface. Its towering cracks and overhanging right face make dangerous drivers out of climbers as they pass through the tight section of the Notch, necks craned and eyes focused on this most alluring of Adirondack cliffs.

The cliff is really an enormous arete-like outside corner. Its crack-lined left face is stepped and generally less than vertical, while its right wall shoots upward, vertical at first, then gradually overhanging, with its crest hovering over the ground hundreds of feet below. Few walls in the East rival the drama of this piece of rock. Naturally, most of the climbing takes place on the more benign left face.

Right of this overhanging northeast face is a section of broken rock that has been home to peregrine falcons. The DEC has instituted annual closures during the nesting season. These restrictions *must* be respected. The particular birds at this site, however, would have closed the place down on their own: The female literally has driven back team after team of battle-shocked climbers, even after the ban was lifted and the warning signs removed.

Park at the dirt pull-off highest in the Notch and right below the cliff. The stream crossing can be challenging at best and hazardous at worst. A long stick or ski poles may be vital for support. There is a vague path, but any route slightly left of center will work; the boulder field off right is best avoided.

There are two descents:

1. Walk into the depression between the overhanging face and *Ausable Arete*. A 75' rappel leads to the base of the big wall.

2. During restricted seasons, the nesting area can be avoided by rappelling your route.

The routes on the southeast face are described right to left from the arete-like outside corner. Note that any number of variations are possible by linking pitches in this section of cliff.

Adirondack Black Fly Rancher III 5.7 A2 350'

This route climbs the thin cracks just left of the arete.

pitch 1 Climb the thin cracks on either side of the arete to a belay on a ledge at 90'.

pitch 2–3 Continue in the cracks just left of the edge until 5.7 free-climbing ends at the large cedar alcove. From here it is possible to join the other routes on the left.

FA Patrick Purcell (solo) 9/88

Fear of Flying II 5.10 350' (E)

This climb originally had an aid start behind the large beech tree at a thin crack, the first on the wall at the outside corner. It is described here as using pitch 1 of *A Touch of Class* to make it a free climb. The essence of this climb is the wide crack: Be ready for parallel-sided cracks in every range from finger to chimney.

pitch 1 The obvious crack just right of the wide flake/crack leads to a fine belay ledge on the right. 5.9 80'

pitch 2 Climb the steep, short face on the right to a birch and curving handcrack to trees. The short, overhanging fistcrack (5.10) on the left ends at stance. 75'

pitch 3 The 4"–5" parallel-sided crack on the right is capped by a block. Exit left. 5.9 50'

pitch 4 Climb the block and tunnel into the cliff, emerging from behind a large cedar and belaying at another excellent, flat ledge. 5.6 50'

pitch 5 Climb the waterworn fingercracks on the black wall to the top. 5.10-

FA Andrew Embick, Al Long, and Al Rubin 9/76

PHOTO BY CHUCK TURNER

MOSS CLIFF

A. FALCONER 5.10+
B. HARD TIMES 5.9

C. A TOUCH OF CLASS 5.9
D. FEAR OF FLYING 5.10
E. CHILDREN AND ALCOHOL 5.11 A2

F. CORONARY COUNTRY 5.11
G. AUSABLE ARETE 5.9

A Touch of Class II 5.9 350' (E) †

This route climbs the main left-facing corner midway up the wall.

pitch 1 Same as for the previous route. 5.9 80'

pitch 2 From this good belay ledge, stay in the thin crack line on lower-angled rock to a hard finish at a large island of trees below the left-facing corner above. 5.9 75'

pitch 3 The fingercrack (5.9) in the corner is followed by a short chimney; then handcrack to a belay on a flat, rectangular ledge. Don't confuse this pitch with *Aerie;* the corner for *A Touch of Class* is hidden from view behind a cedar jungle.

pitch 4 From the right end of the ledge, follow a handcrack to a stance below a cedar-filled corner. Fight through the trees and finish via an easy handcrack. 5.8 100' Alternatively, one may climb the short, thin crack to the right. 5.10

> FA It was recently discovered that Jack Maxwell, Ben Ales, and the late Rocky Keeler climbed a full-length route on Moss cliff around 1968. This may account for "the ridiculous resident piton" that Al Long, Al Rubin and Dave Hoffman reported finding on their 9/8/74 ascent.
>
> FA Mark Ippolito 1988 (var. p.4)

Aerie II 5.12 350' (E) †

Like many other routes on this face, *Aerie* follows a single and direct crack line from bottom to top; its middle pitch, a 5.10 stemming corner, is one of the best anywhere and can be used as a variation for the routes on either side. This is a highly recommended finger exercise with two crux sections. Begin at the obvious right-facing flake/chimney.

pitch 1 The chimney is followed by a thin crack right of *Hard Times'* pitch 1 cedar belay. Climb the short wall mid-pitch via a small left-facing corner (5.11) and belay at the large island of trees. (same as for *Hard Times*) 140'

pitch 2 Right of the *Hard Times* chimney is a left-facing corner that sweeps up steeply at its top. This superb pitch ends in a hanging belay just above. 5.10 60'

pitch 3 Follow the thin crack up increasingly steep rock and angle up right past a series of thin cracks to a belay at a large (but unstable) cedar. 5.12 50' *pitch 4* The thin crack just left of the tree provides another really good pitch. 5.10 90'

FA Don Mellor and Jeff Edwards 9/1/88

Hard Times II 5.9 350' (E) †

This is one of the most direct, interesting, and satisfying of Adirondack climbs. It follows a single line up cracks and corners; it is identified as the major right-facing dihedral on the large wall facing the road.

pitch 1 Begin uphill and left of the prominent outside corner; there is a 4th class approach angling up right to a bushy ledge atop a 40' flake.

pitch 2 Climb a handcrack at a cedar and up corners (5.8) to lower-angled rock. Continue weaving a line to the left end of the island of trees. 140'

pitch 3 Chimney to the top of the 75' flake (belay possible). The crux roof is followed by face climbing and an offwidth (5.8) finish at a flat ledge. 5.9 150'

pitch 4 Handcracks lead to the top. 5.8 75'

FA Al Long and Al Rubin 8/23/75
FFA Henry Barber and Dave Cilley 1977

Spirit of Adventure III 5.11 350' (E) †

This route climbs the arete of *Hard Times,* and finishes up the beautiful shield of rock to the top.

pitch 1 and 2 Take any neighboring route to the tree ledge at the base of the *Hard Times* corner. 150'

pitch 3 Up the right-facing corner to a "hand rail" left onto the arete (bolts) and up to a fixed belay. 5.11 60'

pitch 4 Descend left to a bolt, then up to undercling and hidden bucket. Up right to thin crack, right again 8' to hanging belay. 5.10+ 45'

pitch 4 Climb incredible cracks through the smooth shield to a ledge. 5.10+ 80'

pitch 5 Climb face to overhang and crack; turn the roof and follow a low-angled handcrack to the trees 5.9 75'

FA Dominic Eisinger and Patrick Purcell 8/94

John Wald on the third pitch of Hard Times. Aerie *is the left-facing corner to its right.*

Red Zinger   I   5.9+   150'   (E)

This is an alternate start to *Hard Times,* et al. It climbs the most prominent right-facing dihedral.

pitch 1 Up the corner to a large, loose rock that blocks passage to the tree-covered ledge (exit) above. Angle right over slabs to the island of trees on *Hard Times.*

FA Todd Eastman and Spaff Ackerly 1981

Falconer   II   5.10+   300'   (E)   †

The left side of Moss Cliff is broken up by a forested terrace two thirds of the way up. This excellent route climbs the striking handcrack up the smooth lower wall.

pitch 1 30' left of the huge right-facing Red Zinger corner is a smaller left-facing dihedral. The crux on this pitch is low. Belay at a good, flat stance. 5.10+ 100'

pitch 2 Above are two crack lines. (The original ascent climbed the right-hand crack. 5.9) Climb the steep face to gain the more prominent left-hand crack. Follow this through a steep, thin-hands crux to the forest. 5.10

pitch 3 Walk uphill through the woods for 50' to the final pitch: the flaring corner capped by the right-facing triangular roof. 5.10+ 100'

FA Don Mellor and Andy Zimmerman 6/15/84
FA Don Mellor and Pat Munn 5/29/85 (p.2)

Far Side   II   5.8   175'   (E)

Up and left from the previous routes is a shorter corner/crack system. The route needs tidying up a bit.

pitch 1 Climb a steep corner (next to a cedar with cut branches), past a short chimney, to a sloping belay. 5.7 70'

pitch 2 Continue in the crack line to the woods. 100'

FA Tom Rosecrans, Dave Szot, and Tom Yandon

The following climbs are located on the overhanging northeast face, described left to right from the arete-like outside corner.

Creation of the World   III   5.10+   350'   (s)   †

This is the continuous (read *endless*) offwidth crack that runs up the left side of the big wall, just right of the arete. Oversized, modern protection is necessary. The route begins at a low bolt below a flaring slot.

pitch 1 Climb a short, steep ramp to a small left-facing corner that leads to the sharply flaring chimney. At its top traverse left 15' to a small sloping ledge in a left-facing corner. 5.10+

pitch 2 Traverse left for another 15' to the crack. Follow it as it widens from hands to offwidth, past the giant cedar, to an incredible cave belay. 5.10+

pitch 3 Continue in the unrelenting, overhanging offwidth crack to a ledge on the arete. 5.10+

pitch 4 Head right onto the exposed wall once again to a large, left-facing corner that ends on a ledge. Mantel onto a sloping shelf beneath a short, overhanging wall, traverse to the arete, then climb a ramp to the final right-facing corner. 5.9+

FA Ken Nichols and Chad Hussey 10/10/87

Children and Alcohol   III   5.11   A2+   350'

This aid route climbs slanting cracks in the middle of the biggest part of the wall. Its clean line and exposed hanging belay make it one of our pre-miere big wall experiences. (Please report if this route goes hammerless.)

pitch 1 Climb a left-facing flake system behind a large yellow birch. The bottom of the crack is always wet. Belay at a sloping stance in a left-facing corner. 5.11 80'

pitch 2 Continue in the crack/chimney line to the left end of the bivy terrace, a long sidewalk 150' off the deck. 5.8

pitch 3 From the left end of the terrace, climb past a bolt (quarter-inch) to a crack that leads past a small roof to a belay at two bolts (quarter-inch, can be supplemented with chocks). A2

pitch 4 The crack leads to the top at the cliff's overhanging crest. A2 or A3

FA Mark Bon Signor, Alan Jolley, and Don Mellor 4/81

Mosscalito   III   A3

Begin at the terrace of the neighboring routes.

pitch 2 Aid up above belay, left at first, then up to a right-diagonaling crack; traverse left to the bolt belay of the previous route.

pitch 3 Traverse left and up to a 3" crack/groove breaking through headwall.

FA Dominic Eisinger and Patrick Purcell 9/94

Pan Am III A3 350'

Right of the yellow birch is a smooth wall split by a 150' thin crack. The upper section of this route climbs a smooth and exposed expanse of rock. Not quite *The Shield,* but nonetheless, a big wall experience. Its multiday, first ascent took place in rain and snow, simultaneously with that of *Children and Alcohol.*

pitch 1 Climb the thin crack past a small ledge at 25'. Continue up the obvious line, switching cracks at one point to a belay at the terrace. A2 or A3 150'

pitch 2 Climb the short left-facing corner above the cedar (5.10 or A1). A bolt leads to a crack that goes up and left to a flake/overhang. Follow this left and up to a sling belay. (Bolts, quarter-inch) A3

pitch 3 Follow the left-leaning crack until it fades. A horizontal seam leads right to a bolt and flake that brings one back left to a tricky finish on a slab. A3

FA Mike Heintz and John Sahi 4/81

Coronary Country III 5.11 400' (s)

The only free route on the overhanging face. The route wanders a bit.

pitch 1 Begin behind a large yellow birch, climbing a left-facing corner to its end. Move out past hollow flakes and face-climb questionable rock to a belay at the base of a left-facing dihedral. 5.11 80'

pitch 2 Climb up for 20' until a traverse can be made to the right. Up to the Terrace with fair protection 5.10+ 60'

pitch 3 From the Terrace, step right behind a large cedar and climb short corner. Thrash behind a tree on a long traverse right to a belay above in a large cedar. 5.10

pitch 4 Climb the obvious line of weakness: the corner system above. 5.10+ 120'

FA Al Long and Al Rubin 5/1/77
FFA Bill Dodd and Don Mellor 7/13/84

A Scream from on High III 5.10+ A1 350'

This is the major corner that forms the very right end of the overhanging big-wall section. A total of six pitches led to its top, exiting leftward via the awesome arching roof crack. This section will probably go free if the rock is cleaned. As it is, it's quite an adventure, with the third-pitch chimney especially memorable.

FA Tim Beaman and Sylvia Lazarnick 1994

Ausable Arete II 5.9 350'

The first ascent party wrote: "The object of this route was to climb the prominent ridge to the right of the large gully right of the main cliff. Find the dihedral (visible from the road) which leads up to the base of the sharp ridge. The route follows grooves and cracks just left of the main dihedral. The line of least resistance is still characterized by poor protection, several trees, dirt, loose rock, and several difficult moves. The third (or fourth) pitch, however, is definitely worthwhile and can be reached by scrambling up the right side of the prominent gully. Traverse right and down around the base of the ridge to the base of the groove which leads directly to the ridge crest. (We belayed after the short downward traverse and did the groove as one pitch.) Here the climbing is much more enjoyable than below—the groove has a crack in it! The groove is continuously steep, though; difficulty is sustained right to the crest of the ridge."

FA Al Long and Al Rubin 7/5/75

OLYMPIC ACRES

On the knoll right of the ski center is a large, steep slab. Surprisingly, this central feature remains unclimbed. There are, however, a few short routes nearby. The potential of this area has yet to be realized. Approach by parking at Olympic Acres, the far right section of Whiteface Ski Center. Walk the overgrown cross-country ski trail for about 150 yards and head directly uphill for another 150 yards to a 100' wet wall. This is the ice climb *Polar Soldier*. Just down and left of this is a short, left-facing handcrack/corner capped by a block (FA Patrick Purcell and Ian Osteyee 1986). Just above this route and left of *Polar Soldier* is a cracked, vertical wall with good potential. To get to the higher routes, walk around these cliffs to the right about 100 yards and angle back left for at least another 100 yards. With some luck, this should bring you to the base of the main slab. The real prize here, however, is the short wall on the right.

On this lower righthand section of the cliff are some attractive cracks. The main chimney/gully (5.6) was explored by Pat Munn and John Plausteiner in 1987. The best-looking crack on the left-center of the sheer wall hasn't yet been climbed: its start will be a tough nut to crack. Right of this is a superb crack/corner that ends with unprotected face-climbing (FA Pat Munn). Twenty feet left of this is another excellent top-rope route of about 5.11 (FA Edwards/Mellor 9/88). The two cracks to the right have been climbed as well (FA Pat Munn, Dave Hough, and Mark Meschinelli 1987).

POKE-O-MOONSHINE
A. THE SLAB
B. UPPER TIER AREA

PHOTO BY MARK MESCHINELLI

POKE-O-MOONSHINE

Poke-O has firmly established itself as the premiere Adirondack cliff. Its steep walls, clean cracks, and abundant natural lines make it a crag to rival any in the East. There are three general sections. First encountered when driving from the south is the Slab, site of face and friction routes of about 600'. Around the corner to the north is the Main Face. This is the looming gray wall that stands about 500' high at its highest point and spans over one quarter of a mile. It is here that most of the climbing is done. Above the Main Face are cliff bands scattered toward the summit itself. These are the Upper Tiers. Some of these cliffs exceed 100' and all hold good potential for hard climbs.

Poke-O-Moonshine is located in the northeast corner of the park, near Lake Champlain and about 25 miles south of Plattsburgh. Approach on Route 87, getting off at the Willsboro exit. From Vermont, it is possible to take a ferry from Burlington to Port Kent or from Charlotte to Essex.

Most climbers park and stay at the state campground at the base of the cliff. The best parking is at the campground, where a day-use fee is collected. There are grocery stores in both Lewis, seven miles to the south, and Keeseville, about the same distance north. The closest hospital is the Champlain Valley Medical Center in Plattsburgh (561-2000).

THE SLAB

Also called the South Face by some, this broad slab is the first piece of rock greeting climbers driving north to Poke-O. It stands about 500' high and is dominated by a frowning overlap, an exfoliation arch that runs across the entire midsection of the face. The more difficult routes climb the steeper slab below this; the moderate climbs such as *Catharsis* take rising left-to-right lines to the left. The climbing here isn't true friction; most of the rock is a bit too steep for that. Instead, the rock has weathered to form tiny pockets and edges, though these often seem insufficient to the climber 50' out from his or her last protection. Yes, like most slab areas, the routes here are only fairly protected, but in most cases, it's the exposure and the runout that complete the appeal of the fine individual moves.

Geologically, there are several "textbook" items to watch for. The most obvious is the *exfoliation* of the huge arch and the last pitch of *Catharsis*. Exfoliation is the process by which some rock "peels" or "sheets" like an onion as erosion wears away the surface above. The newly "unloaded" surface responds by shedding its skin on a plane parallel to the surface. And this skin is alive: one group of climbers left a large hex nut fixed under the roof right of *Space Walk* only to find it the next spring on the ground crushed! The arch does more than frown. It yawns and groans under the expansion and contraction of warm days and cold nights.

Less noticeable, but perhaps as interesting, are the ledges that traverse the face. (Examples include the first belay of *The Arch,* the second belay of *Space Walk,* and the fourth belay of *Catharsis.*) They all slope generally downward and they are the result of that same process: exfoliation. Why then don't they parallel the surface? They do. Only in their case, the surface to which they had responded was the preglacial dome-shape that existed before ice cut clean the steep east face of the mountain. After the ice age, the exfoliation began on the newly exposed slab.

In addition to these surface features are several dikes, intrusions of molten rock that filled fissures in the rock when it was deep within the earth. The best example is the short traverse of *pitch 4 Catharsis.* When the hot rock shoots into the cooler, hardened stone, it "bakes" a thin layer of the older rock where contact is made. Look for this "contact metamorphism" where the dike meets the older rock.

Park at the dirt pull-off directly below the slab and walk north for at least 200 yards before heading into the woods north of the face. A path leads back in from the right along the base of the mountain. Descent can be made by heading back from the top of the climb (there is no established trail) and joining the Poke-O-Moonshine hiking trail, which drops from the main summit down the drainage to the north of the slab.

The climbs are described right to left as one approaches.

Space Walk   II   5.9   400'   (D)   †

With excellent and varied climbing every step of the way, this route is justifiably popular. Although the first two pitches are probably 5.9, the consensus holds that the 5.7 run-out of the third lead is the true crux. Begin by scrambling 30' up the left side of a vegetated buttress at the right side of the smooth slab. The start is hidden from the ground.

pitch 1 Climb sharp fingerholds on a water streak past two bolts (one-quarter inch, 1976) to a tree ledge. 5.9 60'

pitch 2 Some route-finding is necessary here. Climb up to a left-facing corner and left to a bolt. Continue straight left to a thin crack and second bolt. Surmount the headwall and belay on the right end of a long ledge. 5.9 80'

pitch 3 Climb into the lower of three grooves (visible from the road). From its top (last nut), head left across a small ledge. Wander upwards to a belay under the overlap. 5.7 120'

pitch 4 Traverse right to the break in the roof at a left-facing corner. Another run-out pitch leads to the trees 5.7 150'

pitch 5–6 Escape right is easy here, but one can also join *Catharsis.* 5.6 200'

FA Dave Hough, Geoff Smith, and Pat Munn 9/76

Le Poisson   II   5.6   A1   400'   (D)

This route begins just left of *Space Walk* and finishes way right on large groove/corners. The first pitch is worthwhile; the upper sections are seldom done.

pitch 1 Climb the obvious line of weakness left of the bushy buttress start of *Space Walk.* Exit right to the trees. 5.6 60'

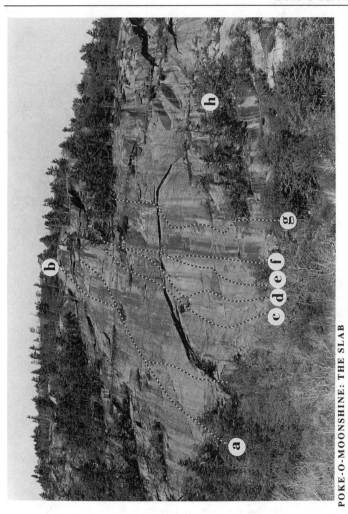

POKE-O-MOONSHINE: THE SLAB

A. CATHARSIS 5.6

B. LAST CHANCE 5.7

C. HUNTER'S MOON 5.10

D. THE ARCH 5.9

E. NEW STAR 5.10

F. TWILIGHT 5.11

G. SPACE WALK 5.9

H. LE POISSON 5.6 A1

PHOTO BY MARK MESCHINELLI

Pat Munn nearing the third-pitch belay on Space Walk:
not a good route for hang-dogging.

pitch 2–3 Head up and right through ledges and trees, exiting (perhaps with aid) via the lower of the two prominent grooves. 200+'

FA Ben Poisson 1957

Twilight   II   5.11   400'   (s)   †

This amazing face climb generally follows the left edge of the obvious black streak in the middle of the face, under the highest point of the arch. Start on the same high ledge as for *New Star.*

pitch 1 Climb out right past small overlaps to a bolt; make a tricky move up to lower-angled rock. Run it out for 50' to a bush and old bolt. The steeper wall above is climbed up slightly right to a right-facing flake and bolt. One more hard move leads to the main traverse ledge. 5.10 150'

pitch 2 Follow a line of four bolts up the sustained, smooth black streak to the two-bolt belay of *New Star.* 5.11 80'

pitch 3 Head up and right, passing bolts through the arch, then up and left to a belay. 5.10+

pitch 4 Join routes out left or rappel.

FA Pat Munn, Mark Meschinelli, and Dick Bushey 10/88

New Star   II   5.10   400'   (D)   †

Right up the middle of the slab under the arch, and just left of the black streaks, is another gem. Like many friction/face climbs, this route has been tamed a bit by the new rubber soles. Nonetheless, it still retains its direct, sustained, and somewhat intimidating qualities.

pitch 1 Begin on a ledge below the highest point of the arch. Climb up to a bolt and left towards a long, thin, left-arching flake/corner. Climb out right to a face with three bolts (quarter-inch) high above. Belay at a narrow ledge. 5.10 130'

pitch 2 Walk right and face-climb up left past two bolts to a corner. Belay above at bolts. 5.10 90'

pitch 3 Break through the roof (as for *The Arch* or *Twilight*) and on to the trees. 5.8 150'

pitch 4–5 Join *Catharsis,* or escape right.

FA Geoff Smith and Dave Hough 9/76

Inner Space   II   5.11   (D)

This route climbs directly between *The Arch* and *New Star.*

pitch 1 Climb straight up toward headwall, belaying just right of the *Arch* crux.

pitch 2 Break through the headwall on the right side of the steep wall to the rap station bolts.

pitch 3 A long pitch climbs straight up from the rappel bolts through the arch as for *Inner Space*. Join upper routes.

FA Patrick Munn and Mark Meschinelli

The Arch   II   5.9   400'   (D)

The scary headwall moves beginning *pitch 2* are just one of the many challenges on this historic route. Begin as for *New Star* on a ledge below the highest point of the arch.

pitch 1 Climb up left on flakes and holds to a ledge. 5.8 100'

pitch 2 Walk a few feet right and surmount the headwall, and step left across a good ledge and belay high above at the higher of two bushy ledges. 5.9 75'

pitch 3 Traverse right, either high or low past a bolt, and break through the arch at the obvious weakness. Belay where possible. 5.8

pitch 4 Easier rock leads to the tree ledge.

pitch 5–6 Join *Catharsis* or escape right. 5.6 200'

FA Dick Wilmott and Brian Rothery 1958

Hunter's Moon   II   5.10   300'   (D)

This route was more likely put in on a full moon. It is a good line, but the climbing here doesn't put for sleeping at the wheel. Begin about 40' right of the huge arch/corner.

pitch 1 Head up, slightly left on loose slabs, then back right to the belay of *The Arch*. It is best to belay above a bit on the highest bushy ledge under the arch. 5.8 150' (D)

pitch 2 Traverse up right (same as for *The Arch*) to a bolt left of *The Arch's* roof pitch. Unlikely and somewhat strenuous moves lead through the break above the bolt and up unprotected, easier rock to *Catharsis*. 5.10 150' (D)

The thin face-climbing on New Star. Climber: Dick Bushey.

PHOTO BY MARK MESCHINELLI

PHOTO BY MARK MESCHINELLI

Climbers low on Last Chance. Catharsis *generally
follows the diagonal fracture above.*

pitch 3 Head right through the trees or join *Catharsis* or *Last Chance*.

FA Pat Munn, Dave Hough, and Mark Meschinelli 10/87

Arch Traverse   II   5.8   250'   (s)

It is possible to climb to the roof of *The Arch* by following the huge overlap right from its start on the left. It was even envisioned once that a route could follow the entire frowning overlap, ending back on the ground. A perverse traverse indeed.

FA Geoff Smith and Dave Hough 9/74

Last Chance   II   5.7   400'   (D)

This route follows much of the same terrain as *Catharsis*. It is possible to join that route at almost any point once up on the face.

pitch 1 Just right of the bottom of the arch/corner, climb to a block below a tree. Traverse left over the roof and up a wide crack to a belay at the edge of the face. 5.7 90' Alternatively, one can start as for *Catharis,* and walk right across a high ledge to the crack (5.6) that forms the flake belay pedestal.

pitch 2 Face-climb with no protection up and slightly left to the belay with *Catharsis* at the small tree under the left-slanting overlap. 5.6 100'

pitch 3 Same as for *Catharsis:* Angle right to Dead Oak Ledge, a bushy terrace in the middle of the left face. 5.5 150' There are many variations possible.

pitch 4 A long, unprotected run-out on pure friction will test both your nerve and the rubber compound on your feet. Admittedly, most parties opt for *Catharsis* here. Exit right. 5.7 (or harder?) 150'

pitch 5 The low-angled black corner just to the left breaks through a short headwall to the top.

FA Rocky Keeler and Rick Weinert 1970

Catharsis   II   5.5 or 5.6   450'   (D)   †

It is no surprise that this has been the most popular route at Poke-O. It is a long, continuous, and varied line with choices available on every pitch. This has helped divert the inevitable traffic during crowded weekends. The most distinguishing feature of the climb when viewed from the road is the triple-layered yellow arching corners at the top of the slab. This is the crux pitch.

Approach by scrambling up dirty ledges and corners to a tree-covered ledge under the left face.

pitch 1 Climb a vague crack to steeper face holds and a belay in a small niche. 5.5 100'

pitch 2 Follow the vertical crack to its top, then face-climb right to gain a left-facing corner. Belay at its top at a small birch. 5.4 120'

pitch 3 Climb right over the overlap at the belay and head straight up to the base of a left-facing dihedral at about 100'. From its base, traverse straight right to Dead Oak Ledge. 5.5 140'

pitch 4 Traverse right across the dike ledge to a belay in a short right-facing corner. 4th class 50' (Easy exit to the right.)

pitch 5 A hard friction move is followed by a leftward traverse and up to an overhang. Climb out and into the left-arching yellow overlap/corners. Stay in these until it is possible to break straight up and over the friction finish. 5.5 or 5.6 150'

Note: The above is only one of many ways to ascend this route.

FA John Turner, Frank Garneau, and Ben Poisson 1957

MAIN FACE

Above and north of the campground is Poke-O's main attraction, the long, clean rock face that stands over Route 9. Here, straight-in cracks and towering dihedrals breach the blank walls that span each of the several traverse dikes.

The dikes (a horizontal intrusion is actually a "sill"; climbers have so long abused the terminology that I'll stick with the erroneous "dike" here) rise left-to-right across the face, forming narrow bands of dark, often loose rock.These distinctive features play a key role in climbing at Poke-O: some routes, *SRT, The Garter,* and *Half Mile,* for example, follow them up and across the face. Other pitches, like *Great Dihedral* and *Paralysis,* end thankfully at rope's end on the ledges at the base off one of the dikes. (The spacing of such intrusions is amazingly well-suited to the length of a climbing rope.) The dikes are mostly diabase, intruded into the main metamorphic granitic gneiss of the cliff. Note the fault in the largest dike by *Gamesmanship.* This is evidence that the intrusion of at least some of the dikes pre-dates the metamorphism that gave the present characteristics to

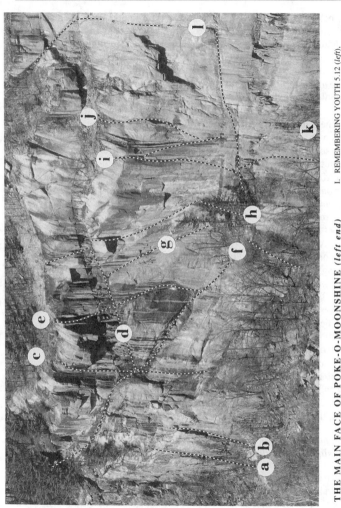

THE MAIN FACE OF POKE-O-MOONSHINE *(left end)*

A. CERTIFIED RAW 5.10

B. PHASE THREE 5.9

C. A WOMB WITH A VIEW 5.11

D. GARTER 5.7+

E. SLIME LINE 5.9+

F. SNAKE 5.4

G. PSYCHOSIS 5.9+

H. MICROWAVE 5.10+

I. REMEMBERING YOUTH 5.12 *(left)*,
   FORGET BULLET 5.11 *(right)*

J. RATTLESNAKE 5.10

K. PILLAR

L. FREEDOM FLIGHT 5.10

the rock. Note also, however, that these horizontal dikes with their shattered rock run across the entire cliff, exposing anyone below to the dangers of rockfall. Be especially wary when climbers are above in the dike areas.

The main rock itself is quite well-suited to climbing. Its vertical cracks and exfoliation corners mark most of the climbs done so far. Although some of these corners seem unlikely from below, there are numerous square-cut holds peppered on the walls that allow easier than expected climbing. *Bloody Mary* and *Sailor's Dive* are two of the best examples of this.

The standard approach leaves the north end of the campground and follows a short path to the cliff's base below *Discord*. Descend by walking back south and scrambling down the enormous eroded dike above the campground, or by rappelling a line just near the center of the cliff: Start from a pine 100' down and left of *Gamesmanship;* rappel to a tiny stance on *Cooney Norton* (bolts); on to the main dike ledge of *Half Mile* (bolts); down left of *Ragtime* to the Sting Ledge; 4th class off left or one more rap to ground. Two ropes are required. For climbs in the "big wall" area, one can also rappel *The Gathering*.

Private land runs nearly to the base of the wall in the left-hand and central portion of the cliff. Please respect this by parking at the campground, paying the fee, and staying within the path at the base of the rock. Climbers have *not* been granted permission to cut directly to the cliff through the talus. Under *Snow Blue* at the right end of the "big wall" section is a survey marker in the wall. This designates the end of state land. The routes right of this lie on private land but are nonetheless included because they have traditionally been part of the climbing here. As such, however, the routes north of *Snow Blue* are subject to any restrictions chosen by the landowner. Obviously, our good behavior is vital.

Finally, we can expect annual closure of selected sections for peregrine falcon nesting. The authorities have agreed to keep the restrictions as narrow as possible in order to let us climb. If we are irresponsible in this regard, they will simply lock tight the whole cliff.

The route descriptions begin on the waterfall face, the wet, black wall above and slightly left of the ranger's cabin.

Note: Some of the bolts at Poke-O and elsewhere have been removed; thus several routes may not exist as described. It is expected that climbers will, sooner or later, replace these missing routes, and so the climbs will be described as they were originally established, keeping route names, grades and first ascent records. The descriptions will simply note: "bolts missing". *Remember that the description applies only if the bolts are in place, and climbers are advised against starting a route without knowing for sure that the bolts are there.* Even on bolted routes, the Poke-O rack includes at least a full set of RPs.

High and Dry   I   5.9   140'   (s)

This and the next few routes are located on the huge, black, waterfall face left of the descent gully. This route follows the crack on the right side of the cleft that breaks up the center of the wall. The wall is seldom dry enough to climb until well into the summer.

pitch 1 Begin right of the huge boulder at the base of the wall and follow the right-hand crack to the top.

ACB Don Mellor and John Wald 8/30/85

Bushmaster   I   5.12   140'

This is the left-most of three awesome climbs by Martin Berzins. They are located at the right end of the waterfall face in the vicinity of *Bushido,* the obvious large dihedral high above.

pitch 1 This is a "face-stemming" pitch up cracks in the pillar left of *Bushido.* Start 15' down and left of *Bushido* at a curving flake below a slab. Climb slab (no protection) to ledge. Step right and up to small ledges until it is possible to move left to an obvious hole. On to the top.

FA Martin Berzins and Dave Lanman 9/4/89

Big Buddha   I   5.12   140'

A tremendous climb between *Bushmaster* and *Bushido.* Follow *Bushmaster* for 35' until it moves left. Step right instead and follow cracks to a poor rest. The difficult wall above is capped by a roof that is turned on the left.

FA Martin Berzins, Richard Felch, and B. Griffiths 7/28/91

Bushido   I   5.11   140'   (E)   †

This is a superior climb with pure, calf-burning stemming on the second pitch. The route climbs a thin crack to an obvious black dihedral high on the right side of the waterfall face.

227

Bill Dodd on the smooth dihedral of Bushido.

pitch 1 Begin below the large upper corner at a hand-/fingercrack. Follow this through an exciting finish to the terrace above. 5.10 90'

pitch 2 Climb the corner to the top. 5.11 50'

History Mike Heintz solo-aid-climbed the thin crack to the right and on up the finish corner in 1984. Dave Georger free-climbed the upper corner (7/10/85), and Don Mellor and Bill Dodd added the variant free pitch one (1987).

Bodacious   I   5.12   140'   (x)

The second pitch is unprotected and at least 5.12+ for anyone under 6'1". Good Luck.

pitch 1 Complex climbing (and protecting). Climb the original aid route of *Bushido* to gain the large ledge. 5.12

pitch 2 Climb the blank wall right of the classic dihedral via a *very* long reach. Hand-traverse right and to the top.

FA Martin Berzins and Richard Felch

Pearly Gates   I   5.9   140'   (E)

This is the last crackline on the right end of the waterfall face just left of the outside corner and descent gully.

pitch 1 Follow the initial fingercrack and remain in the line of weakness to the trees.

FA Todd Eastman and Don Mellor 7/82

Kaibob   I   5.8   70'   (E)

Up inside the canyon that forms the descent gully (standard descent) is a narrow, right-facing corner on the left (south) wall.

pitch 1 Follow the corner to an overhanging finish, ducking left under an unstable roof/block.

ACB Don Mellor and John Wald 8/30/85

Battle Creek   I   5.10   80'   (s)

On the right side of the entrance to the descent gully, opposite *Pearly Gates,* is a right-slanting inside corner. Begin at a tree stump.

pitch 1 Climb the corner to a stance up right and follow a straight-in handcrack to the top. Walk back and scramble into the gully for descent.

FA John Bragg and Dave Cilley 1977

Certified Raw   I   5.10   150'   (s)

This route climbs the right-facing corner left of the more prominent *Phase Three*. The crux is the corner, but the rock above is frighteningly hollow.

FA Gary Allan 1978

Mother's Day Variation   I   5.9+   120'   (D)

This route climbs the easy initial section of *Phase Three* and heads left on flakes and thin cracks parallel to and left of the regular pitch.

FA John Bragg and Dave Cilley 1977

Phase Three   I   5.9   120'   (E)

This is the very obvious right-facing corner just left of the top of the approach trail. It is recognized by the overhang halfway up.

pitch 1 Climb easy rock to the crux overhang and finish the 3"–4" crack to the top.

FA Pat Munn and Dave Hough 7/75
FFA Gary Allen, Tom Schwarm, and Dave Hough

Bastard   I   5.11-   90'   (s)

pitch 1 Begin at the base of *Phase Three*. From left end of boulder-cave, climb through small roof and angle right to bolt. Face-climb to a stemming exit at *Ladder.* (Bolt missing.)

FA Dennis Luther and Joe Szot 7/88

Ladder   I   5.7   150'

pitch 1 This is the left-facing corner right of *Phase Three*. Climb up past a scrawny cedar. Join *Snake* to finish.

Discord   II   5.8   250'   (s)

This route begins a few feet right of where the approach trail meets the main face and climbs a series of right-facing flakes and corners up the black slab.

pitch 1 Angle up and left in grooves and easy rock to a belay at a tree. 5.4 50'

pitch 2 Climb up and out right on hollow flakes, exiting into a right-facing corner. Belay on a large ledge above. 5.8 100'

pitch 3 The dark corner above is often wet and usually avoided. It is reported to be free at about 5.8. 75'

FA Brian Rothery and Bob O'Brien 1958

A Womb with a View II 5.11 250' (s) †

Just right of *Discord* is a wide black slab leading to *Snake* traverse ledge. This route climbs the slab on its left side and breaches the impressively steep wall above.

pitch 1 Climb up steps toward the obvious right-facing flake/corner of *Discord*. Break out onto the slab past two bolts to a belay on *Snake* traverse. 5.9 150'

pitch 2 On the wall above is a huge right-facing dihedral. This is *Discord*. To its right is a smaller, steep, right-facing corner. Climb this to its top and step left to vertical cracks. At the bolt, head up and right to an unlikely and hard finish.

FA Don Mellor, Jeff Edwards, and Patrick Purcell 6/14/90

Bathtub Virgin 5.9 80' (D)

Right of the previous route slab is a thin crack. This is an alternate start to the Snake Ledge.

FA Jeff Edwards and Don Mellor 6/12/90

Garter II 5.7+ 200' (s)

This route breaks off right on a right-rising traverse line as an alternate finish to *Discord* or *Snake;* the route begins at the junction of these two. Two or three pitches across the large orange dike lead to the exit.

FA John Turner, Brian Rothery, and Peter Thompson 1960

Snake I 5.4 300' (s)

This is Poke-O's easiest climb. It ascends a left-rising traverse line across a dike under the steep walls above. Begin about 100' right of *Discord,* just before the trail heads downhill from the open area.

231

pitch 1 Climb to Snake Ledge by means of a vertical crack and friction. Belay at large trees. 5.4 75'

pitch 2 Traverse left across easier terrain to a belay at the corner or above.

pitch 3 Scramble off left towards the descent gully.

FA John Turner and John Brett 1957

The next series of routes begins from Snake Ledge, a tree-covered terrace that begins about 100' right of where the approach trail meets the rock. All are reached by climbing pitch 1 of Snake.

Slime Line   II   5.9+   200'   (s)   †

This route climbs the left-slanting groove in brown rock up the steep wall, 50' left of *Firing Line* above Snake Ledge. The climb is often wet. Otherwise, it is clean, sustained, and highly recommended. Don't let the name turn you away.

pitch 1 Same as for *Snake*. 5.4 75'

pitch 2 Traverse left a few feet and set up a suitable belay. From here, make a hard series of moves with no protection to gain the corner. Stretch the Achilles tendons up the sustained corner to a belay at the base of a corner. 5.9+ 120'

pitch 3 The final corner is steep and classic. 5.8

FA Geoff Smith and Drew Allan 9/78

Firing Line   I   5.11   100'   (E with 5.8 x start)   †

This is the very obvious towering left-facing corner seen from the open area right of the approach trail.

pitch 1 Same as for *Snake*. 5.4 75'

pitch 2 Wander up to the base of the corner 5.8. Climb the corner with excellent protection (5.11) and exit right or finish to the top of the corner. Join *Psychosis* or use that route's bolt for a short rappel to Snake Ledge.

FA   Jim Dunn, Geoff Smith, and Gary Allan 1977

Psychosis   II   5.9+   200'   (E)   †

This is the slanting layback corner facing left above Snake Ledge. It can be seen from the ground to the right of *Firing Line*. The rating continues to evoke argument: it has been followed by beginners and it has spit experienced leaders out into space. In other words, the difficulty of the moves isn't necessarily the difficulty of the lead.

pitch 1 Same as for *Snake*. 5.4 75'

pitch 2 Follow the slanting corner for about 50' to a belay/rappel or continue the line on easier rock to a belay on *Garter* dike.

pitch 3 Join *Garter*. 5.7+

FA Claude Lavallee and John Turner 1958
FFA Jim McCarthy and Richard Goldstone 1967

Microwave   II   5.10+   200'   (s)

This is the left-sweeping corner seen from the road parallel to and right of *Psychosis*. The route begins below the right end of a huge, left-rising flake atop Snake Ledge. The climb is invisible from below.

pitch 1 Same as for *Snake*. 5.4 75'

pitch 2 Climb to the fragile flake with no protection, and traverse left to its top. Face moves right lead (5.10+) to the major corner and a belay at rope's end under the roof high above. The two bolts above the flake provide protection for the crux traverse, but having been placed on the aid ascent for a tension traverse (5.8 A0), they aren't in the best position for free-climbing.

pitch 3 A short but strenuous pitch leads out the fistcrack roof. 5.1 25'

FA Geoff Smith, Pat Munn, and Dave Hough 9/76
FFA Geoff Smith and Gary Allan 1978

Remembering Youth   II   5.12   250'   (E)   †

An excellent route: steep, continuous, and spectacular. This is one of the prize routes at Poke-O.

pitch 1 Start down and left of The Pillar, gaining the ledge above the bulge. Belay here or continue up slab past a bolt, past overlap (two more bolts) to the belay at the right end of Snake Ledge, common with *Freedom Flight*. 5.9

pitch 2 Straight above is a vertical face with several bolts. Belay at base of overhanging right-facing corner. 70' 5.11

pitch 3 The unrelenting right-facing corner (mixed gear and bolts) is followed by a step right and an easier finish. 75' 5.12

FA Patrick Munn and Gary Allan 8/93

Forget Bullet   I   5.11   (s)

Gary Allan, known by his friends as Bullet, was instrumental in putting in the hardest routes of the late seventies. His annual sojourns back from his home in California have ensured that this route name will remain unlikely.

pitch 1 Gain Snake Ledge by any of several routes.

pitch 2 Start as neighboring routes at a bolt belay on the far right end of Snake Ledge. Follow the upper of two horizontal dikes right for 30' (quarter-inch bolt) to a groove that is climbed straight up to a belay. 65' 5.10 Some loose rock.

pitch 3 Climb to left-facing corner, stepping left at ramp into the finish corner of *Remembering Youth*. 80' 5.11

FA Gary Allan and Patrick Munn 8/91

Rattlesnake   II   5.10   250'   (s)

This is the serpentine flake that rises above Snake Ledge and is easily seen from the road. It stands on an alarmingly small base and is probably as unstable as it looks.

pitch 1 Same as for *Snake*. 5.4 75'

pitch 2 Same as first pitch of *Forget Bullet*.

pitch 3 Cross the slab right (quarter-inch bolt) to the base of the pillar. Climb the right side to a bolt belay at its top. 5.10

pitch 4 Easier rock scrambles to the trees.

FA Geoff Smith and Pat Munn 9/76

Freedom Flight   II   5.10   400'   (E)   †

Originally called Freedom Fighter, this route's name changed to fit a common outcome of the battle. It is one of the finest routes at Poke-O, combining a long, thin traverse with a 100' fingercrack up a blank face.

pitch 1 Same as for *Snake*. 5.4 75'

pitch 2 From the right end of Snake Ledge, traverse right over the void on

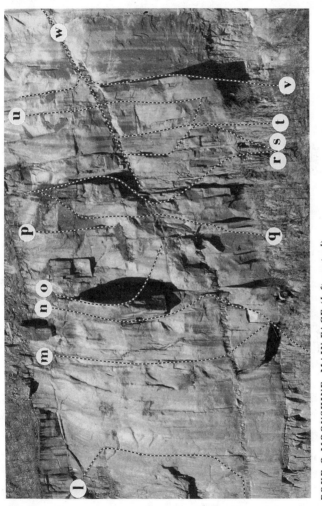

POKE-O-MOONSHINE: MAIN FACE (*left central*)

L. FREEDOM FLIGHT 5.10
M. SUMMER SOLSTICE 5.11-
N. WILD BLUE 5.11-
O. SKY TRAVERSE 5.8
P. SILVER STREAK 5.11
Q. HOMERUN DERBY 5.11
R. FM 5.7
S. BODY SNATCHER 5.9

T. THE SNATCH 5.10
U. KNIGHTS IN ARMOR 5.10+ A0
V. GREAT DIHEDRAL 5.9+
W. SPECTACULAR RISING TRAVERSE (SRT) 5.8

the lower of two horizontal dikes for 70'. From the third bolt, climb up (5.10) to the upper dike and continue to a belay at a small ledge.

pitch 3 Climb the left side of a very hollow flake to a stance. Step right into the fingercrack and belay just above the steep section. 5.10 100'

pitch 4 Unprotected but easier rock leads up and left to a final short corner. 5.6 140'

FA Geoff Smith and Dave Hough 9/76

Pillar I 5.7 70' (E)

This is the fragile finger of rock that leans against the cliff below and right of Snake Ledge. The grade applies to either side. Rappel or join *Superstition Traverse*.

Autumn Flare I 5.10+ (D) 70'

pitch 1 This is the serious route up the central groove on the face of *The Pillar*. It is infrequently led.

FA Gary Allan and Patrick Munn 1977

Superstition Traverse II 5.7 200' (S)

This line to nowhere crosses the large horizontal dike from the top of *The Pillar* to meet with the Nose Apron far to the right. Three pitches are required.

FA Geoff Smith, Gary Allan, and Dave Hough 10/75

Spooks I 5.11+ 70' (S)

This is the very thin crack line 18' right of *The Pillar*. Many tiny nuts and much skill in their use must be acquired before jumping on this one.

FA Alan Jolley and Bill Diemand 4/81
FFA Dave Lanman 8/87

The Howling I 5.12 70' (E) †

Right of *Spooks* by 8' is a thin bolted line that becomes a narrow, right-facing corner.

FA Dave Lanman 6/88

Salad Days   I   5.13-   100'   (s)   †

30' right of *Pillar* is a flaring left-facing corner on overhanging rock. It represents the hardest climbing yet done in the Adirondacks.

FA Dave Lanman 9/88

Pentecostal   5.12

This is a one-pitch bolted face on the sheerest part of the smooth wall right of the previous routes.

FA Gary Allan 8/92

Verdon   I   5.11   75'   (E)   †

At the very right end of the bulging blank wall is a steep, finger-ripping bolted face climb on tiny flakes and sharp holds.

FA Julien Dery and Pierre Gagnon 11/1/87

Right of the huge bulging wall and under the roof of Summer Solstice *is a lower angled slab with some bolted face climbs. This popular top-roping area is called the Nose Apron. The Nose is visible above and right.*

Homecoming   I   5.9   60'   (s)   †

This route traverses in from the right and climbs the right-facing corner past three bolts.

FA Geoff Smith, Dave Hough, and Pat Munn 8/76

Ukiah   I   5.9   60'   (s)

This is the line right of *Homecoming*. It is an intimidating lead for the grade. (Bolts missing.)

FA Geoff Smith and Mark Meschinelli 1977

Raindance   I   5.7+   60'   (D)

This is the left-facing corner just right of *Ukiah*.

Libido   I   5.11-   60'   (s)

On the slight bulging wall just right of *Ukiah* and *Raindance* is a good route with two bolts. The route climbs past a lower crux to a good ledge, finishing more easily to the trees.

FA Julien Dery 8/18/85

Snake Slide   I   5.7 or 5.8   60'   (E)

This is the left-facing corner toward the right end of the Nose Apron.

Scorpion   I   5.11-   50'   (S)

This is the thin crack right of the *Snake Slide* corner. Begin atop boulders. (These rocks, by the way, were once the undercling second pitch of *Wild Blue,* which fell in Spring 1987. A sobering thought indeed.)

FA Jim Dunn 7/78

Rodeo Man   III   5.10+   A2   400'

This rarely-done route begins above the Nose Apron and climbs left under the big roof and up the left-facing corner.

pitch 1 Climb up to the roof, aid left and up to a tree.

pitch 2 From this point a lasso maneuver was used to reach the upper corner.

pitch 3 Continue in the corner to join *Summer Solstice.*

pitch 4 Follow *Solstice* (5.10+) to the top.

FA Geoff Smith, Dave Hough, and Gary Allan 9/75

Summer Solstice   III   5.11-   400'   (S)   †

This climb is regarded as one of Poke-O's best, requiring a full repertoire of climbing skills. It challenges the climber with a strenuous roof, several sections of thin face climbing, and a spectacular, steep offwidth crack. The route is identified from below as the huge, red overhanging corner above the right end of the Nose Apron. Approach via *Snake Slide* or traverse in easily from the right.

pitch 1 Climb broken rock to the overhanging left-facing dihedral that breaches the huge roof above. Climb out right and belay in slings just above. Dunn: "5.10+++" 50'

pitch 2 Climb up and across the blank face left to a belay at a tree. 5.10-70' *pitch 3* The offwidth above leads to a sloping stance or, by stretching the pitch, a belay high above at a good ledge. 5.9+ 150'

pitch 4 Climb the thin crack past a bulge (5.10+ quarter-inch bolt with RP back-up nearby) to an easy but unprotected finish in the trees. 150'

FA Geoff Smith and Jim Dunn 1977

Wild Blue   III   5.11-   400'   (s)   †

The sister route to *Solstice,* this too calls for every technique in the book. It is highly recommended and really demanding.

pitch 1 Same as for *Summer Solstice.* 5.11- 50'

pitch 2 This was once a superb undercling/layback pitch known as *Shakey Flakes.* The name was prophetic indeed: a large section broke away, leaving a prominent 15' x 15' scar. The rerouted pitch face climbs right to a bolt, then runs it out (5.10) to the corner above, traversing right under the pillar, climbing its right side, and belaying at its top. The two old bolts should be backed up with chocks off right.

pitch 3 Face-climb up and left to a belay in the corner formed by the left side of the Nose, the huge block that dominates the upper central part of the cliff. 5.9 80'

pitch 4 Climb a fistcrack up the wall of the Nose itself and into a 20' flaring, sharp-edged, overhanging offwidth crack. Sounds fun, doesn't it? Belay at a large, tree-covered ledge. 5.10 75'

pitch 5 Step right out into the void to the edge of the Nose. A hidden handcrack leads up the ridge to the top. 5.9 100'

pitch 6 Cross the gap back onto the cliff proper and climb wet, grassy rock to the top. 75'

FA The history of this route is a long one. Dave Hough and Mark Meschinelli aided the now nonexistent pitch and the thin cracks right of the offwidth. Geoff Smith and Dave Hough free-climbed the fallen undercling in 5/78. (If you can find it at the base of *Scorpion,* try it. It was a superb pitch.) Steve Larson and Don Mellor free-climbed the upper pitches as described on 6/13/83. Pierre Gagnon and Gelu Ionescu resurrected the route after the rockfall by placing a bolt on the fresh scar and climbing through to the pillar 6/87.

Home Run Derby   II   5.11   400'   (s)   †

Between *FM* and *Summer Solstice* is a sharp vertical pillar with dihedrals on either side that mirror each other. This route follows the left corner, and would be the obvious direct start to *Silver Streak*.

pitch 1 Up easy, unprotected rock to the difficult left-facing corner. From its top, face-climb out right past bolt (difficult clip), then up crack line to dike belay (or continue right to Triangle Ledge 145'). 5.11.

pitch 2 Face-climb back left to obvious left-facing flake, then up slab and loose crack to huge grassy ledge. 5.9

pitch 3 Join *FM*.

FA Don Mellor, Jeff Edwards, and Bill Dodd 6/30/89

Karmic Kickback I 5.11 140' †

pitch 1 The right side of the previously described pillar offers another good route. Start about 75' right of the Nose, and 50' left of *FM*. Up past bolts to join the higher crux of *Homerun Derby*.

FA Gary Allan and Patrick Munn 8/91

FM II 5.7 400' (s) †

Even with its loose rock and dangerous sections, the *FM* route is a Poke-O classic. It was the first major route on the main face, and it continues to be popular, offering varied climbing and several interesting problems. The name of the route originated on the first ascent when Hugh Tanton stepped on a block on *pitch 4* which broke loose, leaving him hanging from Turner's belay. Tanton screamed "____me!" Most people see the crux as being the insecure step on *pitch 2*, but this is by no means the only challenge this fine route has to offer. Begin about 100' right of the Nose, in a shallow depression at the top of the hill (about 75' left of the *Great Dihedral*).

pitch 1 Climb broken dike rock in the back of a broad alcove to a left-facing corner that leads to a good ledge belay. 5.6 60'

pitch 2 Climb up a few feet into the left-facing corner above and traverse a small ledge left, around an outside corner and up toward a loose slot. Struggle up and left past a loose flake, finally traversing up and left to a superb belay, the Triangle Ledge. 5.7 100'

pitch 3 Hard moves up the corner (or more easily, out left onto the face) lead to a narrow ramp that snakes up right to a belay on loose rock in the major, forbidding corner. 5.7 100'

PHOTO BY MARK MESCHINELLI

Ann Eastman on the second pitch of FM.

pitch 4 Climb this corner past an enormous hollow flake, finally emerging out left before climbing to the trees. 5.7 100'

pitch 5 An easier scramble brings one to the top. 5.2 50'

FA John Turner and Hugh Tanton 6/57
FFA (crux traverse move) Claude Lavallee and Michael Ward 1957
(Michael Ward was the expedition doctor for the successful 1953 Everest first ascent.)

There are numerous variations to the FM *route:*

FM Direct   5.9   150' (E)

This is an alternate start that bypasses the first two pitches. Left of the normal start is a large right-facing flake/crack that leads to a fingercrack on the wall above. This long pitch joins the Triangle Ledge belay.

FA Geoff Smith and Dave Hough 9/78

Sky Traverse   I   5.8   100'   (x)

This is the wild climb up the bridge of The Nose. Although it can be reached by rappel, it is really a variation finish to the routes below (*Wild Blue, FM* or *FM Direct*). This is a good route, but a serious lead.

pitch 1 From the ledge on the right side of the Nose, traverse out and up over flakes to the crest. Follow a thin crack to the top.

FA Geoff Smith and Pat Munn 9/76

Nose Traverse   5.7

From the Triangle Ledge belay weave a line across the face to the left, joining the Nose. Finish *Sky Traverse* or continue up the hideous corner formed by the Nose and the main face.

Silver Streak   5.11

This is the vertical crack that runs up the wall to the top of the cliff right of the Nose. It is distinguished by the white, chalk-like deposits clearly seen from the road. It's hard, but not as appealing as it looks from below.

FA Gary Allan and Dave Hough 10/76

Spectacular Rising Traverse (SRT)   5.8

Instead of finishing up the major dihedral at the top of the *FM,* it is possible

PHOTO BY MARK MESCHINELLI

One of Poke-O's most spectacular positions: the bridge of the Nose.

PHOTO BY MARK MESCHINELLI

The committing Sky Traverse. *Climber: Patrick Munn.*

to traverse right along a rising dike for two pitches. The left-facing corner finish at the end of the traverse is a good one, but careful rope management is required to climb up and out left at the corner's top. Alternatively, one can continue under the roof system to an overhanging and bottomless chimney. Originally, this was a double jamcrack formed by a block. After many ascents, the block dropped out in the late seventies, creating the present finish; and even this is fairly unstable and scary. Like so many other examples at Poke-O and elsewhere, this can only remind us of the dynamics of the landscape and the temporary surface upon which we tread. No doubt future climbers will read this guide and search in vain for features on the cliff that we now climb and depend on. "Solid as a rock": Whoever coined this phrase never climbed.

Body Snatcher   II   5.9   250'   (E)

Right of *FM* and just before the trail drops downhill is an attractive left-facing corner about 60' up. This route approaches from the left, and climbs out just right of the main corner into a smaller, hidden corner.

pitch 1   Traverse a rising line from the left to the base of the corner. Head out right at a block and follow the small corner up to a long traverse left and a belay behind giant blocks. 5.9 150' This pitch is usually split.

pitch 2   From the stance behind the blocks, climb a long right-facing corner to the *SRT* line.

pitch 3+   Finish *FM* or *SRT*. 5.8 100'

FA John Turner and Wilfried Twelker 1960
FFA John Stannard 1968

The Snatch   II   5.10   250'   (E)   †

This is the direct line up the attractive corner of *Body Snatcher*. Begin 45' left of the *Great Dihedral* at a vertical crack.

pitch 1   Climb a handcrack in dike rock directly below the corner; follow the crack to the top of the dihedral and handtraverse left to the huge block belay. 5.9 140'

pitch 2   Reverse the traverse back right and climb the magnificent left-facing dihedral above. 5.10 100'

pitch 3+   Join *FM* or *SRT*.

Variation **Snatch It** 5.9   An alternate second pitch to *Body Snatcher* or

245

The Snatch climbs the thin crack line up the face between those two routes.

FA Gary Allan, Geoff Smith and Pat Munn 1977
FA Dominic Eisinger, Mike Wray, and Anthony Smith 8/91 (var.)

Knights in Armor II 5.10+ A0 450' (E) †

This route has been long in the conception and creation. Its main feature is the incredible fingercrack left of *Great Dihedral*. Getting there proved to be another story. It was originally solo-aid-climbed (A4) out the roof. This dangerous approach will see few takers. Later, rappelling in from above became the norm for the few ascents that this climb saw. Now, it can be approached more sensibly from the ground, and with the addition of a final pitch, it is now a full-length route.

pitch 1 Same as for *The Snatch* to *Body Snatcher* block belay out right. 5.9 80'

pitch 2 Traverse directly right to the base of the fingercrack; this involves tension, hammerless aid, clawing, dangling, etc. A0 40'

pitch 3 No doubt, this is one of the best fingercracks at Poke-O. Belay 100' above. (same as for *Great Dihedral*.) 5.10+

pitch 4 Directly above is a crack system that starts from loose blocks. The climbing is hardest down low on this pitch. 5.8 150'

FA Pat Munn (roped solo, winter 1977)
FA as described Patrick Munn and Don Mellor 9/9/88
FFA Gary Allan 10/78 (p.2)

Great Dihedral

II 5.9+ 450' (E or D with the direct finish) †

Few pitches at Poke-O are more obvious or enticing; this is the right-facing corner that seems to go on forever left of the open, grassy area of *Positive Thinking*. Although the corner itself has endless good nut placements, the traverse of pitch 3 is quite committing; many parties opt for the *SRT*.

pitch 1 Climb cracks and blocks through dike rock to a belay hidden in a niche below the roof. 5.8 100'

pitch 2 Hard moves and Houdini work lead to the main corner.

pitch 3 The original route climbed the *SRT* dike to the right for two or three

Dick Bushey follows Great Dihedral.

PHOTO BY MARK MESCHINELLI

pitches. The direct finish heads right about 15' before angling back over the belay with no protection to a bolt. Face-climb (5.8) past the bolt to an easier finish. It is also possible to walk left a few feet and climb *pitch 4* of *Knights in Armor.*

FA Geoff Smith and Dave Hough 10/75
FFA Richard Goldstone and Ivan Rezucha 7/76
FA Geoff Smith and Dave Hough 8/76 (p.3)

Changing of the Guard   I   5.9+

The sharp edge of *Great Dihedral* had long attracted notice. It is one of the area's most striking aretes.

pitch 1 Same as for previous route.

pitch 2 After escaping from the hole at the bottom of the corner of *Great Dihedral,* break left onto the bolted arete.

FA Patrick Purcell and Gary Allan 8/93

Sea of Seams   III   5.8   A3 (or 5.12+)   450'

Formerly an aid route, this line now has some hard free climbing. Begin by climbing to the top of the pillar of *Half Mile.* Combined with *Sea Tips,* the route is even more continuous.

pitch 3 From the top of the pillar, climb up left heading for a loose flake. Continue right, then up to a sling belay. 5.12+

pitch 4 Follow a line of bolts to the *SRT.* 5.12

pitch 5 Finish either of the two 5.8 *SRT* options.

FA Dave Hough and Mark Meschinelli 11/78
ACB Gary Allen and Patrick Munn 8/93

Half Mile   III   5.7   600'   (s)

This is a long natural line that follows the largest of Poke-O's dikes from left to right. Though the general line is clear, the specific line leaves route-finding decisions to the leader. Begin below *Great Dihedral,* just before the trail drops to the low, open, grassy area under *Positive Thinking.*

pitch 1 Wander up and right to a belay at the left-facing corner at the base of the pillar. 5.4 75'

pitch 2 Climb up to the top of the rock, then either down-climb, rappel, or lower to a belay at the other side. 5.6 80' The second can pendulum here to avoid the climbing. (Alternatively, an exposed 5.9 traverse leads around the base of the pillar.)

pitch 3 Harder face moves (5.6) lead up and across to a large belay ledge beneath the huge cave of *Positive Thinking*.

pitch 4 One more horizontal pitch leads to *Gamesmanship*.

pitch 5 Climb up broken dike rock, heading for a tree-covered ledge below a prominent white birch. 5.4 100'

pitch 5 The crux handcrack leads up the outside of the block to the very obvious white birch and up to a belay near rope's end. 5.7

pitch 6 An easy, unprotected slab ends at the woods. 5.1 150'

FA John Turner and Claude Lavallee 1958

Sea Tips I 5.10+ 120' (E) †

This and the next route are excellent, bolt-protected face climbs up the black wall. They end at rappel stations on the *Half Mile* dike.

pitch 1 From the top of the hill, traverse out right along a ramp and up the steep wall above.

FA Patrick Purcell and Mark Meschinelli 1991

Mogster I 5.12 165' (S) †

A parallel route right of *Sea Tips*. Begin down and right at the bottom of the hill.

pitch 1 Follow a line of widely-spaced bolts that gains the ramp of the previous route and breaches the unrelenting wall above the *Son of Slime* slab bolt.

FA Dave Lanman 7/92

Son of Slime II 5.10 500' (S)

Some of Poke-O's best climbing is on the wet walls. In summer, routes like *Bushido,* on the waterfall face, become dry and clean. The deep chocolate rock is rough and textured, and the climbing is excellent. This route is perhaps the best of the bunch. It climbs directly up the *Positive Thinking* ice route itself, just left of the summer hand- and fistcrack. Begin uphill to the left.

249

pitch 1 Traverse the upper of two broad ramps out right. A bolt en route protects the hardest move. Set up a semihanging belay at the end of the traverse. 5.9+ 75'

pitch 2 Fascinating climbing up waterworn rock ends on the huge traverse dike. There are two bolts (the first, quarter-inch, 1984, is a joke) along the way. The run-out from the second bolt (three-eighths, 1988) is breathtaking but secure. 5.9

pitch 3 Straight above is the third pitch. Climb the dike left of the *Positive Thinking* cave pitch, past some loose rocks, to gain the left-facing flakes and corners. Face climb past a bolt (five-sixteenths, 1988) and traverse left to a good stance.

pitch 4 Climb up to the bottomless (and unstable) chimney to the top. 5.8 150'

FA Mark Meschinelli, Pat Munn, and Ann Eastman 8/88

Positive Thinking I 5.9

Better known as an ice route, this line follows the single hand-/fistcrack on the right side of the smooth wall. Only the first pitch is described here. The original route climbed the cave above to the top, but this is rumored to have been altered by rockfall. No recent reports exist on this upper section. Begin at the open grassy area.

pitch 1 Climb the crack to the large ledge 5.9 165' (E)

FA John Turner and Dick Wilmott 1959

P.T. Pillar I 5.8 100' (E)

pitch 1 A left-facing corner stands just right of *Positive Thinking* as a one-pitch climb.

Dave Hough and Geoff Smith 5/78

Macho I 5.11 90' (s) †

pitch 1 Just right of the *PT Pillar* corner is a superb fingercrack. Begin by face-climbing steeply from the lower left end of the long ledge system that runs across to the top of *The Sting*. This is a recommended and challenging climb that requires control, especially on the lower half. (Bolts missing.)

FA Julien Dery 6/7/86

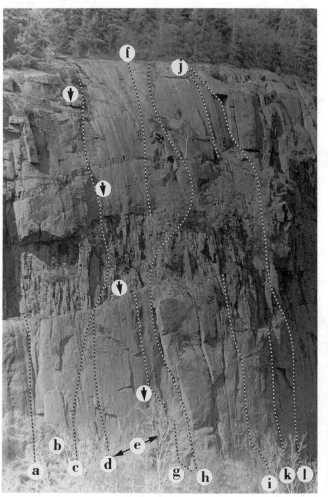

POKE-O-MOONSHINE: MAIN FACE (*central*)

A. POSITIVE THINKING 5.9

B. P.T. PILLAR

C. COONEY-NORTON FACE 5.10

D. COSMOPOLITAN WALL

E. STING LEDGE (arrows show central rappel route)

F. TRUE GRIT 5.11

G. THE STING (5.8) TO RAGTIME (5.10+)

H. GAMESMANSHIP 5.8

I. SOUTHERN HOSPITALITY 5.11+

J. GOOMBAY FINISH 5.10

K. BLOODY MARY 5.9

L. FASTEST GUN 5.10

P.T. Pillar Right   I   5.8   90'   (E)

The right-facing corner of the *PT Pillar* block is usually grass-filled and not too inspiring.

FA Patrick Purcell and Mark Meschinelli 4/19/91

To the right of this route rises a huge flake ledge that provides access to several routes on the upper face and was originally the indirect start to Gamesmanship. *It is known as Sting Ledge. 4th class*

Cooney–Norton Face   II   5.10   450'   (s)   †

On the blank wall right of *Positive Thinking* is a series of slanting slashes. Most climbs with names like these commemorate the first ascent party; this one celebrates a heavy-weight title fight. Yet most climbers find it more a pleasure than a battle.

pitch 1 Begin on the left end of Sting Ledge. Stem two shallow corners facing each other before heading up right on the slashes. Two bolts protect the crux face moves left to the dike. 5.10 160'

pitch 2 Traverse up and right across the dike to a block belay. 100'

pitch 3 Climb up and left to a flaring corner, breaking through to the slab above, passing by the fixed slings of the Central Rappel Route.

FA Mark Meschinelli, Dave Hough, and Todd Eastman 7/82

Cosmopolitan Wall   I   5.10   80'   (s)   †

pitch 1 Begin part way across Sting Ledge, the left-to-right rising flake system between *Positive Thinking* and *Gamesmanship*. Climb thin cracks and a shallow left-facing corner to a small roof. Continue up and slightly left to finish with *Cooney–Norton,* or break right via a bolted face (5.11 Gary Allen).

History Gary Allen, Geoff Smith, and Dave Hough climbed the good lower section in 1975; the upper section joining *Cooney–Norton* was completed later.

Unnamed   I   5.11   140'   (D)

From the middle of Sting Ledge, follow a sharp-edged, hard crack into a shallow right-facing, hollow corner. Bolts lead up a headwall to the traverse dike of *Half Mile*.

Central Rappel Route

1. Start 150' down and left of the top of *Gamesmanship* at a large pine (slings) below a block. Rappel to two bolts and a foothold stance straight below. 100'
2. Straight down to the dike ledge of *Half Mile* and two bolts. 90'
3. From anchor, straight down sheer wall (between *Ragtime* and *Unnamed* 5.11) to Sting Ledge. 165'
4. Stay connected to rappel rope and tip-toe left to left end of Sting Ledge or rappel 75' to ground, just left of *The Sting*.

Below Sting Ledge are four short routes.

Two parallel (and grass-filled) unnamed cracks mark the left end of the wall directly below *Cosmopolitan Wall,* gaining Sting Ledge below the previous routes. The left is 5.9; the right is 5.11.

Excitable Boy   A2   60'

The thin crack that starts from a 5' cave.

FA Tad Welch (roped solo) 9/30/84

Save the Rock for Uncle Sam   5.12   (top-rope)

An extreme face climb about 35' left of *Gamesmanship.*

FA Julien Dery 6/88

Ragtime   I   5.10+   250'   (s)   †

This is a logical extension to *The Sting,* climbing the wall left of *pitch 2* of *Gamesmanship.*

pitch 1 Follow *The Sting* up and left to a ledge belay (bolts). 5.8 150'

pitch 2 Climb past a bolt and thin flake. The climactic finish of this pitch involves a crux mantel to a second bolt. 5.10+ 100'

pitch 3 From the *Half Mile* traverse dike, rappel or join *Gamesmanship* or *True Grit,* etc.

FA Patrick Munn and Dominic Eisinger 1987

True Grit   5.11   (s)

Combined with *Ragtime* from below, this would make a logical and excellent, sustained linkup. The route as described climbs the sheer wall left of upper *Gamesmanship.*

pitch 3 From the top of *Ragtime,* at the huge dike ledge, climb up right through dike and belay near the top of the dike at a ratty fixed anchor. Back it up.

pitch 4 Climb a mixed gear/bolted face (visible from *Gamesmanship*) to a two-bolt belay.

pitch 5 5.9 face (tricky protection) leads to the top.

FA Dennis Luther and Steve Bailey 7/20/91

The Sting   I   5.8   75'   (E)   †

pitch 1 About 100' right of the large, open, grassy area that is the annual bomb zone from the falling ice of *Positive Thinking* are two parallel handcracks. This route climbs the left-hand crack by traversing in on a fingertip crack from the left. Above, join *Gamesmanship* via 5.6 face climbing, or traverse (4th class) left across Sting Ledge to the ground.

FA Geoff Smith, Gary Allan, and Dave Hough 8/75

Gamesmanship   II   5.8   500'   (E)   †

A continuous and direct line, this route is one of Poke-O's finest; its first pitch has few peers. Begin at the bent "belay seat" tree. Traversing into the route from Sting Ledge creates a sustained 5.7 to the top of the cliff. British alpinist Doug Scott, after a long career of some of the most daring climbing in history, was recently heard muttering angrily at the base of the route that the rockfall that just missed him from the above was as close as he'd ever been to getting killed.

pitch 1 Getting off the ground is the technical crux of the route. Climb the right-hand vertical handcrack for a seemingly endless pitch of jamming to a small stance with pitons. 5.8 140'

pitch 2 Join a left-facing corner system above and belay at the ledges of the *Half Mile* traverse dike. 5.7 120'

pitch 3 Broken rock through the dike must be handled carefully. Angle up and right to a belay at trees under the left-facing corner. 5.4 100' *pitch 4* Step right to the block's outside face and climb a pure handcrack to the obvious white birch (easily seen from the road) that grows above. Belay at rope's end at bushy ledge. 5.7 140'

pitch 5 Easy, unprotected slabs lead to the trees. 5.1 150' (D)

FA John Turner, Brian Rothery, and Wilfried Twelker 1959

Gamesmanship Direct Finish

The huge left-facing corner above *pitch 3* is 5.8.

fa Gary Allan and Dave Hough 1975

Southern Hospitality   II   5.11+   300'   (E)   †

This route began as a winter aid climb that ended high on the blank wall right of *Gamesmanship*. Piece by piece, the climb has been freed to the main dike line. It is now one of the best and most demanding routes on the cliff.

pitch 1 About 60' right of *Gamesmanship* is a short fingercrack. At its top, traverse left to a roof move and a small stance. 5.11 60' Alternatively, climb straight up from the crack (bolts), joining the original route about 40' above the roof. (5.11+)

pitch 2 Follow the crack up until an unlikely traverse leads to the right-hand crack and a good belay. 5.10 75'

pitch 3 The crack above becomes increasingly difficult until a traverse takes one left to the prominent finish corner. 5.11+ 75'

pitch 4 A pitch of lesser difficulty and quality passes the bolts of the old route's high point and ends on the dike. 5.8 100' (s)

pitch 5 It may make more sense to rappel here. To finish, however, climb really loose blocks to join upper *Fastest Gun* or *Gamesmanship*.

History Geoff Smith and Mark Meschinelli aided most of the route in a midwinter siege (2/76). (Meschinelli, during a solo ascent, broke a quarter-inch belay bolt by simply loading it with body weight, leaving him hanging from a single small bolt.) Later, Smith, Gary and Drew Allan free-climbed the first pitch (9/78). Don Mellor and Patrick Purcell pushed the route through to its top using one point of aid (1987). Martin Berzins and A. Gale freed that one move in 1989 (5.12 bolt missing). The current line with its higher traverse on pitch 3 was established by Patrick Munn in 1990.

Patrick Purcell solo on The Sting.

PHOTO BY MARK MESCHINELLI

Psalm 32   II   5.12   (A0)   †

This route climbs open rock just right of *Southern Hospitality*. Two good pitches lead to a very hard series of moves. *Psalm 32* is the song of forgiveness, though high on the route, you'll be pleading for mercy.

pitch 1 Start right of the previous route in a dike near the right end of the wall. Follow weakness past bolts to a higher dike. Belay or head right 10' to a ledge below a roof and a bolt belay. 5.11 60'

pitch 2 Pass the roof on the left and follow bolts to arete and a higher belay at a small ledge. 5.12 90'

pitch 3 Follow shallow right-facing corner to headwall. So far, about 10' remains to be free-climbed.

FA Patrick Munn and Dominic Eisinger summer '94

Bloody Mary   II   5.9   500'   (E)   †

100' right and up around the corner from *Gamesmanship* is a flaring high dihedral with a curving crack on its right wall. For more than 15 years, this stood as the hardest route in the Adirondacks.

pitch 1 Climb a broken corner to a belay below the corner proper. 5.6 50'

pitch 2 This pitch is a gem. Sustained, but never desperate, climbing leads up the corner and wall on the left to a small, semihanging stance in the corner above. 5.9 100'

pitch 3 Climb the tight dihedral to a belay on easier rock. 5.8 75'

pitch 4, 5, and 6 Scramble over loose rock, left to join *Gamesmanship* (5.7), or right to meet *Fastest Gun* (5.10).

FA John Turner, Dick Strachan, and Dick Wilmott 1959

Gun Control   I   5.11   100'   (s)

This is a one-pitch climb that joins *Fastest Gun*. Begin 20' left of that route.

pitch 1 Climb a right-facing corner to a seam; traverse right to the thin, sharp crack. Join the corner above and continue past a prominent birch to the block belay atop pitch 1 of *Fastest Gun*.

FA Mack Johnson and Paul Boissonneault 9/3/88

Fastest Gun   III   5.10   500'   (E)   †

Taken separately, each pitch of this route would be considered among

Poke-O's best. Linked together they create an experience that seems too good to be in the East.

pitch 1 Climb the obvious right-facing flake/crack behind a large tree about 60' right of *Bloody Mary* and about 150' right of *Gamesmanship*. From the top of the corner, traverse left and up to a belay atop the blocks. 5.9 100'

pitch 2 The twin cracks just left snake upwards, past a roof/slot to the broken dike. Belay here or continue up and slightly left to a flake/ledge just above the dike. 5.9 140'

pitch 3 Climb a thin crack on the right on good rock past a quarter-inch bolt (5.9+) and run the rope out to the base of the large left-facing corner capped by a roof. 165'

pitch 4 A hard roof move leads to the corner. Exit left past unstable flakes and up to the top. 5.10- 150' (Exit right 5.10 below the roof is possible.)

Variation **Goombay Finish** 5.10 (s) 150' The steep slab left of the prominent final corner of *Fastest Gun* is marked by thin vertical cracks, each actually a shallow right-facing corner. The right one is a black seam that is probably unclimbed. *Goombay* takes the middle crack.

Variation **McCarthy Offwidth** 5.10 It is also possible to climb the offwidth crack right of the corner (the other side of the towering block). This 1960s lead was one of the most impressive of the era.

FA Geoff Smith and Dick Bushey 1/77 (p.1 & 2)

FA Jim Dunn 1978 (p.3 & 4)

FA Don Mellor and Bill Dodd 1990 (var. 1)

FA Jim McCarthy (var. 2)

Pinhead I 5.9+ 60'

pitch 1 About 20' right of the obvious *Fastest Gun* crack and 8' left of *The Cooler* is a right-facing corner with a triangular roof 15' up. Unfinished.

FA Mark Meschinelli

FFA Todd Swain and John Thackray 7/85

The Cooler III 5.8 600' (s)

Just before walking under the Big Wall section, Poke-O's highest vertical

POKE-O-MOONSHINE: MAIN FACE (*right central*)

I. PSALM 32 5.12 A0

K. BLOODY MARY 5.9

L. FASTEST GUN 5.10

M. THE COOLER 5.8

N. THE GATHERING 5.11

O. SAILOR'S DIVE 5.11

P. MESSIAH 5.12

Q. IT DON'T COME EASY 5.11

R. SNOW BLUE 5.11

wall, one passes a right-facing corner/chimney. This is *The Cooler,* an ominous slot from which refrigerated breezes pour, even in summer. This seldom-done route demands varied techniques, route-finding sense, and even a dash of courage.

pitch 1 A short, tree-filled lead ends at a ledge below the crack. 40'

pitch 2 Climb the chimney/groove to the dike ledge. 5.8 150'

pitch 3 Head up and right through the dike, passing a really scary wedged flake. Belay on a good ledge under a roof up and left. 5.8 80'

pitch 4, etc. Hand-traverse out left from under the roof and head up left to join *Gamesmanship.* 350'

FA John Turner and Dick Strachan 1961

The Gathering IV 5.11 500' (E) †

This is an outstanding long free climb, not to be missed. Start 20' right of *The Cooler* at a shallow left-facing corner that leads to a large right-facing corner.

pitch 1 Climb to the right-facing corner about 25' up (tricky protection). Follow corner through bulge (bolt); traverse left to another right-facing corner and up to a belay. 5.10 60'

pitch 2 Straight up to bolt (hard), then right-facing corner to block/roof. Traverse right under roof and up to belay. 5.11 85'

pitch 3 Traverse right into another right-facing corner, up through dike to belay. 5.9 75'

pitch 4 The face pitch follows bolts up and left under overlap to a left-facing corner. Up corner, out right at overhang, and up left side of the block to good ledge. 5.11 75'

pitch 5 A huge right-facing corner ends at a large ledge. 5.9 60'

pitch 6 Up left on slab to deep left-facing corner and bolt belay above. 5.9 40'

pitch 7 It is possible to finish via obvious line of weakness, but it is preferable to rappel from this point.

FA Patrick Munn and Dominic Eisinger 9/93

Extreme Unction I 5.11 A0 175' (E)

Start as for *Sailor's Dive,* the long, left-to-right rising staircase. The route finishes part-way up the wall; rappel or join *The Gathering pitch 3*.

pitch 1 Up a left-rising line to gain a right-facing corner. Belay at bolts. 5.7 60'

pitch 2 The corner leads to left-facing corner and then up right following bolts. Reaching for the final bolt is the "last right" of the climb.

pitch 3 This links with the previous route for those in need of further annointing.

FA Patrick Munn and Dominic Eisinger 9/93

Sailor's Dive   IV   5.11   500'   (s)   †

This is a really good big-wall free climb. In the middle of the sheer, dark Big Wall section (up and right of the corners of *Bloody Mary, Fastest Gun,* and *The Cooler*) are two black, flaring corners, the upper of which being above and left of the first. Call all of your friends and borrow their RPs.

pitch 1 About 60' right of *Fastest Gun*, a right-rising dike pitch ends below a horrifying flake. 5.7 75'

pitch 2 Traverse left across the face to gain the crux right-facing corner. At its top, head left to a belay (three one-quarter-inch bolts, 1976) or continue (5.10) up the second corner to a belay at a sloping ledge in dike rock below the "orange shield." 5.11 140'

pitch 3 Exit the roof above on the left and climb the right-facing corner to a roof move at a block at a left-facing corner. Belay here or continue out right to an open and sloping ledge. 5.10 140'

pitch 4 Slightly right are twin cracks that end in a low-angled, left-facing corner. 5.9 60'

pitch 5 The easy corner ends at a tricky exit move right. Scramble to the top. 5.11 100'

FA Dave Hough, Mark Meschinelli, and Geoff Smith Dec.–Jan. 1976
FFA Don Mellor, Patrick Purcell, and Mike Heintz 5/87

Calvary Hill   II   5.12   250'   (E)   †

On the sheer wall right of *Sailor's Dive* are two awesome routes. Locate the prominent pillar of *It Don't Come Easy,* the most obvious feature in the central part of this section of the wall. It begins about 150' up and runs a full pitch up the cliff. Start 40' left at a thin vertical seam. Supplement rack with RPs.

pitch 1 Head up seam, eventually heading left on a good ledge to the dike (or straight up to the dike), then right to belay at base of Pillar. 5.12 90'

pitch 2 Climb up left into a short right-facing corner, to a left-facing corner, gaining fingercrack, then up and right to the top of the Pillar. 5.12 100'

pitch 3+ Join one of the next two routes or rappel.

FA Patrick Munn, Dominic Eisinger, Mark Meschinelli (p.1)
FA Patrick Munn and Bill Dodd 1992 (p.2)

Messiah   IV   5.12   500'   (s)   †

This route is simply amazing. Pitch after pitch of hard, varied, thought-provoking climbing combine to make it one of the East's hardest long routes. Combined with the first two pitches of *Calvary Hill,* it is unquestionably the finest long-route achievement so far in the Adirondacks. Start below pillar.

pitch 1 Face-climb past bolts to a belay at the base of the pillar. The last bolt move is quite hard. 5.12 90'

pitch 2 Up the left side of the pillar. A full rack, including much hand-sized gear required. Some stacked blocks. 5.9

pitch 3 Known as the Crystal Traverse, this pitch climbs left from pillar, staying low (bolt misplaced), and up to left end of arch to gain the large right-facing corner. Belay at large block.

pitch 4 Up the corner, then ramp leading across right to double finger-cracks (these are passed from the other direction on *It Don't Come Easy*). Up fingercracks, traverse right to a slot, then up to a stance.

pitch 5 Battle the fistcrack through a downwardly inclined roof directly above to a ledge at base of left-facing corner. 5.12 (roof free-climbed with a hang—awaits clean lead).

pitch 6 Up corner to grassy ledge, then left to finger flake. Belay or continue slabs up and left to rim.

FA Patrick Munn and Geoff Smith 1991

Foreplay   I   5.11   140'   (E)

This is a superior start to the next route.

pitch 1 Directly below the right side of the pillar is a small right-facing corner with a piton. Continue a short layback, then left on steep rock to a belay.

pitch 2 Above the dike are two bolts and face-climbing to the base of the right side of the pillar.

FA Dennis Luther, Dave and Joe Szot, and Tom Yandon

It Don't Come Easy   IV   5.10+   500'   (E)

Even though this is easier than its neighbors to the left, this route still doesn't "come easy"; instead, it throws challenge upon challenge, each different from the last, and only the most persistent top out. The main feature of the route is the pillar that runs up the right-center of the big, steep wall. Start at a black chimney 12' right of the surveyor's benchmark in the wall.

pitch 1 Belay about 100' up and well right of the column's base. 5.9+

pitch 2 A slightly descending traverse along the dike leads left to the pillar. 5.4

pitch 3 A sensational pitch up the right side of the column continues through a brief off-sized section, steps left and follows a groove to one of Poke-O's most spectacular belays. 5.10- 140'

pitch 4 Face-climb up right past two bolts (quarter-inch, 1976) to broken cracks, ending at a roof. Crux face moves straight left; end at a sheltered belay. 5.10+ 100'

pitch 5 Turn the "coffin" block on the right (if you dare), and head for the top. 5.9 150'

FA Geoff Smith and Pat Munn (Aid was used to
clean the route of some huge, unstable blocks.) 9/76
FFA Geoff Smith, Gary Allen, and Dave Hough 1978

Snow Blue   IV   5.11   600'   (E)

A long and a bit devious (read *tedious*), this route has one outstanding pitch: the fingercrack on the narrow buttress right of *It Don't Come Easy*.

pitch 1 Right of the benchmark at the base of *It Don't Come Easy* and left of the broken rock in the *Worse Than Real* area is a flaring, right-facing dihedral. 5.8 75'

pitch 2 There are two options here: the first and original is reserved for those who trust large hollow flakes. Climb directly up to a stance below and right of the fingercrack buttress.

OR:

pitch 3 The more timid will prefer instead to traverse left to a 5.10 hand-crack in black rock. Then traverse right under the roof under the buttress to the stance mentioned in pitch 2. 5.9 60'

pitch 4 Up the corner to the tree, then blindly out left onto the edge (razor sharp: clever double-rope work mandatory) to gain the fingercrack. This crux crack ends on the perch above. 5.11 75'

pitch 5 Head left over bad dike rock and up a left-facing corner to breach the roof band. The move into the corner isn't too frightening: you won't realize what you've just mantled until you look back. 5.8 100'

pitch 6 Scramble left over bushy terraces, aiming for the obvious hand-crack in the wall above. Climb this to a belay below the summit barrier wall. 5.7 100'

pitch 7 Out left is a bottomless wide crack. This leads to a scrambling finish. 5.8 150' (D)

> FA The route was originally solo-aided by Pat Munn to the high point at the top of the fingercrack. (1982) Munn later followed the crux pitch free. Don Mellor and Chuck Turner made the FFA of the route and added the trashy finish in 1983.

All routes right of Snow Blue *are on private land and are subject to restrictions.*

Worse Than Real   II   5.6   400'

Well named. There is a series of tree-filled, broken left-facing corners right of the Big Wall section and before the trail drops downhill past the left-facing chimney of *Neurosis*. This route finds a way up these corners and depression above.

Raptor's Scream   I   5.12   80'   †

This is a sustained route that follows bolts about 20' left of the obvious *Neurosis* left-facing chimney. Some gear needed up high.

FA Patrick Munn and Dominic Eisinger 8/93

POKE-O-MOONSHINE: MAIN FACE (*right end*)

A. POMME DE TERRE 5.10
B. SCALLION 5.10
C. GREEN ONION 5.9
D. LA SPIRALE 5.11
E. THUNDERHEAD 5.10+
F. AMONGST THE CROWD 5.11
G. PARALYSIS 5.8
H. MOONSHINE 5.10+
I. SUNBURST 5.8+

Neurosis II 5.6 400'

This is a seldom-climbed route that makes its way up the broken depression. Climb the left-facing chimney to the gully exit a few hundred feet above. Or better yet, wait till winter.

FA Frank Garneau, Ben Poisson, and John Turner 1957

The next climbs end on the brushy dike ledge. Descend via rappel with two ropes.

Free Swing I 5.10 175' (S or D)

The giant fallen tree at the base of this one was once an integral part of the climb: the first ascent party threw a rope over a branch to protect the traverse. The tree fell in the early eighties (perhaps from holding so many "free-swingers"?). The long hand-traverse start of the original line was finally repeated in 1988, the same year the climb was given a direct start.

pitch 1 Begin right of the left-facing chimney. Climb out over steep rock to gain the more secure traverse crack. Climb up right to a belay at a tree around the corner. 5.10 100'

pitch 2 Step back left onto the face and follow a prominent crack to the terrace.

Variation A direct start climbs a steep face to a pin, then follows a slight groove left to join the crack. 5.10+

FA Geoff Smith and Pat Munn 4/77
FA Gelu Ionescu 5/29/88 (var.)

Royal Savage I 5.10 150' (E)

Right of the left-facing chimney and left of the always wet, left-facing corners is a smooth wall. This route climbs up to the right-facing corners high and left.

pitch 1 Start at a shallow left-facing corner and crack that angles slightly right. Up this to a traverse left to the base of the corner. 5.9 75'

pitch 2 Follow the corners past two bolts (one-quarter-inch, 1980) to a crux finish. Rappel with two ropes.

FA Mark Meschinelli and Drew Allan 1980

The Natural   I   5.10   80'

Locate the obvious wet left-facing corner of *Neurosis Direct* and the bolted line of *Home Rule.*

pitch 1 Up thin crack, face-climbing past two bolts to the shared belay.

FA Patrick Purcell, Jen Collins, and Dan Stripp 1993

Home Rule   I   5.10   165'   (E)   †

pitch 1 On the brown face left of the prominent left-facing corner is an excellent face route. Climb past several bolts to a belay.

pitch 2 Another pitch leads up the face. Rappel.

FA Patrick Purcell and Bill Dodd 7/92

Neurosis Direct   I   A1   175'

This is the always wet, left-facing corner that makes up the direct start to the ice climb. It would no doubt be free if someone gave it the effort.

FA Mark Meschinelli (roped solo) 1980

Pomme de Terre   I   5.10   175'   (s)

The low wall right of *Neurosis* contains some of Poke-O's best short routes.

pitch 1 Begin just right of the wet *Neurosis Direct* corner. Climb a crack to a tree ledge. 5.7 40'

pitch 2 This pitch climbs the beautiful curving dihedral on the open face above right. Traverse right onto the face and run it out over easy rock to the left-facing arch. (Small nuts can be arranged in the arch, but it is an expanding flake. Better protection is offered by the crack of *Scallion* to the right.) Climb the arch and belay high above.

FA Don Mellor and Bill Dodd 8/84

Scallion   I   5.10   150'   (s)   †

pitch 1 Begin under a flaring corner above a roof about 15' up. Enter the corner and stay in the line past two bolts. The crack line ends at a fixed anchor. Rappel here or climb dirty rock to the terrace. It is also possible to traverse right from the belay past a quarter-inch bolt to join *Macintosh.*

FA Drew Allan, Pat Munn, and Mark Meschinelli 9/80

Macintosh   I   5.10+   175'   (D)   †

pitch 1 This is a superb face and crack climb. Start just right of *Scallion's* bottomless corner. Climb the corner/crack and make a seemingly endless run-out to a belay on lower-angled rock. 5.10 90'

pitch 2 Climb the slab above and turn the roof via the obvious fingercrack. 5.10+

FA Gary Allan and Geoff Smith 1977

Green Onion   I   5.9   180'   (s)

This route begins in a flaring, right-facing corner and finishes out the right side of a square notch in the large roof at the top of the slab.

pitch 1 Up the corner to a belay 30' below the roof. 5.7

pitch 2 Traverse right on easy rock with no protection to an overhanging exit on the right side of the notch. Belay here to cut rope drag, or continue on the dirty face to the trees.

FA Geoff Smith and Pat Munn 1977

The section between Green Onion *and* Sunburst Arete *has had many routes erased by the removal of bolts. The status of these climbs may change as the bolts are replaced.*

Grapes of Wrath   I   5.11   150'   (s)

pitch 1 Two bolts on a steep face just right of *Green Onion*. It wanders a bit, but it's a good route.

FA Joe and Dave Szot 1993

A.S.   I   5.10

Between *Green Onion* and *Quo Vadis* is a high dihedral.

pitch 1 Ascend face to bottom of the dihedral. (5.10 bolt), then up arete 5.8 left of the corner, then face-climbing past two more bolts to belay at *Green Onion* just under roof. (Bolts missing.)

FA Gelu Ionesco and Pierre Gagnon 9/89

Quo Vadis   I   5.11   80'

pitch 1 Just left of the black arete of *La Spirale* is a black, right-facing corner. Begin down and left, following cracks and small corners to the base of the black corner. Continue past two bolts slightly left at first, then right to the belay of *Thunderhead*. (Bolts missing.)

FA Gelu Ionescu and Pierre Gagnon 6/12/88

La Spirale   I   5.10+ or 5.11   80'   (E)   †

pitch 1 Follow the very obvious black arete that makes up the right end of this section of rock past seven bolts to the *Thunderhead* belay. (Bolts missing.)

FA Gelu Ionescu and Pierre Gagnon 8/87

Thunderhead   II   5.10+   150'   (E)   †

Surprisingly, the giant roof is about the easiest section on this route.

pitch 1 Climb the main black corner under the roof. Undercling and jam left to a belay just above. 5.10 80'

pitch 2 Stay in the crack through the second roof and continuously difficult crack-climbing above. 5.10+ 60'

FA Gary Allan and Dave Hough 9/78

Lightning   II   5.9   150'

pitch 1 Begin as for *Thunderhead*. Climb cracks in the black wall on the right to a narrow, sloping ledge below the huge roof. Traverse right to a jamcrack that ends at the good ledge belay common to *Cirrhosis*. 5.9 75'

pitch 2 Climb the obvious dirty corner above. 5.6 75'

fa Ken Nichols, Mike Heintz, and Mark Meschinelli 9/21/84

Cirrhosis   II   5.9+   150'   (E)   †

Right of the obvious *Thunderhead* is a black wall with a bolt at 20'. The classic second pitch climbs the long, right-facing flake above and right.

pitch 1 Climb past the bolt to a belay at a good, flat ledge in the corner. 5.9 75'

pitch 2 Traverse right to gain the flake. Only after they had taken to the wing did it occur to several leaders that this section isn't as straightforward as it looks. Traverse left to the belay. 5.9+ 75'

FA Dick Williams and Dave Loeks (early '70s?)

269

End Game   I   5.10+   150'   (s)

Above *Cirrhosis* is a forested ledge. Start here at a dangerous flake.

pitch 3 Up to a right-facing corner to a bolt belay. A committing pitch. 5.10+ 75'

pitch 4 Continue same line to the trees. 75'

FA Dennis Luther and Dave Szot

Dicentra   I   5.10   75'   (D)

Named for the bleeding hearth found in the crack, this face climb is an alternate start to *Cirrhosis.*

pitch 1 About 15' right of *Cirrhosis,* climb up and left on a slab to a bolt, then follow a right-facing corner to the top of pitch 1 *Cirrhosis.* (Bolt missing.)

FA Pierre Gagnon and Jean-Luc Michaud 5/28/88

Amongst the Crowd   III   5.11   400'   (E)   †

Absolutely phenomenal, but often wet. Every pitch is a treat, and no pitch is a giveaway. Begin left of the huge block that forms the approach for *Paralysis.*

pitch 1 Climb a right-facing corner to a roof at about 40'. Belay above at a flake. 75' 5.10

pitch 2 The crux narrow corner above is obvious: unrelenting climbing up a right-facing corner to a belay up and right. 5.11

pitch 3 Climb up and right to white streaks, gain roof, and climb the crack out to headwall and bolt belay. 5.11

pitch 4 Face-climb up and right, then back left following slight weakness. 5.10

History The original first two pitches by Patrick Purcell, Herb George, and Mark Ippolito 8/88 ended at the dike. The aptly named *Amongst the Clouds* (pitches 3 and 4) were added by Patrick Munn and Mark Meschinelli. 1991

Paralysis   III   5.8   475'   (s)   †

This and the next few climbs begin on the large block/ledge at the base of the large amphitheater. *Paralysis* is one of the Poke-O originals. It takes advantage of both of the cliff's most distinguishing features: the straight-in crack and the traverse dike. The challenges here are sustained and varied.

pitch 1 Approach the block from the right. 4th class 50'

pitch 2 From the left end of the block/ledge, climb the vertical crack for a full pitch to the traverse dike. 5.8 140'

pitch 3 Traverse right to a belay in a left-facing corner. 5.6 75'

pitch 4 Stay in the horizontal dike around a corner and up to a block belay. 5.7 75'

pitch 5 Climb the steep, imposing bulge on the left and follow easier rock to a chimney finish. Many climbers reach this point and just can't believe the route goes out so unpromising an overhang. It does. 5.8-

pitch 6 A short pitch up a corner above a tree ledge leads to the woods.

FA John Turner, Brian Rothery, and Dick Strachan 1959

Annie's Dilemma 5.11

A direct finish to *Paralysis,* this route starts at the main traverse dike.

pitch 3 Climb up and left, then back right to a break through the roof. Belay at a stance in fingercrack or up to next roof, climb through and belay above.

pitch 2 Climb up and right on the large upper wall to gain upper *Moonshine.*

FA Patrick Munn and Ann Eastman 1991

Orchestra I 5.10 150' (D)

pitch 1 Climb the face just right of the crack of *Paralysis,* past three bolts, until it is possible to join upper *Maestro.* Though a bit run out, it is easier than its neighbor to the right. (Bolts missing.)

FA Patrick Purcell and Ed Palen 9/87

Maestro I 5.10 140' (E) †

pitch 1 In the center of the blank face right of *Paralysis* is a superb face climb (seven bolts). It may well be the best of its genre at Poke-O. Exit left to *Paralysis* or right to *Moonshine.* As with many other face climbs here, a rack of small nuts will help.

FA Julien Dery 7/87

271

Macrobiotic   I   5.10-

pitch 1 This is the face right of *Maestro*. Three bolts. (Bolts missing.)

FA Julien Dery

Moonshine   III   5.10+   350'   (s)   †

This is a superior, full-length route that climbs cracks and corners on the right side of the *Maestro* wall and breaches the unlikely overhangs above.

pitch 1 From the right side of the *Paralysis* block/ledge, climb out right to gain a left-facing corner and a large belay ledge above. 5.7 75' (D)

pitch 2 Climb past two bolts (the first is three-eighths inch, the second is one-quarter inch) to a right-facing corner. Follow this line until it becomes a left-facing corner. At its top, run it out right to the dike ledge (same as pitch 3 *Paralysis*). 5.10 90'

pitch 3 This lead finds a relatively easy way through the huge overhangs. Climb (5.10+) up past two bolts (quarter-inch, 1970s) and hike a left-rising ramp to a pullover at its end. 100'

pitch 4 Climb either of two cracks to the woods 5.8 80'

FA Don Mellor, Mike Heintz, and Mark Meschinelli 9/1/85

Tachycardia   III   5.12   350'   (s)

A bolt ladder up high led to one of the Adirondacks' most spectacular and exposed pitches. More recently, after the removal of the bolts, the roof was reached by free-climbing in from the right.

pitch 1 Climb the huge, left-facing corner that forms the right-hand boundary of the *Paralysis* amphitheater. Belay below the steep hand/fist crack. 5.7 90'

pitch 2 Up the always wet and grassy crack to the dike belay. Most parties will prefer to skip these annoying pitches and approach via one of the previous lines. 5.10 70'

pitch 3 The first ascent aided to the roof and free-climbed left out (at least 25') the roof on an amazing adventure that has numerous hidden rest stops along the way. Later, the wall to the right gave free-climbing access to the roof. Belay above the lip at an exposed, flat stance. 5.12

pitch 4 The final pitch is an excellent, run-out face climb on sharp black holds. 5.7 100' (D)

FA Mark Meschinelli, Pat Munn, and Drew Allan 1980 (p.1 & 2)

FA Roof and beyond Don Mellor, Bill Dodd, and Patrick Purcell 8/15/86

FFA Craig Smith 9/5/92

Sunburst Arete   II   5.8+   300'   (S)

On the right edge of the amphitheater is a black buttress; this route climbs the outside edge and joins upper *Paralysis*. This route comes highly recommended.

pitch 1 Begin on the left wall and climb up toward the edge and a belay ledge about halfway up.

pitch 2 Continue in the crack line to the dike belay.

pitch 3 and 4 Join *Paralysis* above the dike.

FA Geoff Smith and Pat Munn

The Real 208   II   5.9+   150'   (E)

pitch 1 Just around the corner of the black buttress of *Sunburst Arete* is the first prominent crack on the wall right of the amphitheater. Belay under a roof at 50'. 5.9+

pitch 2 Turn the small roof and follow the crack up a beautiful right-arching corner and belay on the loose traverse dike. The obviously cleaned strip above was the intended finish, but the flaky band above the dike blocked progress.

FA Mike Heintz and Don Mellor 5/5/85

Paper Walls   II   5.10+

Start about 75' right of the broad *Sunburst Arete* on a 15' vegetated tier.

pitch 1 Climb an extremely thin crack just right of a spruce tree. Surmount block and climb a crack to easier ground, heading left to the oak island. 5.10+ 80'

pitch 2 Up obvious corner to the loose dike. 5.9+ 50'

pitch 3 Climb (bolt) obvious right-facing corner with a handcrack. Belay at lip of overhanging section or continue low-angled crack and slab to oak tree belay. 5.10+

FA Jeff Achey and Patrick Purcell 10/22/94

En Vivo   5.11+

200' right of *Sunburst Arete* is a line with three bolts and a thin crack that leads to the upper end of *Keep Off Flake,* one of the remaining prizes on the cliff. Details sketchy.

FA Gelu Ionescu and Pierre Gagnon 5/1/93

Rare Earth   I   5.9   150'

This route begins about 300' right of *Sunburst Arete.*

pitch 1 Climb a short, overhanging left-facing corner for 30' to a bushy ledge. Move left to a thin crack and a tree ledge high above. Rappel with two ropes.

FA Dave Hough and Mark Meschinelli 1982

Parabolic Cats   I   5.12-

About 100' right of *Rare Earth* is a large, 30' left-facing corner capped by two huge roofs.

pitch 1 From the top of the handcrack corner, head left to the crack that goes out the roof. There is a fixed anchor above.

FA Bill Lutkus and Jim Damon 7/88

Lichenstorm   I   5.9   150'

About 150' right of *Rare Earth* is an obviously cleaned left-facing corner system about 75' up.

pitch 1 Climb the brushy slab to a small overhang. Continue over this into the corner above, switching right into another corner. Move left at the top.

pitch 2 Rappel with two ropes or continue on easy rock.

Variation It is possible to finish more directly via friction (bolt).

FA Mark Meschinelli and Dave Hough 1982
FA Pierre Gagnon and Gelu Ionescu 1988 (var.)

UPPER TIERS

If they weren't dwarfed and overshadowed by the magnificent Main Face of Poke-O, these bands of cliffs near the summit of this fire tower peak would be among the most popular and best-known up here. Numerous cliffs, some over 150' high, line up, one over the next, across the mountain above Main Face and on around south to the summit itself. The step-like profile of the upper cliffs depicts the classic uplifted block structure that makes up Poke-O-Moonshine Mountain. Here the purity of crack-climbing and the unrelenting steepness of most of these cliffs make for a far better area than their present traffic would suggest. As things stand now, no paths lead to their base, lichen still covers much of the rock, and just what's been done hasn't been fully sorted out. Although this isn't really a wilderness cliff, the climbing here retains many of the elements we associate with the wilder and more remote crags of the backcountry.

Because of the limited reporting of the past, many ascents aren't documented or described accurately. The descriptions that follow are an incomplete survey of what's been done in the recent seasons. It is likely that many of the descriptions here are simply rediscoveries of earlier, nameless climbs.

Described here are only two of the more obvious walls near the summit: the Sun Wall, and the Headwall (the cliffs that run the length of the cliff above the Main Face remain undocumented). Both can be approached via the summit hiking trail that leaves from the ranger's cabin. The steep uphill approach takes about 30 minutes. On the way, the trail passes under a short cliff called Hospital Rock. The main crackline behind the boulder is called *First Aid* (5.9 FA Meschinelli/Bushey '77.) Right of this is a large roof. *Incision* climbs this out left via a handcrack (5.10 FA G. Allan, Munn, Hough '77.)

THE HEADWALL

Directly below the fire tower and at the left end of the cliff is a huge right-facing corner with a flaring chimney at midheight. Above this is a lower-angled face. This corner is the key to finding routes in this area. The first route begins around left of the corner on a vertical wall split by interesting-looking cracks. Above this is a low-angled slab that leads to the steel poles drilled into the summit rock.

Flashback Crack   I   5.9   40'   (E)

Off in the woods left of the hiker's trail is a 40' slab with a crack in the middle. It is about 150' left of *Telegraph Crack*.

FA Mark Meschinelli, Pat Munn, and Dave Hough 1978

Telegraph Crack   I   5.11   100'   (E)

This is a narrow, somewhat flared hand and fingercrack that becomes offset a bit to the right before rising to the top of the wall. Just below the offset, traverse left with difficulty to a flake/corner facing right. Finish on a low-angled crack, then left to parallel cracks.

Variation It is also possible to finish up directly.

FA Ken Nichols and Mike Heintz 10/7/84

FA Bill Pierce 1988 (var.)

Telepathy   I   5.8   100'   (E)

This is the more moderate handcrack to the right.

FA 1970s

About 100' down and right of the right-facing corner is a beautiful finger-crack line on a less-than-vertical face. This is Fairview.

Radio Face   I   5.10   80'

30' left of *Fairview* is a superb top-rope climb on discontinuous flaring cracks and friction.

FA 1970s

Fairview   I   5.8   100'   (s)

This hard-to-miss and harder-to-resist climb begins in the right-hand of three thin cracks and finishes in the higher, left-hand crack. A short runout at the top is the psychological crux of this route.

Geoff Smith and Don Layman 4/77

Rainbow Crack   I   5.10   90'   (D)

About 200' right of *Fairview* is a huge flake just left of a birch. The face of the flake has a thin vertical crack (crossed by a horizontal one). The flake forms a right-facing, offwidth corner.

pitch 1 Climb the thin crack until it intersects the edge of the flake; continue up left to stacked blocks. Pull over the tricky bulge and finish up left on a low-angled, 2" crack. The right-facing corner to the right can be used as a downclimb for those wishing to stop after the good fingercrack.

FA Ken Nichols 10/30/87

Snowbound   I   5.10+   75'

Just right of the right-facing chimney/corner is an excellent top-rope route up a flaring crack to hard face climbing.

FA Mike Heintz and Mark Meschinelli (top-rope) 1986

Gusto Crack   I   5.6   75'   (D)

This is the obvious and ominous wide chimney that arches left. Climb the slab on its left side.

FA Geoff Smith and Dave Hough 1976

The following climbs are on the largest part of the Upper Tiers. A landmark in this section is the huge diagonal low roof; right of this is the obvious Adirondack Crack. *Up and left of the huge roof is* Solar Energy, *the large corner with a wide crack high up.*

Solar Energy   I   5.6   75'   (E)

This is an obvious route that begins below a large corner and wide crack. Follow the corner to its top.

FA Gary Allan and Tom Caramia 1975

Hot Saw   I   5.9   75'   (E)

The upper section of this route is the very obvious wide fistcrack high on the wall.

pitch 1 Begin 9' right of *Solar Energy,* following a short thin crack past a huge perched flake. Traverse right under the roof and finish the fistcrack.

FA Mark Meschinelli, Dave Hough, and Pat Munn 1978

Adirondack Crack   I   5.11   100'   (S)

About 100' right of the previous routes and just right of the large, diagonal, low roof is a steep, shallow crack that ends at a small roof. This is a test-piece of flaring jams and minimal rests.

pitch 1 Climb the crack to the roof; turn this and reach high left to gain the easier, unprotected face-climbing finish.

FA Ken Nichols and Marco Fedrizzi 10/14/84

Mechanical Hydraulic Control   I   5.10   100'   (s or d)

About 30' right of *Adirondack Crack* (and the huge low roof) is a left-facing corner. This is a superb route, but the crux moves up the ramp are not well protected.

pitch 1 Climb the corner with the handcrack to a bulge. The steep ramp up right leads to a finish up a series of right-facing corners and flakes.

FA Mark Lemons and Ken Nichols 10/13/84

Down and right of these routes is a wall split by thin cracks that end on a ledge below various upper corners; to the right of these is a wavy dihedral that also gives access to the upper section. At this point the south-facing wall begins to bend around face east, out toward Lake Champlain. The descriptions below are reconstructions of early, less direct connections of these cracks and corners; obviously, there are numerous combinations.

Fear of Gravity   I   5.9   100'   (e)

pitch 1 The left-most crack begins in a low stepped, right-facing corner and passes an awkward slot at the top. 5.9 40'

pitch 2 Climb the jamcrack in the right-facing corner above the left end of the ledge, finishing in a short 5.9 crack. The pitches can be combined.

FA Gary Allen, Geoff Smith, and Dave Hough 1976 (with approach from the right)
FA Direct Start Ken Nichols and Chuck Boyd 10/8/84

Dutch Masters Direct   I   5.9+   100'   (e)

pitch 1 Climb the most attractive, right-hand fingercrack to the ledge. 5.9+ 40'

pitch 2 Continue in the left-facing handcrack corner above. The final right-facing corner is a short 5.8 offwidth.

FA Mark Meschinelli, Geoff Smith, and Pat Munn 1977

Thunderbolt   I   5.9   100'   (s)

pitch 1 Any route to the ledge at 40'.

pitch 2 *Thunderbolt* takes the right-facing corner above pitch 1 of *DMD* (and just right of that route's finish.)

FA Marco Fedrizzi 10/13/84

Hydrophobia   I   5.9   110'   (E)

The route's obvious start is the wavy corner at the right end of this good section of cracks and corners, just right of the *DMD* fingercrack. Originally, the earliest climbers here headed left to link up with upper *Fear of Gravity*. The route described below finishes via the often-wet, left-facing corner up high. Obviously, this and the other routes on this part of the cliff can be linked at will, creating any combination of pitches that seems appealing.

pitch 1 Climb the wavy right-facing corner. 5.7 35'

pitch 2 Diagonal up left to a left-facing corner and final face-climb above. 5.8

ACB Chuck Boyd and Ken Nichols 10/8/84

Adirondack High   I   5.8   160'   (S)

This is a good route that heads slightly right from the start. It was the first route on the upper bands at Poke-O. Begin 80' right of the wavy corner of *Hydrophobia* on a large boulder.

pitch 1 Climb the thin flake/crack. Step right from its top (crux) and climb a corner to a huge, sloping ledge. 70'

pitch 2 Climb the obvious chimneys above. 5.7 80'

FA Pat Munn, Dave Hough, and Geoff Smith 1975

The next routes are on the imposing east-facing section of the Headwall. Walk down and right around the corner for about 300' past the Dutch Masters Direct *section. (This section of the wall is clearly visible to climbers who are descending across the top of the Main Face, just before reaching the descent gully.) The most obvious route here is* Plate Tectonics, *the huge right-facing, offwidth chimney high on the left side of this vertical wall.*

Continental Drift   I   5.10   160'   (E)

Start at a large flake 15' left of *Plate Tectonics.*

pitch 1 Climb the flake and small left-facing corner to a bulge and a small ledge. Continue the edge of another flake that forms a right-facing corner and traverse left to a good ledge (possible belay) at the base of an overhanging right-facing corner. Follow the corner to a stance on a narrow ledge; step left at the overlap above and finish via a slightly overhanging crack.

pitch 2 Finish up the huge left-facing corner with the offwidth crack. 5.7 40'

FA Ken Nichols 9/27/87

Plate Tectonics   I   5.10+   180'   (s)

This ominous route is one of the most spectacular up here; the route is easily identified as the right-facing flake chimney capped by a right-facing roof.

pitch 1 Climb an unprotected friction ramp to large flakes that lead to a belay at a fragile, thin flake. 5.6 40'

pitch 2 Pull over to a hollow flake/fingercrack and on into the huge flake above. Hand-traverse right under the roof to the top. This is a scary and sustained lead. 5.10+ 140'

FA Ken Nichols 9/29/84

Dark Lord   I   5.8+   180'   (s)

This is the prominent, black, left-facing corner with the off-width chimney at its base. It is often wet, but it nonetheless is one of the best routes here.

pitch 1 The first 15' of the route is the crux; it is also the only section for which protection is limited. The pitch ends on a small ledge at 140'.

pitch 2 A short pitch leads to the trees.

FA Ken Nichols and Marco Fedrizzi 9/29/84

Flash Flood   I   5.8   180'   (E)

Begin in a small left-facing corner 40' right of *Dark Lord*.

pitch 1 Climb the corner to a flat-topped spike of rock; continue up a steep crack to a triangular ledge.

pitch 2 Follow the large corner above the left side of the ledge until it becomes a ramp. Finish the vertical crack.

FA Ken Nichols and Bruce Jelen 9/27/87

Retrograde Motion   I   5.9+   180'   (s)

About 65' right of the very obvious *Dark Lord* is a large left-facing corner system that runs full-length up the cliff with an offset in the middle formed by a ledge.

pitch 1 Ascend cracks about 6' left of the lower section of the corner to a friction ramp leading to the large ledge. 5.9+ 80'

pitch 2 Continue in the main corner past an awkward bulge. 5.9 100'

FA Ken Nichols, Mike Heintz, and Carold Nelson 10/6/84

Worlds in Collision   I   5.9   180'   (E)

This route climbs the lower half of the corner of *RGM* and finishes in a smaller, right-facing corner on the right wall.

pitch 1 The first pitch is a full rope-length and ends at a sloping slab.

pitch 2 Climb a crack in the shallow corner to the right.

FA Ken Nichols, Mike Heintz, and Carold Nelson 10/7/84

Fracture Zone   I   5.10   (E)

Start this route about 120' right of *Worlds in Collision* or about 200' right of *Dark Lord* below the left end of an undulating ramplike face.

pitch 1 Diagonal right on the face to the left side of a large ledge with a perched flake. Climb the overhanging fingercrack above to low-angled face and a good ledge. 5.10

pitch 2 Head up right about 10' and follow a steep hand- and fingercrack to the trees. 5.9

FA Ken Nichols and Chuck Boyd 10/27/87

Odd Nine   I   5.9   170'   (E)

About 50' beyond, or about 250' right of *Dark Lord,* is an obvious crack facing south.

pitch 1 Climb the leaning, right-facing corner/crack to a sloping belay at a 3" crack. This exposed belay is simply a great place to be. 50'

pitch 2 Climb the crack; traverse left to a good fingercrack on a slab. A final short jamcrack leads to the top. 5.9 120'

FA Geoff Smith, Gary Allan, and Dave Hough 1977

Atlantis   I   5.9   100'   (E)

Around to the right of *Odd Nine* is a left-facing corner system.

pitch 1 Climb the corner to the top.

FA Geoff Smith and Gary Allan 1976

From this point it is easy to descend via the standard descent gully as for the Main Face off to the right; simply head down the drainage. Conversely, it is typical to approach climbs at this end of the cliff by climbing up the descent gully and bushwhacking up left.

SUN WALL

A little over halfway to the summit on the hiker's trail it is possible to see a steep cliffband through the woods. This is the cliff below the Headwall. Approach directly through the woods. Once at the cliff it may be possible to get oriented by finding the three parallel cracks of *Octoberfist* (the handcrack with a roof start), *Foam Flower* (the steep crack 20' right), and *Eastman-Kodak Crack* (the offwidth 8' right).

Smoke Signal   I   5.11   100'   (E)

About 250' left of *Octoberfist* is a very obvious crack that splits a large bulge (or roof) and finishes up a difficult overhanging face.

FA Ken Nichols 9/22/84

Cosmic Arrest   I   5.10   100'   (E)

Begin 50' right of *Smoke Signal* below a large orange dihedral with two overhangs, at a shallow chimney formed by the right edge of a huge flake.

pitch 1 At the top of the chimney and flake, follow the orange corner to a wild hand-traverse left.

FA Ken Nichols 8/26/87

Teamwork   I   5.10-   100'   (D)

Start this one on the top left side of the huge block that bridges the trail, 50' right of *Cosmic Arrest.*

pitch 1 Climb a series of small, steep left-facing corners up the black waterstreaks to lower-angled rock and a fingercrack finish.

FA Bruce Jelen and Ken Nichols 8/16/87

V for Victory   I   5.10   100'   (E)

pitch 1 Begin just right of *Teamwork,* under the block that crosses the trail. Climb through the hole and follow the large right-facing corner to a nasty V-slot finish.

FA Ken Nichols and Bruce Jelen 8/16/87

Black Crack I 5.11 100' (E)

pitch 1 About 100' past the block that bridges the trail is a black wall. Climb the crack over a bulge to lower-angled rock. Finish the crack (or the ramp up left).

FA Ken Nichols 9/16/87

Octoberfist I 5.10 75' (E)

This is the most prominent handcrack on the separate, right section of the cliff.

pitch 1 Surmount the low roof and follow the sustained and steep crack to the top.

FA Mark Meschinelli 1970s

Foam Flower I 5.10+ 75' (E)

pitch 1 20' right of *Octoberfist* is another vertical crack. The going gets steadily more difficult toward the crest.

FA Don Mellor and Mark Meschinelli 6/85

Eastman-Kodak Crack I 5.10 75' (S)

pitch 1 This is the offwidth just right of *Foam Flower,* the third crack in this series.

FA Ken Nichols and Todd Eastman 10/84

Lazy Crack I 5.9

pitch 1 Climb a low-angled slab right of *Eastman-Kodak.* Finish via the vertical crack. Right of this it is possible to scramble up around to the Headwall.

FA Ken Nichols and Mike Barker 9/16/87

MENTAL BLOCKS BUTTRESS
   A. RUBICON 5.10
   B. MENTAL BLOCKS 5.12
   C. BMZ 5.9 A2

WALLFACE

Towering over Indian Pass, this cliff, the state's largest, is a remote and wild place, a place where explorers find almost limitless expanses of rock, where aspiring wall climbers find the magnitude that is lacking in most other Eastern areas, and where climbers of all abilities find solitude. Wallface has long been a focus of explorers to the region: Adirondack lore is filled with accounts of the chaotic boulders, impenetrable forests and awesome cliffs of Indian Pass. The stories and paintings that depicted the Pass made it the place that perhaps best typified the Adirondacks in the public perception.

Today, with the exception of a good trail, little has changed. Climbers still must fight, both to get to the cliff through the tangle of trees and boulders, and to stay on route on a cliff that resists clean description. It seems that Wallface is the place where climbers define themselves. Some have seen it as the best of Adirondack adventures; others, having gotten lost both on the cliff and in the woods above, have vowed never to return. Those who like their climbing tame should avoid Wallface. If, however, you think that bushwhacking is fun, that loose rock here and there makes it more like the big mountains, that uncertainty is a spice, then you just might find climbing on Wallface worth the effort.

Wallface stands over 600' high and stretches the length of Indian Pass. At its right end are a series of buttresses (*Mental Blocks* taking the cleanest one) that are divided by shrub and block-filled depressions. In the cliff's center is a massive slab of rock that spans crackless for hundreds of feet under an ominous series of overhanging corners. Here are *Eastern Shield* and *Pleasure Victim.* Closer to the left end of the cliff is the very obvious *Diagonal* ramp, left of which are the chimneys of *No Man's a Pilot.* Finally, on the extreme left end of the cliff is a lower-angled, less threatening section of long-neglected rock that has only recently seen climbers.

Approach the cliff from the north or south via the Indian Pass Trail. From Tahawas to the south, it is a 4.5-mile trek to the Pass; from Heart Lake and Adirondak Loj near Lake Placid, the hike is about 6 miles.

Most parties set up camp at Indian Pass to allow an early start on the routes. Those who are quick hikers and know the cliff and its approach can figure on about three hours from car to rope-up if they decide upon a more alpine-style day trip.

It is essential to get a good look at the cliff before dropping into the talus maze. The best view of most of the climbs is from Summit Rock, an open terrace one-half mile south of the height of the Pass. Once the route is clearly found, it is possible to choose a line to its base. Though there are no well-established paths to the cliff, a common approach drops downhill from a campsite just north of Summit rock and follows a line of cairns.

Descent can present as big a problem as the climb itself. Most climbers opt for the wicked bushwhack north (farther back from the edge is easier), back toward Indian Pass Brook. Allow about an hour to regain the trail at the foot of the steep section. It is also possible to rappel most routes, and the copious slings around trees and blocks indicate that just about every possible descent has been used at least once by someone.

A common descent from the *Diagonal* is described below. Some of the tree anchors are rather small and climbers should consider leaving gear if there is any doubt.

Start from the top of the last pitch, about 50' below the actual rim.

1. 150' down last two pitches of *Diagonal*. End at huge ledge.
2. From birch clump at the left side of the grassy ledge at the top of the ramp, drop down huge overhanging *Gourmet* dihedral. 120'
3. From birch to the north of the wide ledge, rap 120' down slabs to bushes.
4. Move south 30' to large birch. 120' to next ledge.
5. 80' to ground.

Although every rock climb has its dangers, routes here are especially committing. There is loose rock on every route. There are numerous broken, easy sections where falls would be disastrous. Rescue is a day away in the best of circumstances and impossible in the worst. Consider that three of the four Adirondack climbing fatalities to date have been on Wallface.

The routes are described right to left as one approaches from Adirondak Loj. *Note:* Several of the routes see little traffic and a few route descriptions are unconfirmed. These are thus described in general terms.

North-End Route   II   5.6

Right of a smooth, waterstreaked wall with arched ceilings is a shallow corner about 40' right of a spring. There is no confirmation of a second ascent.

pitch 1 Climb the rotten corner to an overhang and traverse left 10' to another corner that ends at a good ledge.

pitch 2 4th class climbing leads up and left to another ledge.

pitch 3 Scramble to the right-hand of two crack/corners in the steep wall above.

pitch 4 On to the top.

      FA John Dickson, Gil Griffes, Dwight Bradley, and Jeff Rainey approx. 1970s

Right Place, but Must Have Been the Wrong Time   II   5.5   A2

250 yards right of *Mental Blocks* is a large corner. No confirmation of second ascent.

pitch 1 Climb the left wall to a vegetated ledge.

pitch 2 Aid the right side of the wall to another corner above.

pitch 3 Follow the left wall to the top.

      FA Frank Abissi and Steve Baker 7/1/75

BMZ   III   5.10   500'   (s)

The distinctive twin cracks diagonaling up the clean face on the right side of the Mental Block Buttress will aid in locating this route. The climbing is arduous and loose at times. Otherwise, it's a big and exposed route up a huge piece of rock. Begin as for *Mental Blocks,* at a right-facing wide crack leading to bushes.

pitch 1 Up the short crack to the bushes 30' above. Face-climb right to better rock and up to a bushy belay right of the zigzag handcrack of *Mental Blocks.* 5. 140'

pitch 2 Step left past a bolt to gain the steep corner. At the roof, make hard moves left to a bushy corner and a sheltered belay. 5.10 90'

pitch 3 Thin cracks on a steep ramp lead up and right to a block-chocked chimney that breaks a roof. A briefly dangerous section through the roof is rewarded by a spectacular belay (semihanging) at the base of the twin cracks. 5.8 90' *pitch 4* Climb the diagonal twin cracks (very exposed), past some loosely wedged blocks, to a steeper series of flakes that allow access to a large block/ledge on the right. 5.8 125'

pitch 5 The aid ascent described a vertical crack from the left end of the ledge, leading to a 30' traverse left and a right-leaning corner. 5.7 A1 165' The free route described walks right across the sloping ledge to a 30' face-traverse (5.10), gaining the gully and easy climbing to the top.

FA David Martin, D.J. Bouyea, and Steve Zajchowski 9/2/78
FFA Don Mellor and Ian Osteyee 6/6/95

Mental Blocks III 5.12 or 5.7 A2 600' †

This is simply an outstanding route. It involves all of the big wall maneuvers—hanging belays, overhangs, a pendulum—as it makes its way up a most remarkable 500' vertical buttress. The rock is impeccably clean and sound. The route is intricate but clear; if aid is used, the artificial portions are short and obvious. Everything about this climb adds up to make it one of the East's best routes. If aided, the route goes easily with the modern clean gadgets. A large free rack will suffice; hammers and pitons are nowhere necessary. Begin at the base of the huge fist-shaped buttress, the major feature of the cliff's north end.

pitch 1 The north-facing zigzag handcrack of the first pitch is a landmark to find the climb. Climb a dirty crack (or any line, for that matter) and head for the zigzag. At its top is a good belay. 5.7 140'

pitch 2 Traverse left across the orange wall under the huge roof to a stance. A2 or 5.11+

pitch 3 Two cracks diagonal left-to-right, the lower of which going at 5.10. It is possible to aid either one to get to the large slab. Unprotected face moves (5.7 x) lead to a belay at the short headwall.

pitch 4 A short pitch up an overhanging fingercrack ends at a ramp. The free-climbing possibilities here are height-dependent: If you're under 5'11", it's 5.12. If you're over 5'12", it may be under 5.11. [Shorter climbers might consider the exciting *Rubicon* (bolt) around to the left 5.10.]

pitch 5 Climb the fistcrack out right as it shoots spectacularly (5.8, and

WALLFACE

A. NO MAN'S A PILOT 5.9

B. DIAGONAL 5.8

C. LEWIS ELIJAH 5.9

D. HANG TEN–GOURMET–CABIN 6
(lower section is only approximate)

E. EASTERN SHIELD 5.9 A2
(left start is 5.10)

F. PLEASURE VICTIM 5.11

G. WIESSNER 5.4

H. FORTY-NINER 5.7

I. CASE ROUTE 5.3

Wallface

289

what a place to be!) across the blank face to a fixed nut/biner. Pendulum or down-climb right to a hanging belay.

pitch 6 A ropelength of moderate crack climbing leads out the overhanging start and on to the summit. 5.7 150'

FA Paul Harrison and Chris Winship 10/26/70
FFA Don Mellor 7/27/91

Rubicon   III   5.10   500'   (s)   †

Just left of *Mental Blocks* is another excellent adventure. It consists mainly of variations of the former route. Highly recommended. The climb begins steeply uphill and about 100' left of *Mental Blocks*. At the top of the scramble, look for a shallow, brushy corner with good climbing potential on its right wall.

pitch 1 Climb the low-angled right wall of the corner to cedar ledges, then up a short handcrack to a headwall and large flake. Set up for the next pitch by traversing down to the right to a semihanging belay under a roof crack. 5.7

pitch 2 The roof crack (5.9) is followed by a flaring groove and an excellent, airy belay ledge. 50'

pitch 3 Climb an aesthetic right-facing corner, emerging right at its top. Here is the short fingercrack of pitch 4 *Mental Blocks*. Climb out left and up past a bolt to a ramp belay. (This 5.10 face move is safe but exhilarating; alternatively, one could grab a sling or two up the *Mental Blocks* crack and make the route 5.9 A0)

pitch 4 From the alcove at the top of the ramp, climb an overhanging handcrack/corner to gain the summit chimneys. 5.8 165'

FA Don Mellor and Brad Hess 9/3/91

Case Route   II   5.3   800'   (E)

Most of this historic route is tree-covered 4th class; as such, it will appeal more to those who appreciate good general mountaineering and Adirondack lore. It was the route of Wallface's first ascent. Case found the route by "looking around the corner" on an early attempt to reach the Wiessner chimneys. He felt that it was so obvious a line that someone must have wandered up it before his ascent in 1933. However, considering the exposure and the difficulty of one move high up, it is doubtful that a hiker without mountaineering experience would have attempted it; first ascent credit thus almost certainly goes to John Case.

The route is best described as a continuous zigzag up the wide buttress right of the Wiessner depression. (Wiessner's route takes the central depression just right of the giant, clean slab of *Eastern Shield,* the blankest section of the entire cliff.) Begin at a high point of the wide depression and traverse across ledges to the right to the woods. Walk this ledge through the trees until it breaks sharply back left, heading toward the depression once again. Angle back right and around a broken buttress. (It is also possible to climb this buttress on its left side.) Cut back left over steep rock (5.1) and continue past odd 5th class moves to a right-rising ramp or groove. This is the crux; the section above is about 5.3 with a full 600' of exposure. From the end of this "zig," turn left once again to a grassy finish. All told, there are three full zigzags.

FA John Case, Elizabeth Woolsey, and John Case, Jr. 1933

Forty-Niner   III   5.7   500'   (s)

This represents one of the most inspirational stories in the annals of Adirondack climbing. In 1941, Gerry Bloch made his first attempt at what would become something of an obsession: a route on the steep section of rock between *Case* and *Wiessner.* If completed that year it would have been one of the biggest climbs of the era. Several times he would return to his route, sometimes with a partner and sometimes solo, and each time he was turned back either by bad weather or route-finding difficulties. Gerry had his eye on the overhanging pinnacle corner visible to the right of the *Wiessner* chimneys. One time he made it to the top of the pinnacle only to be turned back by the prospect of the unprotected summit face pitch. His attempts were made during the forties, fifties and sixties. In 1990, at the age of 73, Gerry returned and finished his route. The final success, 49 years after the saga began, is a tribute to a top climber of his generation.

The route's lower sections have grown in badly, and it is now best to approach as for the *Wiessner Route.* From a point below the chimneys, the pinnacle is all too clear: it is the huge, overhanging, left-facing corner. This 5.7 pitch is followed by an unprotected 5.5 summit pitch of about 165'. (Note: Gerry holds the record for the oldest climber up El Capitan at age 69. His 1993 Christmas card described a recent leader fall at the Gunks during which he hurt his knee—but remember, Gerry is only 75 and he expects to be back next season still pushing the sharp end of the rope!)

FA Gerry Bloch and Don Mellor 6/90

Wiessner Route   III   5.4   500'   (s)   †

The earliest attempts to climb New York's largest cliff aimed at the right-facing chimneys at the top of the huge, bowl-shaped depression near the center of the face. It was here that John Case and Jim Goodwin first explored. It is a good and historic route, but there is abundant vegetation and loose rock. The judgment required exceeds the technical difficulty.

The climb begins with *Case Route,* traversing the ground-level ledges right into the woods and heading sharply back left to gain the middle of the depression about 200' up. From here, it is possible to see and plan a route for the right-facing chimneys that finish the climb.

Variation **Direct Start**   5.6   (D)   The slab at the base of the depression leads logically and directly to the upper chimneys. The protection is poor, and dry conditions are necessary.

Variation **Direct Finish**   5.6   Right of the third-to-last chimney is a left-facing crack/flake. This leads to a left-facing corner and the top. This is a recommended finish to avoid the often-wet chimneys.

FA Fritz Wiessner, Bob Notman, and M. Beckett Howorth 5/38
FA Fritz Wiessner (var. 1)
FA Butch and Jeanne Kinnon 8/10/86 (var. 2)

Pleasure Victim   IV   5.11   700'   (s)   †

This is one of the best long routes in the region. It takes a direct line to the huge, blank slab called the Shield, and finishes in a climactic, overhanging corner. The rock is generally excellent throughout. Finding the start may be a problem. (It is possible to walk 4th class left onto the ledges below the Shield, find the route, and rappel to its base for the first two pitches.) Please respect fixed gear left for rappel descent.

pitch 1   Begin left of the Wiessner scree cone. Climb a face to a left-leaning corner/crack, finishing on a ledge under a cracked bulge. 5.7

pitch 2   Climb through the bulge (5.9) and up the crack until a traverse left leads to a hanging belay in a small corner.

pitch 3   Easy rock leads up to the first large traverse terrace. This is also accessible from the base of the Wiessner amphitheater. 5.1

pitch 4 The next pitch begins at bolts atop a short tower of rock on the huge Shield slab. Climb left at first, then up past several more bolts to a two-bolt belay. 5.10

pitch 5 Head left (bolts), then up to a bolt before traversing right and up on easier rock to the base of the second traverse terrace at the top of the Shield. (5.9) It is possible to exit right here over very loose rock.

pitch 6 Climb a long corner to a hard exit left (5.11) and up a good crack to a fixed belay.

pitch 7 This climactic pitch climbs the right-facing corner with the roof near the top. Climb up to the base of the corner on very steep rock. A spectacular finish up the corner and around the roof ends on the flat summit. 5.11

Descent This route has a fixed rappel descent. It is marked by bolts at the top of the cliff. The first rappel overhangs severely.

Variation Left of the original start is a face climb with about eight bolts. 5.10- This joins the route after a pitch.

FA Michael Dimitri and Michael Sawicky 8/84–6/29/86

Eastern Shield   IV   5.9   A2   800'   (s)

This route has the potential to be one of the region's finest, but two problems exist. First are the bad bolts on the shield pitches. Instead of useless, partially driven, quarter-inch bolts every 10 feet, there should be fewer, more responsibly placed, stronger bolts. The present bolts were probably installed in the mid-sixties and were discovered by the first recorded ascent party. The second problem is the original crack finish. It looks as though there has been some shifting of the huge flake at its base, making the crack dangerous to approach.

pitch 1 Begin about halfway between the *Diagonal* and *Wiessner* at an open slabby area beneath huge, orange overhangs. Follow a step-like series of ledges and flakes leading to a ledge. 100'

pitch 2 Follow the line of weakness to the large terrace below the Shield. 130'

pitch 3 Near the left side of this sheer face is a left-facing dihedral. Climb this to a ledge at its top, and move right onto the slab, belaying at bad bolts. 5.8 120' *pitch 4* Continue up the slight depression, tending left a bit, past many worthless bolts. Belay high on the left at the base of a right-facing corner. 5.9 120'

pitch 5 Continue up slightly right on slabs and corners to a belay at the steep wall right of the towering offwidth crack.

pitch 6 Climb over the flake and up the crack. Some aid was used here. 5.9 A2 85' (A recent party estimates that the huge flake has shifted and is **unsafe**.)

pitch 7 Walk left to a corner and on to the top. 80'

Variation **Atlas Shrugged** This allows for a safer exit. Instead of climbing the offwidth crack, climb the right-facing corner (dubbed the "toilet bowl") for 10', then step right onto freshly exposed rock. Thin and unprotected climbing leads to the base of the final steep corner, marked by an overhang at midheight. The final pitch climbs this corner as a fitting finale to the fine route below. [This may well be the same corner as for the finish of *Pleasure Victim*. If so, then the original rating of 5.10 given by Wade, Bandorick, and John Kravetz (FA 5/79) is certainly conservative. Others have thought that hard 5.11 might be closer to the truth.]

FA Bruce Bandorick and Scott Wade 5/23/78

AG   III   5.7   800'

Little is confirmed on this old route. It climbs easy, vegetated and broken rock from tree-covered ledges in the middle of the cliff up left toward the final corners of *Diagonal,* passing the "white spot" on its right. It is reported to climb the corner just left of last *Diagonal* pitches.

FA Art Gran, Ira Schnall, Mary Sylvander, and Bob Graef 1957

Gourmet   IV   5.6   A2   800'

This 1964 route has seen little traffic lately; the original route description hasn't been confirmed. A major feature of this climb is the large open book below the *Diagonal* exit corners. When planning for this route, it will be useful to find this feature as well as the "white spot" near the center of the *AG* route. Below and right of the *Diagonal* ledge is a large, smooth slab with a black streak in the middle and "wrinkles" or roofs at the left end of the slab. Begin below these.

pitch 1 Climb a corner for 15', then traverse right onto easy ledges.

pitch 2 Aid over a small roof and continue easily to a belay at trees. 5.6 A1

pitch 3 Climb down and left, around a corner and up a crack. Easier rock leads left to a belay.

pitch 4 Scramble left to the base of the large, obvious corner.

pitch 5 Mixed climbing leads up the dihedral and exits left. Continue up slabs and small aid roof, belaying on *Diagonal*.

pitch 6 Directly above is a steep mossy corner.

pitch 7 At the top of the corner, head left to a chimneying finish.

Variation **Cabin 6, Capacity 10** 5.9   From the *Diagonal* at the top of *Gourmet's* sixth pitch, it is possible to climb the big corner left of the mossy dihedral. There is a fixed anchor at the top of the corner, at the base of a very mossy slab in a flaring, right-facing chimney. The first ascent climbed to the top of the cliff, tunneling under a chockstone en route; free climbs have ended at the mossy slab.

FA Ants Leements, Geoff Wood, and Dave Isles 9/64
FA Peter B. Harris and Roger Bowman approx. 1970 (var.)

Hang Ten   III   5.10

In essence, this is a free ascent of most of the *Gourmet*. After a slightly different start, it climbs the awesome overhanging dihedral of that route's 5th pitch. Directly below the *Diagonal* summit corners is a prominent black streak on a large blank slab. The route starts in right-facing corner at the base of the black streak. (Note: LaForge and Sugiyama called this their "lost route" at Wallface, not remembering quite where their route went. Their notes seem to describe the *Gourmet* area exactly, and thus the author matched their notes to the area described below.)

pitch 1 Start high in the corner and traverse upwards and right for a full rope-length to the tree ledges. (5.7 x) 165'

pitch 2 Angle back left towards the landmark overhanging corner. 5.7 100'

pitch 3 Up the amazing corner: wide cracks followed by a spectacular exit left. At the lip of the overhanging corner, you'll be "hanging from ten fingers." 5.10 90'

pitch 4 The angle lessens as the climb joins *Diagonal*. 5.8

pitch 5 *Gourmet* climbs the mossy corner. The first ascent of *Hang Ten* led much of *Cabin 6 Capacity 10* free before being turned back by rain.

FA Larry LaForge and Linda Sugiyama 9/82

Lewis Elijah   III   5.9   700'   (s)   †

Named after the Indian guide who brought prospectors through the Pass in 1826, this excellent route parallels the *Diagonal* ramp, taking obvious right-facing corners that ultimately join the upper corners of *Diagonal*. The linkup provides a significant option for those who find the ramp pitches too easy, and who are looking for a more sustained adventure to gain the upper corners. Locate the obvious black streak running down a wide slab under the *Diagonal*.

pitch 1 Gain a tree-covered ledge below the black streak by climbing the obvious right-facing corner. 5.8 75'

pitch 2 Face climb up right to the edge of the black streak, then left past a bolt. Belay in the trees high above. 5.7 (D) 100'

pitch 3 4th class up to the base of the clean, right-facing corner. 75'

pitch 4 This begins the obvious corner: climb up and right to a belay at the base of a corner (to avoid rope drag) at about 50'. 5.7

pitch 5 Up the corner, traversing (crux) right to easier ground. 5.9 75'

pitch 6 Climb easily to the base of the upper corners of *Diagonal*.

pitch 7 and 8 *Diagonal*. 5.8

FA Don Mellor and Ian Osteyee 8/94

Diagonal   III   5.8   700'   (E)   †

This is the most obvious and well-traveled route on Wallface. The ramp pitches are direct and easy; the final corners exposed and sustained. From Summit Rock, it is easy to see the long, diagonal ramp. From a distance, it looks narrow and difficult. Actually, it is over 20' wide. It will take about two roped pitches of scrambling to reach the ramp, and this will be much easier if a general line of approach has been determined from afar.

pitch 1 and 2 Head to the base of the ramp. Mixed 4th and 5th class. 200'

pitch 3 Up ramp to a tree belay on the left at 140'.

pitch 4 Face-climb up and the right side of the bulge to a ledge belay. 5.4. 150' *pitch 5* A short pitch ends at the large, grassy terrace. Above is the mossy *Gourmet. Diagonal's* corners are visible and are reached by walking right 50' to an alcove with a tree.

pitch 6 A hard boulder move past an old pin leads into right-facing corner and chimneys to a large open ledge. 5.8 50'

pitch 7 The large, right-facing dihedral ends on a good ledge below the rim. Another short scrambling pitch out right is necessary if a walk-off is planned. 5.8 110'

Variation **Direct Start** Begin at the lowest point on the left-hand end of Wallface.

>*pitch 1* Climb the blocky corner for 60' to a tree belay on the right.

>*pitch 2* Up and left over a short steep section; then follow a diagonal ramp right to a good ledge capped by a large roof. 140'

>*pitch 3* Traverse left 20' and climb the crack/groove to an overhang. Above this, traverse right 40' to an obvious corner. Up to the belay. 120'

>*pitch 5* Climb the weakness to the right and join the *Diagonal* near junction with *No Man's a Pilot.* 75'

FA *History* Trudy Healy first wrote up the route for *Diagonal* after her ascent with Alvin Breisch and Craig Patterson in 1965. They described finding pitons along the way. Shortly thereafter, Joe Rutledge reported that he too had found pitons when he, Tom Morgan, and Jane Morgan climbed the route in 1962. Healy guessed that they were the work of either Harry Eldridge or Dave Bernays. It was typical of both to be reticent about their achievements. In fact, she wrote to Rutledge that Harry always claimed never to remember quite where his routes went. Eldridge and Bernays both died relatively young, and the mystery continues.

ACB Ken Reville and George Carrol 8/26/83 (var.)

Jaggar-Richards   5.9   A2   150'

This is an unfinished (can't get no satisfaction) route that follows the crack and corner that rise between the *Diagonal* ramp and the crux chimney of *No Man's a Pilot.*

pitch 1 From a belay on the ramp, climb cracks, then aid past a pod into the

The rappel down upper Diagonal *shows just how steep the final corner is.*

dihedral. "Thrilling" stemming and laybacking lead to more aid and a poor bolt belay. Rappel.

FA Tad Welch and Bill Widrig 6/86

No Man's a Pilot   III   5.9   600'   (E)   †

This is an obvious line up a right-facing chimney system that leads up left from *Diagonal* ramp.

pitch 3 After the initial approach pitches, leave the lower section of the huge ramp and head up toward the chimney. Belay at its base.

pitch 4 Originally rated 5.8, this pitch has turned back several parties at "the 5.10 section". The climbing involves unusual moves out stacked blocks and wedged flakes, typical of many of the Yosemite chimney routes.

pitch 5 Continue in the narrower chimney to a sheltered belay at a diving-board flake. 5.8 100'

pitch 6 The original ascent aided out the overhang above. The free variation heads left (really?) out of the alcove via a thin crack. This airy pitch is perhaps the most thrilling 5.3 you'll ever do.

FA Pete Metcalf and Lincoln Stoller 8/74
(with free exit by Alan Spero and Dane Waterman 11/12/75)

Wrapping around left of the steep main wall is a long slab that will no doubt reveal many good routes in the future. It probably would have already if it were not dwarfed by the larger, steeper main wall. The rock here is lower-angled and the slabs are distinctly different from the broken, freshly exposed cracks and corners that typify the main cliff.

Out with the Boys Again   II   5.7   350'   (E)

From the base of *Diagonal,* walk left beyond the lowest point of the cliff, then uphill past a sheer expanse of rock capped by overhangs. Left of this is a large, broken, right-facing corner and face beyond with a solitary crack.

pitch 1 This good pitch climbs the zigzag crack and hand-traverses left to a belay below the overhang.

pitch 2 A short pitch leads over the ceiling and past blocks to a roomy belay on the highest ledge.

pitch 3 Climb the straight-in handcrack to the right-facing flake/corner. Follow this to the tree ledge.

pitch 4 Finish directly up the clean, knobby face.

Variation From the belay for pitch 2, a left-slanting crack may be climbed to the tree-covered arete. 5.6

FA Jamie Savage, Tad Welch, and Bill Widrig 5/13/86 (p.1–4)

Moon Unit   I   5.5   150'   (E)

Uphill from the preceding route is a nondescript, textured face. Surprisingly, the climbing here is protectable, unique, and worthwhile.

pitch 1 On the right side of the face is a grassy ramp. From its end, climb up and left on enormous holds and knobs. Follow the twin slanting cracks, then continue up, right, and over the overlap.

FA Tad Welch and Mike Cross 10/18/86

THE NORTHWEST

This is to be considered a "region" only in the broadest sense: the climbing here is spread out over a huge section of the Park, and there is no central location from which to base your operations. However, the growing list of climbs here adds to the diversity of the Adirondack experience and shows climbers that there's a whole lot more to the Park than the roadside crags of Keene Valley.

AZURE MOUNTAIN

Azure Mountain is a pointed knob standing above the open forests between Santa Clara and St. Regis Falls. Presently, it is the only rock-climbing on Forest Preserve land in the entire northwest corner of the Park. As such, it fills an important gap in Adirondack rock-climbing. And it fills this gap impressively. The main face stands about 200' high and overhangs dramatically in the center. On the right side are some short, unclimbed walls with steep crack lines that will no doubt soon yield hard climbs. The actual central section of enormous blocky overhangs has been home to both ravens and falcons; copious whitewash marks their perch. Climbers, however, haven't made much headway here. To the left is a lower-angled face that has some good routes. Added to this are an entrance wall on the approach and a good series of short summit crags.

Access to Azure is from the Blue Mountain Road, which leaves highway 458 halfway between Santa Clara and St. Regis Falls (about 35 miles from Potsdam to the west and the same from Saranac Lake to the east). Drive south for almost 7 miles (just past a bathtub spring pipe) to a narrow dirt road opposite a tin-roofed garage. This leads shortly to a gate, where parking for the hikers' trail is available. Walk about 100 yards up the trail to the ranger's cabin. The summit trail leaves here. Instead, turn left at the cabin and skirt the mountain's base for about one-half mile. The route to the Main Face is marked by cairns. The path that turns right up the ridge at 0.2 miles leads to the cliffs on the South Face.

SOUTH FACE CLIFFS

The southern cliffs are located just 0.25 miles west of the ranger's cabin. Follow the path toward the main face to the crest of the ridge. Walk up a few hundred yards to a short, dark wall. This is the Sidewalk Cafe Area of winter ice routes. There are three distinct walls here. So far, only the middle cliff, the Equinox Face, has seen any traffic. The other faces will need some cleaning.

To reach the Equinox Face, walk left (west) from the Sidewalk Cafe for about 60 yards to a steep scramble leading up to the cliff. The routes are described right to left.

The Other One   I   5.6   50'   (E)

pitch 1 At the extreme right end of the cliff is an easy-looking face below a shallow, left-facing, zigzag corner. Climb the easy face near the corner to a ledge; finish via the A-shaped overhang.

FA Jon Bassett and Tripp Leiby 6/12/88

Equinox   I   5.3   125'   (E)

pitch 1 Begin at the right end of the face where the cliff's base is highest. Climb an easy corner past a ledge and overhang. Continue up and left before stepping back right to a steeper crack. Follow the slabby ridge to the left; from the birch climb the orange slab on the right to the steeper wall. Finish left.

FA Jon Bassett and Rob Washbourne 3/24/88

You're No Spring Chicken Head   I   5.4   125'   (E)

This route threads its way between its two neighbors; it is possible to link these at several places. Start at the maple below an A-shaped undercling 12' up.

pitch 1 Climb to the undercling, step right to the top of the loose boulder and up to the ledge. Climb over the roof right of center. The face above involves excellent, knobby climbing and a short crack left of the birch.

FA Jon Bassett and Andy Legg 6/8/88

Sunshine Daydream   I   5.4   135'   (S)

Start at a birch left of the previous route, just right of the cliff's lowest extension.

pitch 1 Climb face to a ledge at 20'. Step easily back left below the overhang, up a few feet, than back right to the smallest of three left-facing corners. Continue up the face between the water-streaked wall to the left and the big knobs on the right. A large crack leads to a ledge below the top.

FA Jon Bassett and Jim Olsen 5/6/88

Diamond C   I   5.7   125'   (S)

The highlight of this route is the steeply leaning inside corner that dominates the center of the face. The crux is well-protected; easier upper and lower sections are quite run out.

pitch 1 20' left of the cliff's lowest extension is a face that leads past the left end of a large ledge and on into the corner. Exit the corner above and right. Diagonal left, then head straight to the top.

FA Jon Bassett and Andy Legg 9/8/88

MAIN FACE

The Main Face has four distinct sections. Its east end is generally vertical or slightly overhanging, and the rock is solid. The most easily distinguished feature here is the natural rock shelter formed by a large slab that leans against the wall. The center of the cliff is an impressive amphitheatre beneath huge ceilings, but the rock here is unstable. Left of the amphitheatre, the lower section becomes more slabby and the upper section is a featureless vertical wall. The west end is a complicated assortment of blocky corners and chimneys. The cliff is about 400 yards long. The routes are described east to west, or right to left as one approaches from the ranger's cabin.

Unnamed   I   5.12   100'

The prominent arete right of *Planet Claire* is reported to have been climbed by Andy Frankenstein. It begins by gaining a handcrack about 10' up, passing a pin and a bolt, and exiting via a second crack.

Planet Claire   I   5.5   165'   (E)

This is the huge vertical inside corner on the right side of the amphitheatre. The first pitch has grown in some; this can be avoided by traversing in from *Weenie Jam.*

pitch 1 Climb the corner past a tight chimney and trees to a ledge on the left. 5.5 70'

pitch 2 Climb cracks in the face to the right to a horizontal crack 6' below the top of the huge block that forms the chimney. Hand-traverse left and up a slot to the top of the block. Easy rock leads to the top.

FA Clarkson Outing Club early 1970s

Unnamed   I   5.10 or 5.11?

No details on what appears to be an impressive climb on the left wall of the huge *Planet Claire* dihedral. Follow a crack to a bolt and a pin to another crack.

Weenie Jam   I   5.1–5.6   165'   (s)

Also known as *The Gully,* this route climbs the prominent ramp right of the amphitheatre roofs.

pitch 1 Start high on the blocks at the base of the gully. Face-climbing options of varying difficulty lead to the birches at the top.

FA Clarkson Outing Club early 1970s

Rare Treat   I   5.6

About 60' left of *Weenie Jam* is a short rock face that can be top-roped.

FA Bill Moratz and Kevin Steele (top-rope) 3/8/86

Holiday in Cambodia   I   5.8   50'

This is an unfinished route in the big wall section.

pitch 1 About 100' left of *Weenie Jam* is a crack system leading to a short dihedral. Discontinuous cracks above end on a spacious ledge. Rappel.

FA Bill Moratz 4/19/86

The next climbs are located at the left side of the amphitheater. First locate Flubby Dub, *the 2–3" crack on a short face capped by bushes.*

First Feast   I   5.7   125'   (s)

Directly above the left end of the talus is a large sloping ledge at the base of the wall. This is known as the Dinner Table. *First Feast* starts here at a small face below a triangular overhang, 7' right of the largest outside corner.

pitch 1 Step up onto sloping holds and traverse left to a flaring groove. Climb straight up the outside corner until blocked by the roofs. Step awkwardly right to a diagonal slot in the roof. Above this and the face above is a good ledge. From here, follow a large diagonal crack up left until a step back right leads to steep rock and the ledge finish.

Forward to Death   I   5.10

Around the corner about 30' to the right of *Flubby Dub* is an outside corner, an inside corner, and a thin dihedral. The beautiful dihedral is about 5.10, though cleaning on the lead forced the first ascent party to use aid here. There is room to push this climb higher in a dihedral above.

pitch 1 Up dihedral, mantel a ledge, and up to the top of the block. Traverse left to large flake, up flake and face above, then up a left-slanting crack (same as for *First Feast*) to the *Flubby Dub* belay.

FA Bill Moratz 4/19/86

Flubby Dub   I   5.7   100'   (E)

The base of this climb is easily located by finding the first large tree to the left of the talus field. Directly above is the 2–3" inch crack.

pitch 1 Climb the awkward crack until a traverse is possible left (10') to another crack. Finish above to the broken ledge.

FA Bill Moratz and Kevin Steele 1985

Hidden Truths   I   5.7   135'   (E)

To reach this climb, it is necessary to ascend the steep woods 55 yards left of *Flubby Dub*. Continue up and left over a slab, and scramble over bushes to the base of the steep wall. Walk left past a crisp orange corner and over more slabs to an elevated ledge with two birches below.

pitch 1 Climb the easy face to a bushy ledge. Step right and up past a boulder to a large ledge. Chimney behind a balanced block and up to the top of the second block in the corner. 5.3 85'

pitch 2 Climb the steep corner to the flakes. Finish up and left. 50'

FA Jim Olsen and John Bassett 8/27/87

LAKE LILA

On Smith Mountain above the shore of this beautiful and remote lake is a 100' cliff of about 70 degrees split by good crack lines. The cliff takes some work getting to and rock is a bit dirty: you won't have to worry about a waiting line so far back from civilization. The cliff can be approached by boat or by the following description. From the Lake Lila parking lot walk along the road for 2.9 miles to the lean-to on the lake shore. Backtrack 50 yards to an overgrown road off right. Hike this for 150 yards to an old railway house. Walk the tracks left for another 150 yards to an old concrete foundation. The cliff is visible above.

HITCHINS POND CLIFF

This steep slab lies at the end of either a 2.6-mile hike along an old road or a slightly longer (and far more rewarding) flat-water paddle up the meandering Bog River. Both approaches emanate from Route 421, southwest of Tupper Lake. Below the cliff are the ruins of buildings once owned by Abbot Low, a New York shipping magnate. These buildings are to be razed by the state (1995) and the land returned to wilderness status. An easy bushwhack up the slope behind the ruins quickly reaches the cliff. The rock is south-facing, offering moderate slab climbing and featuring long runouts on sound rock. Shorter, better protected routes seem likely toward the ends of the face. The rock is surprisingly clear of lichen. Description by Jim Vermeulen.

Fun-Hogs from Hell   I   5.4   180'   (s)

The first pitch of this pleasant two-pitch route ascends the initial slab on the cliff's right side. At a large vegetated ledge, walk right for 80' to finish up either a right-facing corner and crack, or the harder steep slab and overlap to its right.

FA Jim Vermeulen, Bill Morris, and Willard Moulton 10/90

JENKINS MOUNTAIN

Jenkins Mountain is a small peak NW of Paul Smiths, and seen from Route 30 across Barnum Pond. It is located on state land, but access is owned by Paul Smiths College and leased to the state for the Visitor Interpretive Center (VIC). There are two approaches: The first is from the east at the VIC. Park on Route 30 (for the gate is locked at night) and walk toward the VIC to the unmarked, gated dirt road. Continue about 2 miles where the road ends at a beaver meadow. The second approach is from the west (Keese Mills Road). Park at the trailhead for Black Pond, following the trail and the Esker Trail to the beaver meadow. To reach the slabs, cross the meadow on a vague path that leads to the summit. Leave the trail after a short distance to follow the brook. About halfway to the notch, leave the brook, cutting right across the slope and passing a huge boulder before reaching the rock. The climbing here is somewhat dirty. Description by Dick Tucker.

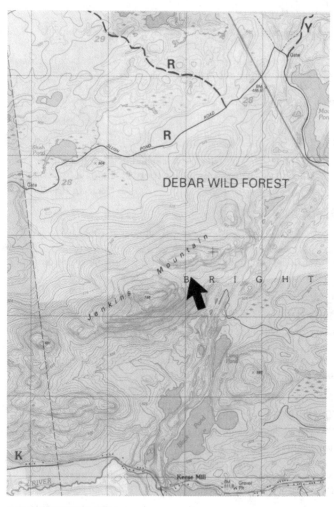

JENKINS MOUNTAIN

Sennet   I   5.2   30'

At the corner of the low, black wall at the left end of the cliff is a face and broken groove.

FA Dick Tucker 6/18/88

The Slot   I   5.4   25'

30' right of *Sennet* is a wide, broken chimney.

FA Dick Tucker 7/26/92

Fly Away   I   5.4   60'   (E)

50' right of *The Slot* is a shallow V beginning a few feet off the ground. Climb the V to a ledge and a bulge on the right. Finish in the corner.

FA Dick Tucker and Tim Riley 7/25/92

Amnesia   I   5.5   130'   (E)

About 125' right of *The Slot* is a small chimney starting on a ledge.

pitch 1 Climb the bulge to the ledge and up face left of the chimney. Above the bushes, follow a vertical crack, moving left on dirty rock to finish.

FA Dick Tucker

Forty Winks   I   5.6   240'   (E)

At the right end of the overhangs is a wet, right-facing corner.

pitch 1 Climb corner, cross blueberries, and over a bulge to an easier slab. Continue up steep bulge at a vertical crack (very dirty). 120'

pitch 2 Finish on easy slabs.

FA Dick Tucker and Tim Riley 7/25/92

Epilogue   I   5.5   240'   (E)

30' right of the previous climb the rock ends at some bushes and a right-facing corner.

pitch 1 Climb the edge of the rock to the trees. Step left and up to the brushy crack, and on to an easy slab. Belay at trees on the right.

pitch 2 Finish on easy slabs.

FA Dick Tucker and Tim Riley 7/26/92

BAKER MOUNTAIN

This is a small red crag near the village of Saranac Lake and seen above the river from the road to Bloomingdale just out of town. The cliff is broken and steep; some sections are cracked into classic cracklines; others need some cleaning. Nonetheless, it fills a void for Placid and Saranac climbers looking for a couple hours on the rock.

From Main Street in Saranac Lake, take Pine Street to East Pine, over the wooden bridge to Moody Pond, where the trailhead for the summit begins. Follow the trail under the power line until it forks; the vague left fork leaves the summit trail and leads across to the top of the cliff. It is possible to cut left and down the hillside to its base before the path crosses the clifftop. The approach takes under 15 minutes.

Most of the climbing lies on the largest outcropping, and routes will be described right to left on this main face.

The property along the base of the cliff (and perhaps including parts of the rock) is privately owned. Please do everything possible to preserve the beauty of the property and our right to use it. Campfires, litter, and tree-cutting are forbidden and will force the owner to close the trail. For now (1995), we have at least temporary permission to walk along the base of the cliff, but please obey any and all postings.

Waterhole # 3   I   5.4   70'   (s)

This is a wandering line up the lower-angled wall of the wide open corner that makes up the right end of the cliff.

Easy Edge   I   5.4   60'

A large birch grows from a crack in the outside corner just right of the largest section of rock. Climb the crack or face.

TB or Not TB   I   5.7 and 5.9   65'   (E)

The right side of the main face sports two parallel cracks about 6' apart. The curving right one is the harder of the two. The left-hand route is actually the right side of the *Cure Cottage* block.

Cure Cottage   I   5.8   70'   (E)

This is the most prominent line on the crag: a left-facing corner with a large wedged block partway up. Steep climbing past the insecure block leads to a right-facing corner where the previous routes merge.

Bubba Does Baker I 5.11 75' (s)

A superb line up the sharp edge (beware the rope) about 40' left of the previous routes. Start in a left-facing corner, and gain the arete as low as possible (bolts), finishing out a thin crack crux at the top. It is possible to skip the finish, making the route easy 5.10.

Saranac 1888 I 5.9+ 75' (s)

This is the clean, left-facing corner at the left end of the main face, just left of the previous route.

Saranac Saber I 5.10 60' (E)

A hundred or so feet left of the main face is another good crag. This fine route climbs the blunt arete past several bolts.

Doctor Y's I 5.9 60' (E)

An excellent and very obvious pitch up a right-facing corner left of *Saranac Saber.*

AMPERSAND

A steep 2.7-mile hike from Route 3, about ten miles SW of Saranac Lake, is rewarded by memorable views of both the High Peaks to the south and east and the lakes region to the north and west. The trail, despite it rigors and its erosion, is a popular one. The open summit was once wooded, until Verplank Colvin removed many of the trees to establish a survey station. Erosion finished the job and left the summit bare. The best climbing story to come from this peak involves, not a climber, but a lost dog. Several years ago, Ron Doell was approaching the open summit, and as climbers do, scoping out the rock wherever openings in the trees afforded some view. High on a ledge sat an emaciated dog, obviously having slipped to a spot from which he couldn't descend. It was clear that the dog was stuck and in bad shape. Upon reporting in to the DEC, Ron discovered that the dog had been reported missing almost two weeks earlier, and its owner, frustrated in his efforts to find his pet, had returned reluctantly to Connecticut. The next day, Ranger Clyde Black joined Ron to effect a roped rescue while the owner sped back to the Adirondacks. The happy ending was reported in the local press. The climbing here isn't extensive, but the beauty of the location may inspire more exploration.

Table Scraps   I   5.6   (E)

This route is found left of the trail about 150' before it leads on to the open summit rock. The prominent feature is the 40' wide roof. Climb a blocky crack to the roof, and traverse right to exit over a bulge. The route name was suggested by the feeling that the traverse felt "like sneaking under the dinner table"; but I'm sure the stranded pup would appreciate the irony.

FA   Dave Furman and partner

Summit Snacks   5.11   (top-rope)

This is the obvious sharp fingercrack.

FA   Patrick Purcell 5/93

BLUFF ISLAND

Few cliffs match the charm of this place. It has long been a popular destination both for canoeists and climbers. The cliff rises about 60' from the deep waters of Lower Saranac Lake and is accessible only by boat. The climbing is easily top-roped. Sharp holds, endless variations, and clean rock in the 5.3–5.7 realm make this a superb outing.

Take Route 86 from Saranac Lake village to either of two launch sites, one about 1.5 and the other about 3 miles west of town. The second of these is closer to the island. In fact, it is possible to get a glimpse of the cliff from the bridge on Route 86.

The Cleaveland area of Good Luck Cliff.

THE SOUTHERN ADIRONDACKS

The recent discoveries in the vast southern half of the Park have added a significant dimension to Adirondack climbing, and it is here that the most exciting prospects for the future lie. Scattered throughout the region are countless outcrops, cliffs, and slabs, all inviting exploration. Some, like Roger's Rock and Moxham Dome, have become quite popular. Others are really remote and of lesser quality for climbing. Perhaps soon, as climbing populations in the areas surrounding the Park increase and as climbers seek out alternatives to Keene Valley and Poke-O-Moonshine, many of these crags will see new cleaned lines, making them worthwhile destinations in their own right. As for now, however, most of the climbing will appeal more to climbers who relish solitude and who don't mind the inconveniences of uncertainty and less-than-perfect rock.

PHARAOH MOUNTAIN

On a clear day from the Northway, look off towards the east, across Schroon Lake. Pharaoh Mountain's rocky flanks appear in the distance as an enticing and surprisingly large cliff. Climbing here consists of either short routes on the summit tiers or long explorations down below on the main face. This lower expanse of rock is somewhat discontinuous, and full-length routes won't come easy. Although the main face does not yet have the high-quality routes that it may someday see, and though the summit cliffs are perhaps too short to justify the long approach, the intrepid wilderness climber may discover secrets here that will be worth the effort.

The Pharaoh Wilderness Area is one of the largest and most beautiful in the Park. The mountain rises dramatically above a landscape dotted with lakes and connected with attractive hiking trails. It has also been "ground zero" in the war between conservationists and land-rights activists. The road to Crane Pond was closed as part of the state's masterplan because it allowed vehicular traffic into a designated wilderness. The huge boulders moved into place to close the road were quickly removed and deposited onto the lawn of one of the park officials, bearing the inscription "stones of shame." Just driving toward the Crane Pond trail one is reminded of how hot the issue is, with American flags waving proudly, and anti-Park Agency slogans painted on makeshift signs. The people of the area have long used the Crane Pond Road for increased access to hiking, fishing, hunting, and camping, and they feel deeply violated that an outside regulatory agency would come in and impose upon them such a restriction. For now (1995), they seem to have the upper hand: The road is open and obviously professionally groomed, with culverts and gravel—clearly not the work of neighbors toting shovels and rakes.

There are several approaches to the climbs, all long and all requiring a good sense of route-finding. Perhaps the surest way is to hike the summit itself, leaving from the Crane Pond Road north of the mountain. At a brisk pace, the summit is reached after about an hour and a quarter. From here, head SSW (magnetic 240 degrees). Generally following the ridge line, one passes the Upper Tiers before emerging onto the flat above the main face. Rappels down to its base are easy to establish from the many tree ledges.

Another approach starts on the Crane Pond Road and parks at the Goose Pond Trail at Plank Bridge Hill. A short walk to Goose Pond is followed by a bushwhack to the south. This might be the shortest way to the

317

face, fighting through Desolate Swamp but avoiding the summit hike. Alternatively from the west, the mountain can be approached via Spectacle Pond Trail off East Shore Road. Two miles of good trail lead to Spectacle Pond, and a two-mile bushwhack through a notch to the east leads right to the face.

The fourth option has been to approach from the town of Adirondack to the parking lot at Beaver Pond. This is the southern access to Pharaoh Lake. Follow the Pharaoh Lake trail to the horse trail that exits left before the lake is reached and before the bridge. Follow this for about 0.75 mile, and head northwest for another half mile. The cliff should soon come into view. Before mountain bikes were prohibited from all Adirondack Wilderness Areas, a bicycle approach to Pharaoh Lake made this the quickest route. Whichever way is chosen, plan for careful route-finding involving good map and compass skills. The routes are described left to right.

MAIN FACE

Walk Like an Egyptian   II   5.10   275'   (E)

This is the first route recorded on this large face. On the high section of rock at the left end of the wall, locate a large right-facing corner and smaller corner to its right. Begin 75' left of the large corner on a wooded ledge. (On the edge 20' left of the large corner is a bolted route of unknown origin or grade.) The upper crack is an obvious feature and a landmark to find the climb.

pitch 1 Climb a left-leaning handcrack for 25' and make a hard move left to a right-facing corner. Move up and left to a loose-block belay. 5.10

pitch 2 Step up and right on the slab to a flake and then back left to a large tree ledge. 5.5

pitch 3 From the left end of the ledge, climb the "pod" through a roof to a diagonal fistcrack and vertical crack finish. 5.9+

FA Jeff Edwards and Patrick Purcell 8/87

Stones Of Shame   II   5.10+   350'   (E)   †

Near the center of the cliff, at its highest and most dramatic section, is a rectangular and vertical buttress, whose right edge makes a sharp-edged

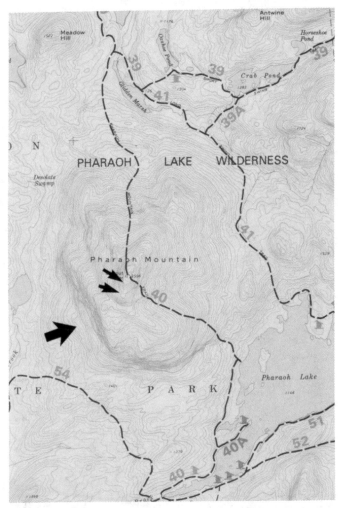

PHARAOH MOUNTAIN

The second pitch corner of Stones of Shame. *Climber: Patrick Purcell.*

blade of rock. Down below and right is an unmistakable white corner. The route is exceptionally good, though the hanging flake of *pitch 4* continues to present a danger.

pitch 1 Locate the corner and head over mossy slabs to a belay to its right. 75'

pitch 2 The corner pitch ends in a large birch to its left. 5.10

pitch 3 Traverse down and left, then up a bushy right-facing corner to a good ledge. 50' 5.4

pitch 4 Climb a steep corner to below the flake. (The first lead aided around from the right in order not to touch the flake; the second on the rope tossed fate to the wind and free-climbed the pitch using the flake.) Continue out a roof to a very exposed fingercrack and flake on the outside of the buttress to a semihanging belay. A wild pitch and a spectacular position. 5.9 (A0)

pitch 5 Make a hard face move right from the belay to gain the blade's edge, then move right to a corner and final headwall. 5.10+

History Tom Yandon and Bill Coryer did most of the work. Don Mellor and Patrick Purcell completed the route, with Purcell free-climbing the flake. 8/3/94

Trick or Treat   I   5.10   120'   †

This good route begins about 200' left of the right (south) end of the cliff, about 50' left of a 50' arete.

pitch 1 Climb a corner with a fingercrack on its left wall. Belay at the base of an overhanging handcrack. 5.8 60'

pitch 2 Climb the steep crack to a grassy ledge. 5.10 60'

FA Patrick Purcell and Ann Eastman 10/31/92

Halloween Cracks

To the right of the arete are two cracks in white rock that end at a small platform about 50' above. The clean cracks (5.9+ and 5.9) bulge steeply about 15' up.

FA Patrick Purcell and Ann Eastman 10/31/92

SUMMIT CLIFFS

The summit cliffs are reached by a marked three-mile trail from Crane Pond. Approach from I-87 on Exit 28 east. From Route 9, take Alder Meadow Road past the small airport for about two miles. Take the left fork to a dirt road marked "Crane Pond." The trail is reached after two miles.

All the routes done so far were put in by Patrick Purcell, who spent two seasons as the mountain's firetower ranger (the tower has since been removed).To find the routes here, go first to the summit. The climbing on these mountaintop cliff bands is concentrated on three separate levels below.

First Tier. The very small first rock is reached by walking about 100 yards, or about five minutes from the summit.

Wilderness Work   I   5.10+   30'

This is the obvious and difficult crack just right of the outside corner. The clean line switches cracks right at mid-height.

FA Patrick Purcell (top-rope) 8/83

5756 in Service   I   5.8   30'

Around left is an overhanging wall. This route begins in the dihedral at the left side of the face above a mud hole. From the top of the corner, traverse right on good holds.

FA Patrick Purcell (top-rope) 8/83

Second Tier. Approximately 25 yards south of the First Tier is the top of this cliff. Here is currently the greatest concentration of climbs. Spruce trees have sprouted up against the cliff since the earlier ascents. The routes are described right to left.

When Clouds Part   I   5.6   65'   (E)

At the right end of the crag is an overhanging section about 20' up. This route begins in a right-facing corner under the overhang. Follow the crack to the right edge of the roof to the arete-like ridge and the top.

FA Patrick Purcell and Karen Bomba 8/83

Pharaoh Winds I 5.8 65'

Begin 5' left of the previous route. Climb the vague crack directly through the roof.

FA Patrick Purcell and Andy Zimmerman 7/84

Slippy Slidden Away I 5.8 65' (E)

8' left of *Pharaoh Winds* (the left side of the roof) are parallel cracks.

FA Patrick Purcell and Andy Zimmerman 8/84

Tuna Fish Crack I 5.11 65' (E)

Next in the series of cracks (10' left of *SSA*) is an all-too-obvious fingercrack. It is an excellent and difficult route.

FA Patrick Purcell 8/83

Pharaoh Ocean Wall 5.7 A2 75'

There are some rivets on a blank section left of *Tuna Fish Crack*. Life in a fire tower can be boring indeed.

FA Patrick Purcell 8/83

Shredded Wheat I 5.10+ 80' (D)

At the left end of the cliff, slightly uphill, is an outside corner. A horizontal crack joins *P.O. Wall*. Climb to a series of holds that lead right for 20' to a mantel and face-climbing finish.

FA Patrick Purcell and Andy Zimmerman 8/84

Third Tier. This has the most rock of the summit bands, but no recorded routes exist.

ROGERS ROCK

Located on the upper end of Lake George, Rogers Rock is surely one of the prettiest and most unusual cliffs in this guide. The slab rises out of the lake with almost 700' of high quality rock, and the views of the deep blue water below the climber's feet almost tempt a jump on hot summer days. The slab is virtually inaccessible from land; an approach from the campground involves slabs, short walls, and even rappels. To approach the cliff by a short paddle isolates the climb and adds an element of removal and solitude that is unparalleled in so populated an area. Your only visitors will arrive by boat as they pass below and spy those "fools up there on the cliff." From their perspective you seem to be flies on a curtain; from yours the boats appear as toys, lending relation to the fabulous exposure below. In the summer the sun blasts the face and there is always a race down the rappel route to drop into the cool water with ropes still hanging from the tree above.

To approach Rogers Rock, begin at the northernmost end of Rogers Rock state campground three miles north of the town of Hague on Route 9N. Paddle past Juniper Island from a small cove (the island is almost a peninsula) and head north for about ten minutes. Route-finding on a fairly featureless slab can be difficult; it is even more so to explain. Instead of the usual pitch-by-pitch descriptions, the accompanying photograph and note should be sufficient. The routes described here were done mainly in the early 1970s.

There are two major features that will help in finding one's way: the large, diagonal, tree-filled crack that splits the face near its left side, and the thin fingercrack that runs nearly the full length of the rock to its right. The tree-filled crack serves as a descent, and the thin crack is *Little Finger,* the most popular route here.

There are three descents: it is possible to pick up a path that heads back to the campground, but this is hard to locate from above. The tree-filled crack can be descended with a short rappel here and there. This is direct, but the nasty junipers are unforgiving. (Recently, there was a well-worn waterski rope hanging from one section, placed either to facilitate descent or inadvertently by an unfortunate passerby.) The third and perhaps easiest descent rappels down the north end of the slabs via trees.

Finally, there are rumors of rattlesnakes in this section of the state, and although the authorities at the campground deny that any risk exists, there have been enough sightings nearby to deserve mention here.

Grace and Commitment 5.8 A3 300'

This first route described is the only one listed on the steep south face of Rogers Rock. All others in the guide are on the slabs, far around on the right, and reached mainly by water. The route is a prominent line that climbs out two right-facing ceilings on its upper section. Because it was climbed as

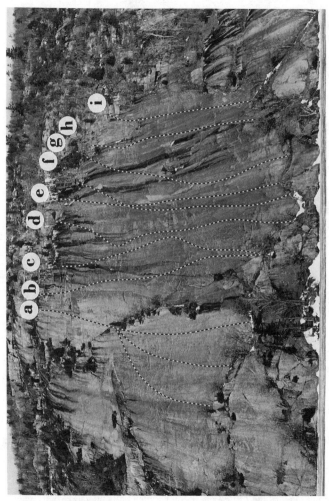

ROGERS ROCK

A. TONE-BONE'S TENNIES 5.7

B. ZIPROD 5.7

C. NOSLOM 5.6

D. SCREAMING MEANY 5.7

E. LITTLE FINGER 5.5

F. LITTLE FINGER DIRECT 5.7

G. TWO BITS 5.6

H. UNNAMED

I. SLIP TEASE–SKID ROW 5.8

325

an adventurous rope-solo, its free potential hasn't been realized. Several fixed pins mark the way, and more cleaning will be necessary if this is to go all free.

pitch 1 Climb a long right-to-left diagonal pocketed seam (crossing a more direct bolted face pitch) to its top. Move back right to a belay. 75'

pitch 2 Continue up and over a bulge (crux) past a fixed blade, heading up right to a belay at piton anchor (160' to ground). 80'

pitch 3 From the belay stance, climb up left, then back rightward up the dirty wide crack, belaying out right at a two-bolt/chain station. 50'

pitch 4 The spectacular roof pitch climbs out a good crack to the righ to another smaller roof and the trees. Two long rappels bring one back to the ground.

FA Sean McFeely 10/94

Tone-Bone's Tennys II 5.7 (D)

The climb has three separate starts; the right-hand one has the least protection and is the hardest. The crux is on the upper face.

FA Tom Rosecrans and Tony Goodwin 1975

Ziprod II 5.7 (D)

The route might seem too close to the tree-filled crack. Protection is fair, and there are variations possible up high.

Tom Rosecrans and Dave Cilley

Screaming Meaney II 5.7 (D) †

This is a recommended route with a couple of unknown bolts along the way.

ACB Tom Rosecrans, Joel Clugstone, and Pat Meaney

Little Finger II 5.5 (E) †

This is by far the most popular line here. It is clear and very well protected. Make sure to head right at the bulge; the direct fingercrack is much harder.

FA Jim Kolocotronis and Bob Perlee

Little Finger Direct II 5.7 (s or D) †

Stay just right of the *Little Finger* crack (some bolts may have been added) until the bulge/headwall; here join the fingercrack past pins, while *Little Finger* opts for an easier exit right.

FA Joel Clugstone and Tom Rosecrans

Two Bits   II   5.6   (D)

Wander to a new two-bolt anchor; the third pitch climbs a tree to get to the crack.

FA Jim Kolocotronis and Bob Perlee

Unnamed

Easy lower pitches lead to the always slimy exit crack.

FA Joel Clugstone and Tom Rosecrans

Slip Tease–Skid Row   I   5.9   (S)

Good, clean face-climbing past several bolts on the right end of the slab.

FA Tom Rosecrans and Joel Clugstone

Last Hurrah   5.9+

A bolted face climb on the right edge of the slab.

FA Dave Aldous and Tom Rosecrans 11/94

BARTON HIGH CLIFF

This may well be one of the best finds in the southern half of the park. It is big and steep, and so far, very little of its potential has been realized. The approach via state land is slightly indirect, generally taking Spuytenduivel Brook from Route 8 between Brant Lake and Graphite. The brook heads north from a rusted guardrail a little over two miles from the eastern end of Brant Lake. A fair path parallels the brook and leaves the road 200 yards east, just past a low roadcut and at the start of a wire guardrail. After about a quarter mile, the better path crosses to the west bank of the stream. To get to the rock, skirt the beaver pond to the right (the rock wall visible from here isn't the main wall; it does have some potential for short overhanging desperates). Follow another lovely stream up right through a hemlock forest before breaking left to find the cliff. The approach may take about an hour and a half if you stay on route.

The Columbine Terrace Wall is the shield of rock first encountered on the lower right side of the crag. *Twinflower Traverse* is the obvious cleaned crack just right of center.

The best views of the cliff are from the low, rocky knoll directly across from it. From the upper of these vantage points across from the wall, the lines of *Excellent Adventure* and *Final Frontier* are unmistakable.

Bloodroot   I   5.10   50'

pitch 1 To reach this climb it is necessary to scramble up and right through trees to an upper tree ledge. This top-roped route involves thin face and fingertip crack work. Needs a little more cleaning.

FA Jamie Savage and Bill Widrig (top-rope) 5/19/91

Twinflower Traverse   I   5.9   120'   (E)

pitch 1 This is the cleaned fingercrack beginning right of center on a high ledge. Walk out the ledge and follow the crack to the top.

FA Bill Widrig and Tad Welc 10/1/92

Columbine Crack   I   5.6   100'   (E)

pitch 1 Begin on the left side of the wall at the top of a hemlock-covered terrace. Follow a wandering crack line to a handcrack finish. The crack is visible from the knoll.

FA Bill Widrig and Jamie Savage 5/19/91

Continuing left along the base of the cliff, one finds a high-angle face 200' past Columbine Terrace.

Ali-Kat   I   5.10   130'   (s)

Start 10' left of a broken right-facing corner, 25' below a prominent 20' white pine.

pitch 1 Face-climb up the right side of the smooth wall heading for a thin vertical crack. Continue to the level of the white pine, then make exciting moves left on small holds to the obvious crack.

FA Bill Widrig and Tad Welch 5/93

BARTON HIGH CLIFF

Final Frontier   II   5.8   300'   (E)   †

This full-length route follows a relatively moderate line up the most impos-ing section of the cliff. The centerpiece pitch ascends the solitary crack high above the overhanging orange wall. Look for the most prominent tall pine high above the second pitch.

pitch 1 Start uphill 25' from the left corner of the orange wall at a short wide crack leading to vegetated ramp. Belay behind a block and small tree.

pitch 2 Up outside corner, following a crack on the main face and past the overhang (some loose rock). The airy crack gets progressively easier and ends at a huge ledge.

pitch 3 The "Gunks" pitch climbs a face behind the pine, then left around ceilings and up the short nose to the top.

FA Tad Welch and Bill Widrig 4/24/90

Spit and Drivel   I   5.10+   140'   (S)   †

The long section beyond *Final Frontier* is loose and capped by big roofs. Past these is an unmistakable arete, the remarkable right face of which of-fers a lot of potential for good thin crack and face climbs.

pitch 1 Start in the most obvious, slightly diagonal crack (same as for the next route). At the yellow spot about 15' up, head left on thin holds and tricky protection to the next crack. Follow this to the top, traversing left a few feet as it crosses the *Excellent Adventure* hand-traverse.

FA Don Mellor and Dave Furman 8/12/94

Excellent Adventure   I   5.8+   160'   (E)   †

This recommended route finds a way to climb the upper arete. Begin in the most obvious crack.

pitch 1 Climb the crack to a hanging belay under a block about 50' up.

pitch 2 The hand-traverse left is obvious and exciting. Once on the crest of the arete, continue up the edge to a ledge below overhangs. Exit left, or right 10' under loose rock to the final crack of *Spit and Drivel.*

Variation Climb the main crack, joining upper *Spit and Drivel* for a more sustained 5.8 to the top.

FA Bill Widrig, Tad Welch, and Chuck Yax 6/89

BARTON HIGH CLIFF

A. SPIT AND DRIVEL 5.10+

B. EXCELLENT ADVENTURE 5.8+

Reckless Endangerment   I   5.7   80'   (E)

There are several cracklines on the high wall on the left side of the low-angle, brushy corner down and left of the previous route.

pitch 1 Follow the left-hand and easiest crack to a tiny alcove. Move left and up a lichen-covered face to a short crack/corner finish.

FA Tad Welch and Chuck Yax 4/20/89

The next destination is the left (east) end of the cliff, another 300' along the base. Routes can be located by finding a 40' right-facing dihedral.

Animal Logic   I   5.7   160'   (S)

30' right of the corner is a short face with unusual brick-colored holds.

pitch 1 Beautiful moves on incuts lead to lower-angled rock and a hemlock tree. Stay left of the corner by climbing a short rib, then up past a series of horizontals to the top.

FA Tad Welch and Chuck Yax 4/19/89

Son of Cirrhosis   I   5.8+   60'   (E)

pitch 1 6' right of the inside corner is an unmistakable layback; at its top go left through roof.

FA Tad Welch and Chuck Yax 4/19/89

Sunset Arete   I   5.7   150'   (S)

This route climbs the fin left of the previous route.

pitch 1 From fallen tree, climb up the right margin of the face and follow edge to a blocky ledge (loose rock).

pitch 2 Climb best-looking line above, staying left of tree-filled groove.

FA Tad Welch and Chuck Yax 4/19/89

Isosceles   I   5.8   50'   (E)

pitch 1 Start 40' left and uphill from the previous route on a smooth 50' wall. Up to upper right-slanting crack line to a tree belay at ceiling and right-facing corner.

FA Tad Welch and Bill Widrig 9/92

Pythagoras I 5.9 50' (E)

pitch 1 Start as for previous route, then finger-traverse right and below *Isosceles* to the common belay.

FA Tad Welch and Bill Widrig 5/93

TONGUE MOUNTAIN CLIFFS

Tongue Mountain is the sharp-edged ridge that extends into central Lake George from the northwest. Although known for its population of timber rattlesnakes, it is still a popular hiking destination, offering a rigorous ridge climb with good views of the lake. The cliffs described here face southwest overlooking Northwest Bay, and they can be seen from Route 9N as one drives north from the town of Bolton Landing. The single-pitch routes done so far are reported to be hard, generally well-protected, and recommended.

The Tongue Mountain Trail begins from Route 9N about 5 miles north of Bolton Landing. Follow the trail for a few minutes to a fork (the ridge trail offers a loop here). Head right (south). After 10 or 15 minutes, the trail climbs a steep shoulder of the mountainside. Just past the top of the hill, the trail descends to a small stream with a footbridge. Here the 30-minute uphill bushwhack begins. Follow the dominant stream course, avoiding the smaller feeder streams. There are plastic markers (origin unknown) that lead most of the way to the cliff. Toward the top, the stream dries up and the cliffs become visible through the trees.

The southwest cliff exposure runs diagonally up the mountainside for several hundred yards. The middle portion is loosely characterized by several large corners. To get a bearing from the downhill end of the crag, follow the base uphill to a large face with several distinct arching cracks. To the right is a small right-facing corner capped by a small roof 30' up. This is *Tartar Control*. Above is an obvious crack system.

All routes done so far were by Fred Abbuhl and Doug Douglas 1992.

Tartar Control I 5.10+ 80'

pitch 1 Climb past the small roof, finishing at a large pine.

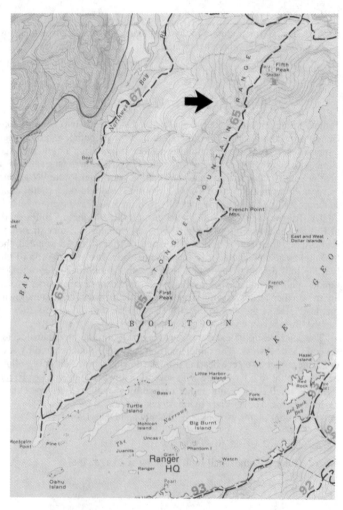

TONGUE MOUNTAIN

Taste Buds   I   5.9+

pitch 1 From the ledge atop the previous route, move left 30' and climb a face with vertical and horizontal cracks.

Tongue Lashing   I   5.11

pitch 1 Start on the ledge atop the previous route, about 10' left of the large pine. Face-climb (hidden nut to the right) to pin and follow cracks to good hands finish.

Slip of the Tongue   I   5.12   (top-rope)

pitch 1 About 75 yards uphill is a large corner with a distinct orange face on its left wall. A 20' thin crack is followed by a move right and a crux bulge. Finish up and left.

Tongue and Groove   I   5.10+

pitch 1 On the right face of the corner is another good route. Begin at a steep bulge below a series of horizontal cracks. Follow cracks and seams up lower angled face to a bulge with a pin. Fingercrack up and right to finish at large pine. (Black streak to the left was top-roped at 5.10.)

Grid Lock   I   5.9+

About 50 yards farther along the base of the cliff is a hidden gully.

pitch 1 On the right wall of the gully is a "stairstep" fingercrack. At its top, climb through a maze of thin cracks.

MOXHAM DOME

Moxham Mountain is a long ridge running east to west about 5 miles north of the village of North Creek. The eastern terminus of the ridge is a steep slab known as Moxham Dome. Climbers approaching from Route 87 will use Exit 26 to Pottersville to reach Route 28N, which runs along the base of the cliff, offering a clear view of the climbs. Follow the dirt road on the south end of the dome to a fork; the right fork leads to a quarry and the vague path across to the rock. The key to finding many of the routes is the Midway, a vegetated ramp leading up and then across the slabs at its midpoint. Just left of the Midway is *Back Space. Beast* starts down and to the right, taking two pitches to reach the Midway. The climbs on the right side of the face are keyed by the *Nexus/True Grit* slab, easily distinguished by its prominent black streak. (Some descriptions are taken with permission from the author from *Adirondack Rock and Ice Climbs* by Thomas Rosecrans, 1976, now out of print.)

As is typical with slabs, routes here abound with variations, and it is likely that your line will combine sections of more than one route. Expect to do some wandering. Also note the fresh scar that runs across the middle of the face. The rock fell here in 1977, and it probably affected routes around *Grotto*. Be ready to detour if the route in the 1975 description seems to have vanished.

The routes as described here begin left to right. In order to begin locating these, it will be helpful to find a feature known as the *Lizard's Tongue*, a tongue-like rock pinned between slabs at the base of the prominent diagonal overlap toward the left end of the slabs.

Moonflap   I   5.4

This route is about 150' left of *Lizard's Tongue,* beyond a confusion of small slabs and clumps of trees. Start in an open book at the top of a wide inverted V. There is a vegetated 4" crack in the corner.

pitch 1 Climb the corner past a small tree to a wedged boulder. Traverse right 20' to another crack; climb the right-facing corner behind the birches to a hollow oak.

pitch 2 Move right, then up along the right side of the flake to a smooth, brown slab. Cross the slab to the right and then up to the end of a large flap. Head up and left over broken rock to finish.

FA Dick Tucker and Eric T. Laurin 7/30/78

Touched   I   5.6

This route parallels *Moonflap,* but it is more rewarding. It will be even more so as lichens wear away.

pitch 1 Climb the slab left of the previous route past the wedged boulder. Traverse right to the prominent nose. Climb this arete up unprotected rock (or move into the corner for safer going). Belay at the hollow oak.

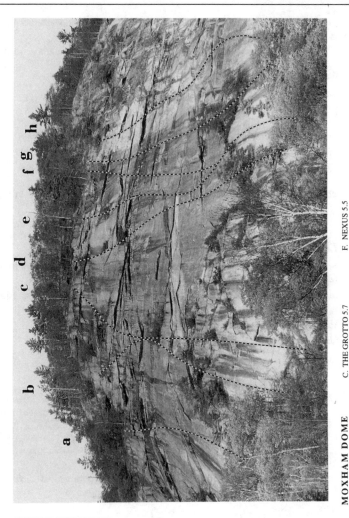

MOXHAM DOME

A. BACK SPACE 5.4
B. THE BEAST 5.5
C. THE GROTTO 5.7
D. TRUE GRIT 5.5
E. TRALFAMADORE 5.6
F. NEXUS 5.5
G. SKID ROW 5.5
H. BLUE JAY WAY 5.5

PHOTO BY CHUCK TURNER

pitch 2 Traverse left into a right-facing corner. Follow cracks upward, then right on a rising, narrow ramp.

FA Dick Tucker and Tim Riley 6/28/88

Vivid Imagination   I   5.8   300'   (s)

Start 50' left of *Lizard's Tongue.*

pitch 1 From an oak on the left end of the vegetated ramp, friction up to a right-rising, slightly overhanging flake. Undercling right, then up to a small oak belay. 5.6 100'

pitch 2 Follow a thin crack up and right about 85'. Leave the crack and face-climb left to an oak belay near a large pine below an overhang. 5.6 125'

pitch 3 Surmount the overhang on the right and climb dirty rock to the top. 5.8 80'

FA Jim Harrison, Tim Harrison, Michael Bolitho, and Rick Villeneuve 8/25/86

Lizard's Tongue   I   5.5   270'

So named for a slim boulder pinned between slabs sticking out like a long reptilian tongue.

pitch 1 Start at a vegetated ramp left of and above the Midway, at the foot of a right-rising flake. Climb the corner to a pin below two ramps rising left and right. 150'

pitch 2 Climb up left ramp to friction on slab to the top of a right-rising overhang. Traverse left to finish. 120'

Variations

Lizard's Tongue Left   I   5.6   300'

pitch 1 From the young oak above the ramp (and left of *Lizard's Tongue*) follow a right-leaning flake to the tongue. Surmount this feature left to right. Climb over flake onto steep friction.

pitch 2 Climb up and left, joining *Lizard's Tongue.*

Tongue and Cheek   I   5.6+   (E)

Surmount the right-rising flake above the double ramps of *Lizard's Tongue,* about 25' up and left of the top of the ramps.

Lizard's Tongue Direct   I   5.5   (s)

pitch 1 About halfway between *Back Space* and *Lizard's Tongue,* there is a vegetated crack system that offers several easy possibilities. Climb thin flakes on its right side to a large oak.

pitch 2 Follow a flake and crack to their end; continue unprotected friction to the base of the double ramps of *Lizard's Tongue.*

FA Unknown

FA Rick Villeneuve and Jim Harrison (var. 1)

FA Rick Villeneuve 8/24/86 (var. 2)

FA Alex Rosenberg and Rick Villeneuve 8/7/86 (var. 3)

Half Space   I   5.4   300'

Start on the vegetated ramp above and 30' left of the start of *Back Space.*

pitch 1 Climb the slab to an inverted V notch. (Watch that rope doesn't jam). Follow crack to its end, and continue up slab past tiny right-facing flakes. Belay at small right-facing flake and grass clump. 5.4 140' (E)

pitch 2 Climb the slab to a pin belay at the end of the second pitch of *Back Space.* 40'

pitch 3 Climb the flap at a low point to the left, and climb the slab to its end at steeper rock. Traverse up and left to a bush belay. 5.4 100'

pitch 4 Climb the right-rising ramp behind the large tree, finishing at the awkward crack. 5.3 30'

FA Dick Tucker and Tim Riley 6/28/88

Back Space   I   5.4   300'

At the left end of the cliff is the Midway. *Back Space* starts at the low point of the slab just left of this feature and crosses the previous route partway up.

pitch 1 Climb the slab to the beginning of the crack. Continue to a small ledge just left of the trees.

pitch 2 Ascend the slab to a right-rising flap and belay.

pitch 3 Climb the flap and slab beyond, and then a complex series of overlaps to a tree grove that ends the climb.

FA Ken Jackson and Tony Brown

Beast II 5.5 (D)

Unfortunately, the rock here is not as clean as on other routes on the slab. Start at the low point of the slab immediately right of the Midway start.

pitch 1 Follow the seam, crack, inside corner, and crack to a small stance.

pitch 2 Climb up the small inside corner and work left from its end, then back right making for the high point of the slab.

pitch 3 Scramble through the trees to the highest clump.

pitch 4 Climb up 10' to cracks and flakes. Climb over the outside corner and diagonal up right to trees and horizontal crack. Climb straight up from here past an island of trees to a belay in a second island.

pitch 5 Straight up over the flap to an unstable clump of birches. Head left through recent rockfall, gaining a crack system. Climb back and then up under overhang. Traverse left until the overhang can be surmounted. Finish up and left.

FA Tom Rosecrans and Janet Beachman 10/74

Grotto II 5.7 (s)

Start a short distance right of *Beast*.

pitch 1 Climb disconnected flakes and slab to the broken tree area.

pitch 2 Scramble through the woods, and climb over flaps and slabs to a tree ledge.

pitch 3 Continue through a shattered area, and climb flaps, making a crouching traverse left (same as for *Beast*) to a ledge.

pitch 4 Finish by diagonaling back up right, ending below the obvious, rectangular "grotto."

FA Doug and Blue Foy, Steve Angelini, and Al Rubin 5/75

True Grit II 5.5 (s)

A climb that required some unearthing, this one has, nonetheless, some good moments. Start at an oak and pine growing together at the base of the clean white slab with the black streak.

pitch 1 Climb the easy but unprotected slab up the left side of the black streak. 145'

pitch 2 From the ledge, diagonal and traverse left into a small flap facing left that arches upward. Climb this to its apex and exit straight up, climbing through another overhang. Continue to a large curving flake that is followed right to its top. 150'

pitch 3 Climb up and over the next flap and pass a right-facing corner on the right. Continue over easy rock to the large overhang, belaying in the corner/niche 5' to the left of the perched block and 25' left of the garden belay of *Nexus*. 135'

pitch 4 Surmount the overhangs behind the belay to a left-slanting corner and tree belay. 70'

pitch 5 Diagonal left and up to the left end of the next vegetation island. Continue the line to a corner/ceiling, ascending right through this and finishing as desired. 130'

FA Tom Rosecrans and Mike Dry 9/10/74

Tralfamadore II 5.6

This route was probably the first on the slab. It starts just right of the black streak in the clean white slab near the right central section of the rock.

pitch 1 Climb excellent but unprotected friction, staying about 10' right of the black streak, to a tree belay. 150'

pitch 2 Diagonal up left and over a flap, eventually belaying at a left-facing pointed flake visible from the base. 60'

pitch 3 Wander up right to a ledge under a wall. 70'

pitch 4 Traverse left under the overlap, then climb through a notch right of the largest overlap. 80'

pitch 5 Make another big step onto the slab above and climb to yet another short wall. Traverse left until it is possible to exit up right.

FA Joe Bridges and Mike Landau 9/5/72

Nexus II 5.5

This good climb is fairly protected on all pitches except the first. It shares much of the same terrain as *Tralfamadore*.

pitch 1 Same as for *Tralfamadore*.

pitch 2 Walk left to the first flap, heave onto the slab, and continue diagonaling left to a second overhang. Traverse left under this until a small, grassy horizontal crack can be seen above. Climb over the flap and diagonal right to a belay in the "eye." 100'

pitch 3 Climb straight up over four flaps and friction to the left end of a vegetated ledge. The belay is somewhat tenuous as the vegetation doesn't offer the foothold that it would seem to suggest. 145'

pitch 4 Climb up to a large overhang with a flat shelf on top, and surmount this from the right side. Diagonal up right to the trees (upper group), and then to a small corner. Ascend this easily and exit up right.

FA Tom Rosecrans and Doug Leith 9/74

Skid Row   II   5.5

Start at the low point of the north end of the slabs.

pitch 1 Climb up the center of the slab, tending left at about 50' and reaching a tree belay at 150'.

pitch 2 Scramble up left for 50', surmount flap, slab, and flap to a small tree belay.

pitch 3 The climb continues up to a prominent garden.

pitch 4 Finish up right.

FA Tom Rosecrans and Rob Norris 6/6/75

Blue Jay Way   II   5.5

Start at a three-trunked oak 35' right of *Skid Row* at a small overhang near the ground.

pitch 1 Climb easy friction to the left end of the flap above and belay. 100'

pitch 2 Ascend the slab for 75' to the next overhang. Climb this where it forms a small corner with a step on the left. Continue to a series of small flaps and on to a large overhang that is followed left to an inverted V with bushes on the right. 150'

pitch 3 Traverse up and left below or through trees and continue left under the overhang until under the island of vegetation. 140'

pitch 4 Climb up left for 15' over the hang into the jungle. Ascend the slab up and right over two small flaps diagonaling right into an inside corner finish.

FA Tom Rosecrans and Mike Dry 9/74

Eneyaw   II   5.5

Start at a small right-facing corner 30' up right of *Blue Jay Way.*

pitch 1 Climb the slab to the left of bushes below the overhang. Climb it here and the slab above to the right end of the second overhang.

pitch 2 Climb around the next overhang on the right and then traverse back left to a sharp break in the flap. Climb this and the crack above and then straight up to the trees.

pitch 3 Climb right to a wide crack and up the big finish corner.

FA Tom Rosecrans and Mike Dry 9/74

HUCKLEBERRY MOUNTAIN

There is a lot of exposed rock here on this ridge off Route 8 south of Wevertown. Countless exposed faces and slabs, separated and somewhat diminished by tree-covered ledges and bushy cracks, span for a half mile around the southern flanks of the mountain. The climbing here is in its early stages of development, but the potential for high-quality routes of all grades and kinds is obvious.

From Johnsburg, take the South Johnsburg Road to Hudson Street. Park at the anglers' turnout at the bridge over Paintbed Creek. Take the uphill dirt road (Paintbed Road) on the left. Though it is possible to drive beyond, the land is private. Please park below on Hudson Street so as not to jeopardize access. Walk uphill to a clearing with a big tree. Take the left-hand fork about ten minutes to another fork; take the left option and, shortly thereafter, look for a yellow-blazed tree. Seventy-five yards beyond is a more obscure tote road heading off left. (The main road continues to Snowshoe Pond.) The cliff begins to appear off to the left after about 15 minutes along this old road.

The cliff wraps around the mountainside, and the first rock seen (though the foliage of summer may obscure any views) is that on the west end of the mountain, referred to as the Boneyard Cliff. (This appellation and those of many of the route names emanate from Dick Tucker's close encounter with two nasty dogs who chased him up a boulder and who refused to retreat until bombarded with rocks.) The left end of the cliff is complex and virtually impossible to describe; one could wander around forever before finding anything recognizable. On the other hand, the Hard Guy Wall has several distinct bolted routes and is thus easily recognized. For this reason, climbs will be described in relation to this fine section of cliff. Once this is located, one should be able to head left or right to discover the neighboring routes. The most direct route to the Hard Guy Wall begins at an obvious lone boulder just left of the tote road and follows widely-spaced red markers on trees to *Hammerdog*. The following descriptions are mainly Dick Tucker's. It was he who saw the potential, did much of the work, and kept the detailed notes.

The Hard Guy Wall (HGW) stands toward the left end of the cliff. Several steep bolted face routes just left of an attractive prow serve as landmarks. The first routes included here are described left to right from the HGW.

NO-NAME WALL

Slightly uphill and right of the HGW, past the gully and huge boulders, is a 150' face with a solitary vertical crack.

Down in the Mall   I   5.6   150'   (E)

pitch 1 Climb the weeds to the overhang (or hand-traverse in from the left) and follow the obvious crack. *Variation* it is also possible to climb the short dirty wall behind the pine.

FA Bill Widrig and Tad Welch 10/27/91

MIDDLE WALL

One hundred feet right of No Name Wall is another small face about 100' wide and 80' high.

LAST WALL

About 100' right of the Middle Wall is yet another slab, the last good rock before the height-of-land. There are well-defined, vegetated cracks on each end of this face.

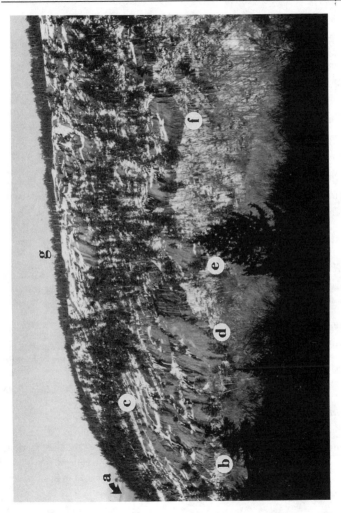

PHOTO BY DICK TUCKER

HUCKLEBERRY MOUNTAIN

A. BONE YARD CLIFF
B. MAIN CLIFF AREA

C. TOP OF THE GREAT DIHEDRAL
D. HARD GUY WALL
E. NO-NAME CLIFF

F. LAST WALL
G. WHITE SLAB

Demitasse   I   5.5   85'   (E)

About 15' right of the left crack is an incipient crackline that starts with solution pockets.

pitch 1 Climb pockets and crack to its end; traverse left to crack, cross sloping ledge, and finish via V notch.

FA Dick Tucker and Jeremy Munson 6/16/90

Untitled   I   5.8   85'   (top-rope)

pitch 1 Climb face 20' right of previous route.

FA Hobey Walker 6/16/90

Opening Moves   I   5.6   85'

pitch 1 This is the crack at the right end of the slab. Climb up past tiny roof.

FA Hobey Walker and Jim Bender 6/16/90

FACTORY SLABS

At the height-of land opposite the ruins of the paint factory lie two small slabs 80–150' high. The northern slab lies out of sight up to the left; the southern slab is just above the height-of-land on the right.

Willy   I   5.3   60'

pitch 1 In the center of the northern slab is a brush-filled right-facing corner. Traverse in from the left, and follow clean rock along the right edge of the slab left of the corner.

FA Dick Tucker 5/3/92

Untitled   I   5.8   130'   (top-rope)

This and the following route lie on the southern slab.

pitch 1 Climb the crack above the roof on the left side of the slab. Start on the left at a vertical crack or clean slab to the right.

FA Dick Tucker and Tim Riley 5/10/92

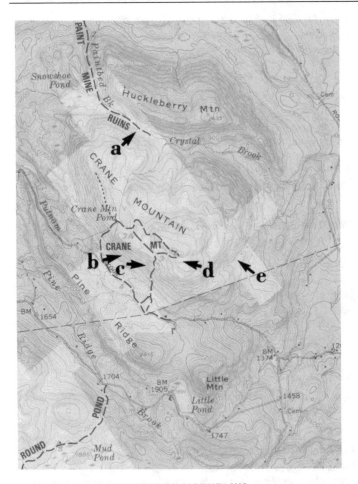

CRANE AND HUCKLEBERRY MOUNTAINS

A. HUCKLEBERRY MT.

B. BEAVERVIEW WALL

C. VIEWPOINT CLIFF AND SLAB

D. SUMMIT RIDGE

E. SOUTHEASTERN CRAGS

It's a Puzzle   I   5.7   130'   (top-rope)

pitch 1 This is the crack on the right behind the large pine. Slab to offwidth, finishing rightward via flakes and slab.

FA Dick Tucker and Tim Riley 5/10/92

WHITE SLAB

Directly above the Hard Guy Wall is an expansive slab that leads to the summit of the ridge. It is the highest and widest of several tiers.

A Walk In The Sky   I   5.1   200'+

Climb the knobby, black streak, just left of center.

FA (solo) Tad Welch and Bill Widrig 10/27/91

The following routes are described right to left, starting at the obvious Hard Guy Wall.

Horror Show   I   5.9   130'   (E)

Well named and formidable. Start uphill from the bolted wall near two large trees below the big vertical offwidth. Bring gear from RPs to large cams.

pitch 1 Climb leftward into the cave, slab climbing until forced out to the offwidth. At its end, climb the outside corner left of the roof to the vertical offwidth and chimney to top.

FA Jim Bender and Patty Li 11/3/91

Barney is the Antichrist   I   5.10+   85'   (E)   †

pitch 1 This is an excellent bolt-protected route up a series of discontinuous flakes, cracks, and edges in the center of the wall.

FA Hobey Walker 7/25/93

Big Purple Rat   I   5.11-   70'   (E)   †

Climb leftward past the "birdbeak" flake to sloping ledge. Follow thin crack line to chain anchor. (It's possible to connect to the previous route 5.10+.)

FA Hobey Walker 7/25/93

Apollo Tucker   I   5.11-   70'   (E)   †

pitch 1 Start on right-facing flake near left end of wall, following six bolts
to chain anchor.

FA Hobey Walker 10/16/93

Insomnia   I   5.11-   140'   (E)   †

This is perhaps the best hard route here, following the edge between the
HGW and the face to its left.

pitch 1 Start at the low, outside left edge of the Hard Guy Wall. Superb
climb (mixed gear and bolts) finishing with slab moves to a pine.

FA Dave Furman and Hobey Walker 10/23/93

Darmok Indirect   I   5.9-   125'   (E)   †

pitch 1 The initial handcrack leading to the low pine is a very distinct feature.
From the tree, head right into a shallow corner, gaining a vertical crack.
Where the angle lessens and the corner veers right, climb straight up
good face holds to finish.

FA Don Mellor and Dick Tucker 10/30/93

Darmok   I   5.7+   100'   (E)

pitch 1 Take the excellent, but too short, handcrack to the pine. Continue
up dirt-filled corner, roof, and offwidth, and face to the left.

FA Dick Tucker and Dave Furman 10/16/93

Tallywhacker   I   5.4   240'   (E)

A two-pitch, dirty gully that diagonals up to the right, providing access to
the top of HGW. The second pitch climbs the slab right of the gully

Variation **Codswallop**   5.6   100'   (E)

pitch 2 Take the fistcrack from the ledge (after a ropelength on the previous
route) and up the left side of the slab.

FA Dick Tucker, Lois and David Legg 9/28/91
FA Dick Tucker, Patti Li, and Jim Bender 11/2/91 (var.)

GPD (Geriatric Profanity Disorder)   I   5.10-   75'   (E)

Begin at the height-of-land. Follow a perfect fingercrack to a rightward traverse, a bolt, and a second fingercrack. Two more bolts lead to a tree.

FA Dave Furman and Mike Dunkerly 5/28/94

Twenty-One   I   5.9   50'   (E)

Start as for *Tallywhacker* to the second step. Move left into the right-facing corner. After 20', move left across slab to crack and bolt anchor.

FA Dave Furman and Dick Tucker 10/16/93

Potato Chip Flake   I   5.11   50'   (E)   †

pitch 1 The name alone should help in finding this one. Climb past four bolts to a fixed anchor.

FA Dave Furman 10/16/93

I'd Rather Be in Iowa   I   5.8   65'   (E)

Begin 10' left of the thin potato-chip flake. The clean right-facing corner marks the route. Five bolts lead to an anchor.

FA Dave Furman 7/94

Escape from Iowa   I   5.12-   40'   (E)

The blunt arete holds a recommended and hard route. Four bolts to anchor.

FA Dave Furman 7/94

Dark of the Sun   I   5.7   150'   (E)

About 100' left of HGW is a short wall with two attractive thin cracks.

pitch 1 Climb the easier and excellent left-hand crack to a terrace. Belay here or continue the inside corner to a short crack and "moonrock" to the top. Recommended.

Variation The 35' thin crack to the right is 5.10.

FA Tad Welch (roped solo) 9/28/91
FA Bill Widrig and Ed Palen 10/30/93 (var.)

Teflon Wall   I   5.11   75'   (E)   †

About 150' (more or less) left of HGW is a right-facing vertical wall marked by horizontal cracks. Bring gear to supplement bolts. Recommended.

FA Hobey Walker 11/3/91

FBW I 5.10 100' (E)

Around the left from the previous route is a steep buttress wall with a striking thin handcrack through a roof. This is *Huckleberry Hound*.

pitch 1 Climb thin cracks near the right edge of a face in a prominent right-facing corner to a ledge. Above, take the thin crack on the left.

FA Jim Bender and Jim Pittman 10/27/91

Huckleberry Hound I 5.10 100' (E) †

From the ledge described above, take the obvious thin handcrack through the roof.

FA Don Mellor and Dick Tucker 10/30/93

Untitled I 5.8 100'

The left edge of the prominent buttress of the previous routes is a brushy, broken corner rising as V. It is a dreadful route that serves best as access to the top of the other climbs.

FA Jim Bender and Jim Pittman 10/27/91

Some 200' left of HGW is another outcropping of decent rock between tree-covered and broken faces.

Jealous Dogs I 5.6 150' (E)

First locate *Hammerdog* on a steep narrow face with two cracks forming a cross. Begin 5' right, behind a clump a trees in a right-facing corner.

pitch 1 Scramble the corner and undercling right to a bombay chimney. Stay in the dihedral, moving right at its top to pine. 80'

pitch 2 Climb slab right of the *Hammerdog* crack to the upper fingertip crack and continue to small tree. Rappel or join the next route.

FA Tad Welch and Bill Widrig 10/27/91

Hammerdog I 5.9 270' (s) †

This is one of the best routes here. Start below vertical crack.

pitch 1 Climb face to horizontal crack, move right, then up and left to easier rock. 5.9 90' (s) *pitch 2* Ascend excellent handcrack, easy slab and the first overlap. Belay tree at left. 5.6 90' (E)

pitch 3 Climb second overlap and slab to overhang, which is climbed at the V.

FA Hobey Walker and Dick Tucker 6/8/91

Lucille   I   5.5   120'

Just left of the previous route is a right-facing corner leading into a slot.

pitch 1 Climb the corner and up into the wide slot, exiting left and up slabs to a ledge below junipers. Rappel.

FA Dick Tucker (roped solo) 10/20/91

Just left of these climbs is an enormous, very low-angled right-facing corner, one of the largest features at Huckleberry. This is referred to as the Great Dihedral.

Aunt Polly   I   5.6   275'   (s)

Immediately right of the Great Dihedral is an arete; 20' right of this is a grassy crack on a steep slab.

pitch 1 Climb crack and slabs to overhang. 5.6 130'

pitch 2 Pass overhang via notch to easier slabs and the top.

FA Hobey Walker and Dick Tucker 6/8/91

Weenie's Way   I   5.5   310'   (s)

About 50' left of the Great Dihedral at the right edge of the slab is a series of cracks.

pitch 1 Climb cracks along edge of slab, moving left to small left-facing corner. At top, scramble across dirt to tree. 5.5 120' (E)

pitch 2 Step right and scramble along edge of slab to offwidth in the overhanging wall. Move right into corner behind small pine. 90'

pitch 3 Climb corner and slabs to trees.

FA Dick Tucker and Hobey Walker 11/3/91

Mister Buzzard   I   5.5   90'   (E)

65' left of the Great Dihedral is a square-cut, right-facing corner at the left edge of the slab.

pitch 1 Climb corner to steepening top, then traverse off right.

FA Dick Tucker and Bob Hey (with upper *Weenie's Way*) 6/23/91

Hat Rabbit   I   5.7   85'   (E)   †

This is a good route on clean rock. Start at the tree several feet left of the previous route (or harder from lowest point on slab).

pitch 1 Climb slab and crack to trees.

FA Dick Tucker and Jim Pittman 10/26/91

The next routes are located well left of the previous ones, on a section known as the Boneyard Cliffs.

Mister Toad's Wild Ride   I   5.6   120'   (E)

This is the attractive crackline right of the arch in the upper face. Seen through the trees when the leaves are down, it is one of the more appealing features on the left end of the cliffs. Unfortunately, it starts from a ledge about 50' above the top of *G-String*. The best approach, therefore, is probably via helicopter or rappel from the top.

pitch 1 Follow the crack to its end, move right at the horizontal and up to finish on hollow flake.

FA Dick Tucker and Karen Kuhn 10/23/93

G-String   I   5.8 (?)   120'

About 20' right of a large, left-leaning, left-facing, shattered corner is a dirty, broken open book.

pitch 1 Up the corner, passing through roof and up flaring offwidth.

FA Jeremy Munson 11/4/91

Desperate Passage   I   5.7   290'   (E)

Start below the prominent chimney formed by a sharp, left-facing flake about 120' up. This feature is also visible and obvious from the approach when viewing is possible through the trees.

> *pitch 1* Climb the slab right of a line of bushes and through a steep zone of right-facing flakes to a brushy ramp at the base of the chimney. 5.7 120'
>
> *pitch 2* Climb the chimney through overhang to ledge with poplar. 5.7 70'
>
> *pitch 3* Follow handcrack left to pine, then up easy rock to choice of corners. 5.3 100'

FA Dick Tucker and Bob Hey 10/9/93

Blueberry Scramble   Class 4

To the left of the previous routes is a route to the top of the Four Pines Buttress.

FA Dick Tucker 6/7/92

The last routes described here, those on the left end of the slabs, are described in relation to a feature known as Four Pines Buttress, a huge, left-facing corner overhanging at the top.

Double Vision   I   5.6   125'   (E)

On the right edge of the Four Pines Buttress is a small, broken corner behind two oaks.

> *pitch 1* Climb the slab behind the oaks and move right to two parallel cracks. Traverse left on the tiny brushy ledge to a corner and easy rock to the top.

FA Dick Tucker and Tim Riley 8/8/92

Motoring with Mohammed   I   5.7   140'   (E)   †

Despite a rough beginning, this is one of the better routes here.

> *pitch 1* Start at the lowest point of Four Pines Buttress at two left-facing corners and a roof. Climb the corner next to the roof and up the wall on the right to a slab several feet below the small pine. Follow cracks to second pine, then take right-rising fingercrack to small ledge. Belay or head upwards, staying left of easier rock.

FA Dick Tucker and Tim Riley 9/12/93

Devil Dogs   5.6   200'   (E)

This is a good friction route that starts on the narrow, clean slab 20' left of the huge Four Pines Buttress corner.

pitch 1 Up past 3 bolts to a small oak on the left. 120'

pitch 2 Up slab past 2 more bolts to a V, then right up broken rock to wide chimney finish.

FA Dick Tucker and Tim Riley 6/13/93

PUFFER MOUNTAIN CLIFF

The cliffs of Puffer Mountain near the Kings Flow region of the southern Adirondacks offer true wilderness climbs for intrepid bushwhackers. Girdling the south and southeast shoulders of the upper mountain, the expansive 70- to 180-foot cliffs have potential for a variety of one- and two-pitch climbs in an untrodden, remote environment. The easiest approach begins at the north end of Kings Flow near Chimney Mountain south of Indian Lake and follows the trail south along its eastern shore. Passing the Puffer Pond trail, continue south until the trail veers right and descends to Humphrey Brook. This is about three miles from the trailhead. Bushwhack up Humphrey Brook, staying to its left as it climbs around into a small valley below the south face of Puffer and reaches a two-tiered beaver pond. The left end of the cliff is now visible; a camp here would provide quick access for those wishing to spend some time exploring. Description by Jim Vermeulen.

Cream Puffer I 5.6 180' (s)

This is a good friction route on clean rock. At the base of the rightmost slab visible from the beaver pond lie several large detached boulders. A left-facing vegetated gully is the beginning of *Cream Puffer*.

pitch 1 Scramble the gully a few feet, then step left onto the face. Climb a left-arching crack to a stance and move up right to a fingercrack. Stay in the crack up and right to a small ledge. 5.6 80'

pitch 2 Traverse left and up to an overlap. Step left and turn the overlap beneath a right-facing corner. Continue in the crackline past a dead fir and on to the top. 5.5 100'

FA Bill Morris and Jim Vermeulen 9/19/88

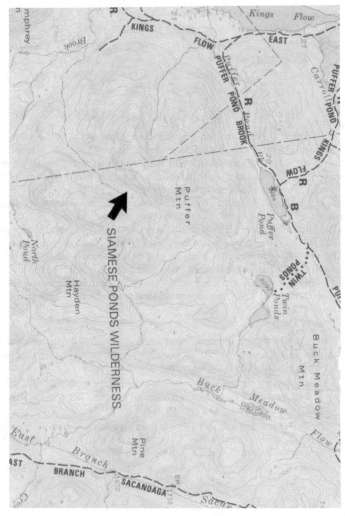

LONG POND CLIFF

This 80- to 150-foot cliff rising above Long Pond offers perhaps some of the best undeveloped rock in the southern Adirondacks. There are two approaches to this remote crag. The southern approach requires a four-wheel-drive vehicle for the 8-mile East Road north of Speculator, leading to state land and a moderate 3-mile hike past Rock Pond and on to Long Pond. (This road lies on the property of International Paper Company, and a $4 fee is required. Permits can be obtained in Speculator at IP offices on Old Route 30 or at Tanner's Outdoor Sports on Route 8.) Once at the pond, one may find a leaky boat for the crossing; otherwise, skirting the pond to its left avoids a swampy area to the south. Alternatively, to approach from the northwest, one can paddle across Indian Lake to John Mack Landing and follow a 3.5-mile trail to the pond. This is a true wilderness rock-climbing area that has nevertheless been despoiled in several places by indiscriminate anglers and campers. We climbers should demonstrate a more mature appreciation for this spectacular environment.

The routes are described left to right.

Pyromania   I   5.7   150'   (E)

Left of center is a big right-facing, broken corner. This route stays right of the corner.

pitch 1 Climb two dirty ledges, then traverse right 8' to a left-facing corner. Up corner and face, over bulges to the left end of a sloping ledge. Belay off right at trees.

pitch 2 Up the crack and corner system to the top.

FA Neal Knitel and Neal Lamphear

Loon Roof   I   5.7   80'   (S)

This climbs the most obvious feature on the cliff: the long roof that resembles an inverted L at the highest section of rock.

pitch 1 Climb the vegetated right-facing corner to the roof, exiting left and up a crack past some trees to the top.

FA Neal Knitel and Jonas Morelli 7/95

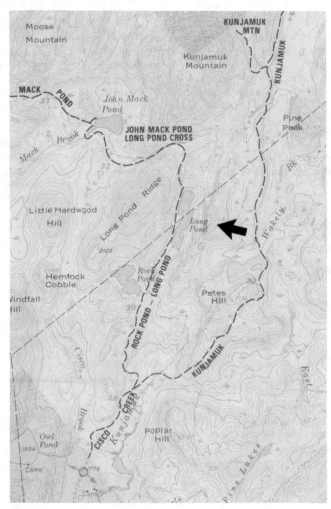

LONG POND CLIFF

Short-Term Memory   I   5.6   60'   (E)

Start on the same ledge as for the previous route.

pitch 1 About 75' right of the corner, climb a left-slanting fingercrack to the top, finishing about 20' right of the huge roof.

FA Neal Knitel and Jonas Morelli 7/95

Nut 'n Left   I   5.5   120'   (E)

Start right of the ledge of the previous routes on a slab on the left side of a talus slope.

pitch 1 Climb a crack to a flake, over a bulge via a crack, passing a detached flake to a leftward vegetated ramp.

FA Jonas Morelli and Jared Thayer 7/95

Little Ado   I   5.3   80'   (E)

This was described as probably "the worst possible route" on the face. It has been used for descent as well. Start at the highest point of the large tree-covered talus slope between the south buttress and the large smooth central face.

pitch Climb the chimney and rock rib left of the steep south-face buttress. There are three finishes: the chimney 5.0, the outside corner 5.6, and the handcrack to the left 5.8.

FA Dick Tucker and Eric Laurin 9/16/89

Too Close for Comfort   I   5.8+   (E)

Right of center is a large buttress with a tree-covered talus slope to its left.

pitch 1 Scramble up and right under the yellow face to a tree ledge. Climb a right-facing corner on the right side of the yellow face to a white pine. 5.6

pitch 2 Climb the fingercrack (good direct finish potential here), and traverse left to a tiny roof that is breached via a left-slanting fingercrack.

FA Neal Knitel and Neal Lamphear

Strike Zone   I   5.6   110'   (E)

Begin on the same ledge as for the previous route.

pitch 1 At the right end of the ledge is a short fingercrack. Angle right to-

359

LONG POND CLIFF

(*Note: Routes are approximate and unconfirmed*)

A. PYROMANIA 5.7

B. LITTLE ADO 5.3

C. TOO CLOSE FOR COMFORT 5.8+

PHOTO BY DICK TUCKER

wards the large left-facing corner. Keeping left of the corner, climb to a vegetated ledge. From here, climb a fingercrack to the top, or the chimney right to escape.

FA Neal Knitel and Tom Cuminski 7/95

Way of the Peckerheads I 5.6 190' (E)

This is a typical Adirondack "recon-climb" that bypasses several challenging options on the second pitch traverse. Locate the southernmost buttress; scramble above the first rock band to a point directly beneath the right side of the overhanging buttress.

pitch 1 Climb up a few feet, then right into a narrow outside corner chimney. Ascend the chimney to a birch and haul past the tree to a large wedged block. Belay above and left on a sloping ledge beneath a vertical crack. 5.5 90'

pitch 2 Down-climb left into a gully, and up left around a corner to another large ledge. From its left end, climb an inverted V slab to a short jamcrack. Finish right. 5.6 100'

FA Jim Vermeulen and Bill Morris 7/9/88

CRANE MOUNTAIN

This mountain has long been popular with hikers who prize it as one of the best climbs in the southern Adirondacks. The mountain forms the southern half of a larger massif that includes Huckleberry Mountain, whose climbs lie in the steep notch that separates the two. Unlike Huckleberry, the Crane Mountain climbs can be seen from many vantage points along the road. The Garnet Lake Road, which flanks the mountain to the south, offers good views of the Beaverview Wall, the Viewpoint areas, and the Summit Ridge; whereas the South Johnsburg Road off Route 8 gives glimpses of the Eastern Cliffs, where the best viewing is from the Baptist Church in Thurman.

Typical of many southern areas, the climbs here lie on good rock interspersed by tree- and bush-covered ledges. Many of the routes are also in need of a good scrubbing. The faces described below are not the only climbable areas here. Clearly, development here is in its infancy, and the new-route potential is endless.

From Northway Exit 25, take Route 8 west to Johnsburg, a few miles past Wevertown and the junction of Route 28. Turn south on the South Johnsburg Road (Hudson Street breaks right toward Huckleberry) for about 8 miles, past the Baptist Church in Thurman and right on Garnet Lake Road. Proceed 1.9 miles, then take Sky High Road up steeply to the right for 2 miles to the trail parking.

Descriptions come from Jay Harrison, who soloed many of the routes during his explorations of the mountain. Unless otherwise noted, the first ascent credits go to him. Jay also welcomes inquiries from anyone who wishes further information on the climbing at Crane Mountain. His guide service is located on Sky High Road on the way to the trailhead.

TABLEROCK SLAB

About a half mile up the summit trail is an open face to the right. The cliff is so named for the large flat rock that sits in the trail. The vague corner system above is 5.3. A ledge just above the trail leads to more potential routes, but the rock deteriorates beyond the Pine Tree Corner (5.3)

TRAILSIDE SLAB

Not really a technical rock climb, this dark slab can lure hikers into a troublesome finish at the headwall. The rock parallels the trail about five minutes above Table Rock.

VIEWPOINT CLIFF AND SLAB

Above the Trailside Slab the trail steepens up a streambed, crosses it to the left and emerges out left at a trail-sign arrow for a good viewpoint. This is the top of the Viewpoint Cliff, with the Viewpoint Slab about 100 yards beyond to the northwest. The cliff lies at about 2,500 feet elevation. Approach by descending sharply from the trail to the southeast side of the rock. Climbs are listed right to left.

Puzzle   I   5.4   80'   (D)

A short vertical crack fades out as another appears to its left. Up the crack, then left to the next crack and up to a ledge on the left. The face between the two cracks above the overhang is covered with good knobs.

Every Creature's Theme   I   5.5   90'   (s or D)

At the lowest point in the cliff is a left-facing corner that fades out at 30'. Climb the corner, then follow big scruffy knobs up right to the lookout ledge.

Morning Stars   I   5.1   200'   (s)

The next routes are described right to left on the large expanse of low-angled rock referred to as Viewpoint Slab. Approach by bushwhacking from the bottom of the previous climbs, skirting the face on a brushy ledge above a dirty 70' slab. From the top of the climbs, bushwhack directly up to the Pond Trail.

pitch 1 A thin crack goes up through an overlap and belays before the protection runs out. 90'

pitch 2 Easier, unprotected climbing leads to the top. 110'

Up on the Mountain   I   5.1   200'   (D)

Just to the left of the next climb a thin seam slants leftward, passing through a dirty section down low.

Daybreak   I   5.2   250'   (s)

Toward the slab's left edge, a line of trees and brush divides the rock. From the center of these rises a thin crack. From its end, step left into the brush or more pleasantly out right on rock.

BEAVERVIEW WALL

Below and about a third of a mile from the Viewpoint Slab is a long expanse of rock that can be reached either by a careful bushwhack from the slab or by cutting off from the outlet trail just below the overlook on Putnam Barn. A direct bushwhack from the beaver pond above Putnam Brook is steep, but possible. The routes are described right to left.

Heart Thrills   I   5.3   300'   (s)

More a steep, dangerous hike than a technical climb, this is a right-to-left exploratory traverse. Near the right edge of the cliff is a blocky corner that leads to a steep ramp of grass and trees.

pitch 1 Up the corner. 150'

pitch 2 Up to the headwall, traversing left to the notch, up and left over the void to the top of the next route.

Fade and Flee   I   5.6   200'   (s)

Near the center of the cliff, just before it drops steeply, is a small open book leading to a wide crack in an overhang. The route finishes on the right side of a very prominent overhang.

pitch 1 Up the seam and corner, stepping left around blocks and up to an overhang. Traverse left around the roof (no protection), then back right to a belay at the crack. 90'

pitch 2 Continue in the fading crack, through the bushes, and diagonally right to the obvious gap. Beware loose blocks. 120'

FA Jay Harrison and Rick Villeneuve 7/95

SUMMIT RIDGE

The greatest concentration of good rock lies on these six crags along the summit ridge. They are described left to right.

Pondview. From Crane Mountain Pond, take the ridge trail to a point just beyond the steep section to a path that leads out to a clifftop with a good view of the pond and Huckleberry Mountain.

Dartmouth. This long, confusing wall can be approached by cutting off into the woods from the summit trail a few yards above the smaller ladder. The cliff is named for Harrison's discovery of the word "Dartmouth" inscribed at the top of a certain "first" ascent. Approach cutting into the woods from the summit trail a few yards above the little ladder, aiming for the section's left edge.

Wretched Wanderer   I   5.4   100'   (E)

A few yards right of the rockfall area is a 20' block with a handcrack. Traverse to the crack and on to the ledge, following the line of least resistance to the top.

Brighter Visions I 5.6 50' (s)

Staying close to the main face wherever possible, a difficult bushwhack leads to a steep alcove with a steep wall on the left. A crack slants from near the corner of the alcove up left towards the center of the wall, fading to a seam before ending at an overhang. Climb to the overhang, traversing around right and up the short face. Other options exist here.

FA Jay Harrison and Gabe Linncourt 5/95

Diagonal Wall. The right edge of Dartmouth is bounded by a large, looming face that begins 20' up the cliff and slants left toward the top. To its right is the Firecamp Area.

Paltry Show I 5.4 150' (E)

Just below the wall's lower right edge is an open book. Climb the corner, stepping left to the ledge under the wall. Traverse up and left to finish.

Mortal Strife I 5.7 A2 170' (E)

Start as for the previous route.

pitch 1 Step to the left and up the arete to the ledge below the Diagonal Wall. A handcrack shoots up and around to the steep face above and right. Aid to the lower angled face and belay 20' below the top. 150'

pitch 2 Easier rock to finish. 20'

FA Jay Harrison and Gabe Linncourt 6/95

Firecamp Area. Just right of the Diagonal Wall lies a large face with vertical cracks (*Mortal Strife* is one). Access is difficult.

Thank You, Cindy I 5.7 150' (E)

A few yard's right of *Paltry Show's* start is a 12' flake, forming a small cave. From the top of the flake, step right to a 6' open book capped by an overhang. Go over this and up the right-facing corner. A crack in the left wall gives access to the steep face around left. Finish up vertical grooves.

FA Jay Harrison and Paul Medici 6/93

True Summit Area. There is no distinct division between the Firecamp Area and the True Summit Area. The big ladder delineates the area's right-hand boundary. Bushwhacking left from here is the best approach.

Chicken Flake   I   5.7   170'   (E)

About 50 yards from the big ladder's base is an open spot with a small talus mound. Climb the left corner and center crack of the alcove through the opening above. (Use the thin flakes cautiously.) The second pitch traverses left and up.

FA Paul Medici and Jay Harrison 6/92

Folly Stricken   I   5.4   150'   (S)

An exploratory hike with some exciting moments. Left of the *Chicken Flake* and another right-facing outside corner. Begin in the inside corner to its left, traversing around the outside corner over the wide crack. Up 10', then left to the nose and up toward the chimney to the right which leads to the top.

FA Jay Harrison 7/95

Nose Area. To the right of the big ladder lies some of the best climbing done so far. Head right a few yards below the ladder. Two 20' cracks make exciting optional starts to the other climbs.

Rock Of Ages   5.7   (top-rope)

Above the 2 cracks is the biggest prow. The route ascends the right side of the arete.

FA Jay Harrison and Paul Medici 6/92

Cornerstone   I   5.5   90'   (E)

On the right side of the lower, right-hand prow is a chimney crack that runs to the base of the cliff. Thrash to the base of the chimney, up and left to finish.

FA Jay Harrison 7/95

SOUTHEASTERN CRAGS

Here are some of the longest routes on the mountain, and there is obvious potential for more. The bushwhack to the climbs is also long. Check these faces from the South Johnsburg Road before driving up to the trail for the approach. From the trail parking, walk east past the outhouse along the base of the mountain, generally maintaining an elevation. After about ten minutes, the mountainside swings north, away from the depression. Turn with it up the slope and gain the crest of a ridge that parallels the east side. A boulder-choked gully separates the ridge from the actual mountain. Stay on the ridge until the cliffs of the Slanting Cracks Wall can be glimpsed through the trees.

There are three main faces: the Black Arches Wall, with its obvious overhangs; the Slanting Cracks Wall, dominated by a huge left-facing corner; and the Waterfall Wall, a 90' slippery slab down and right. Descriptions begin here.

Waterfall Wall. Two routes have been done here, one a 5.7 pocket and knob climb just left of the water, and the other a 5.4 on the right. Both have bleak protection.

Slanting Cracks Wall. From the smooth Waterfall Wall, hike up around to the left (about 5 minutes), or approach directly from the ridge bushwhack. The prominent feature is a huge left-facing corner with a crack line *(Providence)* separating it from the crack face itself.

In the Beginning   I   5.7   350'   (E)

Start 10' left of the corner at a right-facing flake.

pitch 1 Up the flake to its junction with a vertical crack. Climb this to a dike and traverse left and up to a friction traverse left to a small oak 5.6 100'

pitch 2 Climb the corner and crack above the belay, stepping around left to climb stacked blocks or continuing in the corner, to a birch below an overhang. 5.7 150'

pitch 3 Stay in the crack or step right to the prow and up the arete (no protection). 100'

FA Jay Harrison and Brian Westenberger 9/19/93

Straits of Fear   I   5.8   320'   (D)

pitch 1 Start as for the previous route. At the dike, step left and up the crack and groove. The crack eventually cleaves the corner, creating a 3" fin of rock. Pinch this to a slanting ledge belay. 5.8 150'

pitch 2 Step left of the fin onto the knobby face, up a left to a short crack, and finally left to a small belay at the junction of the headwall and the slab. 5.4 120'

pitch 3 The easy slab leads to the woods. 50'

FA Jay Harrison and Brain Mosher 9/8/94

Providence I 5.6 300' (s)

The major crackline in the large dihedral is better than it appears, though dry conditions are desirable.

pitch 1 Follow the crack to a belay at 165'. 5.6

pitch 2 Climb the face to the right, angling gradually left toward the crack, then right to a flake at the overhang. 5.6 135'

FA Jay Harrison and Brian Westenberger 9/25/93

Fits and Arms I 5.5 60' (E)

This is the wide crack on the right wall of the huge dihedral, passing a wedged block en route.

FA Jay Harrison, Ron Briggs, and Don Mellor 7/95

Prone To Wander I 5.7 180' (s)

Around right of the big corner is a narrow rising ledge past a big arete, and then a smaller arete just beyond.

pitch 1 Start right of the smaller arete, traversing the horizontal crack left to the outside corner. Up 25' then back right and down to a belay under a roof. 80'

pitch 2 Follow the right-slanting crack through the right side of the overhang and over the big left-facing corner. Climb this to a horizontal crack and hand-traverse out right to the outside corner (exciting). Then up easily to the woods. 100'

FA Jay Harrison and Gabe Linncourt 4/95

Black Arches Wall. The approach is best from the top of the Slanting Cracks Wall. Alternatively, one can traverse left from the base of the Slanting Cracks Wall for 20 minutes, until it's possible to head back right and up. Black Arches is split into four sections, the left of which is separated by a tree-filled gully.

Tribulation   I   5.5   200'   (E)

This is the corner created by the left side of the buttress against the main face.

pitch 1 Up the corner, staying out of the crevice, to the top of the buttress. 5.4 90'

pitch 2 Up the short face above via a left-slanting seam to a ledge. Climb the next short face and on to the thick spruce above. 5.5 110'

FA Jay Harrison 7/93

SHANTY CLIFF

Shanty Cliff is the remaining wall of an eroded dike, the largest in the southern Adirondacks. The crag is becoming popular for its very climbable rock and generally easy grades. The rock is an abrasive mixture of slabs, faces, cracks, and overhangs, with an open summit knob offering excellent views. The cliff is located off Route 8 about 8 miles north of the intersection with Route 30. Get a good look at the summit knob from Route 8 before fording the East Branch of the Sacandaga and bushwhacking the half mile to the rock.

Blue Toes   I   5.4   100'   (E)

At the right end of the textured face is a broken corner that can serve as a descent route. Begin just left in a fern-choked crack.

pitch 1 Climb the crack and the right-leaning crack above to the top of the face, then move back left over easy slabs. A harder variation traverses 10' left from the tiny birch and up the face to the top.

FA Jim Vermeulen and Mike Cross 11/9/86

Vernal Imperatives   I   5.6   100'   (E)

This "directissima" route ascends the slanted wall between *Blue Toes* and *Little Gem Dinner.*

pitch 1 From its lowest point, climb the thin face to a slight bulge, step up left through the bulge and follow weaknesses to the top.

FA Jim Vermeulen and Bill Morris 10/10/94

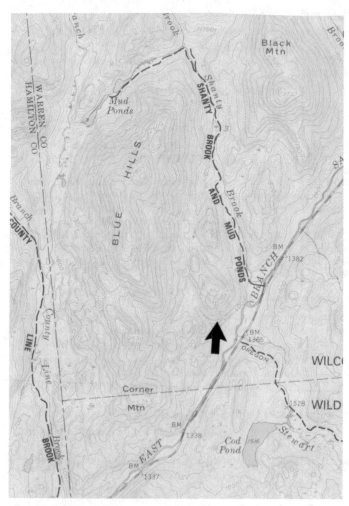

SHANTY CLIFF

Little Gem Diner   I   5.6   110'   (E)

pitch 1 15' left of Blue Toes, near the large gully, is a prominent left-leaning crack. Climb the diagonal crack and face above to a stance below a small overhang and bulge split by twin cracks. Take the lefthand crack (crux) to easier rock and a leftward traverse up sloping ledges toward the summit block.

FA Jim Vermeulen and Bill Morris 6/14/87

Howdy Doody   I   5.3   80'

pitch 1 Halfway up the large chimney (nearly under the chockstone) is a crack system leading past a tiny birch. Climb past the tree and follow slab leftward, staying between cracks.

FA Dick Tucker 7/4/90

C & E   I   5.5   70'   (E)

Near the midpoint of the cliff, just left of a tiered amphitheater with steep walls, is a face with a large tree at its base.

pitch 1 Climb into a dirty, right-leaning ramp and up along a small rib. Follow the crack above to the top.

FA Jim Vermeulen and Mike Cross 11/9/86

Soweto   I   5.8   130'   (E)

At the highest point in the cliff is an arete capped on the left by a giant roof. This route begins on the right side of the arete, climbs to the roof, breaking it on the right. Moderate face-climbing leads to the top.

FA Jim Lawyer, Stuart Williams and Eric Dahn

Gullet   I   5.3   110'

The central buttress is bounded on its left by an obvious chimney with a fern-filled fan below. Climb the chimney.

FA Dick Tucker 7/4/90

The following routes begin on a gravel- and blueberry-covered fan above the overhanging wall left of the chimney. They cannot be seen from below. Access is via the chimney.

371

Fizzle   I   5.2   80'

Left of the chimney is a rib; follow the crack system to its left.

FA Dick Tucker 7/4/90

Wanderer   I   5.4   100'   (D)

pitch 1 Climb the smooth face left of the previous route to easy rock. Traverse left to another face to the top.

FA Dick Tucker and Dave Legg 9/19/82

The following routes are located on the west end of the cliff. There, a headwall drops off to a sweeping ski-jump-like slab with an overhanging drop at the bottom.

Circuitous Shit   I   5.4   140'   (E)

Don't be put off by the name; this is a pleasant route.

pitch 1 20 yards below *Flying Friends* is a squattish slab, severely over-hung at its base. Begin on the left side of the slab in a broken corner. Pull onto the slab and traverse right to a crack arching right. Traverse onto the crest and up to a small birch. Right of this is an easy layback finish. It is also possible to finish directly above the birch.

FA Eric Dahn, Stuart Williams, and Jim Vermeulen 5/7/88

Flying Friends   I   5.7   110'   (E)

60' left of the previous routes is a crack cleaving the vertical base of the overhang.

pitch 1 Take the jamcrack onto the slab and traverse left to the base of the headwall. Follow a vertical crack to a rightward hand-traverse (crux) finish.

FA Stuart Williams, Eric Dahn, and Jim Vermeulen 5/7/88

Bo Peep   I   5.4   75'

pitch 1 10' right of *Sleepwalk* at the beginning of the overhanging wall is a shallow crack. Climb the crack to the slab where a leftward intrusion leads to a crack. Finish past loose boulder.

FA Dick Tucker 7/4/90

Sleepwalk I 5.2 40' (E)

At the upper end of the cliffs are rolling slabs. *Sleepwalk* is on the leftmost slab.

pitch 1 From a point midway up a narrow, grassy tongue, hand-traverse across the slab via the deep crack. At the middle of the slab, head straight up cracks.

FA Jim Vermeulen 5/7/88

Shanty Knob. This delightful "lunch rock" lies 100 yards south of the Shanty Cliff dike and offers not only boulder problems but a scenic warm-day lounge site.

thing 1 5.6 20'   From a left-side corner, follow a hand-traverse crack right and up.

thing 2 5.5 18'   Climb the 18' right-hand crack.

FA Jim Vermeulen and Bill Morris 10/10/94

MITCHELL PONDS MOUNTAIN

These Moose River Cliffs offer limited climbing potential, but combine a great day in the southern Adirondack wilds with scenic canoeing. Perseverance to the clifftop is rewarded by ranging views of the Moose River Plain. From Limekiln Gate on Route 28 just east of Inlet, drive the Moose River Plains Road 8.5 miles to a T intersection. Take the right (south) fork and drive 0.7 miles to a campsite on the road. A 0.4-mile carry along a yellow-marked trail behind the camp puts you on the South Branch of the Moose River. Paddle west several miles, following the winding channel until the 80'–120' cliffs near the crest of Mitchell Ponds Mountain come into view.

The rock is steep and blank in the central section. Some dirty cracks offer promise. The western end is more broken and slabby, but lichen is abundant. Description by Jim Vermeulen.

Moosed You I 5.3 80' (s)

This easy route on the western end of the cliff begins where a grass-covered ledge running above the lower slab peters out.

FA Jim Vermeulen and Bill Morris 7/90

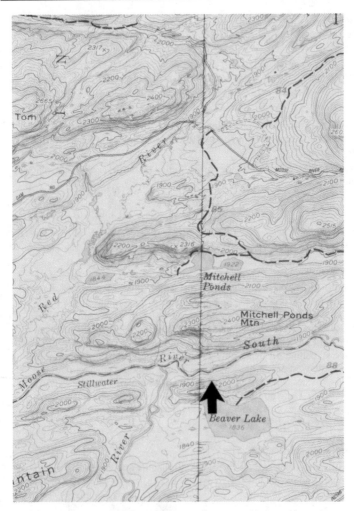

MITCHELL PONDS MOUNTAIN

ECHO CLIFF

This scenic crag overlooking Piseco Lake with its challenging crack climbs heralded the beginning of southern Adirondack rock climbing. Approach from Route 8 and follow West Shore Road around the west side of Piseco Lake. The trail begins about a half mile south of Little Sand Point State Campground. Hike toward the cliffs and Panther Mountain, bushwhacking right to the cliff's base. The climbs are described left to right and are located on or adjacent to the obvious and sheer main wall.

West End Brewery I 5.8 40' (E)

pitch 1 This route climbs the largest rock formation left and uphill from the main face (at the top of a recent dirt slide). Follow the short, strenuous handcrack to a ledge. Weave left around blocks to the top.

FA Tad Welch and Jamie Savage 5/10/85

Misspent Youth I 5.8+ 40' (E)

This route is around the corner, uphill from *Yax Crack* and a few feet left of the stunted beech tree that marks the start to the *Yax Crack* variation.

pitch 1 Climb the crack to the tree ledge. Rappel.

FA Tad Welch and Pat Clark 5/8/86

Yax Crack I 5.10- 90' (E)

pitch 1 On the left side of the slightly overhanging main face is a fingercrack. A short crux leads to a shallow right-facing corner and on to the top.

Variation Traverse into the squeeze chimney from the beech tree up and left. 5.7

FFA Tad Welch 1985

Prisoner in Disguise I 5.9 100' (E)

A recommended route offering memorable moves on steep rock.

pitch 1 Begin at the next crack and corner system to the right. After a committing mantel, escape up the corner (fixed pin) and bulging crack.

FA Tad Welch 11/2/85

Life during Wartime   I   A1   100'

pitch 1 Climb the thin crackline that begins at wedged blocks forming an inverted V just above the ground.

FA Tad Welch and Bill Widrig 3/31/85

Carrion Crawl   I   5.8   (E)

pitch 1 Begin 40' right of the previous route, scrambling up a gully to an alcove with a crack above. Up the crack and right to a good ledge with a small maple. 5.7 45'

pitch 2 Climb the overhanging corner system to short, dirty corners and the top.

FA Neal Knitel and Mykel Ruvola

Tennis, Anyone?   I   5.7   60'   (E)

Around right of the main wall and just right of a steep gully is a distinctive wedge of rock close to the ground.

pitch 1 Climb the attractive crack on the right side of the wedge. After the short overhang, follow the handcrack to the trees.

FA Tad Welch and Mike Cross 11/2/85

GOOD LUCK CLIFF

This unique cliff is located near the easternmost summit of Good Luck Mountain in the very southwestern corner of the Park. The high, steep walls of the central face and its two bordering buttresses provide good crack and face routes, with future potential mainly limited to the harder degrees of climbing. The trailhead for Good Luck Lake is on Route 10 at a parking area one and a half miles north of Arietta, just past the second bridge. From the highway, the marked trail leads about a half mile to a junction and hiker's register. Follow the left fork toward Spectacle Lake. After a gradual descent, Good Luck Lake becomes visible on the left. After the lake, watch closely for two streams that cross the trail. Just before the long wooden bridge that crosses the second stream, head upstream along an obvious path on the right-hand bank. The trail soon crosses the brook and climbs steeply to the cliffs. Though it's tempting to head directly to the cliffs through the

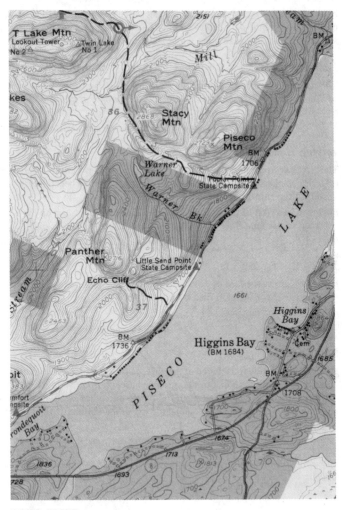

ECHO CLIFF

boulders, it may be easier to orient oneself if one stays on the trail to the top of the hill where the path comes within a few feet of the rock. This approach should take just under an hour. Climbs will be described left to right.

Lady Luck   I   5.7   40'   (E)

This is an obvious and impressive short, right-facing, open book with a roof at its top. It is located just left of a "stonehenge" rock formation and right of the dirty descent corner.

FA Jim Lawyer and Stuart Williams 1990

Talking Heads   I   5.6   150'   (S)

The first two routes on the larger main face to the right climb a series of offwidth cracks. This route begins at the short cave with a beech tree, about 18' left of the chimney.

pitch 1 Climb left of the cave and up to a large tree. Continue up the wide crack to a stump. Stay in the crackline to the top.

FA Jim Vermeulen and Bill Morris 11/30/86

J.J.'s   I   5.6   150'   (E)

pitch 1 Begin as for *Talking Heads.* Traverse left from the stump to parallel cracks. Belay down left on a large block. 95'

pitch 2 Take the jamcracks to the top.

FA Jim Vermeulen and Jim Lawyer 5/9/87

Bon Chance   1   5.8+   140'   (E)   †

pitch 1 Dominating the left end of the cliff is a full-length, narrow chimney, an awesome feature that has no recorded ascent. *Bon Chance* begins as for the chimney, but escapes out right via a thin crack. A short offwidth section above finishes the route at the top of the chimney. An excellent pitch.

FA Don Mellor, Brian and Ed Ballentine 8/1/93

Above the chimney is a short face with two cracks. These end at the hikers' lookout.

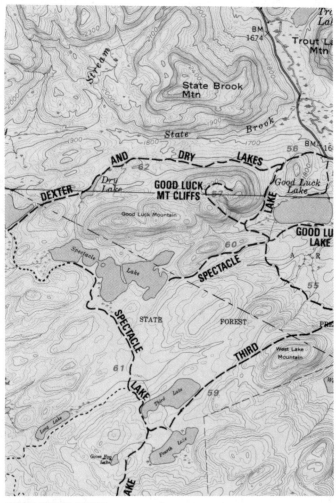

GOOD LUCK CLIFF

Stonewall Brigade   5.9

pitch 1 The thin crack on the left is good and sustained.

Appomattox Crack   5.9

pitch 1 This is the handcrack with the vague start.

From the chimney, the path leads along the base of the cliff and past a tree-filled inside corner.

Curbside Crawl   I   5.7   90'   (E)

Start this route at the base of the tree-filled corner.

pitch 1 A short crack leads into an alcove capped by a small roof. Climb out left past a large dead tree and up to a hidden ramp and jamcrack finish.

FA Tad Welch, Jim Lawyer, and Jim Vermeulen 5/9/87

Cleaveland   I   5.8   150'   (s)   †

Near the center of the cliff is a very impressive slanting, right-facing dihedral. To its left is an offwidth crack in another right-facing corner formed by a huge flake.

pitch 1 Swing up into the wide crack (the original ascent used a dead tree to gain the crack; good luck now that it's gone) to the jammed blocks. Bypass the upper offwidth section on face holds. Rock steps lead past a large flake to the top.

FA Tad Welch and Jim Vermeulen 4/11/87

The Reach   I   5.10   80'   (s)   †

Toward the right end of the terrace are a pair of vertical cracks.

pitch 1 This is the unmistakable crack just left of *Mystery Achievement*. Contemplating the start of this one, the route name will be painfully obvious. Start as for the other crack and move desperately left into the crack.

FA Tad Welch and Bill Widrig 4/91

Mystery Achievement   I   5.9   80'   (E)   †

This impressive and recommended route takes a plumb-line handcrack on the right side of the main wall and left of the tree-filled corner.

pitch 1 Jam the crack to less strenuous climbing above.

FA Tad Welch and Jim Lawyer 5/9/87

Star in the Dust I 5.10- 60' (E) †

This is the cleaned line on the high-angled face right of the large, left-facing tree-filled corner. To its right is a prominent arete and farther right is a complex series of faces and roofs that offer good new-route potential.

pitch 1 The fingercrack is followed by a face-climbing traverse and a thin crack finish.

FA Tad Welch and Jim Lawyer 5/88

Get a Grip I 5.9 80' (E)

From a viewpoint near the first of several giant boulders passed on the initial approach trail, find a zigzag crack system snaking up the large section of rock. It's tough to get a grip in November: numb hands led to a 20-footer from the top of this one.

pitch 1 Climb the groove to the triangular roof. Follow the cleaned fingercrack as it angles upward to a short handcrack finish at trees.

FA Bill Widrig and Tad Welch 11/93

Good Luck Bolder. Thirty feet off the approach trail directly in front of the main face is a large bolder with an arching crack starting at mid-height.

Lucky Stars I 5.11 R 50'

Starting on top of a ledge on the left side of the boulder, make a series of thin moves right to gain the beautiful fingercrack.

FA Jim Lawyer, Tad Welch and Bill Widrig 1994

Grape Juice I 5.9+ 60' (E)

Climb the left arete to the downward sloping crack and final fingercrack of *Lucky Stars*.

*Yet another secret waiting to be explored:
the unique amphitheater wall of the south side of Basin Mountain.*

REMOTE CLIMBS
IN THE HIGH PEAKS

The High Peaks area of the Adirondacks holds almost limitless possibilities for exploring new lines. Many of these are on the high, slabby faces of mountains such as Gothics, Porter, and Big Slide. Route descriptions have been written for some of these in the past, but a tradition has evolved to leave such areas free of detailed description. The guidebooks were only marginally helpful for these high mountain faces anyway. Sections had either overgrown or been altered by slides, and climbers always seemed to put the guidebook back in the pack and strike out on their own in finding a way to the summit. If the climbers had wanted a tame experience, they wouldn't have trekked so far back in the hills in the first place.

So here is a section that will seem a bit different, and maybe even refreshing, from what climbers are accustomed to in an Eastern mountain guidebook. The faces will be described in only the most general terms so as to allow climbers to find the face, bring the right kind of gear, and allow enough time for ascent. But at the same time, the decisions will be theirs and the exploratory essence of the experience will be retained for all time.

Obviously, a trail map and a compass are essential. So are dry conditions, bivouac contingency plans, and even a wire brush for that handhold that just might keep you from taking the big one.

PORTER MOUNTAIN

Actually, this is not so remote a face. It towers over Keene Valley as a high and tempting slab. It was first climbed (5.5) by Jim Goodwin and Edward Stanley in 1938. It is interesting to note that the second reported route (5.8) was by Jim's son Tony (author of *Guide to Adirondack Trails: High Peaks Region,* also published by ADK) and Todd Eastman 42 years later.

BIG SLIDE

Big Slide stands high above Johns Brook Valley across from Gothics and is reached via the Big Slide Trail, which forks off right just before Johns Brook Lodge, or by the Brothers trail, which leaves the Garden parking lot and follows the very scenic Brothers Ridge to the face. The slab is reached by walking from the junction of these two trails just below the summit. It is a quick bushwhack west to the grassy slope beneath the climbs.

In 1953, Fritz Wiessner and George Austin climbed a route left of the main, stepped, overhanging right-facing dihedral that is the dominant feature of the face. They began about 60' left of the dihedral, continuing up some unprotected face-climbing (5.5) to a tree ledge on the left. Their climb finished above, tending leftward toward the top. The Penn State Outing Club team of Craig Patterson and Oliver Jones varied this by beginning left and joining higher up; later, Trudy Healy and John Chuta finished more directly on an unprotected slab up right.

The smooth main face right of the dihedral has a good route called *Slide Rules* (5.7 Andy Helms and Don Mellor, 1980), which has two bolts per pitch. *Surf and Turf* is an unprotected direct finish up and right for the second pitch. *Freudian Slip* is an excellent, bolted two-pitch direct start that begins from the ground directly below the second belay of *Slide Rules* (5.9 Ed and Ann Palen and Joe Seftel). Additionally, in 1988 Rob Cassidy and Jeb Wallace-Brodeur climbed *Mustard Sandwich,* beginning 60' left of *Slide Rules* at a steep, grassy ramp, continuing left under a roof (5.9) and finishing up the right side of a huge block.

ROOSTER COMB

There is some good climbing on this small summit, the first peak in the Great Range. It was first climbed by Fritz Wiessner and Jim Goodwin in 1949. Their climb (5.3) began in a large corner with a roof above the right wall, meandering up a ramp and a line of weakness for two more short pitches above. Since then, it has seen little traffic, but routes up to 5.10 have been done here. The rock is generally steep and about 150' high. The approach is a steady uphill hike of just under two miles beginning at the huge boulder and bridge of the Johns Brook Road to the garden.

BROTHERS

There is a rock band on Lower Brother that overlooks Johns Brook Valley and is visible from the trail in winter. It is easily located from the open slabs about three quarters of a mile from the Garden where the trail crosses above an attractive, 30' dihedral *(Pringsheim Chimney)*. To get to the main face, head uphill about 100 yards and contour down to the base of the rock. The slabby face can also be seen from the trail just beyond. It has been climbed by Jim Goodwin in the 1930s and the PSOC crew of Trudy Healy and Al Breisch in 1965. The climbing here seems inferior to that of most other established crags in the region.

GOTHICS

It is on this steep and sculpted mountain that some of the most intriguing friction-climbing possibilities exist. Legend has it that the mountain was named by Frederick Perkins and Orson "Old Mountain" Phelps for the gothic architecture suggested by the clean, arching slabs. In fact however, the name Gothics had probably been given to the mountain a few years before Perkins and Phelps inspected it from Mount Marcy. Nonetheless, the colorful story depicts well the ominous but alluring gray slabs that gird the peak. There are wide expanses of open rock on five different faces. These are not the typical slides; instead, they can be true 5th class rock climbs with great exposure and generally little protection. Lichen covers much of the rock, but this thin growth can be dealt with by combining an eye for clean rock with some strategic wire-brushing. Because of the peak's size

PHOTO BY CHUCK TURNER

BIG SLIDE

A. WIESSNER/AUSTIN 5.5

B. MUSTARD SANDWICH
(approximate) 5.9

C. FREUDIAN SLIP 5.9

D. SLIDE RULES 5.7

alone, these have and will continue to be among the most sought-after Adirondack climbs.

North Face

This is the wall that looms over Johns Brook Valley. It is also easily seen from many vantage points in and around the village of Lake Placid. The face is about a quarter-mile wide and over 1000' high. In 1990, an impressive series of slides swept the North Face, changing considerably the nature of the approach and the climbing. The rock is now reached by hiking up the first large streambed after Orebed lean-to on the Orebed Brook Trail above Johns Brook Lodge. Soon the recent devastation becomes obvious as the streambed widens toward the base of the slides. If in doubt, stay right at forks.

(Prior to the 1990 slides, the approach description was fairly complex. It is included in its original form here to assist in the event that the trees reclaim the lower flanks of the mountain. From the Orebed Brook Trail, take the first large stream above the Orebed Lean-to. Bear right at the first fork, left at the next, and right at all others. This brings one to the center of the face where a good view of the face will allow for route planning.)

The first recorded ascent was by Dick Pitman, Dick Lawrence, and Paul Lawrence in August 1956. (Paul's account in *Adirondac*, Nov./Dec. 1957, described the adventure of their 18-pitch route.) Later, Dougal Thomas and Molly McNutt reported an ascent in 1966. Guidebook author Tom Rosecrans teamed up with Ken Jackson in 1973 to climb *Gothic North Face Direct* 5.7, passing a mysterious old bolt on the attractive, bulging wall toward the right side of the face. Theirs was a fairly direct, 10-pitch route. A more recent report (Butch and Jeanne Kinnon, 1988) described a "highly recommended" 5.8, beginning about 300' from the right end of the face, and following slabs, corners, and overlaps on good rock for most of the way, finishing right below the summit after 12 pitches of climbing. Since the 1990 slides occurred, it is now possible to follow an obvious "finger" of the right side of the main face at about 5.1 with clean rock all the way. Off to the left are other options. Refer to the Slides section for the description to the True North Route (3rd class).

West Face

This face consists of the wide disconnected expanse of slides just right of

GOTHICS NORTH FACE

Left to right: TRUE NORTH *(3rd class),* THE STANDARD NORTH FACE WINTER ROUTE, THE NEW FINGER SLIDE 5.1

and parallel to the cable section on the Gothics Trail via Orebed Brook or the Range Trail. The left side is lower, steeper, and wider, providing the hardest climbing. Moves that are 5.6 with *no* protection are encountered here. To the right are longer, easier route possibilities with some protection. The climbing ends at the chimneys on the first rock knob visible from the junction of the Orebed Trail with the Range Trail. Here, at the col between Gothics and Saddleback, it is possible to find some strategic locations from which to view the rock; with a little more effort, one also can get good views from the Saddleback Trail itself. Approach via short bushwhack. Maintain the elevation of the col and skirt around to the base of the wide left-hand slab. The first two ascents on record are Craig Patterson's committing solos in the mid-1960s.

South Face

This one is seen easily both from Upper Ausable Lake and from the summit of Pyramid Peak (the southeast summit of Gothics). From this vantage point, the steep white rock is as tempting as any on the mountain. It has been climbed a few times and all report that it is an outstanding ascent, perhaps the best on the mountain. The climb is best approached from the saddle between Pyramid and Gothics, bushwhacking downhill for about twenty minutes to the base of the rock. The overlap about a third of the way up comprises the principle obstacle. The grade could range from 5.4 to 5.7, depending on the line chosen. The rock is continuous, beginning just right of an obvious dark streak and finishing near the trail via the longest stretch of rock. The route may be around seven pitches on mostly clean rock, and the difficulty could increase dramatically if the line is lost or misjudged.

Pyramid Peak: The South Face

From the air or on a map, Gothics is shaped something like a T, with the North Face on top, the South Face tucked into the left corner, and the Rainbow Slide into the right corner. Pyramid Peak is the summit at the bottom of the ridge, the stem of the T. It, too, has an open south face. The look of the rock is distinctive in that it is split into an upper and lower face by a left-rising, tree-filled gully. The lower sections are smooth and low-angled, whereas the upper half is a steep buttress that may be quite difficult. The approach is steep and straightforward. After a three-mile walk up the Lake Road to Lower Ausable Lake, take the Alfred E. Weld Trail to the col

Gothics overview from the south: The left side is the West Face, with the North Face barely discernable above. The long central stripe is the South Face, and in the lower right of the photo is the Pyramid Peak slide.

between Pyramid Peak and Sawteeth. Bushwhack west to reach the face. (The rising traverse gully is a 2nd class route up Pyramid for those not roped or ready for the exposure above and below.)

Rainbow Slide

The east face of the Gothics is the distinctively striped Rainbow Slide. The 1965 route of Craig Patterson and Ronald Dubay, *Teddy's Trauma* 5.7 (Dubay's dog, Teddy, failed on this one. His friction limit was reported to be 5.4.), took at least seven pitches up the face and through the summit overhang. There is a bolt midway. Approach this slide via the Gothics Trail from Lower Ausable Lake. About halfway to the col between Sawteeth and Gothics, bushwhack right (NE) to Rainbow Brook. There is a lower-angled section of slides before reaching the 5th class climbing above. There have been no recent reports of any ascents to confirm the condition of the slabs.

PANTHER GORGE

No place evokes intrigue like Panther Gorge. The name conjures up images of desolation, tangled blowdown, impenetrable forest, and boulders strewn in tumbled confusion. Tucked in between Marcy and Haystack, this wild place has long been the stuff from which stories are made and legends grow. No one can agree, however, whether the climbing here justifies the work. (Ah, this should inspire a perverse few!) Climbers have approached by the long haul (over ten miles) from Elk Lake. They've also dropped into the ravine from the Range Trail between Marcy and Haystack. It is from Haystack that Panther Gorge looks most alluring. High, steep walls and slabs appear across the vastness of the ravine. Climbers who have been there, however, have come back with a different story. "Did we miss something? Were we lost? Was it worth it?" And then they think back to that view from Haystack, and in a year or two, the temptation and curiosity begin to take root again, and they talk about going back for another look.

AVALANCHE PASS

The huge walls on both sides of the lake are some of the region's best. On the right (west) side when approaching from Marcy Dam is a 200' wall with

AVALANCHE LAKE

A. THE FIN AREA

B. THREE DIHEDRALS OF 3D

many vertical cracks. One section of this cliff is particularly appealing; it is shaped somewhat like the fin of a fish, with cracklines, vertical at first, then arching back left at the top. The "fin" is bounded on its right side by a long, continuous, right-facing dihedral, climbed at 5.8 by Tim Beaman, Jim Cunningham, and Sylvia Lazarnick. The first three cracks to its left, on the "fin" proper, were also climbed by Beaman and Lazarnick. These are in the 5.10–5.11 range.

Well to the right of the "fin" is a very obvious feature: an A-frame roof. Four good routes have been done here.

Straight A's   5.9

Begin on the right side of the 90' pillar at a crack. Belay near the top of the pillar. 5.6 80' Continue to the roof and left-facing dihedral, through the A-frame to the trees. 5.9 110'

FA Dominic Eisinger and Ed Palen 10/94

3D   5.10

This is a highly recommended route consisting of three left-facing dihedrals, thus the name. Begin on the left side of the pillar mentioned above, climbing past two dead cedars to a hidden ledge 5' left of the top of the pillar. 5.9 90' Step right to the pillar's top, and up to the second dihedral, traversing left past a cedar to a belay at the base of the third left-facing dihedral. 5.8 70' The final corner is 5.10 60'.

FA Dominic Eisinger and Ed Palen 11/94

Shaky Flakes Traverse   5.7

An old pin was found in the base of the A-frame; this route could have been the line of that mysterious ascent. Start 60' left of the pillar (near the north end of the lake), climbing a right-facing corner to a ledge with a cedar. 5.7 60' The traverse pitch heads right to a belay at the base of the third left-facing dihedral of the previous route. 5.6 90' The climb has loose sections and requires large protection.

FA Ed Palen and Bob Martin 10/94

Chalk Up Matilda   5.7   150'

Another very good route, beginning as for *Shaky Flakes* in a right-facing corner, climbing straight up an obvious fingercrack.

FA Ed Palen and Paul Brown 11/94

High and left is a series of discontinuous cliffs and slabs that end high above, near the summit of Avalanche Mountain. Separate short routes can be done here, or several bands can be linked (with some bushwhacking) to make a long, scenic tour. Most will be at least 5.8.

Across the lake is a huge wall that is accessible by boat (or swimming, or maybe even by creative traversing). The climbing here is sustained, but seldom desperate (around 5.8), wandering up the steep black wall with scant protection (ACB Bill Dodd and Don Mellor). The central wall has about four pitches of surprisingly good rock before the angle lessens on the slide above. It is interesting to note that the first route reported here (*TV Dinner* 5.8 FA Robert F. Lauder and Jeff Vaughan 7/26/75), taking a thin, right-facing flake on the left end of the wall, fell into the lake in the early eighties. The remnants of the corner may yet provide another option.

In the *Trap Dike* itself (see description in Slide Climbs section) are numerous, high-standard, single-pitch options. These dike walls may well become a destination climbing area by itself as more lines are climbed. The possibilities will probably begin around 5.8 or 5.9 and quickly escalate once the easier routes are established.

Janet Mellor nears the top of the southwest slide on Dix.

SLIDE CLIMBS

Most people view Eastern mountain climbing as either hiking steep trails in the woods or clinging by the fingertips from a precipitous rock face. Yet one of the wonders of climbing in the Adirondacks is that no such dichotomy exists. Instead, there is an unbroken continuum from the flat trails to the steep walls, from the truck road to Marcy Dam to the overhanging Spider's Web. Climbers here have a lot to choose from and can pick from any realm of verticality or remoteness they desire.

Included in this guide is a selection of steep slides in the High Peaks region. These are long, open expanses of rock wiped clean by avalanches. It isn't really hiking; it isn't really rock-climbing. Climbing these slides is, perhaps, closer to classical mountaineering: it generally entails a long approach hike, some steep scrambling on open rock, discretion in route choice, tremendous exposure, perhaps a little rope work for the tricky sections, and best of all, a finish not in some lowland forest, but on one of the Adirondacks' glorious summits.

An avalanche slide usually results from saturation of the wooded slope that clings to the face of the mountain. In an unusually heavy downpour, the shallow soils become heavy and lubricated by the rain. The massive Adirondack anorthosite offers few cracks into which vegetation can extend anchoring roots. The result is a mass wasting that usually starts at a steep headwall and clears a path down the mountain in one calamitous surge. When the rains end and the fogs lift, a new white stripe bears witness to the violence of the event and the dynamics of the landscape.

And it is a living and dynamic landscape indeed. While new slides occur every few years, the older ones become overgrown and a new growth of vegetation invades the open slopes. The lichens, then mosses, and finally the trees that establish themselves on the old slides remind one of the human residents on the San Andreas Fault or the hurricane-ravaged Gulf coast lowlands: the inevitability of another catastrophe doesn't stop the locals from optimistically starting anew. So while some of these routes gradually become too mossy and overgrown to afford good climbing, we may be witness to the birth of a new exposure of some other place in the High Peaks.

The difficulty of these climbs is twofold. First, there is the problem of just finding the base of the slide. It always helps to get a look from afar and plan your route accordingly. (Some people have even brought along a postcard of the slides of Giant and Whiteface to help with route choice.) Second is the difficulty of the steep rock itself. The angle of slope for most of these slides is generally somewhere between 25 and 40 degrees. For the easier climbs one needs only the friction of hiking shoes for ascent. The steeper climbs require all the gear of the rock-climber. It is necessary, therefore, to become acquainted with the grading system before setting out. Remember that Class 2 climbing is generally a steep walk-up, Class 3 is steeper and may require a rope for the careful or timid, Class 4 is certainly a roped climb, and Class 5 requires belay stances and protection points between leader and second.

All slides will require a map and compass, as well as stout clothing for the approach and exit through the bush. A wire brush is very helpful (sometimes mandatory) for the harder or dirtier slides; one cleaned handhold can make quite a difference when you're looking at a long fall. Finally, bring along a good attitude, especially if you're used to tame climbs with easy approaches. Slide climbers get lost, get scared, get torn by nasty little spruces, get bitten by black-flies that hold on all summer long in the High Peaks, and generally have a whale of a good time.

GIANT

The bare expanses of rock on this peak make it one of the most majestic in the Adirondacks. It is especially impressive when viewed from the golf course at the Ausable Club, just a few minutes off Route 73. It is worthwhile to scope it out from this vantage point before heading up any of the slides in the western cirque. The huge slides on the east face can be viewed from afar from Route 9 south of Elizabethtown, but the distance is so great here that one really can't discern any details.

The slides of Giant are also noteworthy because their formation was so recent and cataclysmic. Locals clearly remember the storm in 1963 that enlarged many of the overgrown slides and created the scene we have now. Today, we can see signs of the chaos in the streambed approach, but the open banks of the slide are gradually being reclaimed by birches. Above, however, most of the slides are as fresh as ever. There was even some more scarring in the seventies, which lengthened and cleaned up some of the slidetracks.

Eastern Cirque   Class 3 to 5

The slides on the eastern side of Giant are wide and continuous. They can be approached via the long trail from Route 9N or by simply heading downhill from the col between Rocky Peak Ridge and Giant. This latter route is the quickest, but it makes the trip a bit anticlimactic since one must climb nearly to Giant's summit before dropping back down to the base of the cirque. The trail from 9N passes Owl Head Lookout on its way to High Bank, a distinctive, tall sandbank above the brook about 4 miles from the road. Here, slide climbers leave the trail and follow the brook up the valley to the foot of the slides.

There are endless options on this face of Giant. The easiest slide is probably the one farthest to the left. The central slides are blocked by a barrier wall about midway up. Most routes here will demand a rope and a belay for this section. Far to the right are shorter, steeper slabs where true Class 5 friction climbing leads to the wooded slopes on the northeast shoulder of the mountain.

Western Cirque   Class 2 and 3

This is the postcard face, carved into such fantastic patterns by the 1963 rainstorm. There are six slides on this face; each of the slides has acquired a name according to its shape, and though time, with its invasion of new growth and its resculpting of the avalanche paths, is changing the shapes on the mountain, the names hold on for tradition's sake.

All of these slides begin in Roaring Brook. Park at the hikers' lot on Route 73 and head up the Roaring Brook Trail toward Giant. At the trail junction (about a mile from Route 73), stay in the streambed and follow it into the cirque.

Bottle   Class 2

This is the left-most obvious slide. It lies on a slight ridge left of the main cirque, and climbers seem to have more difficulty finding it than climbing it. Approach this slide at a straight section of the brook where a broad slide enters from the left. The most easily distinguishable feature here is the line where a stand of birch gives way to a mature forest of spruce. It is best to approach about 100' short of this abrupt change in forest. Climb the birch bank to another stream. Follow this, avoiding the first stream that enters from the left. This slide, averaging about 34 degrees of inclination, rises for almost 2,000 linear feet to the summit cliffs which are skirted right toward the top of the peak.

Diagonal Slide   Class 2

Probably more often than not, ascents of this slide are made by frustrated climbers who missed the Bottle. It is looser than many of the other slides here and will be sought only by climbers who have done the others and are seeking new terrain. Like the Bottle, this ends below summit cliffs which are avoided to the right.

Question Mark   Class 2 or 3

No longer does this really resemble its namesake. Approach this as for the Diagonal and head up right. The upper section of very steep slab is avoided left or right, and the summit cliff band is bypassed uphill to the right.

Eagle Slide   Class 3

There is endless debate as to which is the better climb, the *Eagle* or the *Trap Dike*. If the *Trap Dike* is the classic 3rd and 4th class varied rock climb, then the *Eagle* is the classic friction scramble. It is a wide, clean expanse of rolling slabs that end just below the trail. The first 100' is hard, and the short upper headwalls require care as well. Stay in the main streambed to its terminus at the foot of the slide. At any stream junctions, always opt for the biggest. Numerous routes can be selected, with the most direct finishing in the middle finger of the right side. The trail to the summit is only a few more feet through the brush.

Finger Slide   Class 2

This long, narrow slide heads up right from the base of the *Eagle.* To find this slide, head up from the base of the final, steep 200' chute that leads to the open *Eagle* face above. The slide ends at a path that quickly takes one to the summit trail.

Tulip Slide   Class 2

About 300' past the approach to the *Bottle* is a less obvious slide on the right (though an obvious new slide begins nearby but ends shortly above). This slide is one of the easier ones and takes the left-most track at the top to quickly join the hiker's trail on the ridge.

EAST DIX

These easy slides make up the easiest access to the Dix Range from Route 73 to the east. The approach starting at the North Branch of the Bouquet and then joining the South Branch is described in ADK's *Guide to Adirondack Trails: High Peaks Region.* There are two parallel slides, the second of which is the larger and more interesting. The unmarked path that leads up the South Branch of the Bouquet leads generally in the direction of the streambed that drains the slides.

DIX

This beautiful peak has slides on three of its steep faces. Those most obvious to the traveler between Keene and Keene Valley came down during the summer of 1993. Approached via the Round Pond Trail to Dix Mountain, these wide open slabs provide lots of opportunity for exploration. The trail was partially obliterated by the slides, so finding the start of the climbs will be no problem. The slides reach the trail a little over a mile above the lean-to, and about 1.5 hours from the road. Over the last two summers, several groups have climbed these clean slides and report them to be among the very best. A few have even ventured all the way to the summit; a discernible herd path is emerging.

The slides facing southwest toward Elk Lake and Hunters Pass were established in 1970. They offer a direct route to the summit. Approach from Elk Lake, past Dix Pond and the southern Dix trail via the Beckhorn. Above this junction the trail steepens for about a half mile, then flattens. Here it is possible to scope out the various slides and their common convergence at the bottom of the mountain. It is necessary first to locate this notch through which the streams drain the slides on the face. The steep streambed is a fascinating, stepped toboggan slide that leads up to the rubble above. Keep right at the lower junctions. The lower unstable section is followed by a wide slide that branches into three options, the left being the most direct. A short, tough bushwhack over rock steps leads to the ridge between the summit and the Beckhorn spur to the south.

The slides on the east side of the mountain, over the valley of the Boquet River, look wet and brushy, but they may offer some good scrambling.

HOUGH

The slide that faces northeast and is so visible from Dix is one of the steepest slides in the peaks. It is truly a 5th class climb, and it requires a rope, some protection, and a belay. Yet the technical difficulty is only one small part of the challenge here. The approach is a horrendous bushwhack. Take the hikers' trail from Elk Lake as for Dix, and head up the yellow trail toward the Beckhorn (Dix's southern summit spur). Bushwhack southeast to gain the drainage. Check the map (and your sanity) before heading out.

NIPPLE TOP
Class 2

This excellent, east face slide can be seen from many of the High Peaks. Approach via the Lake Road to Lower Ausable Lake. The Gill Brook Trail (at about 1.75 miles) bears left and reaches Elk Pass just over 2 miles later. Here the Nipple Top Trail heads steeply uphill. Instead of taking this trail, head south, downhill, in the steep pass beyond, until at the base of the slide. Resist the temptation to cut straight across, hoping to join the slide without losing elevation: It's pretty tough going. The slide rewards the climber with ever-increasing views, first limited to the wooded wall of Colvin and Blake, but finally opening up the whole panorama of the Great Range.

GOTHICS: TRUE NORTH

This recently created route is well-named: it climbs the actual north ridge of the mountain, left of what is called the North Face (actually the northwest face) of Gothics. True North was made available by the 1990 slides. It currently offers the only non-technical route up this side of the mountain, and it comes highly recommended.

Approach as for the North Face (see Gothics rock climbs). Head up onto the broad expanse on the left-hand side of the face for an exhilarating view, both of the valley below and of the amazing bare face itself. Don't go too high before bushwhacking straight left into the woods; in fact, the higher you go before cutting left, the nastier the forest becomes. After a short wooded section, a small vertical slide is reached. This leads upward to join the wider True North Slide which ends at the northern end of the Gothics summit ridge. The route is becoming a popular winter ski descent, especially for North Face climbers.

SADDLEBACK

The north side of this mountain can be climbed via a slide. From Bushnell Falls, hike up Chicken Coop Brook to gain the open rock. The slide isn't one of the most dramatic, but the trip as a whole through an attractive forest to a Great Range summit comes recommended.

MARCY

The overgrown slides on the south face of Marcy are probably more trouble than they are worth in their present condition. They are included mainly for their historic value: this was the route of "Old Mountain" Phelps as he guided clients to the top of the state's highest peak. Now it has become so grown in that the upper section is a real battle against the brush. The slide is approached via Panther Gorge.

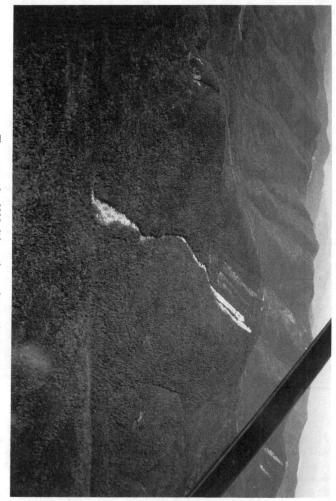

The spectacular 1990 slide on the southeast side of Colden.

COLDEN

Southeast Slide

There had long been a mossy slide on this face of the mountain, but it was drastically improved for climbing by the huge slides of June 1990. In one night, over ten slides were formed, here on Gothics and elsewhere. This trip is a good one and, combined with the Trap Dike, would make for a spectacular traverse. Approach via Lake Arnold, following the trail south and descending to reach the foot of the slide just before the trail reaches the Opalescent River. The slide ends right on the trail itself, so no bushwhack is necessary down low. The lower portions are dirt-covered, winding upwards in several S turns. (It is fast becoming a popular ski descent.) The top slab is steep, and the timid (or smart) may opt left for a safer, dirtier finish.

Via the Trap Dike   Class 3

This is *the* historic Adirondack climb. In fact, many consider it the site of the beginning of Adirondack rock climbing. Here Robert Clarke and Alexander Ralph made the first ascent of Mt. Colden in 1850. The climb is also one of the most interesting features in the High Peaks: it is a deeply eroded dike of gabbro that was intruded into the anorthosite of the mountain. Differential erosion of this more fractured rock left us with a chasm between towering walls and a logical climbing route to the slides above. From Avalanche Lake, this climb is entirely on rock with a vertical gain of about 2000'.

Unlike the uniform slope of most of the other slides, Colden's *Trap Dike* begins with a staircase of steep rock before emerging onto the slide out right. Approach by walking around the far end of Avalanche Lake to gain the tree-covered debris slope at the dike's base. At the top of the staircase, at the first opportunity to escape the dike, the friction climbing is hard. It is much better to stay in until the second outlet is reached; then traverse right across a mossy section to get to the better slides out right. The technical crux is in the dike itself where the waterfall is at its steepest; many groups opt for a rope here. With the exception of the hard friction at the first exit, the slide climbing is fairly easy, but the exposure over the tiny lake below is especially exhilarating.

Wright Peak   Class 2 (with a slightly harder barrier high on the slide)

From Indian Falls on the Marcy Trail, this slide shows itself as a striking white line on the south face of Wright Peak. It's not as long as some of the others, but it is a worthwhile trip nonetheless. The streambed that flows from the valley of the slide enters Marcy Brook a short distance above Marcy Dam. Follow this stream. The slide enters the main stream from the right. It is also common to begin the bushwhack right from Avalanche lean-tos by skirting a small hill on its north side to meet the streambed. The going on this slide is fairly easy save for a barrier wall above mid-height. There are several ways to break through this. Along the way, you are likely to find bits and pieces of a B-47 bomber that crashed into the summit of Wright in 1962.

WHITEFACE

The slides on the faces of the Olympic mountain are familiar sights to every visitor. The southwest slide is an integral part of Lake Placid's visual backdrop, and the eastern slides by the ski area are often confused with the ski trails themselves. Both sides are excellent and clean, and both end easily at the crowded summit. Many climbers seek out the slides of a peak to get far away from it all; this isn't possible at Whiteface. Civilization is always in view and the top of the mountain is packed with people who have arrived by car and elevator. But where else can you approach by boat or chairlift and finish with a chili-dog and a Coke?

Lake Placid Slide
Class 2 (with one Class 3 overlap that can be avoided)

Approach this slide from Whiteface Landing at the end of Lake Placid. A 2-mile hike from Connery Pond off Route 86 or a paddle from the village brings one to the hiking trail. At a point about 1.75 miles from the lake, the trail turns sharply right, away from Whiteface Brook. Leave the trail here by keeping in the original straight line up an old phone line, picking up the pipe and cable shortly. It is possible to cut left to the brook at any point, but don't go much farther than the boulder tunnel of the cable. A short bush-whack west leads to the brook and slide above. The final summit cliff is a textbook example of an arete, the ridge formed by glacial carving of the retreating headwalls on either side of the mountain. The horn-shaped summit of Whiteface is the East's best example of this process. The short cliffs can be avoided to the right.

Ski-Center Slides   Class 2

Right of the ski trails on the east face of Whiteface are several obvious avalanche scars. The main path splits halfway up, with the left-hand route being the widest and most direct. This slide is smooth and white and is intersected at several points by dark ribbons, intrusions of molten rock, called dikes. The slide paths are reached from the ski trails. Walk or take the chairlift to the midstation lodge. From here follow the right-hand chairlift to the building at the base of Lift Six, the highest and rightmost of the chairlifts. Continue up the main ski trail under the chairlift until an obvious service road makes a hairpin turn on the right. From the turn itself an informal path heads directly across to the base of the slide. The top of the mountain is reached after a short, difficult bushwhack.

SANTANONI

This has been called one of the best slide hikes in the mountains. It is certainly one of the most impressive: a very long, very straight gash on the southwest face, well south of the summit itself. The slide resulted from a huge storm in September 1985, and it is visible from Route 28 between Long Lake and Newcomb.

Two problems exist on this trip that will keep away the crowds but at the same time will ensure its intrigue. First, the approach is a long one. The hike from Newcomb towards Moose Pond and up Ermine Brook (take the right fork about a half mile up the brook) is no short stroll. Second, once on top of the slide, the summit is over a mile away and the bushwhack across the ridge may be unreasonable. Most climbers will simply savor the views and then head back down the slide toward the trail.

PHOTO BY MARK MESCHINELLI

Chapel Pond Slab *in winter.*

ICE CLIMBS

"Ice is nice and will suffice." So wrote Robert Frost and so believes the climber who is willing to stand on frozen ledges, stamp his feet and swing his hands wildly in a vain effort to stay warm, all just to be part of the surreal blue landscape and to feel the reassuring thunk of a tool well placed. To such a climber winter isn't the off-season; it's *the* season.

Adirondack ice ranks among the best and most varied in the eastern United States. If there is a center of activity, it's Keene Valley. Visitors often start at nearby Chapel Pond or Cascade Lakes, two of the most reliable areas, selecting from thick and secure top-rope routes, thin low-angled slabs, and steep green gullies. In good winters, Poke-O-Moonshine can offer outstanding hard climbing, and always it's possible to retreat into the high country for the frozen unknown. Along with these options, there are the vast unexplored territories loosely referred to as the southern Adirondacks.

Some (fool-?) hardy souls will spend their nights in tents, maybe sneaking into the warmth of a diner before setting out to climb. More commonly, climbers will find lodging in the numerous bed-and-breakfasts or inexpensive motels in the region. Gear can be bought—and fondled when the wallet is too light—in Lake Placid at Eastern Mountain Sports and High Peaks Cyclery and in Keene Valley at The Mountaineer.

Maybe the saner folks will stay home and train on their indoor walls, readying themselves for more benevolent conditions. But to a certain few, winter in the Adirondacks is a crystalline fantasy.

GENERAL NOTES ON ICE CLIMBING

The rain- and meltwater that we so scorn when they spoil our rock climbing easily make recompense in the winter by seeping from rock walls and flowing down gullies, freezing into excellent and varied ice routes. In good years the major passes, such as Chapel, Cascade, and Avalanche, wear myriad stripes of white, green, and blue, each a potential climb with its own challenge and character.

As in all mountain areas, ice climbing here in the Adirondacks has undergone something of a technological revolution. For years climbers armed with long axes and ten-point crampons ascended the low-angled slabs and slides of Colden, Gothics, and Chapel Pond. These climbs were quite challenging in light of the gear available, and they added a genuine mountaineering element to Adirondack climbing.

Things have changed. Tools of amazing sophistication are now standard, and climbers who punch their way up one of the older routes aided by two slick hand tools, tubular ice screws, rigid twelve-point crampons, and plastic boots can easily forget the difficulty faced by their forebears. Frequently we are all guilty of overkill when we equip ourselves for a route; it's difficult to shun a tool that is going to make our climb easier and its outcome certain. Yet, though these technological innovations have at times replaced our boldness, they have opened up a whole new realm of possibilities. As the curved pick and tubular and reverse-drooped hand tools became available, our eyes for the first time lifted up to notice those magnificent icicles and vertical glazed walls that were inconceivable only a few years earlier.

These new tools of the trade have also had a profound effect on the way climbers are moving on ice. They are the first that really allow down-climbing. Climbers no longer need to view a crux section as a one-way street. They can climb up, check things out, arrange a screw or two, and hook back down in their old holes to a stance for a rest. This has the additional benefit to the ice itself: a route that would be devastated by repeated bashing with more traditional axes can withstand multiple hooking ascents. Although this isn't meant to fan the embers of a needless debate, it is worth noting that the ice climber can now approach more creatively and less violently, and the routes are better off for it.

Any discussion about improved climbing gear can quickly degenerate into debate. Yet while ethics and style are inextricably woven into rock climbing, ice climbers seem to spend more of their energy keeping warm on belays than yelling at each other about how things should be done. The most prevalent of these squabbles, however, involves tying into the tools and hanging in the harness in order to either rest or place protection. Because ice climbing requires hanging onto tools one way or another (from taped handles, webbing wristloops, etc.), any controversy here is an arbitrary contrivance. Your approach affects nothing but your own experience. For the sake of information and history, however, it should be noted that all routes listed in this guide have been led "free"; that is, by hanging onto tools with the arms only and not taking tension from the rope or sitting back on a harness tie-in to rest or protect.

Fortunately, although the tools may be considered the great equalizer of climbers, our technology hasn't yet conquered the elements. Winters are as fickle as ever, and ice conditions change daily. Rock routes stay the same, and once one has mastered their individual moves, the sharp edge of their challenge and mystique has been sanded smooth. Not so with ice. The benign Chapel Slab can become a whirlwind of spindrift on verglassed rock, and the mysterious first pitch of Roaring Brook Falls refuses to wear the same mask twice.

These variables add an attractive element to ice climbing, but they make efforts to describe and grade routes difficult and potentially misleading. Ice routes aren't to be plugged neatly into a decimal rating scale. They change day to day, month to month, season to season. Climbers in the Northeast use a rating system known as the New England Ice System (NEI) that was adapted from the Scottish system principally by Rick Wilcox and Peter Cole for their New England ice guide, *Shades of Blue*. Some may continue to advocate the more general system of "easy," "moderate," and "hard," but as technology leads us to steeper places, so does it demand that we be more precise in our evaluations. Bear in mind that changing conditions can dramatically alter a climb's difficulty. Comparing this fluctuation to rock-climbing equivalents, it is as though a climb can be 5.10 one week and 5.6 the next, simply because of a change in the weather. A brief and deliberately vague description of this system follows:

NEI 1   Easy, low-angled ice. The easiest ice for which a belay rope could be used.

NEI 2   Harder, low-angled ice. Still climbable without front-points on crampons.

NEI 3   Steeper ice. Some continuous front-pointing with perhaps the assistance of a hand tool in conjunction with the ice axe in places. Generally allows protection screws to be placed from comfortable stances.

NEI 4   Difficult and sustained with vertical sections. Requires two tools and usually demands that screws be placed while on vertical or near vertical ice.

NE 5   The hardest category. These routes are usually several pitches in length and have sections of vertical ice in excess of 50'.

(A plus or minus sign may be added to further delineate the grade.)

Naturally, these grades are subjective. So is the advice about what gear is used for each grade. Such information is included only to help paint a picture of the challenge presented by a climb. It is in no way a prescription as to how one should approach a route. Look the ice over yourself and take what you think you'll need. Keep in mind, however, that curious but absolute law of ice climbing: It's steeper than it looks.

Where possible, many of the descriptions in this edition include some suggestion as to the reliability of the ice climb. The direction that a route faces and the elevation above sea level are factors that can help you plan. Look also for notes next to the rating that indicate the likelihood of the route's being in shape in a typical winter. Such suggestions include:

Reliable:	Forms most years
Unreliable:	Has formed somewhere between 3 and 6 of the least 10 seasons
Rare:	Once in a decade
Forms early:	Usually by Christmas
Easy top-rope:	Recommended as a suitable site with easy access and good tree anchors

Granting first ascent credit creates a slippery issue because poor records have been kept and ice climbs vary from year to year. Icicles quickly heal from the axe wounds we inflict, so unlike rock climbs, there is no trace of previous passage. Also, many climbers have, owing to neglect or modesty, failed to record their exploits. Perhaps the ephemeral nature of ice, that here-today, gone-tomorrow nature of it all leads us to feel that our accomplishments melt away each spring, so permanent route credit should fade also. This is especially true of the lower-angled routes that have been popular for a longer period of time. The more extreme routes have, by the very nature of the tools required, been climbed more recently, and therefore one can be more certain of their origins.

This guide will assign credits only hesitantly. The standard FA (first ascent) designation will be reserved for those routes whose histories are fairly certain. Otherwise, ACB (as climbed by) will denote the first recorded ascent, and though this may or may not be the first, it will help future historians piece together this puzzle for those who care to know. Many of the popular routes, however, will remain on their own, with no connection to a specific climbing party. This might not be so bad: After all, a route isn't a possession. Nobody "puts up" these climbs. They were here when we arrived.

Finally a word about judgment. Climbers here and everywhere should be aware that ice is variable and unpredictable. They should realize that simply because a climb has been acknowledged here in print does not imply that the route is safe or recommended. The slab might explode under water pressure, the pillar might collapse under body weight, or the previous ascent parties just might have been damned foolish. Add Adirondack weather to this picture and you have a situation that may demand only the best decisions. You be the judge.

GREATER KEENE VALLEY
ALONG ROUTE 73 AND
I-87 SOUTH OF CHAPEL POND

The following routes are described north to south, beginning on Route 73 south of Chapel Pond Pass.

Round Pond Trailhead
NEI 2   100'   faces SW   el. 1600'   (reliable)

In low-snow years, there is some visible ice a short distance from the road about 50 yards north of the Round Pond/Dix Mountain trailhead parking lot south of Chapel Pond. The streambeds are often snow-covered.

Two-Below Honey   NEI 4

High in the cliffbands across the road from Round Pond/Dix Mountain

Trailhead is a sizable piece of ice. It is reliable, visible from the road, and quite a beat-out if the snow is deep.

FA Chuck Turner and Dom D'Angelo 1983

So What   NEI 3   70'   faces SW

Close to the Dix Mountain trailhead on the east side of Route 73 is an ice route low in the boulder field. Climb up beneath a rock ceiling; traverse left around the overhang, and chimney to the top.

FA "The usual suspects" 1/3/88

Sheik of the Burning Sands
NEI 4-   120'   faces SW   (unreliable)

This climb is located just left of Spanky's Wall. First locate a small pull-off on the east side of the road 1.5 miles south of Chapel Pond. The top of this route can be seen from the road a short way north of the parking area. Approach directly through the steep woods (10 minutes), passing *Ahab the Arab* on the way. The climb ascends a steep wall for about 90' to a good ledge. A final 20' wall leads to the top.

ACB Patrick Purcell and Don Mellor 12/85

Ahab the Arab   NEI 3   70'   faces SW   (unreliable)

This is a smaller slab above and right of the *Sheik,* and left of a vertical wall with a prominent ceiling at mid-height.

ACB Patrick Purcell and Tom Skrill 12/85

Camel Clyde's Goober   NEI 3   50'   faces S   el. 1300'   (reliable)

This climb is located on the southernmost slab of the Whitewater Walls rock-climbing crags. These are just south of the bridge over the North Fork of the Bouquet River. The slabs are across the river and slightly below road level. *Clyde's Goober* is a distinct strip of ice on the right of the group.

ACB Patrick Purcell (solo) 12/85

Rites of Passage   NEI 4   80'   faces SW   el. 1200'   (reliable)

About three quarters of a mile up from Exit 30 on Route 73, and just below the Underwood Club, is a crag in the woods. A careful eye as one drives by will locate this attractive blue line dripping from the crag's right end. Climbers had long noticed this route, but thought it to lie on private land. Fortunately for climbers, a jog in the property line just below the route places the ice on state land. It necessitates, however, an indirect approach. Park at the King Philips Spring lot just off I-87 and walk Route 73 north to the Forest Preserve sign posted on a large pine. Follow the property line diagonally, across the river and uphill to a point near the climb.

ACB Don Mellor, Mark Meschinelli, and Gary Spesard 4/9/86

Left of Passage   NEI 3+   90'

Climb the buttress left of the chimney to a pillar and chockstone finish.

ACB Tad Welch and Bill Widrig 1/29/95

Exit Thirty Gullies
NEI 3-4   50-150'   faces W   el. 1100'   (reliable)

There is a large, craggy wall off to the right of I-87 just south of Exit 30 that leads into the Keene Valley region. The ice here is very good and there is plenty of variety. The problem is the prohibition of parking on the interstate. Perhaps an approach could be effected from Route 73.

Another Roadside Detraction   NEI 3+   70'   faces SE   el. 1100'

This small roadside cliff lies on the southbound side of the Northway about 1 mile south of Exit 30. As with Exit Thirty Gullies, parking is a problem. One solution is to park at the exit and walk. There are usually three routes on this uniformly smooth, steep slab, all similar in difficulty.

Left to right:
Another Roadside Detraction   NEI 3+
Over My Dead Battery   NEI 3+
Another V&T Violation   NEI 3+

ACB Alan Jolley and Patrick Purcell 2/3/85

Mineville Pillar   NEI 4   100'   faces SE   el. 1200'   (reliable)   †

One of the best pitches up here, this steep and thick column is located near Exit 30. From the exit, drive east for a few feet, then turn immediately left on Route 6 toward the town of Mineville. The obvious route stands about 2 miles up the road on the left. The climb is only barely on state land.

If recent boundary markings are correct, your right tool may be trespassing at times. Walk in from the left to keep your approach legal.

CHAPEL POND AREA

The area around Chapel Pond (elevation 1700') is perhaps the most popular and varied in the Adirondacks. Here one can practice French technique on the 700' *Slab Route* or, at the other end of the spectrum, fry the arms and mind alike on the columns of *Power Play* and *Big Brother*. And there's everything in between to satisfy all levels of ambition. The ice in this region is as reliable as any in the Adirondacks, and it forms early: *Chouinard's Gully* and *Chapel Pond Slab* are often climbed before Thanksgiving.

The routes are described south to north as one approaches on Route 73.

Cheese and Crackers   NEI 4+   120'   faces E   (unreliable)

Driving north, just before reaching Chapel Pond, one looks straight up at the huge Emperor Slabs before cresting the hill and descending to the pond. At the left side of these slabs, where the cliffs turn uphill to the King Wall, is an icicle barely visible from the road.

FA Tom Yandon and Glen Villeneuve 1986

Emperor Slabs   NEI 3   500'   faces NE   (unreliable)

This expansive slab rarely ices very thickly; the few ascents so far have tiptoed on thin ice with little protection. Actual route choice will be dictated by conditions. Nonetheless, for those who thrive on the insecurity of glazed rock, this route might be just the answer.

Chapel Pond Slab
NEI 2–3   700'   faces NE   (reliable, forms early)   †

This low-angled slab offers the area's best easy and moderate ice climbing. The first route to form usually begins at the major left-facing corner and continues up the line of *Victoria*. Later in the season other possibilities exist, the most challenging of which is *Thanksgiving*.

The slab, though relatively easy, does present some problems and dangers. Avalanches sometimes sweep from the more benign-angled slopes above and have taken more than one unsuspecting party to the ground. And as noted in the 1983 edition, there is also a possibility of tapping high-pressure water under the slab. Three years after I wrote those words, I was about 20 feet out from the belay, about level with the *Empress* crack, when I fell victim to the very thing I had warned others about. A 15' x 15' slab exploded in a gush of water with me in the middle, and my fall (or swim) was limited to 40' by a belayer who held on despite the battering he was taking from the ice blocks. Since then there have been at least three close calls, each in a different location and during different conditions. These hazards are part of any ice climb, but they should be considered especially here. The apparent ease of the climb can lead one to forget the risk.

As in all ice areas, a combination of ice conditions and ambition decides the route of ascent. A note to early season crazies: by following the line of *Victoria* (see Rock Climbs, Keene Valley section), one can dig out some nut belays, helpful especially below the bulge. Descend as for the summer routes.

FA Jim Goodwin and Bob Notman 1936

To the right of the Slab is Chapel Pond Gully. In this drainage above the left end of the pond are the following routes. They are located on the right-most slopes of Chapel Pond Slab, across from the Chapel Pond Gully rock climbs.

Cold Warrior   NEI 3   80'   (typically thin)

Left of the next route is a right-slanting corner with an ice ribbon in it. Delicate climbing leads to a traverse below overhangs to a block belay.

Forest of Azure   NEI 1-2

This follows the long, most prominent wide gully whose lower portion is essentially a snow climb. The upper ice bulges are more challenging. For those who know the northern descent route in summer, the climb crosses the descent just above the birch rappel.

Tahawas   NEI 3   250'   (unreliable)   †

This climb stands directly across from *Right-Hand Route* on the Gully Cliff. It is the widest flow, with an abundance of ice. Climb a 12' vertical wall (this can be hard when thin) to lower-angled slabs. Another pitch up and right leads to the trees.

TYPICALLY LEAN CONDITIONS AT CHAPEL POND

A. CHOUINARD'S GULLY

B. POWER PLAY

C. BIG BROTHER

D. RHIANNON

The Mason-Dixon Line   NEI 4   40'

High in the gully, across from *Tennessee Excursion,* is a wide curtain of steep ice.

Crystal Ice Tower   NEI 4   60'   faces NE   (reliable, forms early)   †

Left of the pond on the low rock walls that ultimately lead up to the Chapel Pond Gully Cliffs is a reliable and obvious ice route. This climb is visible from the Chapel Pond parking area, and though it is possible to link with the following climb, most parties treat it as a single-pitch route.

White Line Fever   NEI 3   350'   faces NE   (typically thin)   †

The former route can be extended for several more pitches by climbing the classic gully just above and right to the tree-covered terrace that runs along the base of the Tanager Face and that is often used for descent from *Chouinard's Gully.* From here one can walk about 100' up to a higher gully that often yields mixed climbing all the way to the top of the Gully Cliff. The whole route in the right conditions is quite an expedition.

Necktie Party   NEI 4-   70'   (typically thin and mixed)

This is the transparent smear of ice that drips from the large overhang just left of *Parallel Gully.* Unprotected crux.

FA Tad Welch and Bill Widrig 2/4/95

Parallel Gully   NEI 3-   160'   (unreliable)

Left of *Chouinard's Gully* is a series of corners and ridges. This route climbs the left-facing corner at *Tilman's Arete.*

ACB Tad Welch and Mike Cross 2/84

Dogleg Buttress   NEI 3   80'   (typically thin and mixed)

In some years it is possible to climb the verglassed rock down left of *Dogleg* to the cedars. From here, an easy traverse right leads to a pillar.

FA Tad Welch 3/4/87

Dogleg   NEI 3+   200'   faces NE   (unreliable)

Actually a left-hand variation of *Chouinard's Gully,* this route sometimes offers a good alternative to its more popular neighbor. Ascend walls and slabs up and left through the trees. Because the upper section is a snow gully, most parties opt to join *Chouinard's Gully* about halfway up.

Chouinard's Gully

NEI 3   300'   faces NE   (reliable, forms early)   †

Owing to its length and continuous moderate climbing, this is one of the most popular lines in the region. It rises prominently above a tree-covered scree cone across the pond from the parking area. (If the pond isn't safely frozen, it is still possible to approach by skirting the shore and climbing a short 5.4 wall to a tree ledge from which a 30' rappel will bring one to the scree cone.) The crux is the short, near-vertical section low on the climb. Above, easier ice with good tree belays leads to the top. Be very careful if a party is above on this route: Ice inevitably rockets down unseen from above the first pitch. Higher up the danger lessens. Two long rappels (careful on the first as the ropes barely make it) descend the left side via fixed slings on trees. Alternatively, it is possible to hike down and left (stay roped across upper *Dogleg* gully) to the Tanager face and down into Chapel Pond Gully.

ACB Yvon Chouinard 1969

Chouinard's Right   NEI 3+ or 4-   300'   faces NE   (unreliable)

From the base of *Chouinard's Gully,* it is possible to climb steep walls interspersed by lower-angled sections, heading up and right, making this a fully separate line.

Pacman   NEI 4+   200'   faces NE   (unreliable)

The left side of the impressive *Power Play* wall has a steep route that joins the main climb high up. The top bulge resembles the shape of the video creature for which the route was named. Start on the steep left-hand ramp and up to a rock belay. Then out left on icicles to join the final large sloping ledge. Finish with the last pitch of *Power Play.* Bring rock gear.

FA Tom Yandon and Ed Palen 1991

Power Play   NEI 5   250'   faces NE   (unreliable)   †

This is one of the Northeast's major ice routes. It is the all-too-obvious line of icicles that drip multitiered down the black wall that dominates the mountainside across from the parking area. Early ascents climbed the

Pushing in another ice season: Patrick Purcell and Chouinard's Gully in early November.

right-rising ramps, exiting right into the woods (NEI 4). A direct attack, however, is one of the Adirondacks' most difficult climbs.

pitch 1 Climb normally thin ice up a right-rising ramp to a belay at the vertical wall. 120'

pitch 2 Head up the steep wall above (the ramp continues up, exiting with difficulty off right) to a belay on the next sloping ledge. 80'

pitch 3 The final columns lead to the woods. 50'

FA Direct Route unknown
Ramp Variation ACB Mark Meschinelli and Pat Munn 1979

March of Folly   NEI 3   200'   (typically thin and mixed)

Down and right a few feet of *Power Play* is an easier, mixed route. Begin in the short squeeze chimney. A ramp above leads to the first belay.

FA Tad Welch and Bill Widri 1/4/87

Patey's Gully   NEI 3+   220'   (rare)

This inobvious line starts between *March of Folly* and *Big Brother* at a left-facing corner.

pitch 1 Climb the thin strip of ice above the slab to a stance. Traverse rock around the outside corner to a cedar.

pitch 2 Move up and left over bulges and enter a long ice groove that ends on a ledge just below the top.

pitch 3 Exit up left.

FA Todd Swain and Tad Welch 12/14/86

Big Brother   NEI 5-   250'   faces NE   (unreliable)   †

This is a fickle but spectacular icicle that forms on overhanging rock about 100 yards right of *Chouinard's Gully*. Not to be confused with the massive *Power Play,* this route is a pencil-like drip to its right. "Big brother is watching you," especially on the first day of 1984.

pitch 1 Climb mixed rock and ice on moderate terrain to a belay in the woods below the pillar. 120'

pitch 2 Climb steepening ice to the icicle itself. There is a small stance on the rock wall about 20' from the top.

FA Don Mellor and Chuck Turner 1/1/84

Rhiannon   NEI 4   175'   faces NE   (unreliable)   †

Below and 50' right of *Big Brother* is a broad, right-facing groove.

pitch 1 Climb the slab past a short pillar and a tree belay (about 30' right of *Big Brother*). 100'

pitch 2 The second pitch has in some years been good and thick; at other times there's no hint of ice. Rock climbing out right of the belay leads to a 40' vertical section.

FA *pitch 1* Tad Welch and Mike Cross 1/2/87

Lilith   NEI 4   220'   faces NE   (unreliable)

Another fickle route right of *Big Brother.*

pitch 1 Climb up and left on slabs to a belay at a large dead tree.

pitch 2 Walk right to the base of the pillar and up to the top.

FA Alan Jolley and Rachael Lawrence 2/17/85

Seldom Scene   NEI 3   90'   (typically thin)

To the right of the big route area is a low cliff band close to the pond. This is an obscure, but easily accessible route, hidden in an inside corner behind a screen of trees at the pond's edge. Bring rock protection.

ACB Tad Welch 2/11/91

Spittin' Image   NEI 3+   40'   (typically thin and mixed)

Right of the previous route is a glazed chimney in a left-facing corner. Wriggle to the overhang and fixed rappel.

FA Tad Welch and Bill Widrig 3/94

As You Like It   NEI 3+   80'   (typically thin and mixed)

An exercise in rock climbing with ice gear. Approaching the outlet channel of the pond, one reaches a final scree cone and high rock wall. The wall is cut by a diagonal slash easily seen from the parking area. A tricky start is followed by easier climbing up the groove and an ice overhang. The flared slot above is the crux.

FA Tad Welch 12/91

High and right of the big wall area, and above the outlet channel of the pond, are three distinct pieces of ice. The approach begins about midway up the outlet channel below a short ice cliff on the right. In low-snow years, the very steep hike takes about 15 minutes. All routes are fairly reliable.

One Giant Step   NEI 3–4   80'

This, as the name suggests, climbs steeply to a huge terrace, and steeply again to the top. It is the left-hand of the three most obvious ice routes.

Red Stringer   NEI 3+   150'

A wide slab leads to a headwall. This is the most prominent and largest of the three.

Dead Rabbit   NEI 3–4   75'

The upper and right-hand of the three routes, about 75' right of *Red Stringer,* has a moderate left side and a steep wall to the right. Named in memory of a snowshoe hare.

FD Bugs Bunny 12/94

CHAPEL POND CANYON

There is popular and accessible ice in the canyon of the Beer Walls at the apparent outlet of Chapel Pond. The routes are generally a half-rope in length with grades in the NEI 4 realm. These climbs come into shape early and are quite reliable. One can approach any of several ways: the most obvious walks from the pond parking area down the lake into the narrows. If the lake isn't safe, it is possible to walk up the road across from the Lower Washbowl Cliffs to get to the outlet of the pond. By crossing the stream just past the camping area, one can continue through the woods into the pass. Finally, it is possible to approach as for the Beer Wall rock climbs, but this is only recommended for *Positive Reinforcement,* which lies across from the Upper Tier rock climbs. The climbs are listed as one approaches from Chapel Pond.

Whales in the Jungle   NEI 3+   80'   faces NE   (unreliable)

This is the thin sheet that often ices up 20' left of *Lions on the Beach.*

Lions on the Beach

NEI 4   80'   faces NE   (reliable, forms early)   †

This is the first large ice route one encounters. For a longer mixed variation, climb steep steps in a tight tree-filled corner to the right.

Lowe Expectations   NEI 4+   100'

There is a sheer wall just right of *Lions* that drips with tantalizing ice. As part of an organized clinic, Lowe began by climbing the broken right-facing corner to reach the thin ice above. The more dramatic start just to its right still awaits either better conditions or another visit from the West.

FA Jeff Lowe, Mark Stampiglia, and Tad Welch 2/94

Hot Shot   NEI 4   60'   faces NE   (reliable, forms early)   †

Begin below a large right-facing corner. The thick steep ice is approached by 50' of snowy ramps.

Ice Slot   NEI 4   75'   faces NE   (reliable)   †

Right of the more appealing *Hot Shot* is a steep, thinly iced wall that leads into a steep, left-facing wooded slot.

Positive Reinforcement

NEI 3+   100'   faces NE   (reliable, forms early)   †

Continuing north through the height of the pass, one encounters several short steep pillars on the left. Beyond is this most impressive route. It is a very obvious waterfall cascading down the left wall of the canyon from Round Mountain. There are several ways up the falls, all ending at a large tree. Above is an easier, often neglected pitch.

Haggis and Cold Toast

NEI 3+   80'   faces NE   (typically thin and mixed)

At the northern end of Chapel Pond Canyon, across from the Case Wall, is a 4'–5' wide chimney. Rock protection is required for this mixed route. Though this is close to the parking lot across from Roaring Brook, use access to Case Wall as described in Rock Climbs, Keene Valley section so as to avoid trespassing on Ausable Club property. Named after a classic Scottish breakfast.

FA Bill Widrig and Tad Welch 3/93

The following routes are on the east side of the road, beginning across from Chapel Pond Slab.

Dipper Brook   NEI 3   35'   faces SW   (reliable, easy top-rope)

Not really a climb, more a practice area, this waterfall stands close to the road across the road from *Chapel Pond Slab*. It has erroneously been called Dipper Brook, which is in fact the major stream to the south.

Tarantula   NEI 4+   75'   faces SW   (unreliable)

This is the vertical ice sheet on the left end of the Creature Wall.

Whip It Good
NEI 4   75'   faces SW   (unreliable, more likely in early season)

There isn't much ice potential on the Washbowl side of the valley: it seems that the splintered crags that are high and dry during the summer months channel run-off between them rather than over the faces. The rock climber is grateful for this; the ice climber is frustrated. The only regular ice-up on this side of Chapel Pond Pass drips from a small, steep cliff up and right of the Spider's Web. Conditions can be ascertained from the road. Approach as for the Spider's Web. Climb the thinly iced right-facing corner to a ledge, then up the pillar to the top.

ACB Alan Jolley (solo) 1981

Roaring Brook Falls   NEI 3+   350'   faces W   (reliable)   †

This is the very scenic falls that cascades from the cirque on the west face of Giant Mountain. It is also the scene of the tremendous slide of June 1963, which scoured the face and left bare the distinctive slide paths. Evidence of this violence can still be seen as the fresh debris high on the route. The climb is easily viewed from the road; in fact, there are often cars stopped on the hill, with people snapping photos. Park at the spacious hikers' parking lot on the east side of the road at the bottom of the hill. Approach via a flat and easy trail that breaks right from the hikers' path up Giant. Descend via the hikers' trail. Keep in mind that there is water pounding under ice all winter and that only a prolonged and deep freeze will bring the climb into shape for the season. Falling through the ice and into the abyss would surely be fatal. The route can be completed in three or four pitches.

FA Unknown   (Attempted in December 1932 by Jim Goodwin and Bob Notman)

CASCADE PASS

Cascade Pass (elevation 2100') on Route 73 between Lake Placid and Keene hosts a variety of good ice-climbing possibilities. Both slopes above the scenic Cascade Lakes drip with ice of all angles that forms early and remains late in the season. The approaches from the road are easy and many routes can be top-roped. The one element of the area that's not wholly friendly is the weather: the wind frequently howls down the lakes and the alpine feeling of the place could make one forget that a hot drink or a good cheeseburger is only a few minutes away.

The routes are described south to north, beginning with the right side of the road when approaching from Keene.

Pitchoff Quarry Wall
NEI 4+   75'   faces SE   (reliable, forms early, good top-rope)   †

This is some of the hardest ice in the pass and its photographic possibilities are superb. The old quarry is located close to the road 100 yards right of the Pitchoff Chimney Cliff. The ice is nearly vertical and has several options for climbing. Conditions can be discerned from the road.

Pitchoff Right
NEI 3–4   30'–70'   faces SE   (reliable, forms early, easy top-rope)   †

Right of the Chimney Cliff and easily seen from the road is this very popular area, probably the most heavily used in the park. The long wall is a good angle for learning steep ice technique, and there is room here for several ropes. Above and right are lower angled slabs that can offer good climbing. Expect other climbers here, and be ready to move elsewhere when the face is draped with ropes.

Rugosity   5.8   NEI 4   150'   faces SE   (unreliable)   †

This route rarely comes in, but when it does, it is not to be missed.

pitch 1 The climb begins in the left-facing chimney of the summer route (do not confuse with The Great Chimney to its left). Aid may be necessary to turn the 5.8 move out to the block belay.

pitch 2 Slither out of this sheltered belay onto the open ice above.

Variation **Juan Valdez** 5.5 A1 NEI 4 (unreliable)   As the name suggests,

The intimidating Pitchoff Quarry Wall.

start with *Coffee Achievers* and aid right to reach the ice.

ACB Mark Ippolito, Alan Hobson, and Don Mellor 12/22/83

ACB Don Mellor and Mark Meschinelli 1990 (var.)

Pitchoff Left

NEI 3–4   60'   faces SE   (reliable, forms early, easy top-rope)   †

This is the waterfall that flows just left of the Roaches Wall rock climbs. The ice is steeper than at *Pitchoff Right*.

Bowser   NEI 2–3   50'   faces SE   (reliable, forms early)

100' left of *Pitchoff Left* are two minor slabs.

Buster   NEI 2+   200'   faces SE   (reliable, forms early)   †

Uphill to the right of *Sisters* is another popular route. The first pitch ascends steep steps. Above is a long streambed that could be considered a pitch; higher is a short vertical headwall (NEI 3–4).

Sibling Rivalry   NEI 3+   40'   (typically thin and mixed)

Around and up right from the *Sisters* is a steep, minor route on mixed rock and ice.

FA Tad Welch and Mike Cross 3/11/89

Sisters Right   NEI 4   80'   faces SE   (reliable, forms early)   †

A few hundred feet north of Pitchoff Chimney Cliff stands a rock buttress with two good ice climbs. There is parking across the road. *Sisters Right* is an excellent and demanding lead. Hint for early season climbers: There are good nut placements under the icicles just left of the lower crux.

Sisters Left   NEI 3+   100'   faces SE   (reliable)

This route branches up and left of the previous line in a series of steps and grooves. In lean conditions, it can be pretty hard.

Cysty Ugler   NEI 4   150'   faces SE   (typically thin and mixed)   †

A very narrow strip of ice often fills the prominent corner around and left of

THE SISTERS

A. CYSTY UGLER
B. SISTERS LEFT
C. SISTERS RIGHT
D. SIBLING RIVALRY
E. BUSTER

the *Sisters*. The route is an exciting mixed adventure on mainly rock protection. The second pitch finishes up right.

FA Tad Welch, Chuck Yax, and Kili Sherpa (Nepal) 12/94

Roadside Gullies

NEI 2–3   75'   faces SE   (reliable, forms early, easy top rope)

These are rather insignificant but reliable climbs with a "Bastille Crack approach." Several gullies rise almost right out of the road onto the rocky, tree-covered slopes above. The area offers ample tree anchors and interesting climbing, but is somewhat diminished by its proximity to the road. Park as for *Sisters* or *Pitchoff,* and walk 200 yards toward Lake Placid. These stand directly across the lake from *Three Flows*.

Indiscretion   NEI 3+   60'   faces S

This is an obscure but easily approached ice route. It is across from the middle of Upper Cascade Lake and tucked in a tight rock groove above the road. The left side of the rock has become known as the Ice Age Wall (see Rock Climbs, Cascade Lakes). The ice can be glimpsed briefly as one drives south into the notch (by the passenger, not the driver, please).

ACB Alan Jolley 2/24/85

The following climbs are described south to north on the left side of Route 73 as one approaches from Keene. The climbs between Quasi-Climber *and* Cascade Cliff *form only rarely.*

Three Flows   NEI 3–4   100'   faces NW   (reliable, forms early)   †

This most obvious ice stands one-half mile north (meaning toward Lake Placid on Route 73) of the Pitchoff Chimney Cliff. Early in the season these are three distinct climbs of NEI 3, NEI 3+, and NEI 4. They often merge later in the winter. The sloping base makes this a hard site to manage for top-roping or groups. Park as for Pitchoff and walk up the lake.

Naked Head   NEI 3   120'   faces NW   (typically thin and mixed)

About 200' right of the very obvious *Three Flows* is a brushy-looking slab. Start in a gully and move left onto the slab. Finish at a birch.

FA Jeff Edwards and Charlie Cohen 2/95

Magic Hat   NEI 3+   120'   faces NW   (typically thin and mixed)

Stay in the gully line, finishing either on turf or via the short pillar. The route is marked by the large left-facing corner that borders the slabby area.

FA Jeff Edwards and Charlie Cohen 2/95

Reliable Thing   NEI 3   60'   faces NW   (reliable, forms early)

300' left of *Jaws* roof, and fairly close to the lake, is a short yellow flow that squeezes around a block to wider finish. Not too significant.

Quasi-Climber   NEI 3   100'   faces NW   (reliable)

This and the next climbs are located on the large expanse of rock left of Cascade Cliff. The most distinctive feature in this area is the dripping overhang of *Jaws*. *Quasi-Climber* is the wide flow highest on the left, up in a right-to-left gully and just visible from the road.

ACB Alan Jolley 2/83

Feeding Frenzy   NEI 4   120'   faces NW   (unreliable)

Just left of the roofs is a line of ice up a narrow rib of rock.

Jaws   NEI 4   A2   150'   faces NW   (rare)

This one climbs the obvious icicles dripping from the middle of the large overhang. Because the fang wasn't fully attached at the base, this ascent aided out the roof and onto the icicle.

FA Jim Cunningham 2/2/84

Killer Whale   NEI 3   160'   faces NW   (rare)

This route begins below the *Jaws* roof and opts for an easier course by heading out right to finish.

ACB Jim Cunningham 2/3/84

Wetfoot   NEI 4   180'   faces NW   (rare)

Down and right about 100' from the *Jaws* roof, at the lowest point on the rock, is a straight two-pitch route. The first is a sustained 80-degree wall; the upper pitch is easier through some trees.

ACB Bill Dodd and Alan Hobson 12/23/83

Cascade Ice Dance   NEI 4-   200'   faces NW   (unreliable)   †

This outstanding route flirts with us each year and only seldom comes into shape. It is the enticing ice line that drips from the wall high and just left of Cascade Cliff, actually at the head of the large gully separating the cliff from the previous ice routes. Two moderate pitches lead to the rim. A good mixed variation, *Dances with Darkness* (NEI 4- Tad Welch, Chuck Yax, and Bill Widrig '95) climbs thin ice up a corner and ramp to the left, joining the route up high. Rappel is possible with one rope.

ACB Don Mellor and Mark Ippolito 12/20/83

Green Gully   NEI 3+   80'   faces NW   (reliable)

Right of the huge Cascade Cliff is the Cascade itself, a waterfall that drains the slopes above and which can be seen above the picnic area between the lakes. *Green Gully* is a harder, hidden left-hand variation that is usually approached as one descends from *Cascade*.

Cascade   NEI 2   250'   faces NW   (reliable)   †

This is an excellent two-pitch route that is approached by a trail from the picnic area between the lakes. Descend by scrambling down left through the cedars and into the lower portion of the *Green Gully* streambed. Keep crampons on.

Top of the Lake Gullies   NEI 1   300'   (reliable)

These are the streambeds/waterfalls that flow into the upper end of the Upper Lake. They are good places to learn footwork, but when covered with snow, they probably aren't worth the effort. The left route is longer and easier.

PITCHOFF NORTH FACE
Elevation 2,400', faces NW

This is a major Adirondack ice climbing area. Some have even compared it to Vermont's Smuggler's Notch. It is a high mountain pass, accessible by an easy ski up a dirt road, and its long routes in a remote setting make the outing more a wilderness adventure than simply a technical ice climb. The high elevation and northern exposure bring the conditions in early and make

PITCHOFF NORTH FACE, *left*

A. EMERALD CITY
B. HANGING SPOONS
C. SCREW AND CLIMAXE
D. PEANUT BRITTLE PILLAR
E. SLIPSTICK
F. WEEPING WINDS

the ice as reliable as any in the Park. The climbs rise above the Old Mountain Road, which was a main route into the region before Route 73 was cut into the steep slopes of Cascade Pass. Only the first mile or so is still used by cars in the summer, but since the establishment of the Jackrabbit Ski Trail linking Keene to Lake Placid, the pass has become a very popular ski-touring route. Keep this in mind when planning your trip: Approach on skis or walk clear of the tracks along the way. The Old Mountain Road turns sharply east from Route 73 three quarters of a mile north of the Mount Van Hoevenberg access road. The climbs begin above a beaver pond about 1.5 miles from Route 73.

The routes are described right to left or as one approaches from the trail.

Eye of the Needle   NEI 2   300'   (reliable, forms early)

This is the first slide one sees upon entering the pass. It is presently the only route right of the large rock buttress just before the pond. The lower section is often thin, but a good line can usually be found to the better ice above.

Variation **Thread Line** NEI 3 50' This climbs steep ice hidden in the trees right of the climb's midsection.

acb Jim Cunningham and Chuck Turner 12/81

Red House Ramp   NEI 3   300'   (unreliable)

This is the huge left-facing ramp/corner on the left side of the major rock buttress. The ice is seldom thick enough to climb, and in verglassed conditions the route is considerably harder than its grade suggests. Bring rock protection.

FA Jim Cunningham and Bob Hay 11/12/83

The following climbs are visible from the pond.

Central Pillar of Pitchoff   NEI 4   90'   (reliable, forms early)   †

This is the obvious cascade that falls from above the SW end of the pond. It is far from being the central feature of the area. It has the easiest approach and is quite popular. The route is actually about 200' long, but the approach is low-angled, and the upper section of short steps is usually avoided. The pillar itself has several options; the easiest is usually the right side.

FA Al Long, Al Rubin, and Dave Hoffman 2/17/75

PITCHOFF NORTH FACE, *right*

G. TENDONITIS

H. ARM AND HAMMER

I. CENTRAL PILLAR OF PITCHOFF

437

Arm and Hammer   NEI 3+   150'   (reliable, forms early)   †

Left of *Central Pillar* and still above the near end of the pond is a wall of ice that usually stands thick and blue. The route is approached by a steep streambed directly below. The lower section is lower angled; a 20' wall at about 80' makes up the crux.

FA Al Long, Al Rubin, and Dave Hoffman 2/2/75

Tendonitis   NEI 3–4   150'   (reliable, forms early)

This is the parallel, left-hand variation to *Arm and Hammer.* The profile of the route is similar, though the crux headwall is steeper.

ACB Don Mellor and Pete Benson 12/81

Hammond Egger   NEI 3+   100'

Just left of *Tendonitis,* and actually on the logical rappel descent from that route, is a less significant route. This one climbs easy ice in a left-facing cleft to some trees on the right, then ascends a headwall above.

Moss Ghyll   NEI 3–4   100'

There is a large left-facing corner about 150' left of *Arm and Hammer,* etc. It is the left-most climbable ice before the large section of forest right of the huge *Weeping Winds* slide. The lower section is easy. Above, the corner (or either wall for the ambitious) leads to the trees.

The Blue Chute   NEI 3   200'   (reliable, forms early)

Right of *Weeping Winds* is a hidden gully.

Weeping Winds   NEI 3+   350'   †

This is the large irregular slide that stands above the middle of the pond. The route generally follows the left side. A final steep pitch of about 75' leads to the top, with another NEI 3+ pitch above and right as a final option.

Slipstick   NEI 4-   80'   (reliable)

High and left of the large *Weeping Winds* slide is a line of roofs that top off the cliffs. In the center of these is an offset crack. At the right-hand end of this line of overhangs is a good line of ice. *Slipstick* can be reached by following thin ice and bushes up for 200' from the base. The final 80' makes a good pitch, but the approach is a steep price to pay.

ACB Don Mellor and Pete Benson 12/81

Peanut Brittle Pillar NEI 4 75' (unreliable)

This is the free-standing, yellow/brown icicle that hangs from the left end of the overhangs mentioned above. As for *Slipstick,* it can be reached tediously from below. Perhaps a better approach reaches this pitch on descent from *Screw and Climaxe;* after one rappel, it is easy to scramble through the trees to its base.

ACB Don Mellor and Patrick Purcell 12/28/87

Screw and Climaxe NEI 3+ 350' (reliable) †

This is the area classic. It is the obvious strip of ice that flows down the middle of the enormous slab above the far end of the pond. The route's name was coined in the days when the Climaxe, a hybrid hammer/axe by Chouinard, was the rage. No, the name doesn't refer to what you thought; but it's the closest thing to it behind Pitchoff. Two ropes are necessary for the rappels.

pitch 1 Climb a steep, usually unprotected slab for 120' to a belay at a small ledge. If this isn't in shape, it is possible to rock/tree-climb the buttress to reach the top of the pitch.

pitch 2 Thicker ice bulges up and right to a belay in the trees. 100'

pitch 3 Head up and left, taking any of several lines of varying difficulty up the final wall. 130'

FA Al Long, Al Rubin, and Dave Hoffman 2/15/75

Hanging Spoons NEI 5 (or 5.6 NEI 4+) 300' (unreliable)

High and left of *Screw and Climaxe* is an awesome free-standing pillar that drips for about 60' from the roofs at the top of the cliff. The only ascents recorded to date have stemmed the icicle and the rock to its left, using nuts for protection. The icicle at those times was hardly attached at its base. A headlong ascent up the middle would be a different story altogether and probably the most difficult pitch in the Adirondacks. Two easier pitches lead to the column.

ACB Don Mellor and Jeff Edwards 12/19/86

Emerald City   NEI 4   125'   (reliable, forms early)

This is the wide ice wall that is farthest left and still visible from the pond.

pitch 1 The first pitch is NEI 3 and leads over bulges to a tree-covered ledge.

pitch 2 Take any line up the nearly vertical 50' wall above.

ᴀᴄʙ Bill Simes and Don Mellor 12/81

On the north side of the entrance to the pass, across from the huge rock buttress (Red House Ramp), are two short lines.

Deadline   NEI 4   75'   (reliable)

This is the steep pillar on the left.

ᴀᴄʙ Alan Jolley (solo) 12/82

Harlot   NEI 3+   75'   (reliable)

This is a wider, stepped affair to the right.

ᴀᴄʙ Alan Jolley (solo) 12/82

KNOB LOCK MOUNTAIN
Elevation 1,800', faces N

On the south side of Route 9N between Keene and Elizabethtown (and across the road and to the west of Hurricane Crag) are some ice lines high on this wooded peak. Check from below before making the steep slog.

Starlight   NEI 4   85'

First locate *JW*. About 300 yards left is an ice-filled chimney. The approach is long.

ꜰᴀ Alan Jolley (solo) 1/83

JW   NEI 3+   120'

This is the most obvious line. It is a continuous, straight line of ice seen easily from the road. In many years, however, the ice has failed to reach the ground.

ᴀᴄʙ Jim Wagner 1970s

Unexpected Pleasure   NEI 4   120'

Just right of *JW* is this unusual and intricate route. It is approached via the gully that leads up to the base right of *JW;* continue in the natural chimney line past a pillar and behind a giant chockstone. Clever mixed climbing is required here.

FA Dennis Luther, Edmund Yandon, and Tom Yandon 1/11/86

WILMINGTON NOTCH

Located near the town of Lake Placid, this spectacular pass (elevation 1,600) separates Whiteface Mountain from the wilder Sentinal Range. Here the Ausable River and Route 86 wind their way between the towering crags of Notch Mountain and Moss Cliff. The first three climbs will be described south to north as one approaches from Lake Placid, beginning with the right (SE) side of the road.

Mirage   NEI 4   60'   faces NW

Just right of *Multiplication Gully* is a 30' ice chimney with a narrow, over-hanging exit, followed by a slab.

FA Alan Jolley and Chuck Turner 12/82

Multiplication Gully
NEI 3+   225'   faces W   (reliable, forms early)   †

This is a classic of the region, a narrow runnel cleaving the steep rock walls on the right side of the 300' High Falls Crag. Park 0.75 miles south of High Falls Gorge (this tourist attraction is rented by Cunningham's Ski Barn in winter). A short but tedious bushwhack leads to the ice. Rock protection is helpful but not necessary for the first belay, and a 2"–3" camming device will help below the crux chimney in very lean conditions. Two ropes are needed for the rappel. It is also possible to scramble north and around to descend.

FA Alan Spero and Tom Worthington 2/4/75

Bombcicle   NEI 4+   150'   faces NW   (unreliable)   †

From the center of High Falls Crag hangs this amazing icicle; it flows from a very thin crack in the middle of the wall. Obviously, it doesn't top out, though hard aid could finish the climb.The first ascent was stopped by disconnected ice just below the pillar, which forced retreat and a new approach from ledges on the left. The climb still awaits a direct ascent. It is easily seen from the road.

FA Don Mellor and Mark Ippolito 1/84

HIGH FALLS GORGE AREA

All along the mountainside above High Falls Gorge (or Cunningham's Ski Barn) are short ice routes. About 20 have been climbed here. Easiest and most reliable are the two streambeds directly above the tourist parking lot (NEI 1–2 150'). Above and right is a small 60' amphitheater with good, reliable ice (NEI 4-). Left of the streambeds and spanning the visible flanks of the mountainside are a series of slabs and pillars. The biggest and hardest is *Bear Claw,* an amazing 100' wall of thick blue ice framed by cedars high in the notch about a quarter-mile around the bend to the left of Cunningham's. The top of this route is visible from the road just north of *Multiplication Gully.* Even farther left up the valley is the *Sunrise Notch Route,* an endless streambed that alternates between good ice and flat hiking as it climbs Little Whiteface.This is visible from *Multiplication Gully* itself.

The climbs are possible only after prolonged cold because the only authorized approach is made across the frozen river: be very careful, stay roped, make good decisions. The bridge at Cunningham's is officially closed during winter.

OLYMPIC ACRES

Just north of Whiteface Mountain Ski Center are some rock slabs and ice routes. Some of the ice described here is actually easily seen from the lower chairlift. Enter the ski area and keep right for Olympic Acres. Follow (but don't damage) the cross-country ski trail right for about 100 yards before heading uphill for an equal distance. The wall of *Polar Soldier* should be the first ice encountered.

Chairlift Fantasy   NEI 3   90'   faces SE   (reliable)

The most obvious route from the ski area, this wide slab is located a couple of hundred yards up and left of *Polar Soldier.*

ACB Mike Peabody, Adam Clayman, and Jeff Edwards 1/16/87

Excelsior   NEI 3   100'   faces SE   (reliable)

Seventy-five yards left of the obvious pillars of *Polar Soldier* is a lower-angled slab. The hardest climbing is at the bottom.

FA Patrick Purcell and Ian Osteyee 1/86

Polar Soldier   NEI 4   150'   faces SE   (reliable)

The top of this excellent pitch can barely be seen from the chairlift and more easily from Route 86 south of the mountain. It is a steep wall low and towards the right of the cliff band. This is one of the best single-pitch routes around, and a direct attack on the hollow pillar just left of the line of least resistance would make the pitch an intimidating NEI 5.

FA Patrick Purcell 1/86

Secrets of the Ice Age   NEI 4   80'

This is the left-facing corner just right of *Polar Soldier.*

FA Jeff Edwards, Adam Clayman, and Mike Peabody 1/16/87

Chiller Pillar   NEI 4   100'   el. 2400'   faces S
(reliable, forms early, easy top- rope)   †

This old quarry route is located above the town of Wilmington off the Whiteface Memorial Highway. The ice can be seen from the tollhouse. Drive a few hundred feet over the pass and park on the right where the road curves left. Walk a short, very overgrown dirt road for 100 yards to the ice. This is an especially good route.

FA Dave Cilley, Todd Eastman, and Dave Hough 2/15/77

POKE-O-MOONSHINE

Poke-O (elevation 900', faces E) is one of the major ice-climbing areas of the Adirondacks with some of the longest, steepest routes upstate. There is great variety here, though the greatest concentration of routes is in the difficult realm. With its relatively low elevation, the climbs here come into shape later than other areas. Nevertheless, the ice here is fairly reliable.

Le Poisson   NEI 3+

This route on the south face slab was done in four pitches. (See The Slab photo in rock section of guide).

FA Tom Rosecrans and John Weston 1/80

Forbidden Wall   NEI 4-   300'   (reliable)   †

This is the wide expanse of slabs and overlaps above and left of the prominent *Waterfall Route*. It can be seen across the road from the Ranger's cabin. Approach as for the summit trail, and head right where the trail meets the 50' wall with the roof/fingercrack. In good years, there are many ways up this massive piece of ice.

FA Mark Meschinelli, Pat Munn, and Dick Bushey 1970s

Goat's Foot on Ice   NEI 5   150'   (reliable)   †

This demanding and often thin route lies on a buttress just left of *Waterfall*. Begin just left of a large right-facing corner. Rock protection is useful, and good technique mandatory.

ACB Dennis Luther and Tom Yandon 2/86

Get a Job   M6+   NEI 4+   150'

This will probably be considered a pivotal Adirondack climb, the first to push mixed climbing into the modern age. Jeff Lowe graded the climb according to his new and developing "mixed" scale, designed to define difficulty more accurately when rock-climbing with ice tools is integral to the climb. The name of the route is ironic indeed: It was shouted from a passing pick-up truck while Lowe was high on the route as part of his Northeastern professional tour.

pitch 1 Begin in the prominent right-facing corner below and right of

PHOTO BY MARK MESCHINELLI

POKE-O WATERFALL AREA

A. GOAT'S FOOT   C. DISCORD
B. WATERFALL   D. MID-LIFE CRISIS

Goat's Foot. Up mixed rock and ice to the roof, and out left to gain the thicker ice of *Goat's Foot.*

FA Jeff Lowe and Mark Stampiglia 2/95

Big Mac Attack   NEI 4   150'   (reliable)

Actually a variation to the *Waterfall,* this sometimes forms as a separate and recommended line. It begins left of the huge boulder at the base of the *Waterfall* wall, climbing a steep, thick pitch to a tree belay at 40'. The ice up the corner above is sustained, though not as reliable as that below. It is also possible to traverse right from the belay to join the regular route.

Waterfall   NEI 5   150'   (reliable, forms early)   †

This is the awesome and unrelenting sheet of ice above the ranger's cabin. There are many options, the easiest generally being a slight groove heading up from the left side of the giant boulder below. This is NEI 4+. Otherwise, some of the most demanding leads conceivable can be found by accepting the challenge of the middle sections.

The following routes are located on the cliff bands above the waterfall. Essentially, there are three levels between Waterfall *and the summit as one ascends the drainage above the descent gully. First locate the "handcrack boulder," a split block about 150' above the descent gully. This marks the lowest and smallest band.*

Christmas Gully   NEI 3   150'   (reliable)

Directly above the summer descent gully and 100' right of the handcrack boulder is a band of low cliffs that drip with ice columns. *Christmas Gully* takes the right-hand of these up a 15' vertical wall to slabs and left-facing corners above, finally finishing up and right on open ledges. (Left of the handcrack boulder and drainage are two short climbs. NEI 3+ 35')

Number One   NEI 4   40'

Continuing up the drainage to the next level, one passes a large cave/over-hang on the right. Up and left of this is the next series of climbs. This first one is the steep pencil-like pillar on the right.

PHOTO BY MARK MESCHINELLI

Poke-O-Moonshine's Forbidden Wall

Number Two   NEI 4-   40'

20' left of the obvious icicle of *Number One* is a steep curtain.

Number Three   NEI 3   50'

This is the biggest piece of ice on this level; it climbs a wide flow in a corner left of the previous routes.

Number Four   NEI 3   50'

This is the left-most ice and is similar to the previous route.

From the top of this cliff band one can see an obvious, huge rock wall high and right.

Topless   NEI 3   200'

This is the very obvious line that runs down the middle of the large expanse of rock. It ends in an overhanging corner, and as such, may be impossible to complete.

Run for Your Life   NEI 4-   130'

On the left end of the huge rock wall and just right of the drainage is an obvious line in a broken corner.

ACB Alan Jolley and Don Hurlbert 2/20/83

Landfall   NEI 4   40'

The last ice on the left side of the drainage before it emerges onto the slopes above is a vertical column with a rest at midheight.

The final series of routes stands on the highest band up, about 500' up and 500' left of the drainage. Scramble through the trees and skirt the rock wall to reach the base of the climbs. In this way it is possible to avoid the house-sized boulders and brush below the routes.

Twin Towers   NEI 4–5   100'   †

This is the most impressive piece of ice on the upper bands. The twin pillars (sometimes merging into one) can be seen from several vantage points along the road and above the main face.

Vector   NEI 4   75'

Though there is much ice here, much of it futuristic, this is the most obvious route between *Twin Towers* and *Don't Adze Me*.

ACB Alan Jolley and Don Hurlbert 1983

Don't Adze Me   NEI 4-   75'

In an obvious right-facing corner is a good and reliable ice line. It stands about 100' left of *Twin Towers*.

ACB Bill Simes and Alan Jolley 2/83

The following routes are on the Main Face and all can be seen from the road.

Discord   NEI 4   300'   (lower sections unreliable)   †

This is an outstanding route whose fickle lower sections often bar the way to the superb upper pitch. Mixed free and aid rock climbing can get one to the good ice above, or for the less ambitious, it is easy to approach the final pitch via ledges at the top of the descent gully. The climb is located where the summer approach trail meets the left end of the main cliff, about 100 yards right of the descent gully. It is marked by black slabs and right-facing corners leading to a final steep pitch in a right-facing dihedral.

Mid-Life Crisis   NEI 5   85'

Right of *Discord* and above *Slime Line* is an impressive and frightening icicle that forms on the upper wall. It is reached by rappel.

Joe Szot and Tom Yandon

Positive Thinking

NEI 5   450'   (*pitch 1* unreliable, upper sections reliable)   †

This is perhaps the most sought-after climb in the Adirondacks. It is the near-perfect ice climb with three superb pitches, each using every inch of the rope. Its first, a single 160' dropline of ice pasted on an otherwise blank wall, brings one to a belay on the traverse dike. Above, the central column plunges from the roofs at the top of the chimney. A final and more forgiving pitch runs the rope out to the woods. In lean conditions when the first pitch is too thin, it is possible to join the upper column by traversing in on *Half*

Mile (see Rock Climbs, Poke-O-Moonshine section). The first ascent party instead climbed the 5.9 handcrack because the first pitch had collapsed.

FA John Bragg and John Bouchard 1975

Neurosis

NEI 3+   400'   (*pitch 1* unreliable, upper sections reliable)   †

This is a superb and complete winter climb. The first two pitches may be bypassed by mixed climbing on the left if conditions are too thin. Chocks are necessary for the first two leads. Additionally, a final pitch on the upper tier may be added for the ambitious. The climb is located on the right side of the wall, just right of the largest, steepest section.

pitch 1 Begin in a left-facing corner, actually right of the summer route's squeeze chimney. Belay at a tree ledge at 40'.

pitch 2 Continue the corner, finally emerging out left to a tree belay. 150'

pitch 3–4 Follow easier ice for 200' to the top.

pitch 5 The *Direct Finish* is the steep (NEI 4) column finish to the next level. 100'

Variation **Italian Traverse** If the initial pitches aren't in shape, it is possible to climb the rightmost of three short corners up and left of the chimney. Mixed free and aid leads past trees to a difficult traverse right to the snowfields of the route's midsection.

FA Claude Suhl 1970s (p. 1–4)

ACB Don Mellor and Mark Meschinelli 12/81 (p. 5)

ACB Mark Meschinelli and Geoff Smith (var.)

Hidden Pique   NEI 4   125'

This is the tight and narrow, classically alpine, runnel 100' right of *Direct Finish*.

ACB Don Mellor and Chuck Turner 2/83

For descent: There are two rappel routes from the top of *Neurosis* (below *Direct*). Both require double ropes. One option takes a line just left of the route, using trees for anchors. The other walks right a few hundred feet to the top of the slab at the cliff's edge. A long rappel leads down the slab to a small alcove (tree) beneath a corner. One more rope-length leads to the

Positive Thinking

ground right of *Sunburst Arete*. Make sure this is set up properly: The alcove tree is perhaps the only anchor in this section of rock.

NORTHWEST ADIRONDACKS
SCARFACE

Between Saranac Lake and Lake Placid is this wide, open slide face. In summer it is a wet, mossy mess, but in winter, a distinct line of ice runs up its center. Approach from the town of Ray Brook via the hikers' trail. Skis are recommended. The route is about 300' long and rates in at NEI 2–3. It sees very little traffic.

BAKER MOUNTAIN

See the rock description for this small crag in the town of Saranac Lake. For those in the neighborhood, there are a couple of short ice routes here that are reliable and worthwhile.

AZURE MOUNTAIN

This mountain peak about halfway between Saranac Lake and Potsdam holds a good deal of ice climbing potential for climbers in the northwestern section of the Park. The approaches are described in Rock Climbs, The Northwest section of this guide. There is good ice in the Sidewalk Cafe Area on the approach. *Weenie Jam* is a good route on an iced ramp. Farther left, *Weenie Roast* is the topless pillar that sprouts from the center of the wall. This requires clever mixed work to gain the ice. There is a fixed rappel at its top. Additionally, *Pearl* is a towering column that is seen high and left on the sheer wall above the *Flubby Dub* rock route. Approach this by friction slabs. This excellent route offers a long, steep pitch (NEI 4) followed by mixed climbing up and right to the top. All in all, there are about 10 established climbs here, ranging from 30' to 150'.

PHOTO BY MARK MESCHINELLI

NEUROSIS (with the ITALIAN TRAVERSE marked to its left)

453

SOUTHERN ADIRONDACKS
PHARAOH MOUNTAIN

The few who have done this route regard it as one of the best moderate routes in the Adirondacks. See Pharaoh Mountain rock climbs for approach routes. In winter, the best route to the mountain is probably that from Spectacle Pond: It is direct and the ice can be seen from the lake. Bring skis or snowshoes, get a very early start, and bring enough gear for a night out. The trip is a long one and you will inevitably be breaking trail. A map and compass and good route-finding skills are a must.

The route lies right of center on the major cliff. Its three or four pitches have been compared in quality to Roaring Brook Falls. The crux is low and the overall rating is about NEI 3+.

BARTON HIGH CLIFF

Two mixed rock, sod, and ice climbs have been done here, both appealing only to the adventurous and imaginative. Refer to Barton High Cliff rock climbs (Southern Adirondacks section) for approach.

Cairngorm Corner   NEI 4   130'

The huge corner right of *Excellent Adventure* arete ices in winter to form two pitches of mixed climbing.

FA Tad Welch and Bill Widrig 2/24/91

Men without Ice   NEI 3+   220'

Downhill and left of the previous route is another large, more moderately angled corner. The start is just right of the crack line of *Reckless Endangerment.* Two creative pitches finish with good ice bulges. Rappel *Cairngorm Corner.*

FA Bill Widrig and Tad Welch 2/24/91

ELEVENTH MOUNTAIN

In times of low snow cover, this is a fairly good and easy ice climb (NEI 2). The route follows a very long (several hundred feet), cascading streambed easily seen from Route 8 a couple miles south of the tiny town of Bakers Mills. A direct approach would trespass private land; instead, use the state-owned access east of the Straight Farm, and bushwhack easily to the stream.

ACB Neal Knite 1994

BLUE MOUNTAIN

There is a wide series of short (50') routes on the Northville–Placid Trail off Route 28 and 30, less than 3 miles east of the village of Blue Mountain Lake. Park at the east end of Lake Durant and head toward Tirrell Pond. The approach is a popular ski trail and the ice is seen on the left after about a half mile.

HIGH PEAKS
WALLFACE

When speculation turns to talk about where the biggest, baddest ice climb is going to be, most climbers mention Wallface in Indian Pass (base elevation 3000', faces SE). Someone will get hold of an old winter photo with a white line tracing its way down toward the bottom of the cliff. Someone else will claim that there's just got to be ice up there; after all, it's the highest, widest cliff in the state. Wallface for now, however, must remain in that realm of speculation about how things *could* be in a super winter. It's a long trek in on skis or snowshoes just to get a look at the face, and many of the parties who have made the journey have ended up rock climbing *Diagonal* or *Wiessner* or simply turning around and heading back down the trail. Two ice routes, however, have been recorded, and one, *Grim And Bare It,* is destined to be coveted and classic. And although the ice here may otherwise be a disappointment, there is no better winter training ground for the big mixed routes we fantasize about.

Fire One Up   NEI 4   150'   (reliable)

This route lies on the lower cliff bands well right of the *Mental Blocks* buttress, and near the actual height-of-land of Indian Pass. The route is identified by its first pitch, a steep pencil of ice leading into a tight notch and a

455

belay on lower angled terrain above. The second pitch climbs out right on steep ice to the top.

ᴀᴄʙ Bob Cotter and Paul Stankiewicz 3/11/84

Grim and Bare It   NEI 4+   500'   (unreliable)   †

This is the eye-catching line that in good ice years forms right of *Mental Blocks*. The ice rarely, if ever, touches the ground. Approach the ice from the right over intricate mixed terrain using ramps and ledges. When this one is in shape, it may well be the big daddy of Adirondack winter climbs.

pitch 1 From a large flake gain the ribbon of ice and follow it to a cedar belay.

pitch 2 Spectacular climbing up steep ice leads up past a chockstone.

pitch 3 Moderate bulges bring one to a large ledge.

pitch 4 Follow frozen turf and snow up right, with a direct finish also possible.

ᴀᴄʙ Todd Swain, Mike Cross, and Tad Welch 1/86

AVALANCHE PASS

Five miles from Adirondak Loj at the foot of Mt. Colden is one of the most scenic high mountain passes in the region. The Pass is about 3000' above sea level and Avalanche Lake stands at 2863', making conditions here much different from those lower in the valleys. The first ice climbing here was in the well-known feature that splits the slides of Colden: *The Trap Dike*. This still sees most of the action in winter, but there are a few other options as well. Avalanche Pass is best approached on skis. (Skis and snowshoes can be rented at the Adirondack Mountain Club's High Peaks Information Center by the trailhead.) If a party chooses to walk the distance, they should make sure that they at least carry snowshoes; the trail to the pass is one of the nicest and most popular ski trails in the Adirondacks, and footprints in the trail spoil and make dangerous this excellent tour. Climbers who once post-holed up the ski trail toward the pass were "asked" by the ranger to repair their damage. Two hours of shoveling and raking sapped their climbing energy, and they dejectedly turned back and headed home. The rangers support climbing, but no one should tolerate such inconsiderate behavior.

At the top of the pass, before the lake, is a short yellow ice line. This flows to the ground and splashes in two directions: north to the Ausable River, then on to the St. Lawrence and the North Atlantic, and south to Avalanche Lake, the Hudson River, and New York City. There is sometimes more ice than is described here, and probably good potential for hard mixed routes.

The climbs are listed as one approaches from the pass, starting with the right wall. All climbs listed here are considered fairly reliable.

Slop n' Sweat   NEI 3+   200'   faces SE

This is the largest flow on the NW side of the pass before reaching Avalanche Lake. It is located at the very right end of the steep rock wall, and is the most obvious ice one encounters before reaching the lake. Approach via a steep bushwhack.

ACB Bill Simes and Bob Bushart 11/80

Avalanche Mountain Gully   NEI 3+/4   350'   faces SE

On the right wall of the pass are two wooden walkways that allow passage around the lake in summer. Above the second of these rises a talus cone leading to a good ice route. The first pitch is mainly snow with a steep, 30' bulge en route. The classic slanting corner follows with a sustained and long pitch of about 70 degrees. Finish awkwardly in a tight chimney. Rappel with two ropes, or face a wicked bushwhack.

The next routes lie on the SE or Colden side of the pass.

Unnamed   NEI 3+   150'   faces NW

Just toward the lake from the height-of-land, the trail skirts two rock walls on the right. Directly across from the second of these is an obvious route consisting of short vertical steps interspersed by snowfields and some trees. This is close to and easily seen from the trail.

The Adirondike   NEI 3+   200'   faces NW

This climb rises out of Avalanche Lake from a scree/tree cone and gully left of the more prominent *Trap Dike*. The ice is often thin on the first pitch, and the snow gully above must be watched for avalanche potential. Rappel with two ropes.

Trap Dike   NEI 2   2000'   faces NW   †

This is the popular and classic mountaineering route up Colden's NW face. The climb begins across the lake from the wooden walkways at the top of a huge, tree-covered scree cone at the base of the obvious canyon that comprises the lower portion of the route. The waterfall high in the cleft is the crux. In heavy snow years this is buried; other times it can make for about 50' of ice climbing. Break out right as soon as practical and follow the slide to the top. There have been at least one avalanche accident and three major rescue operations on this route: Treat it seriously. Bring along a map for the descent trail, or follow the tree-filled drainage back into the *Trap Dike* and rappel the short steep section.

FA   Jim Goodwin   12/35

GOTHICS

North Face   NEI 2   1100'   base elevation 3700'   faces NW   †

This is a worthwhile and sought-after climb. A difficulty rating is very subjective here because conditions on this high mountain face are so variable. In compact snow, one can imagine climbing the face without crampons. On verglassed rock, only the best ice technique will suffice. However, in most cases, escape can be made into the trees where a less exposed and easier way can be found to the top in any condition. The ice usually forms only late in the season when more direct sun angles help consolidate the snow cover. The face should be avoided after a snowfall or any time avalanche conditions exist.

Approach from the Garden in Keene Valley as for Johns Brook Lodge and turn left at the ranger's cabin, crossing the suspension bridge to the Orebed Brook Trail to Saddleback and Gothics. One-half mile past the Orebed lean-to, follow a large stream left. It is practical to ski to this point. Beyond, prepare for tough going in deep snow. (For detailed approach description, see Remote Climbs in the High Peaks, Gothics.) Many parties fail by simply missing the approach and ending up high on Armstrong Mountain, having cut too far to the left.

Descend by hiking the trail toward the Saddleback–Gothics trail junction or by careful, roped down-climbing along the trees at either edge of the face. There have been a few noteworthy and more rapid descents: the face has been skied, both with alpine and three-pin gear. And more chilling, one climber fell the entire length of the face after losing his way in the mist. Fearing the worst, his partners slowly rappelled the face, only to find him shivering impatiently at the bottom, bruised but otherwise in good shape. (This is not a suggested option.)

FA Dougal Thomas (via the left side of the face) 3/65

ELK PASS

In the high pass between Nipple Top and Colvin is a 100' ice route hosting options that vary between NEI 3 and NEI 4+. The ice is located on the flank of Colvin, right across from the base of the Nipple Top Slide.

The Trap Dike

Gothics North Face in winter.

Select Bibliography

The following books and articles were instrumental in both my research and the evolution of my own wilderness philosophy.

Carson, Russell, M.L. *Peaks and People of the Adirondacks*. Lake George, New York: The Adirondack Mountain Club, 1973 edition. Out of print.

Goodwin, Tony. *Guide to Adirondack Trails: High Peaks Region*. Vol. 1 of 8 in the Forest Preserve Series. Lake George, New York: Adirondack Mountain Club, 1992.

Healy, Trudy. *Climber's Guide to the Adirondacks*. Gabriels, New York: Adirondack Mountain Club, 1967. Out of print.

Heilman II, Carl. *Guide to Adirondack Trails: Eastern Region*. Vol. 6 of 8 in the Forest Preserve Series. Lake George, New York: Adirondack Mountain Club, 1994.

Jaffe, Howard W. and Elizabeth B. *Geology of the High Peaks Region: A Hiker's Guide*. Lake George, New York: Adirondack Mountain Club, 1986.

Keller, Jane Eblen. *Adirondack Wilderness: A Story of Man and Nature*. Syracuse, New York: Syracuse University Press, 1980.

Laing, Linda. *Guide to Adirondack Trails: Southern Region*. Vol. 7 of 8 in the Forest Preserve Series. Lake George, New York: Adirondack Mountain Club, 1994.

McMartin, Barbara. *Discover the Adirondack High Peaks*. Vol. 1 of 11. Utica, New York: North Country Books, 1986.

Rockwell, Landon G. "Adirondack Slides," *Adirondac* Vol. XIV. Lake George, New York: Adirondack Mountain Club, 1982.

Rosecrans, Thomas R. *Adirondack Rock and Ice Climbs*. Lake George, New York: Rosecrans Outing and Climbing Klub, 1976. Out of print.

Terrie, Philip G. *Forever Wild*. Philadelphia, Pennsylvania: Temple University Press, 1985.

VanDiver, Bradford B. *Rocks and Routes of the North Country*. Geneva, New York: W.F. Humphrey Press, 1976.

Waterman, Guy and Laura. *Yankee Rock and Ice*. Harrisburg, Pennsylvania: Stackpole Books, 1993.

Index

The Adirondack Mountain Club, Inc.
814 Goggins Road, Lake George, NY 12845-4117
(518) 668-4447/Orders only: 800-395-8080 (Mon.–Sat., 8:30–5:00)

BOOKS

85 Acres: A Field Guide to the Adirondack Alpine Summits
Adirondack Canoe Waters: North Flow
Adirondack Canoe Waters: South & West Flow
Adirondack Mt. Club Canoe Guide to East-Central New York State
Adirondack Mt. Club Canoe Guide to Western & Central New York State
Adirondack Park Mountain Bike Preliminary Trail and Route Listing
Adirondack Wildguide (distributed by ADK)
An Adirondack Passage: The Cruise of the Canoe Sairy Gamp
An Adirondack Sampler I: Day Hikes for All Seasons
An Adirondack Sampler II: Backpacking Trips
Classic Adirondack Ski Tours
Climbing in the Adirondacks: A Guide to Rock & Ice Routes
Forests & Trees of the Adirondack High Peaks Region
Guide to Adirondack Trails: High Peaks Region
Guide to Adirondack Trails: Northern Region
Guide to Adirondack Trails: Central Region
Guide to Adirondack Trails: Northville–Placid Trail
Guide to Adirondack Trails: West-Central Region
Guide to Adirondack Trails: Eastern Region
Guide to Adirondack Trails: Southern Region
Kids on the Trail! Hiking with Children in the Adirondacks
Our Wilderness: How the People of New York Found,
Changed, and Preserved the Adirondacks
The Adirondack Reader
Trailside Notes: A Naturalist's Companion to Adirondack Plants
Views From on High: Fire Tower Trails in the Adirondacks and Catskills
Winterwise: A Backpacker's Guide
With Wilderness at Heart: A Short History of the Adirondack Mountain Club

MAPS

Trails of the Adirondack
High Peaks Region
Trails of the Northern Region
Trails of the Central Region
Northville–Placid Trail

Trails of the West-Central Region
Trails of the Eastern Region
Trails of the Southern Region
Trails of the Catskill Region

THE ADIRONDACK MOUNTAIN CLUB CALENDAR

Price list available on request.

Backdoor to Backcountry

ADKers choose from friendly outings, for those just getting started with local chapters, to Adirondack backpacks and international treks. Learn gradually through chapter outings or attend one of our schools, workshops, or other programs. A sampling includes:

- Alpine Flora
- Ice Climbing
- Rock Climbing
- Basic Canoeing/Kayaking
- Bicycle Touring
- Cross-country Skiing
- Mountain Photography
- Winter Mountaineering
- Birds of the Adirondacks
- Geology of the High Peaks
  ... and so much more!

For more information about the Adirondacks or about ADK:

ADK's Information Center & Headquarters
814 Goggins Rd., Lake George, NY 12845-4117
Tel. (518) 668-4447   Fax: (518) 668-3746
Exit 21 off I-87 ("the Northway"), 9N south

Business hours: 8:30 A.M.–5:00 P.M., Monday–Saturday

For more information about our lodges:

ADK Lodges
Box 867, Lake Placid, NY 12946
Tel. (518) 523-3441, 9 A.M.–7:00 P.M.

Visit our Web site at www.adk.org